GIMBEL'S
ILLUSTRATED 1915
FASHION CATALOG

GIMBEL'S ILLUSTRATED 1915 FASHION CATALOG

Gimbel Brothers

DOVER PUBLICATIONS, INC.
New York

Published in Canada by General Publishing Company, Ltd., 30 Lesmill Road, Don Mills, Toronto, Ontario.
Published in the United Kingdom by Constable and Company, Ltd., 3 The Lanchesters, 162–164 Fulham Palace Road, London W6 9ER.

Bibliographical Note

Gimbel's Illustrated 1915 Fashion Catalog, first published by Dover Publications, Inc., in 1994, is an unabridged republication of *Paris London and American Styles*, originally published by Gimbel Brothers, New York and Philadelphia, in 1915. With the exceptions of the illustrations reproduced in color on the covers of the present edition, illustrations appearing in color in the original are here reproduced in black and white. A new Publisher's Note has been written specially for the Dover edition.

Library of Congress Cataloging-in-Publication Data

Paris, London, and American styles
    Gimbel's illustrated 1915 fashion catalog / Gimbel Brothers.
       p.   cm.
    Originally published: Paris, London, and American styles. New York : Gimbel Brothers, 1915.
    ISBN 0-486-27938-3 (pbk.)
    1. Costume—United States—History—20th century. 2. Costume—Europe—History—20th century. 3. Gimbel Brothers—Catalogs. I. Gimbel Brothers. II. Title.
GT615.P37   1994
391'.009'041—dc20   93-51252
                                                       CIP

Manufactured in the United States of America
Dover Publications, Inc., 31 East 2nd Street, Mineola, N.Y. 11501

Publisher's Note

At one time one of the most famous retail operations in the United States, Gimbel Brothers traced its origins to Adam Gimbel, a peddler who opened a dry-goods store in Vincennes, Indiana, in 1842. Eventually the business grew to include large stores in Philadelphia, Milwaukee and New York and "buying establishments" in London, Paris, Lyons and Berlin.

Following the trend in American merchandising, the company published a mail-order catalog, the one reproduced here having been issued for spring/summer 1915. Although the emphasis is on women's fashions, it covers a variety of goods, from pillows and tablecloths to rocking chairs and tennis nets, although not in nearly the quantity or variety of Sears, Roebuck or Montgomery Ward.

The catalog was issued at a moment when women's fashions were following a liberating trend, one that was to be accelerated by the effects of the First World War. Only a few years previously, Paul Poiret had changed fashion by adopting a "natural figure" that did away with the tightly corseted S-curve that had long dominated women's dress. Ironically, he also introduced one of fashion's great peculiarities—the hobble skirt, a long, narrow skirt that severely restricted movement. But, almost immediately, slits and hidden pleats were added to the skirts to make them more practical. The look was further modified to a sheath, over which a tunic top was worn. By the time this catalog appeared, the sheath had been eliminated and the tunic top extended downward to form a dress. (Vestiges of the tunic top can be seen in such items as K-200, page 2, and K-2000, page 20.) It was in this season that hems were raised and skirts widened ("Skirts Again Spring Out into Width at Foot," pp. 32–33).

Although Europe had been at war since 1914, there is little evidence of it in the catalog, which was probably issued before the sinking of the *Lusitania* on May 7, 1915. Some references to the European conflict can be found in the catalog, but only pertaining to the availability of goods: "We have them [dress goods], despite war and . . . other conditions . . ." (p. 133). "Our orders [for dress linens] were placed abroad, before declaration of the war, and we had them shipped weeks ago . . ." (p. 134). "The scarcity of ocean-going ships, the extreme danger of ocean travel, increased marine insurance, and actual detention of goods abroad have caused the foreign linen market to go steadily upward" (p. 141).

The catalog does offer outfits in "the new military fashion lines" (K-101, p. 1; K-900, p. 9; K-2803, p. 28). "The military trend of thought has influenced Miladi towards a liking for the natty, practical tailormade" (p. 27).

The connection to Europe was important, both to Europeans and Americans, for fashion was rapidly becoming an industry. (The original title of the catalog was *Paris London and American Styles*.) American buyers would purchase from London or the French couture with an eye to secure models to be "knocked off" on Seventh Avenue and, although couturiers such as Poiret objected, these purchases did represent considerable business. Thus the Chambre Syndicale de la Couture Parisienne began to organize the shows of collections that continue today. "Every whisper of coming fashion heard in London or Paris is transmitted by Gimbels foreign organization to the Gimbel Stores" (p. 115). Although war did not sever links with Parisian fashion (as it did in 1940–44), it did create gaps that fledgling American design houses were not fully prepared to fill. Some European designers, such as Lucile (Lady Duff Gordon), had already established American branches (New York in 1910; Chicago in 1913) and were able to play a larger part (in addition to dressing Mary Pickford, the Dolly Sisters and Irene Castle, Lucile was also responsible for the look of the Ziegfeld girls.) A reefer suit bearing her name is illustrated on page 27.

Although Gimbel's certainly catered to women concerned with European fashion, it was always keenly aware that these fashions were being bought by American women, who were leading a more active life than their European counterparts, and adapted them accordingly. The shirtwaist-skirt combination is also given prominence. "The women of other lands occasionally wear a shirtwaist—the American woman occasionally wears something else" (p. 44). Since the 1890s, the shirtwaist had allowed the working woman an affordable wardrobe capable of considerable variation.

Despite a brief attempt to return to prewar fashions after the Armistice, the trend in creating freer, more practical dress for women continued, culminating in the fashions of the mid-twenties.

Gimbel Brothers continued as an active presence for many years, closing the New York store in the 1980s, when the nature of retailing had altered significantly and the function of the large urban department store had come under question.

PARIS LONDON AND AMERICAN STYLES

NEW YORK   GIMBEL BROTHERS   PHILADELPHIA

[original front cover]

Three Frocks of Distinctive Charm and of Most Unusual Value

K—001. Woman's Evening Gown of Chiffon Taffeta. Made with modified bolero forming a sleeveless coatee and trimmed with rows of crystal beads. An underblouse of all silk tulle is banded with silver on the exquisite butterfly sleeves. The skirt has an empire waist line and about hip depth numerous rows of shirrings gathering in the fulness of the new flaring skirt. This frock is copied after an imported model with wonderful style features and is a most successful adaptation of the style demands of well dressed women of fashion. The alluring loveliness of this charming gown is one that carries with it the essence of refinement, and at the price is possible only through the Gimbel organization. In fine quality chiffon taffeta in rose, pearl grey, or black. Sizes 34 to 44. **$15.00.**

K—002. Dancing Frock. Accordion pleated girdle that permits of self adjustment and perfect adaptability for the new dances. A rich trimming of exquisite filmy shadow lace forms a fichu with soft flying circular frill over the shoulders and forming smart coatee ripple in back as shown in the small illustration. Beautiful crushed June roses are used to outline the corsage and are also placed in a novel Empire belt effect across the back. Outlining the deep V cut neck is a dainty frill of silk tulle. The wide Empire girdle forms a novel high waist line and also a yoke effect from below which the soft flaring fulness of the skirt hangs in pretty gathers. In pink, white, Nile green or lavender crepe dechine. Sizes 34 to 44. **$15.00.**

K—003. Exquisite Net Lace Frock. Entirely suitable for a bride's maid, or as a commencement dress or general dancing or party frock. Its charm lies largely in the beautiful designing and in the exquisitely filmy fabrics with which it is combined. The thread run tulle lace is hemstitched at the joinings, and hemstitching also outlines the tucks in both skirt and waist. The lace is appliqued to form a most attractive and becoming style. Soft tucked ruffles of net form a bolero and the wide Empire girdle is trimmed with rosettes of silk tulle garnished with rosebuds. Rose tipped rosettes of silk tulle also finishes the neck and sleeves. This frock is built on a net foundation and may be had in cream white or white with pink or blue trimming. Sizes 34 to 44. **$15.00.**

K-001
$15.00

K-002
$15.00

K-003
$15.00

New York — Gimbel Brothers — Philadelphia

[original inside front cover]

Three Peerless Models in Frocks

K-100
$15.00

K-101
$13.75

K-102
$15.00

Sleeveless Coat Effect with Net Underblouse

K—100. A most engaging model is this semi-tailored frock showing the new sleeveless coat effect with underblouse of fine net. A rich hand-embroidery in wool embellishes the Empire waist band, and underblouse of self material further emphasizes the coatee. Filmy net forms the sleeves, vest and frill that is part of the beautifully raised flying collar. The skirt is in the new width with yoke and panel effect forming long graceful lines and on either side is inserted, with slight fulness, a most effective flaring gore. Fancy buttons trim both coat and skirt. We call your attention to the charming back view of this beautiful frock. In soft, rich French cotton crepe in gray, coral and reseda green. Sizes, 34 to 40. $15.00.

Dainty Military Frock

K—101. The snappy lines of this military model are well brought out by this handsome illustration and gives a very excellent idea of how this cleverly designed costume is made. The coat effect is blousy and slightly gathered into a soft gendarme belt which, however, is joined only at the upper edge, then falling in an easy circular cut and finished with a flat bow. The blouse is trimmed with a rich embroidery of gold thread simulating military ornaments. The sleeves are of becoming width tapering gracefully to the bell-shaped cuffs with which they are finished. Long lines of the full skirt are simple and straight with wide overlapping stitched folds and groups of buttons. In fine quality taffeta; navy, brown, or green. Sizes, 34 to 40. $13.75.

Afternoon Frock of Chiffon Taffeta

K—102. An elaborate semi-formal dress with new Empire coatee, beautifully trimmed with oxydized chain ornaments. Has a rich wide belt with pointed tabs of contrasting color and long sleeves of filmy Georgette crepe. A Norman collar stands in soft rolling raised effect and in front the frock is cut with a most attractive low round neck. The graceful skirt is also a special feature, hanging in soft flaring fullness and is finished with wide scallops below which the flat circular flounce forms a still further and very effective ripple. Sand, navy blue or black Sizes, 34 to 46. $15.00.

A rich and refined costume that is an excellent example of value and workmanship that has made the Gimbel organization the admiration and envy of merchandising experts.

New York — Gimbel Brothers — Philadelphia

1

Outing and Afternoon-Wear Frocks of Smartness

K-200
$3.95

K-201
$5.50

K-202
$5.95

Contents of the Spring and Summer 1915 Gimbel Paris, London and American Style Book

This book treats only of merchandise of the better class, the grades that we can confidently guarantee. The merchandise is the same "good goods" that is sold "over the counters" in the Philadelphia and New York Gimbel Stores to the most up-to-date and discriminating city trade, and should not, before ordering, be confused with the inferior qualities largely produced for certain mail order houses. When Gimbel goods are received there can be no confusion as to their style, worth or intrinsic value.

Outing and Afternoon Wear Frocks of Smartness—Illustrated in Colors on Page 2

Gimbels are, this season, showing chic types of dresses and coat suits adapted especially to medium-sized women, also other types more suited to other sizes. The descriptions state sizes to be had in each style. Certain ones are suitable for extra-size women, and if you will write, giving your measurements and style you like, we will quote the extra cost.

K—200. Charming Combination Dress for Women. Pretty rice cloth. Loose bolero of color over a complete white waist. Bolero has a V-shaped neck and fastens in front with crochet buttons and loops, and may be omitted. Waist has set-in, three-quarter sleeves with turn-over cuffs to match bolero. Revers and collar with standing back. Pleated girdle of white with square buckle. Skirt has circular tunic, very full at back, sloping to front, which is open at center showing the underskirt and closes at lower part with three crochet buttons and loops. Wide, plain underskirt with deep hem. White

and rose, white and blue or white and lavender. Sizes, 34 to 44. $3.95.

K—201. Woman's Fancy Striped Cotton Crepe Dress. Very daintily made with set-in vestee of net lace and pleated net ruffle. White pearl buttons down center. Girdle. Cuffs and standing collar of plain messaline. Two rows of small covered buttons down front. Set-in sleeves with lace trimmed cuff. Skirt has three cut flare flounces and pointed yoke. Piped throughout. Silk trimmings are green or rose. Sizes, 34 to 44 bust measure. $5.50.

K—202. Woman's Pure Linen Dress. Made

in "Bolero" coatee effect with extension tabs crossing in front and fastened on hips. Tips are ornamented with loops and ball buttons. Medallion of colored braid gives a dressy effect on each side. The neck may be worn low or collar may be turned to make a V-shaped chemisette trimmed with small covered buttons. Turn-over cuff and covered buttons. Loose box pleat at back of waist gives fullness. A bodice lining attached to skirt. Skirt has a deep yoke all around. Panel down center front and side pleats give fullness and flare. Blue, pink or tan. Sizes, 34 to 44 bust measure. $5.95.

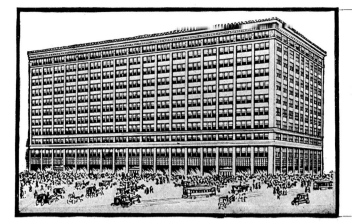

FREE DELIVERY IN THE UNITED STATES OR ITS POSSESSIONS TO YOUR POST OFFICE, EXPRESS OFFICE OR FREIGHT DEPOT

OF ALL GOODS LISTED IN THIS CATALOGUE, EXCEPT ON A FEW ITEMS WHERE AT HEAD OF THE PAGE OR IN THE DESCRIPTIONS IT IS STATED TO THE CONTRARY

At our option as to manner of shipment we will, in the United States or its possessions, prepay the transportation charges on all goods described in this catalogue, excepting on a few items where mention is made at head of the page or in the descriptions that they come under our "Restricted Delivery Offer."

The "Restricted Delivery Offer" is as below, and applies to all goods we carry, whether catalogued or not, that are of a character that would not permit of their coming under our absolutely free delivery offer.

Within 50 miles of New York or Philadelphia: Purchase of $5.00 for every 100 pounds	Within 150 miles of New York or Philadelphia: Purchase of $7.50 for every 100 pounds	Within 300 miles of New York or Philadelphia: Purchase of $10.00 for every 100 pounds	Within 600 miles of New York or Philadelphia: Purchase of $20.00 for every 100 pounds	Within 1,000 miles of New York or Philadelphia: Purchase of $30.00 for every 100 pounds	Within 1,000 miles of New York or Philadelphia: Purchase of 50.00 for every 100 pounds	Within 1,800 miles of New York or Philadelphia: Purchase of $75.00 for every 100 pounds	More than 1,800 miles of New York or Philadelphia: Purchase of $100.00 for every 100 pounds

In the first instance it will be observed if the distance is not greater than 50 miles from Philadelphia or New York and the goods do not weigh beyond 100 pounds for each $5.00 worth we will deliver by freight to your depot, transportation charges paid, or if the goods do not weigh beyond 100 pounds for each $7.50 expended upon them we deliver free of freight charges 150 miles from Philadelphia or New York—and so on.

If the above is not entirely clear to any out-of-town patron, we shall appreciate the writing us, asking for further information on any point involved.

Most of the goods illustrated in this book will, of course, be sent either by parcel post or express.

The goods which come under our Free unrestricted delivery offer in the United States or its possessions will also be sent at our cost for postage to any country that is a member of the International Parcel Post.

Do not send back goods C. O. D. If anything is unsatisfactory, return, sending letter of advice separately, and we will promptly refund the money. If liquids are sent by mail we do not pay the postage or the cost of the retainer.

New York — Gimbel Brothers — Philadelphia

Please Read the Following Carefully

GIMBEL BROTHERS LONDON, ENGLAND

SHIPPING INSTRUCTIONS.—State how you wish goods sent—Parcel Post, Express or Freight. If the goods are to be sent by insured Parcel Post, so state in your order and include the insurance fee of 5c. for a package not exceeding in value $25.00, and 10c. for a package not exceeding $50.00 in value. Our free delivery offer does not include insurance. Goods by Express do not need to be insured.

If your express or freight office is different from the town in which you reside, and goods are to be forwarded freight or express, mention the fact, stating clearly to what address the goods are to be shipped.

VERY NECESSARY.—If you remit with order, make mention of the character of the remittance and the amount. If you want the goods sent C. O. D. so state. If you have an open account with us make mention that goods are to be charged.

IN REMITTING.—*Remittances should be made by* AMERICAN, ADAMS, OR WELLS FARGO & CO. OR THEIR CONNECTIONS, EXPRESS MONEY ORDERS, or by Bank Drafts on New York or Philadelphia, or by Post Office Money Orders. Small sums can be remitted in postage stamps with little risk.

THINGS WE DO AND DON'T.—The Customer's good-will is invariably valued much higher than the money involved, and therefore we gladly accept back for credit, exchange or refund, as the case may be, articles in this book, if returned promptly, except Hair Goods, Rubber Goods, Combs, Brushes, Veilings, etc., which for sanitary reasons are not returnable.

Goods delivered free of transportation are returnable only when return charges are paid by the purchaser unless we were at fault in filling the order. Otherwise we cannot allow the return charges.

Fragile articles will be carefully packed and properly labeled as such, but as the Parcel Post does not guarantee their safe delivery neither can we. WE RECOMMEND WHERE POSSIBLE THAT SUCH SHIPMENTS BE MADE BY EXPRESS. *Except insured, we assume no responsibility for packages lost in the mails, but such losses are of rare occurrence.*

Goods sent C. O. D. or sold with wholesale or other discounts are not delivered free outside the confines of our wagon delivery.

SENDING SAMPLES.—We very gladly send samples of piece goods with the exception of a few things like real laces, high-grade trimmings and bordered goods, where it is impracticable to do so.

State kind of goods wanted, the color or colors, and about the price you care to pay, when we will be able to send you a nice line of samples in the goods you actually want to buy.

SENDING C. O. D.—We gladly send goods C. O. D., when so requested, if in our judgment it is suitable to do so—character of goods, distance, etc., to govern our decision.

ABOUT SUBSTITUTING.—When privilege of substituting is accorded us, and we are compelled to avail ourselves of it, we very gladly try to send a little better article at the same price.

FROM EITHER STORE.—It saves time and often transportation to send your order to the Gimbel store in the city nearest to you—New York or Philadelphia.

GIMBEL BROTHERS, BERLIN, GERMANY

Open a Charge Account With One or All of the Gimbel Stores

A charge account is a convenience for you and for us. We shall therefore appreciate the opportunity of opening one with you at one or all of our stores, if you will kindly make your responsibility known to us by references or otherwise.

Extracts from Letters from Our Customers in the United States, West Indies, Central and South America, Etc.

The Gimbel Mail business covers the entire civilized world, and from all directions have come words of approval—some from near home, some from the further confines of the United States and from its farthest away possessions—then some from Europe, some from Asia, some from Africa. Gimbels ship everywhere, and all over the world their merchandise and methods are favorably commented upon.

GIMBEL BROTHERS, LYONS, FRANCE.

From Luribay, La Paz, Bolivia, South America.
"I hereby acknowledge receipt of the goods ordered, and thank you for same. They are more than satisfactory."

From Taltal, Chile, South America.
"The merchandise sent me is now in my possession; everything came and all please me very much."

From Huila, Colombia, South America.
"Your kind favor at hand also the merchandise that I sent for, and same arrived to my entire satisfaction. Please send me a new catalog, as I wish to send you a large order.
"Your kind favor advising of shipment of goods at hand, also goods referred to just received, and they are very satisfactory."

From Cárdenas, Cuba.
"I received, to my entire satisfaction, the goods ordered some days since, and am very much pleased with everything.
"Take pleasure in again sending a money order for list of articles noted below:"

From Sagua la Grande, Cuba.
"Thank you so much for your prompt attention to my two orders. I especially appreciate the dispatch with which you carried out the Christmas part of it. Everything was *nicer* than your catalog led me to expect, which is not a very common characteristic."

From Harrington, Delaware.
"I've always been treated so courteously by your stores, both at Philadelphia and New York that it is a comfort to know when you get it at Gimbels the *quality* is all right."

From Guayaquil, Ecuador, South America.
"The packages are in my possession, and contents are very satisfactory."

From Honolulu, Hawaii.
"Received the table cloths, napkins, etc., and am very much pleased with them."

From Tegucigalpa, Honduras, Central America.
"The goods that I ordered from you reached me in due time, and everything was very satisfactory."

From Cherryvale, Kansas.
"I wish to thank you for prompt attention given to my order of some time ago for a pleated skirt, and want to say that same is entirely satisfactory. I like it just fine."

From Cambridge, Maryland.
"I received my dress and skirt several days ago and am delighted with them. I could not be more pleased if I had been in your store and selected them myself.
"I have bought several things from you, all before I was married, and have always been delighted with them."

From New Brunswick, N. J.
"Many thanks for the prompt way in which you filled my order. The goods perfectly satisfactory."

From Summit, N. J.
"It may interest you to know that I have not been shopping for two years, as I find I can do it so satisfactorily with you by mail."

From New York City, N. Y.
"I should like to take this opportunity of telling you how efficient I have always found your mail and telephone order department."

From Delhi, N. Y.
"What I like most about your store is your promptness in sending goods ordered by mail, besides the satisfaction your goods give."

From Falmouth, Mass.
"I was very much pleased with everything and you certainly have a fine store, judging from my order. I also appreciate

your charge account, since it is very convenient for me, as I am not very near the Postoffice."

From Lake George, N. Y.
"I must say in all my years of doing mail order business with the different big houses of New York yours is the most prompt and most courteous Mail Order Department of them all, and wish to thank you for your promptness and courtesy."

From Managua, Nicaragua, Central America.
"'Your letter and the parcel post package to which it referred reached me, and all arrived to my satisfaction. Thanks!'"

From Chadbourn, N. C.
"We are all very much pleased with everything; couldn't have been done any better had we been there in person."

From Panama, Rep. of Panama.
"Your letter and the package by parcel post received. I am very much pleased with all, and extend thanks."

From Harrisburg, Pa.
"I received waist and it is perfectly satisfactory. I think it beautiful. It is so good looking. Hereafter I need not fear to send for any garment. I thank you for filling the order so soon."

From Lock Haven, Pa.
"I am pleased to report that the coat which you sent me is very satisfactory and I am more than pleased with the selection.
"I thank you very kindly for your prompt and courteous attention, and can only add that in the future my mail order motto will be—'Gimbel first, Gimbel last and Gimbel always.'"

From Sellersville, Pa.
"The coat you sent me is quite satisfactory in every way. I thank you for the attention you gave to its selection. It is not the first time I have had cause to be grateful to Gimbels Mail Order Section."

From Government House, Porto Rico.
"I wish to state that I am very pleased with both sets of china, and particularly with the large one, which is very pretty."

From Bell Buckle, Tenn.
"Nearly three years ago I visited your store and did all my shopping there. I bought a complete spring outfit for myself, clothes for a young lady daughter, presents for a married daughter and her baby, and everything gave complete satisfaction.
"My daughter at Sagua la Grande, Cuba, has written me that she is more pleased with some recent purchases made from you than from any department store in New York with which she is acquainted. I thought it would gratify you to know this.

From Lee Hall, Virginia.
"My order received and I thank you for your quick response. Everything was satisfactory and am delighted with each article. I have never yet made a purchase at your store which was not satisfactory or what it was represented to be."

Extract from letter of a valued customer at Fayetteville, W. Va., accompanying an order for furniture and a remittance of $204.00 in payment of same:
"This coming spring I hope to buy some more furniture and will write you concerning it, as I find that your Mail Order Department has given me the very best of satisfaction."

GIMBEL BROTHERS, PARIS, FRANCE.

Gimbels Paris, London and American Style Book

Fashions Are Nothing Less Than Delightful This Season

K-800
$5.00

Every innovation has been maintained and frocks are easy-fitting, with soft, graceful lines, yet to all the clinging effects have been added the smart, trig, military lines that are shown in the square shoulder effects, in the charming strapped and braided trimmings, and in the most practical and rational flare that characterizes the hems of skirts as well as the hems of coats and jackets. This is the last touch that was necessary to make the prevailing fashions of the past few seasons absolutely sensible. There is no skimping of materials, lines are full and free, and sensationally lovely silhouettes are shown in a large variety of entirely "different" models.

Gimbel gowns are "different," each with a touch of style that distinguishes it at once as having been created, not merely cut and sewn up after the manner of the careless factory or indifferent dressmaker, and that makes even the most inexpensive of Gimbel frocks a note of gladness and, as the poets say, "A joy forever."

This charming Morning Frock Is A Splendid Example Of Gimbel Style in the famous Gimbel quality and at a money-saving price that is characteristic of Gimbels

K—800. This cleverly designed dress is intended for morning or general wear. It is suitable for neighborly visiting and is one of the daintiest models that our various experts have been fortunate enough to develop so successfully. The dainty broken stripes give excellent long lines and the slightly draped blouse overlays a filmy net lace vestee with soft flying frill edged with velvet. The new standing ruche collar falls in soft raised ripple and has a firm military underband to hold it high and snug about the neck. Same soft net lace frill finishes the sleeve and both are trimmed with bands of velvet ribbon. The graceful skirt has a slightly gathered yoke effect, below which the skirt hangs in rippled fulness and has an exceptionally wide flaring hem. The front of the skirt is laid in wide panel effect, further carrying out the long lines of this charming costume. Smart flat girdle is outlined with velvet and finished with tailored bows. There is a charm about this model that will appeal to the woman of taste. It is entirely suitable for both young and older women and is a delightful summery costume. In a superior quality of broken striped voile, in white with stripes in black, blue or rose. Sizes 34 to 41. Note the price—but $5.00.

and compare them carefully with the styles shown in this book. You will see at once that we have the very best of them reproduced in the many varieties of fabrics, and you will also readily distinguish the clever adaptations that have resulted. Of the hundreds of garments shown, no two are in the least alike, and you would almost think it impossible to create so many novel and becoming styles from what would appear to be the few special features that are generally accepted as style authentic. Whether your choice is from our waist department or from the dresses or suits, or even the most trifling item that may happen to be your need, you will have a world of opportunity for making selections until there is no question of your entire satisfaction.

On this page you see a very simple and youthful adaptation of the striking military effects, and you would hardly think it possible that this simple washable fabric has the possibilities for so smart and substantial a model. Yet you have only to read the description of this frock and look at the picture and you will be convinced that it is a most desirable purchase.

This Smart Frock conforms to the new military fashion lines and emphasizes the clever innovations that are evidenced in the authentic style features that are reproduced in high-priced garments.

K—900. A military frock of excellent style and one that is sure to be very popular. The handsome striped wiry voile used herein emphasizes the long line effect that makes it a most stunning costume. The waist is cut with square military shoulder effect with yoke. Wide stitched tuck gives it the appearance of having a deep yoke from beneath which the blouse appears gathered with slight fulness into the wide military belt. The military collar is also overlaid with handsome turn-over of Indian Tissue embellished with hemstitching. Long sleeves shaped to fit closely at the wrist are finished with hemstitched turn-back cuffs to match. Carrying out the long line effect of this costume is the wide panel of plain voile that extends from the collar to the hem of the skirt, closing with gun metal buttons in a very fashionable arrangement. The skirt is built to carry out the coat effect of this costume, a yoke coming to about hip depth of bias material, stitched and finished with a wide fold to give it the appearance of a coat bottom. This coat effect top, which also has the appearance of a yoke for the skirt, overhangs a soft full circular ripple in which the skirt is finished. The wide military girdle is in contrasting color, giving it an exceedingly smart finish. In wiry crisp voile in black and white stripe. Sizes 34 to 48. **An unequaled value at $5.95.**

K-900
$5.95

Gimbels Paris, London and American Style Book

The Style-Value of Gimbel Quality Attire

At prices that can safely be your guide throughout this book

In creating Gimbel style and maintaining Gimbel value, we do so at a tremendous effort. The various departments represented in this book are each doing their share to give in every item the utmost value so that no transaction can possibly lead to anything but the utmost satisfaction. Satisfying the customer is the foundation of the Gimbel success and has resulted in the world-renowned merchandising organization that is exclusively our own. The Gimbel catalogue is our message to you and is our greeting of good-will, and, furthermore, of the most exacting economy. We consider the economy to you on our part of buying by mail through this book a fine achievement.

We are not overestimating our ability to give you better values than any other organization without duly considering the fact that we can do this chiefly because our organization is, in fact, better than that of any other organization in the U. S. A., as evidenced by our European houses and our tremendous stores in New York, Philadelphia and Milwaukee. Our entire foreign affiliations are busily engaged all the year round in obtaining everything of merit and interest as well as the tremendous quantities of staple and every-day merchandise.

Country Club Dress of High Quality Ramie Linen

K-1000. There is a particularly modish swing to this snappy man tailored dress that distinguishes it as an ideal outing frock, and in its outline portrays the very highest expression of style desired in a garment intended for general outing wear. Made of a superb quality of roughly finished ramie linen, it is much more practical than French linen and will not muss as easily. The blousy waist has prettily rounded lines, closing in side effect, with numerous buttons that also serve as a trimming. The sleeves are set into deep arm eyes and the neck and sleeves are finished with wide, shapely collar and cuffs of white linen, hemstitched with deep, firm hem. The shaped Empire girdle that holds the fulness of the blouse forms slight bodice effect and holds the Empire waist line. The flaring skirt is also the latest development in modish models, fitting smoothly over the hips in straight line fashion and coming to an exceedingly wide umbrella flare. You will thoroughly enjoy this graceful and becoming frock. In fine quality ramie linen in rose, tan, navy blue or white. Sizes 34 to 44. A truly splendid bargain at $5.00.

K-1000
$5.00

Quality-value Is a Most Important Consideration

In maintaining the high standard of excellence that has made Gimbel famous, we appreciate the balance that is necessary to make you a satisfied patron. No matter how excellent the quality of materials, if Style is lacking you are not satisfied. No matter how excellent the style, if Quality is lacking you will not have the satisfaction you have a right to demand in your attire. The psychology of clothes is a science that proves that a large part of your satisfaction in life is derived from being becomingly and properly clothed. This can apply to all times and to all garments. There is no need to have anything but suitable wearing apparel if your selections are made from the many classifications of modish attire shown in this book. Shopping by mail is pleasant and easy and everything goes to you with our assurance of satisfaction with every transaction.

The world-wide connections of Gimbels are of inestimable value even in garments made wholly from American fabrics in the U. S. A., and when you understand all that Gimbel merchandise means, and how often American-made fabrics and styles are dependent in some small way on our foreign connections, you will realize how important they are. Possibly only a trifling touch of something that goes into the fabric is obtainable abroad, and yet, were this small item omitted, the entire character of the thing itself is changed. As an example, a certain fabric may be ever so rich and beautiful, yet if the dyes that go into it are obtainable only abroad any change therein would naturally produce an entirely different result, both in tone of the color and in the finish of the texture.

A Man-Tailored Coat Dress In Your Choice Of

Navy Blue Serge at $10.75

Or Sand Colored Gabardine, $12.50

K-1100
$10.75

K—1100. In this dress you see a superb model that is developed after the ideals of the carefully dressed American woman of fashion. The jaunty Eton coat is in full double breasted style, standing sharply away from the body, and closes with a double row of large ornamental buttons. A clever little handkerchief pocket effect is placed low at one side, also trimmed with buttons to match. A novel raised collar with abrupt Empire revers are of sand colored bengaline silk, the front cut away in a vest effect and underlaid with vestee of hemstitched Georgette crepe. A small back view shows the stylish Empire belt carrying out the high waisted line of this charming design. The skirt has graduated pleats finished with silk arrow-heads coming to about hip depth and forming exceedingly handsome wide flaring hem. Sizes 34 to 44. In fine wool navy blue serge, **$10.75**. In high grade gabardine suiting, **$12.50**.

Here You See Reproduced Two of Gimbels Matchless Models That Will Hold Their Own in Every Fashion Center.

Their grace and charm are the personification of refinement and place them on a par with art creations for individuality and style. Were you to have an artist of high standing create a gown for you for a special occasion, you would not be more successful than has been the style creator of these two most engaging frocks. You can make no mistake in selecting either one and if you choose them both you will be doubly glad and profit by your choice. You will readily see that here is your opportunity to obtain Gimbel styles at saving prices.

Bolero Frock of Crisp White Voile

K—1200. The grace and charm of this one-piece dress are sure to appeal to the woman of fashion. Style is a delightful variation of the military coatee developed in a clever bolero model. Embroidery and filet lace insertions are prettily combined, and Irish crocheted buttons and loops give a military finish. The sleeves are in a charming three-quarter length with fancy flying cuffs with bow. A Directoire collar completes the modish silhouette and a wide girdle of rich moire silk emphasizes the Empire waistline. The long lines of the full, flaring skirt hang in graceful ripples and are finished with two wide hemstitched tucks and deep hemstitched hem. A delightful, summery frock that is in the very best style and of high quality. In white only. Sizes, 34 to 44. $8.75.

Eton Bolero-Dress of Dainty White Voile

K—1201. The popular Eton jacket is developed to meet the demands of the modish loose frocks that are the accepted novelty for summer wear. Nothing more alluring than this charming high-waisted effect that gives opportunity to the modish Empire waistline that is so generally becoming. The crisp French voile that is used in the body of the frock is trimmed with beautiful insertions of rich Venise lace, forming wide points that outline the jacket and are also introduced in flat points on the skirt. A new Oliver Twist collar is a feature of this snappy frock; it has a novel shape and rolls soft and full from either side of the deep lace-edged V that completes the front. Crocheted ball buttons in a continuous row on either side serve as a novel trimming, and the entire harmony of this frock is one that will be most engaging. In crisp white voile. Sizes, 34 to 44. $10.75.

K-1200
$8.75

K-1201
$10.75

New York — Gimbel Brothers — Philadelphia

Under the guidance of fashion experts who are in thorough touch with foreign exponents of style, the Gimbel staff of designers are continually in the foremost rank of those who adapt the extreme foreign models to the demands of American tastes and figure lines. Gimbel styles are authentic, in that they embody the best features of exclusive and high grade models, and in doing so attain supremacy that is unchallenged in its field. The buying power of the Gimbel merchandising organization and their joint efforts are what you receive in the exclusive apparel of which this book is only a small and inadequate representation.

Garden Party Dress—a Richly Embroidered Robe

K—1300. Exquisite filet motifs woven in fine white voile are a special feature of this wonderful dress that is fashioned after the latest hand made embroidered lingerie models. The bolero is in charming loose style and rich insertions and trailing vines of embroidery embellish the entire bolero. A wide girdle of moire forms an empire effect and gives a charming bit of contrast. The skirt is fashioned to fit and embellished with motifs and is embroidered to match. The gores are in a novel arrangement outlined with hemstitching, the skirt falling in a wide, flaring ripple. This skirt is made with cords, making it self-adjusting. Dainty touches of color are in the buttons that here and there trim this exquisite frock and in the girdle. In fine white voile with colored girdle and trimmings. Sizes, 34 to 44. Price $12.75.

Afternoon Frock of Voile Combined With Woven Ratine

K—1301. In this dainty frock you see a wonderful adaptation of the new suspender skirts combined with bodice. The dainty underblouse formed of rows of tucked net and lace and dainty Venise edging. The blouse extends into a high military effect collar, also edged with Venise, and the exquisite sleeves are long and of net embroidered in soft, rich floss. Crocheted buttons are also used to trim both bodice and skirt. Particularly attractive feature of this frock is the woven ratine border of heavily raised stripes that appear on the wide, flaring skirt and also in the empire belt, finishing the fancy sleeves are cuffs, a Lace frill on cuff. An exquisite adaptation of suspender model in voile combined with net lace, in white only. Sizes, 34 to 44. $15.00.

K-1300
$12.75

K-1301
$15.00

Gimbels Paris, London and American Style Book

Two Splendid Examples of Style Value and Intrinsic Worth

If you want the very latest style in dresses for the price, try Gimbels. If you want the best value for the price, you will find Gimbels pre-eminent. If you want the quickest and best service, patronize Gimbels. The huge Gimbel Stores have a working organization that is matchless for efficiency and they can best serve you. Read page 7 for expressions by customers of their complete satisfaction with Gimbel methods and Gimbel goods.

K—1400. Woman's Beautiful Afternoon or Street Dress. Polka dot voile is the fabric used. Made attractively with new "bolero" effect waist, rounded in front and attached at armholes and yoke. Three-quarter set-in sleeves edged with ruffle of net lace and band of black velvet. Front of waist has a hemstitched panel. V neck with neat revers and standing hemstitched collar. Bolero is finished with ball and loop embroidery edging, making a very pretty design. Black velvet girdle belt is connected in front with two straps and white pearl buckles. Wide skirt has panel front intercepting a deep bias fold at bottom in circular effect. Black and white, or blue and white. Sizes, 34 to 44 inches bust measure. **$3.95.**

K—1401. A Wonderful Special. Woman's Very Attractive Silk Dress. Fine quality messaline, substantial and of good luster—a very desirable quality. Dress is made plain with long, tight sleeves, much favored at present. Neat waist with wide peplum belt. New V shaped neck opens below the standing collar, which fastens in front with a strap and is entirely edged with dainty ruffle of figured net lace, giving softness to the face. New full circular skirt, fitted at waist line and flaring at foot, the season's innovation. Navy, black, Copenhagen or brown. This is a most unusual value, only possible through buying in large quantities to supply the big Gimbel Stores. Sizes, 34 to 44 inches bust measure. **$5.00.**

K-1400
$3.95

K-1401
$5.00

New York — Gimbel Brothers — Philadelphia

Two Dresses of Charming Style and Unequaled Value for Women

Here we present two charming dresses, embodying all the newest style features that you are accustomed to find at Gimbels, so cleverly combined that almost any type of figure would look well in them, and they would be becoming to almost every one. And the materials will delight by their beauty and quality. You will have the satisfaction of knowing you are well dressed when wearing a Gimbel frock.

K—1500. Woman's Fashionable Embroidered White Frock. Appropriate for tango, teas or evenings. Designed with a modified bolero in loose jacket effect, very long in the back. Made of medallion embroidery with long, drooping points falling over a satin girdle which has a large bow in back. Front of waist has pin-tucked net vestee trimmed with small black velvet buttons and satin bow at center, to match girdle. Double ruffled net collar at back of neck with band of black velvet around the throat. Embroidered sleeves, with points falling over a deep ruffle of pleated net edged with lace. Small tucks around hips with tunic of embroidery, stitched to plain bottom of lawn with deep tuck and three-inch hem. Skirt is made very wide, after the newest fashion. Sizes, 34 to 44 bust measure. **$4.95.**

K—1501. Woman's Beautiful Soft Messaline Dress. Made with the new loose bolero effect attached at neck to under waist, so nothing intercepts its fashionable lines. Bolero has a piping of contrasting silk and stylish ball buttons in front. Neck is V shaped. Revers, standing collar and cuffs are of contrasting shades of satin. Wide, crushed girdle extends high to form Empire effect. Skirt is designed with a yoke at top, also a panel in front trimmed with buttons. Three pleats at sides give fullness and width to bottom, the distinguishing feature of 1915 skirts. Green, navy, black, or Copenhagen. If you could see the beauty and quality of the messaline you would wonder at the modest price asked. Sizes, 34 to 41 inches bust measure. **$9.75.**

K-1500
$4.95

K-1501
$9.75

Gimbels Paris, London and American Style Book

15

K-1600
$2.95

K-1601
$5.95

K-1602
$1.95

These Three Charming Dresses are described on page 17.

New York — Gimbel Brothers — Philadelphia

Charming, Cool, Comfortable Dresses for Women

It is not only a fine organization, but huge—the New York store with over 6,000 employes, the Philadelphia store with a like number, and the Milwaukee store with about 2,000—then the employes of the Paris, Lyons, London and Berlin houses—the Gimbel connections in Constantinople, Kobe, etc. None of the manufacturing end included in the above figures.

K—1600. Woman's Allover Embroidered Gown. Simple and very attractive. Waist made plain with the embroidered points overlapping a vestee of plain lawn. Invisible front closing. Square lawn collar edged with lace. Back extends over shoulders to form yoke. Set-in sleeve of allover embroidery. Wide satin girdle with large bow in front. Skirt is made with a deep yoke and two flounces of allover embroidery. Cut very full to flare at the lower edge. White only, with white, pink or blue girdle. Sizes, 34 to 44 bust measure. You could hardly find a value to equal this anywhere in the county outside of the Gimbel Stores. Note the remarkably low price. $2.95.

K—1601. Woman's Beautiful Plaid Cotton Crepe Dress. Cross bar design. Very full waist with vestee and lay-down collar of double tiers of embroidery. Yoke at back, with gathers below. Three-quarter full sleeve with quaint double ruffle on cuff and bows of satin. Crushed satin girdle with large loop bow and knotted ends in front. Skirt has yoke all around and two deep folds at bottom. Full flare width. Beautiful plaid combinations with trimmings in green, rose or black. Sizes, 34 to 40 bust measure. A charming and graceful frock that will delight you. $5.95.

K—1602. Woman's Striped Voile Dress. Very remarkable and pretty. One of our best selections at the price offered. Waist is rather plain with a little fullness at front and a pointed yoke at side with two covered buttons of satin. Plain belt of self material. Standing collar of messaline to match material. Open throat with ruffle of fine lace. Satin buttons down front of waist and skirt. Skirt is circular in shape and has yoke broken in front and a wide fold down center. Blue and white, black and white, pink and white, lavender and white or green and white. Sizes, 34 to 44 bust measure. $1.95.

K-1700
$5.50

K-1701
$3.50

K-1702
$1.50

K-1703
$3.95

Misses' and Small Women's Dresses, Modestly Priced

K—1700. Miss's and Small Woman's Linen Combination Street Dress. Full jacket of color with high empire belt. Set-in sleeves, pointed at wrist. Wide turn-over collar that may be worn low or standing. Front of waist, belt and sleeves are trimmed with white crochet buttons, which makes the model very dressy. White skirt attached to an under bodice edged with lace. A deep yoke over hips with a one-inch loose edge. Very full skirt in white with a deep side pleat on each side forms a very full flare. This model is suitable for dressy occasions. Pink and white, blue and white, or tan and white combination. Sizes, 14 to 20 years. $5.50.

K—1701. Miss's and Small Woman's Ratine Dress. Tailored waist with a little fullness at waist line. Round standing fan collar of contrasting material, extending down front to form a vestee. Wide belt of same shade and cuffs on three-quarter sleeves to match. Skirt is a plain flare model with two patch pockets and deep fold down front. Waist buttons through in front with covered two-tone buttons. Skirt is made in walking length. Natural color trimmed with cadet blue or all white trimmed with cadet blue or rose. Button on each pocket. Sizes, 14 to 20 years. $3.50.

K—1702. Miss's and Small Woman's Dress. Made especially for street, also suitable for house wear—indeed, appropriate to use at any time. It is a simple model of fine quality gingham in checks and trimmed with plain gingham. Collar and cuffs finished with beautiful embroidery edge. Collar is also enriched with scalloped Venise edging. Fitted at waist-line with belt. Panel back and front, extending two inches above belt, forms a high waist effect. Front of waist and panel are prettily trimmed with white pearl buttons. Very full skirt widened by pleats. Blue and white or black and white checks. Sizes, 14 to 20 years. $1.50.

K—1703. Miss's and Small Woman's Very Pretty Dress. Made of striped rice cloth, trimmed with plain colored linen. Waist is designed with set-in sleeves, vestee, and fastens invisibly at side front. Yoke effect over shoulder back and front. Square standing collar with hemstitched edge extends into long revers that meet a crushed girdle of self cloth piped with linen to match collar and cuffs. Skirt has Bayadere yoke extending to hip, and a very full lower portion with half-inch pleats at sides and back. Yoke, belt, bodice and cuffs are trimmed with covered buttons of white and color to match. An extremely fascinating model. White and tan, white and blue, white and pink or white and lavender. Sizes, 14 to 20 years. $3.95.

Gimbels Paris, London and American Style Book

Dame Fashion is Partial to Girlhood in Creating Modes

The outfitting of Misses and Girls is yearly growing in volume at the Gimbel Stores. A home corps of experts, augmented by the matchless Paris house, are constantly scouring the markets for becoming, girlish modes. The lowness of manufacturers' prices, induced by the hugeness of Gimbel orders, bring correspondingly low selling prices, that, with the style appeal, make Gimbel clothing peerless.

K—1900. Miss's and Junior Girl's Very Airy and Dainty Dancing Dress. White net over evening shades of peach, Nile or light blue. Model has the new Bebe Empire waist. Skirt set on with a stylish frill and laid into deep tucks at foot. Waist has a wide corsage band of silver thread lace, held in place over shoulder with black velvet ribbon with bow. Soft net shoulders and sleeves. A wonderfully stylish, fascinating and girlish frock. Misses' sizes, 14, 16 and 18 years. Junior sizes, shorter skirts, 15 and 17 years. $10.75.

K—1901. Exquisite and Dainty Dancing Frock for Misses. Softest clinging chiffon, very fine and dainty, over white net with shadow lace. Square neck, giving wonderful charm to the features. Waist is of the chiffon and is gathered on shoulder, falling over the short, full kimono sleeve, ruffled at edge. Shadow lace vestee back and front. The new Empire forms the new Empire. Full tunic skirt, with a band of shadow lace, six inches from bottom, falling over a chiffon flounce. Corn, blue, pink or white chiffon over white net. Sizes, 14 to 20 years. $5.75.

K—1902. Miss's Afternoon or Party Dress. Fine, soft embroidered net. The stylish and pretty waist is in one piece with the loose kimono sleeves. Lace panel in front. Square neck. An under-bodice of net, made tight-fitting, with ruffle of lace to form sleeve effect. Wide princess crushed girdle of messaline. Two-ruffle skirt, an underlining of net,

attaching a deep fold of messaline at bottom to match girdle. This model is made especially for dancing or party purposes. It is simple, yet very attractive and girlish. White with messaline in baby blue, pink or maize. Sizes, 14 to 20 years. $5.95.

K—1903. Miss's and Small Woman's Dancing Dress. Made of chiffon and satin. Waist is the new Empire of folded satin with chiffon folds over shoulders. Feather trimming around arm size and forming mounts for the boutonniere roses. Accordion-pleated underskirt with chiffon tunic over it. Feather trimming around edge of tunic. Light blue, pink, maize, Nile or white. Sizes, 14 to 18 years. $13.75.

K-1800
$11.75

K-1801
$8.95

K-1802
$5.75

K-1803
$2.95

K—1800. Stylish Afternoon Dress for Misses and Small Women. Crepe de chine in new gray, navy, green or black. Model has waistcoat in front, continuing in a girdle shape around to the back, where it is finished with a pretty shirred sash. Front closes with ball buttons. Dainty fancy net vestee. Pleated chiffon ruche at neck. Long tight sleeves with drooping cuff, ball buttons and chiffon pleating. Coquettish boutonniere rose gives finish. Full flare skirt with three encircling tucks. Sizes, 14 to 20 years. $11.75.

K—1801. Miss's Charming Street Frock. Graceful crepe de chine dress. New "bolero" effect with boutonniere rose. A little fullness below the V-shaped neck, with two novelty tassels.

Neck edged with soft lace. Small collar at back. Chiffon veils all-over lace sleeves, which are full length and attached to underbodice of fine lawn. Crepe de chine cuffs. Skirt has four-inch shirring on hips, which makes it very full. Two-inch fold down front is finished with buttons. Navy, brown, Belgium blue or black. Sizes, 14 to 20 years. $8.95.

K—1802. Miss's Beautiful Embroidered White Lingerie Robe. Made with long-waisted jacket basque. Allover embroidery forms front, which closes with small crystal buttons. Girdle is partly concealed by the jacket. A small turn-over collar of same soft satin to match girdle. Full-length embroidered sleeve with cuff of lace insertion and lingerie. Back of

waist is of embroidery, with lace insertion. Shirred skirt of allover embroidery with scallops attached over a bottom of lingerie with lace insertion. Maize, blue or pink girdles. Sizes, 14 to 20 years. $5.75.

K—1803. Beautiful Afternoon Dress for Misses. Neat voile in colored stripes. Set-in yoke of fine ruffled net. Wide crushed girdle of black taffeta. Turn-over revers of white organdie. Three-quarter sleeves, with a cuff of pleated organdie. Pin-tucked, standing collar with hemstitching and ruffle. Very full skirt with yoke effect over hips overlapping full lower portion. Skirt and waist finished with silver ball buttons. Skirt flares and is very wide. Black and white, blue and white or pink and white. Sizes, 14 to 20 years. $2.95.

Commencement, Dances, Weddings, Troop Into the Girl's Life

Whether as a graduate, bridesmaid or one of the merry companions, a girl must be suitably dressed—often a serious matter if there be more than one to provide for. Gimbels have happily combined beautiful, stylish dresses of high merit with very reasonable prices. There is no need for the girl to long for pretty clothes and stay at home from pleasures because she has not got them. Girls should enjoy youth while they have it.

K-1901
$5.75

K-1902
$5.95

K-1900
$10.75

K-1903
$13.75

See page 18 for descriptions of these lovely Dresses

New York — Gimbel Brothers — Philadelphia

19

K-2000
$10.00

K-2001
$13.75

K-2002
$15.00

K-2003
$15.00

These exquisite Dresses are described on opposite page

New York — Gimbel Brothers — Philadelphia

Fit for Lovely Girlhood Are These Gimbel Creations

White is the color of innocence, and best suited for children's festive wear, also good for any occasion. The pretty colored dresses in this catalogue are so stylish and of such appropriate materials that they are quite nice enough in appearance for Sunday, and yet sufficiently sturdy for daily wear. Description of the Lovely Dresses on opposite page.

K—2000. Dainty and Inexpensive Dancing Dress for Misses and Small Women. A lovely creation, prettily decollete, in chiffon and satin combination. New short, full, pointed overskirt of chiffon with satin piping and satin foundation. Spray of coquettish French flowers on deep crushed Empire girdle of the satin with sash ends at the left. Soft chiffon waist and short sleeves. Light blue, maize, pink or nile. You will be delighted with the quality Sizes, 14, 16 and 18 years. $10.00.

K—2001. Newest Afternoon Dress for Misses and Small Women. Combination of soft taffeta and sheer voile of particular beauty and fineness. Short jaunty jacket of taffeta and folded taffeta girdle. Neck is finished with soft net ruche and velvet baby ribbon. Taffeta oversleeves lapping the net puffing at hand. New, full voile skirt made with graduated tucks, a favorite touch this season. New brown, rose or Copenhagen. A wonderfully dressy and pleasing creation. Sizes, 14, 16 and 18 years. $13.75.

K—2002. Miss's and Small Woman's Dancing Dress. Fashionable puffed Empire waist formed by corded shirring and enriched by rose corsage. Hardly a frock this season but shows a trace of the charming Empire period. Chiffon shoulders with silver braid. Braid to match forms yoke back and front. New draped overskirt with touches of flowers in drapery and silver braid edge. Orchid pink, blue or nile green. Sizes, 14, 16 and 18 years. $15.00.

K—2003. Beautiful Combination Dress for Misses and Small Women. Soft, clinging chiffon-striped, corduroy and fine voile. New bolero jacket effect of chiffon-striped corduroy. High collar of delicate white embroidery and soft vestee of white organdie. Stylish long voile sleeves. Jacket and sleeves finished with loops and metal ball buttons. Finished with wide Persian silk belt. New full skirt of voile with chiffon-striped corduroy forming deep fold at foot. Beautiful shades of rose or Copenhagen. Sizes, 14, 16 and 18 years. $15.00.

K-2100
$7.50

K-2101
$9.75

K-2102
$8.95

K-2103
$12.75

K—2100. Exquisite, Dainty Afternoon Dress for Misses and Young Women. Soft white embroidery voile flouncing forms the loose bolero that falls to the Empire waistline. Bolero and sleeves have inset of Venise lace and lace edging. New standing flare collar of embroidered organdie. Soft girdle of white, blue or pink peeping under the bolero. The new full skirt of embroidery has plain deep embroidery yoke, trimmed with buttons. Bottom of skirt has pretty insertion and lace edge. Sizes, 14, 16 and 18 years. $7.50.

K—2101. Miss's and Small Woman's Dainty Imported White Voile Dress. All of the dress shows a combination of dotted and plain voile. The waist is dotted voile, beautifully set in with filet Venise lace on shoulders and each side simulating the new suspender effect, and is also tucked in clusters. The waist is Empire and finished with unique broad ribbon girdle. High standing collar at back. The new flaring skirt of plain voile with Van Dyke yoke and inset panel down front of dotted voile. Finished with two hemstitched tucks and hem. In all white or white with pink, blue or nile green ribbon. Sizes, 14, 16 and 18 years. $9.75.

K—2102. Miss's and Young Woman's Smart Afternoon Dress, also suitable for Graduation. The newest style points have been assembled in this frock. Handsome white embroidered voile forms the new Empire waist, the points cleverly simulating a bolero, which falls over a soft pink, blue or white ribbon girdle. Full-length sleeves and new high collar of embroidery. Skirt of embroidery in two tiers fitted at hips. Lace insertion appears on edge of vest and simulates the deep tier effect on skirt. Sizes, 14, 16 and 18 years. $8.95.

K—2103. Miss's and Young Woman's Dainty Graduation or Dancing Frock. All white, exquisite embroidered net flouncing composes dress. Three rows of puffed shirring give yoke effect to skirt which is stylish and full. The pretty soft waist has net lace frill over a ribbon frill in Empire bolero effect, also soft shirred puffings on waist and short sleeves. Ribbon is in all white, pink or blue. Foundation of net. Handsome bow of the net appears at side front. Finish of field flowers is pretty and quaint. The entire dress is exquisite, and value for the price is splendid. Sizes, 14, 16 and 18 years. $12.75.

Gimbels Paris, London and American Style Book

K-2200
$6.75

K-2201
$5.75

K-2202
$5.95

K-2203
$7.95

Dresses and Coat Suits for Misses and Small Women

The Gimbel Stores have a wonderful line of women's and children's apparel, modes being the most advanced and prices the lowest for equal grade. Supporting this is a service that is the marvel of the mercantile world. The same fine courtesy is extended equally, whether a purchase or exchange, whether order is large or small. Promptness and dispatch characterize Gimbels handling of each commission, and where the very few transactions go astray, every effort is made to satisfactorily adjust.

K—2200. Miss's or Small Woman's Very Stylish White Linen Dress. Waist prettily trimmed with imitation hand-embroidery and the popular hemstiching. New fashionable pointed rever and collar edged with Venise lace. New, modish, shaped yoke skirt with three deep pleats at side, giving fullness and the new skirt width. Soft crushed silk belt. White with pink or light blue girdle. Sizes, 14, 16 and 18 years. The linen is of excellent quality, and in combination with the silk girdle makes a very charming dress. You would not find such a value in any other than a Gimbel store. **$6.75.**

K—2201. Miss's or Small Woman's Youthful and Charming Dress. Soft linen. Short bolero jacket effect, loose in front and

held in position with hemstitched linen peasant girdle in back. Velvet girdle across front. White inner bolero. Dainty, embroidered vestee finished at neck with collar. New yoke skirt with pleats in back and flare bottom in the correct width. White, rose, light gray or Copenhagen. Sizes, 14, 16 and 18 years. Another great value or it would not be offered by the Gimbel stores. **$5.75.**

K—2202. Miss's or Small Woman's Pretty Afternoon Dress. Made of quaint flowered voile in beautiful colorings. Empire bolero effect waist buttoned in back and trimmed in front with small cluster buttons and loops. Soft silk girdle and pipings. New flare tunic trimmed at hips

with loops and buttons, and finished at lower edge with ruffle which overlaps two other ruffles. A charming mode, adopted from the days of grandma's girlhood. Simple, quaint and sweet. Rose or Copenhagen effect. Sizes, 14, 16 and 18 years. An astonishing value. **$5.95.**

K—2203. Smartest of Summer Styles in a Military Trimmed Dress of Cotton Ratine for Misses or Small Women. Circular tunic over a drop skirt with circular ratine bottom. Front of dress and the stylish long sleeves show braiding and large crochet ball buttons. Stylish leather belt. Copenhagen or white with Copenhagen trimming. Sizes, 14, 16 and 18 years. **$7.95.**

K-2300 $16.75   K-2301 $15.75   K-2302 $14.75   K-2303 $12.75

Very Trig Suits for Misses and Small Women

K—2300. Miss's or Small Woman's Smart Military Coat Suit of Gabardine. The nobby short coat is lavishly trimmed with military braid. High flaring standing silk collar. Empire, postillion back with exceptionally high belt and six tucks below. The new skirt has two side pockets and deep side pleats below, and is also trimmed with military braid. Colors, navy or black gabardine, or black and white shepherd check. Sizes, 14, 16 and 18 years. Best value. **$16.75.**

K—2301. Miss's or Small Woman's Calling Suit of Navy, Copenhagen or Black Serge. The new dressy short coat, with high standing flaring collar faced with silk, and trimmed with military straps and

buttons. Front of coat shows yoke with fullness across bust, and cloth revers. Postillion back with belt. Side of coat shows the smartest touch in ball trimming. New flare skirt with belt extending into a flap panel at each side with ball button trimming, to match coat. Sizes, 14 to 18 years. **$15.75.**

K—2302. Miss's and Small Woman's New Covert Cloth Suit. Up-to-date model with very high waist line and narrow sectional belt with buckles and buttons of self material. Military collar, with turn over of black velvet. Buttoned close to neck with cloth covered buttons. Postillion, with two-inch edge and rows of buttons in back. Set-in sleeve with row of but-

tons and neat tab fastening. Peau de cygne lined. New flare circular skirt with deep lapover fold down front. Color, tan. Sizes, 14 to 18 years. **$14.75.**

K—2303. Miss's and Small Woman's Nobby Suit. Good quality serge. Coat has yoke back and front, with two side pleats down back from yoke, enclosing a panel with pleated skirt effect below a wide short belt with buckles of self material. Half belted front to match back, with buckle and buttons. Mannish sleeves, trimmed with bands of self material forming cuff and buttons. New yoke skirt with side pleat down front from yoke. Double box pleat down back from waist opening into fullness. Colors, putty, navy, Copenhagen. or black. Sizes, 14 to 18 years. **$12.75.**

Gimbels Paris, London and American Style Book

K-2400
$10.00

K-2401
$10.75

K-2402
$8.95

K-2403
$9.75

For full descriptions see the opposite page.

New York — Gimbel Brothers — Philadelphia

Descriptions of the Cleverly Designed Suits Illustrated on Opposite Page

As heretofore, the Gimbel Stores will make up suits or dresses to order in extra large sizes at an advanced cost. Write us; stating your measurements and the number you prefer, and we will quote the price.

K—2400. Miss's and Small Woman's Semi-Norfolk Suit. Beautiful novelty mixture. Man tailored collar and revers. Set in mannish sleeves with stitched cuff button-trimmed. Coat belted in at waistline with a wide, loose belt which extends around back to side front. Fullness pleated under the belt in front. Back has pleated panel. Wide circular skirt, straight front, fastens invisibly at left side. Back has wide panel forming full pleats at either side. Girdle top. Black and white novelty mixture only. Sizes, 14 to 20 years. **$10.00.**

K—2401. Woman's Beautiful Empire Suit. Fine quality serge. Man tailored throughout. Coat has a stylish belt of self material, trimmed with a fancy buckle in front. Double panel extends down back from waistline to bottom of coat, finished with tiny buttons. Coat slopes down front forming points. Set-in sleeve, finished with a stitched cuff and tiny buttons. Man tailored collar and revers. Skirt is one of the new full models, cut slightly circular. Fastens over left hip. Girdle top. Sizes, 34 to 44 bust. Colors, navy, black or putty. **$10.75.**

K—2402. Woman's and Miss's Serviceable Suit. Made of exceptionally good quality serge in navy or black. Coat is made on Empire lines in back and has straight front with pointed corners. Mannish collar and revers. Inset handkerchief pocket at side. Deep, comfortable set-in sleeves have stitched cuff trimmed with covered buttons. Inverted pleats in back, at each side, from waist line form panel and are trimmed with buttons. Skirt is made in circular flaring effect. Plain back. Invisible fastening at side. Sizes, 14 to 44 bust. **$8.95.**

K—2403. Woman's Beautiful Suit. Smart shepherd check in black and white. Coat has straight front, and sloping fastening. Panel back. Fitted front. Neat notch collar of heavy black satin trimmed with stitching and covered ball buttons. Inset tailored sleeves have tiny turn-back cuffs trimmed to match collar. Semi-fitted back. Coat lined throughout with peau de cygne. Wide circular skirt with panel front and back. Fastens invisibly under panel. Girdle top. Sizes, 34 to 44 bust. **$9.75.**

K-2500
$14.95

K-2501
$12.50

K-2502
$15.00

K-2503
$12.50

FOUR OF THE SMARTEST MODELS OF THIS SEASON.

K—2500. Woman's Handsome Wool Poplin Suit. The new and popular short coat, in a modified Norfolk effect. Empire lines are induced by a knapsack belt with tab. Box pleated flounce in back. Collar ends in tabs, button-trimmed. Sleeves and cloth buckle in front trimmed to match. Soft revers and invisible fastening. Flare skirt is plain with three box pleats in back. Coat beautifully lined with peau de cygne. Sizes, 34 to 44 bust. Navy, black Belgiun blue, brown or putty. **$14.95.**

K—2501. Woman's Nobby Suit. Black and white shepherd check. Black satin flaring collar trimmed with big cloth bound buttonholes and buttons. Deep set-in sleeves have black satin cuffs trimmed to match collar. Empire effect coat, short front, fastens with cloth covered buttons. Back is cut with a tabeliar and has novelty belt. Two-piece flaring skirt is plain in front and has a sectional belt in back. Invisible fastening at side. Sizes, 34 to 44 bust. **$12.50.**

K—2502. Woman's Stylish Suit. Exceedingly good quality Panama cloth. Beautifully lined with peau de cygne. Coat has simulated vestee in front of corded silk, trimmed with fancy buttons. New and stylish standing Tipperary collar of embroidered net. Fancy belt of self material in back and at sides with fancy ornamented buckle. Tipperary style front closing. Set-in double sleeve trimmed with frog. New circular skirt. Fastened invisibly in front. Colors, navy black or putty. Sizes, 34 to 40 bust. **$15.00.**

K—2503. Woman's Beautiful Suit. Excellent quality storm serge. Empire effect coat is lined in peau de cygne. Front has straight lines, and fastens to one side with three buttons in a pointed outline. Back has small pleats. Set-on flounce is prettily trimmed in back. Self collar button-trimmed. Silk tie at neck. Inset sleeve. Wide two-piece circular skirt with yoke at front and sides, and panel back fastens invisibly at side back. Trimmed in front. Girdle top. Sizes, 34 to 44. Colors, navy, black or putty. **$12.50.**

K-2600
$15.00

K-2601
$19.50

K-2602
$15.00

K-2603
$15.00

For descriptions see opposite page.
New York —- Gimbel Brothers — Philadelphia

Women's Coat Suits, Faultless in Tailoring

Coat Suits have not been so strong as a fashion for years. The military trend of thought has influenced Miladi towards a liking for the natty, practical tailormade. It can be simple and severe or chic and dressy, to suit the individual taste. It is economical, too, in the end, as it can serve so many purposes.

K—2600. Woman's Suit. Gray hairline suiting. Belt at waistline buttons through and is 25 inches long. Three-button straight front. Roll Tuxedo collar of self-material and a flare collar of satin. Turn-over satin cuffs, with three small satin buttons. Circular skirt with shallow yoke at top. Peau de cygne lining. Sizes, 34 to 44. **$15.00.** Also in navy gabardine or white serge, **$15.00.**

K—2601. Woman's Wool Poplin Suit. In black, navy, sand or Belgium blue. Coat is 25 inches long. The skirted tendency in back has pleats at each side below waistline with cluster of small buttons. Peggy pocket on each side. Three-piece sectional belt buttoning through at waistline. One-button fastening. Peau de cygne lined. Circular skirt is semi-pleated. Almost concealed pocket effect at side seams. Deep yoke girdle extends from each side to back buttoned through. Sizes, 34 to 42. **$19.50.**

K—2602. Woman's Suit of Shepherd's Check. Dip pointed front coat with straight lines in back is 24 inches in length. Set-on belt at waistline has envelope point flap pocket effect at each side of front and group of bone buttons across back. Circular skirt with en-velope pocket at each side of front to match belt. Sizes, 34 to 48. **$15.00.** Also in navy serge, **$15.00.**

K—2603. Woman's Serge Suit. Navy, Belgium blue or black. Coat has 26-inch back with yoke shoulders and pleats down each side of panel. Belt from side front around back at waistline. Square flap buttoned through at left side, like a pocket, adds a newness. Single-breasted, four-button front with pleat dart seams from shoulder. Yoke top skirt with lap seam center front and panel back with two pleats at each side. Sizes, 34 to 42. **$15.00.**

K—2700
$18.50

K—2701
$25.00

K—2702
$25.00

K—2703
$19.50

K—2700. Woman's Suit. Coat of this clever and very becoming model is designed and made in a skirted modified Eton tendency attractively worked out by cluster pleats and a tapering turned back fold graduating wider to center back. A group of buttons and wide pocket flaps give smart finish to the fold. Satin collar with additional flare collar of taffeta. Turn-over taffeta cuff on sleeve. Peau de cygne lined. Skirt has a roomy flap patch pocket at each side and a different type inset panel of wide pleats which extends from the pocket to the hem. Back of skirt is shirred at belt. Navy or black serge, also in black and white shepherd's check. **$18.50.**

K—2701. Woman's Smart Model of the New Vigoreaux Gray Gabardine. Made on tailored lines with smart touches, giving it the appearance of a custom-made garment. Coat has stitched patch pocket at each side. Postil-ion back in straight lines finished at each side with two small stitched pleats overlapped by a tab showing military buttonhole and button. Two-piece circular skirt with round yoke in back and narrowing to side, where it is cutaway and finished with buttons. Fastens directly in front under a wide, stitched, full-length pleat. Lined with peau de cygne. Sizes, 33 to 49 bust. Also navy or black gabardine. **$25.00.**

K—2702. Woman's Silk Poplin Suit. Skirt is made in the new four-gore circular model with inverted pleat down front. A shaped yoke across back finished with ball buttons and buttonholes. Coat is short with front ending in a peplum a little below waistline with cluster of gathers on each side above small simulated flap pockets trimmed with uncut buttonholes and drop buttons. Chiffon taffeta silk collar with roll edge.

Postilion back with short waisted tendency created by wide belt across. Long sleeves with wrist vent buttoned through. Peau de cygne lining. This model is an exact copy of a Bernard. Black, navy, beige or battle-ship grey. **$25.00.**

K—2703. "Lucile" Reefer Suit. A combination of the smartest 1915 style tendencies. Back of coat is 25 inches. Straight graceful lines. Fullness is held in at back waistline with Godet tuck pleats. Sectional belt buttoning through. Pointed dip front with slanting buttonholes and link button fastening. Double flap pique top collar. Peau de cygne lined. Collar and long revers of cloth. New bell shaped sleeves. Circular skirt, with just the correct flare, has the new cuff effect at foot with bow finish. Fine gabardine or poplin in navy, black, Belgium blue or sand. Sizes, 34 to 42. A Gimbel leader. **$19.50.**

K-2800
$13.75

K-2801
$9.75

K-2802
$2.00

K-2803
$8.95

For descriptions please see the opposite page.
New York — Gimbel Brothers — Philadelphia

Gimbel Coats at the Prices Defy Comparison

The pictures and descriptions designate for whom the garment is intended. We have endeavored to faithfully present to you a word picture and pen picture of each, but the result seems so prosy to us, who know values and have selected these models from among quantities and quantities of others because they were wonderful specials at the prices. Scrutinize them carefully—you, too, will find them the best you can procure.

K—2800. Woman's Rich Lustrous Black Faille Silk Coat. Very elegantly designed, stylish and suitable for evening or day; in fact, appropriate for any occasion. Made in a three-quarter length with a wide military turn-over collar of moire faced with white dotted silk Bengaline. Large revers of silk moire at front. Broad belt all around coat forms high waistline and is ornamented with two silk cord drops on back to match a large silk cord frog at front. Broad box pleat on back of skirt. Set-in sleeve with fullness below elbow pleated into a deep turn-over cuff. Half satin lining. Sizes, 34 to 44 inches bust measure. **$13.75.** Same in elegant, luxurious black moire, **$13.75.**

K—2801. Woman's or Miss's Dress Coat. Made of novelty cloth, finely adapted to spring and summer wear. Fancy tab collar inlaid with fancy Persian silk. Deep revers of self-material. Set-in sleeves with cuffs inlaid with silk to match collar. New high waistline fitted with wide belt, the newest style feature. Fastened in front. Circular skirt. Navy, brown or black. Sizes, misses', 14 to 18 years. Women's, 34 to 44 inches bust measure. **$9.75.**

K—2802. Woman's Motor Coat and Cap with Goggles. This model is of exceptional quality, natural linene, for the price. Made very full with Raglan sleeves in an armhole extending from neck to waistline. Has belt at back to form Empire effect. Side patch pockets. Tabs on sleeve to match. Finished with smoked bone buttons. Small turn-over collar. Buttons high to neck. Cap has goggles and is pleated into a wide turn-over band. Goggles are finished with cotton tape. Elastic at back of cap to adjust. Sizes, 34 to 44 inches bust measure. **$2.00.**

K—2803. Woman's and Miss's Stylish Natural Covert Cloth Coat. Made in the new military effect with very wide belt. Wide semi-Raglan sleeves with very deep armhole. High collar. Rows of large covered buttons back and front. Diverging panel of pleats in back gives fullness to lower portion. An exceedingly stylish garment. Sizes, misses', 14 to 18 years. Women's, 34 to 44 inches bust measure. **$8.95.**

K-2900 $15.75   K-2901 $10.00   K-2902 $4.95   K-2903 $7.95

K—2900. The Latest Fashion in Coats for Dressy Occasions, Suitable for Misses and Small Women. Made of good quality silk poplin lined throughout with plain satin. The set-on skirt is in flaring effect. Beautiful flaring collar, cuffs and fold at bottom of coat of handsome quality black velvet. Sleeves set in very deep and comfortable armholes. Coat has tablier pleats on each side extending over shoulders from waistline in back to waistline in front, then stitched with slot seam part in front, then stitched with slot seam part way to open into fullness. Navy or putty color with black velvet trimmings, or all black. Sizes 14, 16 and 18 years. **$15.75.**

K—2901. New Sports or Motor Coat for Misses or Junior Girls. New mannish English cut side pockets. Straight front with bone buttons. Narrow, high-waisted belt fastens at either side with button. Raglan sleeves with deep turn-over cuffs trimmed with button and buttonhole effect. Large rolling collar of self-material. Can be fastened high to neck or form into flaring revers. Plain back. Bottom of coat cut on flaring lines. Skeleton lining of self-material. Knee length. English tweeds, tan covert or broken checks. Sizes, 14, 16 and 18 years for misses, and 15 and 17 years for junior girls—girls "large for their age" who wear short skirts. **$10.00.**

K—2902. Miss's or Junior Girl's College Coat. Made of seasonable novelty check. Plain, straight front with mannish collar and revers. Back has yoke with box pleats extending to bottom and wide belt in center. Mannish sleeves have turn-over cuffs. Pockets have flaps. Metal buttons trim belt and effect side-closing. This is a wonderful value at the price we have asked and most effective in appearance. Sizes, 13, 15, 17 and 19 years for junior girls—large girls wearing short skirts—and 14, 16 and 18 years for misses. **$4.95.**

K—2903. Miss's or Junior Girl's Stylish Coat. Tan covert cloth, now so much in vogue, and very economical as it wears well and cleans nicely. Swagger Raglan sleeve with turn-back cuff. Effective broad belt at each side forms pleat back and front. Square collar can be worn open or in military effect. Belt and sleeves trimmed with covered buttons. Sizes, 13, 15, 17 and 19 years for junior girls—large girls wearing short skirts—and 14, 16 and 18 years for misses. **$7.95.**

Gimbels Paris, London and American Style Book

Tailoring in These Skirts Equals Their New and Exceptional Style

K-3000
$1.50

K-3001
$1.00

K-3002
$1.95

K-3003
75¢

These Are Wonderful Skirts as Descriptions Opposite Tell.

New York — Gimbel Brothers — Philadelphia

Women's Practical and Beautiful Skirts—Sizes Will Be Found on Page 35

Tailoring means not only the stitching—in Gimbel skirts careful in the extreme—but the expert draftsmanship that produces correct proportions for a good fit, also fashionable lines.
Styles are always right in Gimbel models, but on the tailoring and value Gimbels truly excel—there is no establishment can equal Gimbels in this respect. Sizes will be found on page 35.

K—3000. Woman's Pretty Ratine Skirt. Deep novelty yoke effect with square tabs on each side sweeps gracefully upwards to back, and a small lap tuck in front of yoke is button-trimmed. Skirt fastens invisibly in center back under a wide seam which extends down to lower edge. This model has the new, fashionable full cut circular flare and is one of our best sellers. At this moderate price it is within the reach of everyone. Go to Gimbels for good values. Skirt comes in white only. **$1.50.**

K—3001. Woman's Natural Colored Linen Skirt. The ever desirable, and ultra serviceable material for summer wear. This fine garment is one of the new circular models. Has deep yoke effect in back graduating upward to

front. Yoke has tuck edge and is ornamented with three beautiful dark color pearl buttons. Straight habit back. Invisible fastening at side front under a tuck effect. Same style tuck extends from yoke to bottom of hem. Decidedly plain, yet wonderfully stylish. Improves with tubbing and thus can always be fresh, crisp and clean. The value is unparalleled. **$1.00.**

K—3002. Woman's Natural Color Linen Crash Skirt. Yoke encircles skirt in an oblique line, showing a stiched edge in graduated depth and is finished at side front with smoked pearl buttons. Fancy shaped pocket is placed at the right, underneath the shorter part of the yoke, and is also trimmed with small pearl buttons. Inverted panel extends down

front of skirt from yoke to foot and is also trimmed with pearl buttons giving the one sided effect. Perfectly plain tailored back fastens invisibly down center. **$1.95.**

K—3003. Woman's Attractive Skirt. Excellent quality white linen. Plain stitched yoke effect, fastened invisibly at left hip. Large square pocket at right side neatly finished with rounded stitched tab and button. The much favored tuck extends down front of skirt from yoke to foot and is finished with pearl buttons. Bottom of skirt is cut full and in the new circular style. Easily laundered. Back is perfectly plain. For an inexpensive garment this skirt cannot be excelled. **75c.**

K-3100
$1.35

K-3101
$1.95

K-3102
$1.00

K-3103
$1.50

K—3100. Woman's Beautiful Skirt. Excellent quality white ratine, an ideal summer fabric. Deep yoke effect finished with a half-inch tuck about 12 inches below waist line. Darts in back give necessary fit at waist. Fastens to one side with pearl buttons and buttonholes. Wide, loose, lapover pleat extends from yoke to foot. Skirt is slightly circular, now so very popular. Made on concealed band. Another exceptional value is to be found in this splendid garment. **$1.35.**

K—3101. Woman's Fine All Linen Skirt. Made in the new circular width and designed in one-sided effect. Skirt has three-quarter inch lap obliquely from right hip at waist

line to center of the skirt then turning down the left side and finished with smoked pearl buttons. Fitted loose belt stitched to skirt. Back has gore down center. Fastening over left hip. Natural color only. **$1.95.**

K—3102. Woman's Ratine Skirt. In white only. Full circular flare bottom. The yoke top is tucked crosswise in three places giving an entirely new and pleasing tier yoke effect, each tuck finished with pearl button. Large rounded pocket on either side with tab, finished with button. Three crosswise tucks near foot give overskirt effect, and each tuck is trimmed with a pearl button. Fastens invisibly in center of perfectly plain back.

High girdle. This is a very charming skirt. **$1.00.** Also in white cordeline, **$1.00.**

K—3103. Woman's Serviceable Skirt. White cordeline of splendid quality is here used. Deep yoke back and front, pointed on either hip, the lap front fastening with buttons and buttonholes. Plain habit back. High girdle. Stitched wide box pleat extends from yoke on either side, opening into pleats at foot and finished half way down by small pearl buttons. Really a beautiful garment and stylish, having the full circular cut at foot. White only. **$1.50.**

Skirts Again Spring Out into Width at Foot

Women are everywhere demanding skirts with the new flare lines and they find the Gimbel Stores amply prepared with an array of beauties. Gimbels foreign and domestic chiefs are first to hear style whispers from fashion centers, and immediately get the Gimbel forces in motion to present them at their famously reasonable prices. Buying materials in quantities and having them made up is one method of lowering cost. Descriptions on opposite page.

K-3200
$2.95

K-3201
$3.95

K-3202
$2.95

K-3203
$2.75

New York — Gimbel Brothers — Philadelphia

Skirts Again Spring Out into Width at Foot

All indications point to a great demand for separate skirts and you will find Gimbels well stocked with clever models at most reasonable prices.

K—3200. Woman's and Miss's Charming Skirt. One of the season's most fetching styles in tan covert cloth. The popularity of this fabric has extended from England to America, and it is much used for smart tailored wear. It gives untold service. Model has deep yoke, also fancy-shaped pocket effect tabs on either side, fastening with buttons and buttonholes. Invisible closing over left hip. Lap-over pleat down center back of yoke and down center front of skirt. Slightly circular at foot. The skirt is neatly finished with buttons. **$2.95.**

K—3201. Beautiful New Model Skirt for Women and Misses. Made of excellent quality silk poplin, with a handsome, rich lustre. Has the fashionable new circular yoke effect with lap in front, and finished with tiny buttons of self-covered material. Back of yoke is plain. Bottom of skirt is box-pleated on to yoke, giving width and spring. Invisible fastening at left hip. A very new model that is quite popular for the spring and summer season, developed in a very stylish fabric. Note the very reasonable price Gimbels have placed upon this skirt. Black or navy. **$3.95.**

K—3202. Woman's and Miss's Handsome Skirt. Made of good quality serge. Cut on one of the new circular flare patterns that Miladi is favoring this season. Yoke has an envelope closing, finished with a large button and buttonhole, and extends downward into points on either side of hips. Braid finishes edges, giving a smart tailored air. Lap extends down center front from yoke to foot and is finished with two clusters of small buttons of self-covered material. Navy or black. Only by purchasing in unity to stock the huge Gimbel Stores could we obtain this low price. **$2.95.**

K—3203. Woman's and Miss's Beautiful Chiffon Panama Skirt. Soft, fine weave, lustrous material that is particularly serviceable. Stylish yoke, featured on so many skirts this season. Lap extending from waist down to foot of skirt, finished with silk-covered buttons. Right side has rounded pocket with two small pleats held in place with two buttons. Straight cut lower portion. Back of skirt is shirred under yoke and has lap seam down center, concealing closing. Black or navy. **$2.75.**

K-3300 $1.50   K-3301 $1.95   K-3302 $2.95   K-3303 $3.00

K—3300. Nurse's or Physician's Skirt. This skirt is one of the most comfortable, convenient and appropriate skirts on the market and the only kind of skirt created for the specific use of nurses or women physicians. It is a plain six gore, panel back and front model with a deep six-inch hem. Deep concealed pocket is inset at the side gore. Open side front, fastened through with white pearl buttons. Attached belt. Made of white motor cloth, non-shrinkable and serviceable. 2½ yards wide at foot. **$1.50.**

K—3301. Distinctive and Stylish Skirt for Women. An attractive model is here shown, made of a good quality white wash eponge. All straight lines are maintained, with good width at foot. A novel effect is given the front, where the typical sports effect is created by flat pocket set in the curve of each side yoke, and finished with a fine quality pearl button. Four buttons close the front through a full-length pleat. Seamless top back. **$1.95.**

K—3302. Woman's Smart Athletic Skirt. This skirt is constructed along standard ideas after painstaking study to devise a model for practical or sports wear. A dressy striped eponge in white of a good grade is the fabric. This skirt makes a wonderful golf or tennis model. Open front all the way down, fastened through with pearl buttons and buttonholes. Stylish slanting patch pockets with buttoned flaps. Separate belt through loops. **$2.95.** Also fine good quality khaki. **$2.95.**

K—3303. Tailored Skirt for Women. There is something very new in this skirt. It is made of a fine, heavy, rich cotton needle cord in pure white, beautifully lustrous, with a silky finish. The style is a tuck-edge, panel back and front one with a diversity of style in the manner of pockets. These are concealed under the front panel by a clever cut of sword points which turn up and button through, keeping pockets flat. Opens invisibly side of back. Skirt is conservative in width. **$3.00.**

Gimbels Paris, London and American Style Book

33

Women's and Misses' Tub and Cloth Skirts for Service

The descriptions on opposite page state whether Skirts are for women or misses.

K-3401

K-3402

K-3400
$3.95

K-3401
$3.95

K-3402
$3.95

K-3403
$5.00

New York — Gimbel Brothers — Philadelphia

Women's and Misses' Tub and Cloth Skirts for Service

Misses' Skirts are made in lengths 35 to 38 inches; waist bands, 22 to 27 inches. Women's Skirts are made in regular sizes from 38 to 43 inches in length and from 23 to 29 inches waist bands. In lengths 38 to 43 we will make skirts with waist bands in extra sizes 30 to 35 inches for 50c additional for cotton or linen, and $1.00 additional for silk or wool. Maternity Skirts will be found on page 49.

K—3400. Woman's High Grade Cordeline Skirt. One of the new sports models, cleverly designed. It is graceful and simple in model and cut in the new circular flare with middle seam back. A graduated Bayadere panel of material running crosswise is inset in the front gore, producing a clever blind opening. Very ornamental and equally useful are the pretty shaped patch pockets trimmed with pearl buttons. Generous hem finishes skirt. High waistline. **$3.95.**

K—3401. Woman's Skirt. Tan Palm Beach cloth of splendid quality is here used. The material, which is so stylish this season, is washable, shakes dust and is as light as mo-

hair. There is something very chic about the model with its new circular flare and lap in front extending from waistline to hem, where it is finished with beautiful pearl buttons. Fancy patch pocket with top shaped into a downward strap, at each side, also trimmed with buttons. **$3.95.** White eponge, same style, **$3.95.**

K—3402. Woman's Skirt. Made of an exceptional quality white eponge of a texture that is good and firm. An especially tailory design selected for the average figure that needs good plain lines. Skirt has a circular flare at foot and fitted closely at top. Back

of skirt is plain with a short strap back trimmed with pearl buttons and a dart pleat at each side. The front is perfectly plain in cut with lengthwise lap from waist to hem, which is trimmed with pearl buttons. An invisible opening in front. **$3.95.**

K—3403. Woman's Skirt. The favorite wash skirt for dress is here shown. It is made of fine white French linen. This skirt is one of the daintiest of the circular models with a deep yoke around sides and back. Panel in front accentuated by slot seams part way and buttons. The lower portion is wide and circular, plain in back and gored on hips. Fastening is through one side of panel. **$5.00.**

K-3500 $3.95   K-3501 $5.00   K-3502 $5.00   K-3503 $6.95

K—3500. Woman's Beautiful Serge Skirt. An unusually attractive model for office or business wear. Perfectly plain in outline, very tailory and good fitting. Excellent style for small women. Circular model attached to a yoke. Plain panel front. Deep tuck in center trimmed with bullet buttons of self material. Invisible front opening. Plain hem at bottom of skirt. High waistline. Black or navy blue. **$3.95.** Also in black and white check, **$3.95.**

K—3501. Woman's Tweed Skirt. An ideal runabout model. Made of a firm, medium weight tweed, a material suitable to fold close and give hard knocks without showing much wear.

Sold in quantities for touring. Made in full circular flare. Fastens all the way down the front with beautiful buttons. Loose girdle belt. Ample patch pocket with small flap buttoning over by two small buttons appears on each side of front. Plain back. **$5.00.**

K—3502. Woman's Handsome Black Voile Skirt. Full circular flare now so much in fashion. A strong revival of voile is evident. It is light in weight, wears well and is strikingly modish. Even the dressiest skirts this season take on a very tailory air, hence this one is ideal with its three bands of satin and ball shape buttons tailored to the finest de-

gree. Small tuck in front conceals closing. Back of model is perfectly plain. **$5.00.**

K—3503. Woman's Dress Skirt. Fine high grade men's wear serge. The tendency for all skirts for the spring and summer season is toward flare without eliminating the straight line effect, and so with this the front is straight, being designed as a panel and extending around side in a very deep yoke effect. The lower portion graduates upwards in back to yoke depth, where it is beautifully set off with tiny buttons to match those on the sides. A lapover pleat down front conceals the closing. Black, navy blue or white. **$6.95.**

The Gimbel Stores buy hugely, and as a consequence, closely. You can get more good, honest value for your dollar in the Gimbel Store than anywhere else. Our customers who have sent in small trial orders favor us thereafter with large and frequent repeat orders, the best demonstration of their satisfaction.

K—3700. Woman's Skirt. Excellent model for the athletic girl. Made with a wide flare at foot to give ample room, while the top, at waistline is snugly and closely fitted. Back is plain, gathered at waistline beneath a loose, narrow belt. Straight patch pocket with a turn-over is button trimmed. High waistline. Wonderful bargain. Tan covert—a fabric so fashionable this season. $5.00. Also in navy blue or black men's wear serge, $5.00.

K—3701. Woman's Semi-Tailored Effect Skirt. Made of black and white or green and white check suiting. Modeled in front into a panel which is trimmed at each side with fancy buttons and buttonholes. Wide circular flare at foot. Habit back. A wide, loose belt

fastening in center back graduates on each side and is caught under the panel. This garment is adaptable for most purposes of wear, and its value is most excellent. $5.95.

K—3702. Child's Rompers. Pink or blue chambray. Wide knees. Strap of white around neck, sleeves, waist and knees. Splendid offering. Sizes, 2 to 6 years. 50c.

K—3703. Child's White Linene Dress. Trimmed with pink or blue checked gingham. Round yoke, kimono long sleeves and small pocket on left side. Skirt made full. Small buttons effect the front closing. A good value. Sizes, 2 to 6 years. 50c.

K—3704. Child's Linen Color Chambray Dress. Kimono style. Turkey red trimming. Neat belt and square low neck. Narrow inset panel

in front of waist is trimmed with turkey red and an embroidery design in center. Fastens in back from neck to hem. Very practical garment for play. Sizes, 2 to 6 years. 25c.

K—3705. Child's White Linen Dress. Trimmed with blue or pink chambray and small pearl buttons. Low belt. A smart model and, indeed, a real value. Sizes, 2 to 6 years. 85c.

K—3706. Child's Shepherd Check Coat. Collar, cuffs and the sash belt which is shirred in center front and at the side are of beautiful Copenhagen messaline. Set-in sleeves. Buttons effect front closing. Model is not very fancy, yet pretty and attractive, and an exceptional bargain for the price. 5 year size. $3.95.

K-3600
$1.25

K-3601
$1.00

K-3602
$2.00

K-3603
$1.50

K—3600. Miss's White Ratine Skirt. Cut in one of the new full effects with a large rounded pocket placed on either side and trimmed with a neat tab set off by pearl buttons. Four loose pleats extend down front from each pocket, giving a full flaring effect at foot. A tuck trimmed with pearl buttons extends from waistline to hem and conceals the front closing. High girdle. Straight habit back. A charming and fascinating model for summer wear, and a wonderful bargain for the low price offered. $1.25.

K—3601. Miss's Skirt. Made of the very serviceable and good-looking material—white ratine. Washes and launders beautifully. Model is in the new combination yoke and circular

flare effect. Front has a full-length side lap which conceals the invisible closing and is trimmed with pearl buttons. Top of skirt forms a yoke with a wide tuck edge, encircling the skirt in oblique lines to a deep yoke in back. Habit back has two neat darts trimmed with pearl buttons to give necessary fit at waistline. Exceptionally fine value. $1.00. In cordeline, $1.00.

K—3602. Miss's Country Club Skirt. Lovely quality, washable white cordeline. Flare model with a wide detachable belt fastening in front by pearl buttons. Particularly new is the pocket trimmed with a tab and button appearing at each side. Plain habit back slightly gathered at the top. Odd-shape but-

tons close the entire front to hem. Ideal for service, and is the equal of a far more expensive model. $2.00.

K—3603. Miss's and Small Woman's Sport Tub Skirt. White repp that launders nicely. A perfect-fitting skirt cut on the full circular flare with the plain habit back slightly gathered at the high waistline. Fastens all the way down front with lustrous pearl buttons. Detachable belt fastening with one pearl button is held at waistline by belt loops. Patch pocket with flap and buttons on each hip. Specially priced and well worth full consideration. $1.50.

K-3702
50¢

K-3703
50¢

K-3704
25¢

K-3700
$5.00

K-3701
$5.95

K-3705
85¢

K-3706
$3.95

For descriptions see opposite page

New York — Gimbel Brothers — Philadelphia

K-3800
$7.95

K-3801
$15.00

K-3802
$15.00

K-3803
$10.75

For descriptions please see the opposite page

New York — Gimbel Brothers — Philadelphia

Gimbels Are Noted for Newest Style and Best Value

Of interest because the styles are authentic and the very latest—because the materials are general favorites for the coming season—because the making is in every way exceptional—because the prices are kept at a most reasonable figure. The Gimbel Stores are large and their orders are correspondingly large, so stock can be bought at original sources of supply at rock bottom cost.

K—3800. Woman's Stylish Coat. Good quality serge in Belgium blue, navy blue or black. Fancy collar of novelty silk. Semi-fitted front with diagonal tab and buttons. Empire effect back—the newest treatment and a very graceful mode. Revers of self material with strap, button-trimmed. Cuff to match on the set-in sleeve. Skeleton-lined. Rounded lower edge. Gimbels have here produced a coat of astonishing merit for the price. Sizes, 34 to 44 inches bust measure. **$7.95.**

K—3801. Miss's and Small Woman's Smart Calling Suit. Good quality lustrous silk poplin, one of the most popular weaves. Made in the stylish short loose jacket with flounce. suitable for slender figures. All the newest and most up-to-date touches are given in the new full flare skirt with inset yoke panel

effect back and front. Sides are finished with belt and deep fold at bottom. Beautiful half ball buttons give finish. Sand, Belgian blue, navy or black silk poplin. Sizes, 14 to 18 years. **$15.00.** All white, Copenhagen or rose ramie linen, **$8.75.**

K—3802. Woman's Fashionable Coat Suit. Developed in Belgium blue, navy blue or black serge also black and white checks. Coat has the chic, semi-tailored lines with the purse-shape patch pocket and half belt on both sides, caught with fancy buttons. Tailored cloth revers and large flaring black satin collar. Strictly tailored, set-in sleeves, finished at hand with black satin cuff and black bone buttons. Lined with good quality peau de cygne. Skirt is a two-piece circular with seam down back and panel in front Stylish,

shaped yoke, very narrow at back and extending deep in front of skirt, continuing into the panel. Narrow belt of self fabric. Sizes, 34 to 44 inches bust measure. **$15.00.**

K—3803. Woman's Covert Cloth Coat. Made after a most up-to-date model, neatly trimmed, and most expertly tailored to preserve the shape and please the eye. Three-quarter length. Tailored collar with revers at front. Broad belt is a continuation of the front piece, and the lower side extends into a pocket flap finished with two buttons and buttonholes covering a small in-set pocket, while the back is stitched down. Has the flare skirt effect at bottom. Tan covert cloth. Coat is half lined with splendid quality peau de cygne. Fastened with bone buttons. Sizes, 34 to 44 inches bust measure. **$10.75.** Same style in navy or black serge, **$10.75.**

K-3900 $3.00

K-3901 $3.95

K-3902 $3.00

K—3900. Woman's Dainty Blouse. Combination of silk shadow Val and chiffon in cream color over flesh, or all sand color. Foundation of this beautiful blouse is of a soft sheer chiffon. Shawl collar of neat shadow lace is very attractive. Very deep folds of lace and chiffon fall gracefully over the chiffon sleeves. Suspender of satin ribbon and fancy buttons trim the front. Dainty three-quarter length sleeves have shadow lace cuff draped with a small ribbon loop, also a band of ribbon above. Pretty odd-shaped buttons effect closing. This blouse is exquisitely dainty and will please you when you see it. Sizes, 34 to 44 inches bust measure. **$3.00.**

K—3901. Woman's Gorgeous and Dressy Blouse. The Gimbel Stores have produced a splendid value blouse for the price in this model. It is made of beautiful white all silk shadow lace over a foundation of silk chiffon in a dainty shade of flesh pink. Between the lace and chiffon are bands of soft flesh satin ribbon arranged in suspender effect, finished off with silver buckles, the whole daintily veiled. The stylish military collar is of lace and edged with a small hem of chiffon. Sleeves are cool and dainty in three-quarter length with picot-edged chiffon cuff. Tiny revers of chiffon. Pearl buttons and buttonholes of braid effect the front closing. Sizes, 34 to 44 inches bust measure. **$3.95.**

K—3902. Woman's Handsome Silk Shadow Lace Blouse. Delicate as a cobweb in appearance, this blouse will give surprisingly good service. The all silk shadow lace falls softy over a foundation of flesh color chiffon in delicate tint. Bands of flesh color soft, narrow satin ribbon prettily trim the lace, and large band of flesh color ribbon with a tailored bow trims the foundation under the lace. Fashionable, cool summer style, with short chiffon sleeves having a neat cuff of lace. Collar of shadow lace with ribbon bands at each side. Four black odd-shaped buttons trim front of this beautiful and stylish blouse. Sizes, 34 to 44 inches bust measure. **$3.00.**

New York — Gimbel Brothers — Philadelphia

Blouses in Ritz and Other New Modes

Blouses with high necks and long sleeves are very strong—Gimbels call them the Ritz model and have produced many charming adaptations. Then, for dressy occasions or warm summer wear, there are the cool, flaring collars and shorter sleeves. Our patrons have always found the Gimbel Stores well stocked with charming, latest-style, and fine-value models.

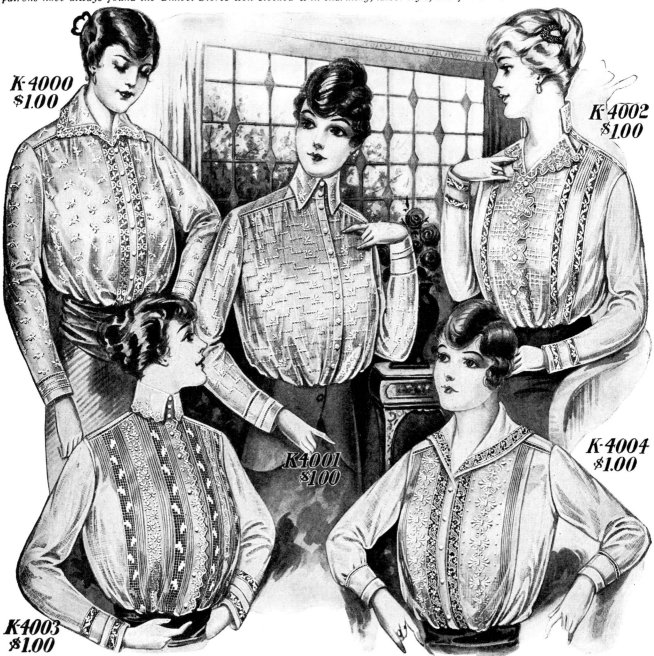

K-4000
$1.00

K-4002
$1.00

K-4001
$1.00

K-4004
$1.00

K-4003
$1.00

K—4000. Woman's Effective and Modish Blouse. Dainty allover embroidered white organdie in floral pattern. Front of this waist has insertions of flat Venise lace and fastens with pearl buttons. Full-length stylish sleeves, have dainty plain hemstitched organdie cuffs. Flat Venise lace trims the attractive and stylish collar. A model of exceptional value is here offered. Sizes, 34 to 44 inches bust measure. **$1.00.**

K—4001. Woman's Smart and Stylish Blouse. Fashionable Ritz model of dainty allover embroidered white voile in a unique pattern, fastening high to the neck with large crochet buttons. Modish collar turns over and is pointed. The full-length sleeves trimmed with a hemstitched voile cuff are set into the deep armholes with neat beading. Sizes, 34 to 44 inches bust measure. **$1.00.**

K—4002. Woman's White Organdie Waist. Made in the newest fashion and is one of the daintiest and most becoming models. Embroidered organdie in the front panel and rows of Val. lace and cluster pleats each side. Pearl buttons through scallops effect the front closing. The stylish collar and revers are of embroidered organdie to match front. Clusters of fine pleats trim the back. Insertions of Val. lace in the shoulders and on the full-length sleeves. Large armholes. A genuine bargain for a waist of beauty and quality as this one is. Sizes, 34 to 44 inches bust measure. **$1.00.**

K—4003. Woman's Chic and Modish Blouse. Very smart and effective. Plain white voile in the fashionable Ritz model with high neck. Fine lace of filet pattern alternating with rows of embroidered voile and clusters of French pleats trim the entire front of this handsome blouse, while the back is neatly pleated. Front fastens with pearl buttons through scallops. Neck has a stylish Ritz collar of French Swiss. Full-length sleeves, set in a deep armhole, are daintily trimmed in lace. Very novel and decidedly new. Sizes, 34 to 44 inches bust measure. **$1.00.**

K—4004. Woman's Elaborate Blouse. Made of a handsome sheer quality of Paris lawn, which is ideal for the hot summer days. Front of this dainty waist has bands of flat Venise lace insertion and panels of embroidered organdie, and the back has clusters of French pleats. Modish collar flares and has insertions of flat Venise lace. French band beading joins the shoulders and the cuffs. Full-length sleeves with a French turnover of organdie. Large armhole. This beautiful and elegant garment cannot be equaled anywhere at the low price we offer. Sizes, 34 to 44 inches bust measure. **$1.00.**

New York — Gimbel Brothers — Philadelphia

Inexpensive Blouses of Artistic and Intrinsic Worth

THINK OF IT! From the Gimbel Stores you can get a charming, stylish blouse, of pretty serviceable dimity, for 50c. You can get a genuine pure linen blouse for $1.00. For $1.00 you can also get a pure silk blouse. Seams are carefully finished—fit is good—blouses are every way most desirable—full Gimbel quality. Choose one of these blouses if you are thinking of sending a trial order.

K-4100
50¢

K-4102
$1.00

K-4104
$1.00

K-4101
85¢

K-4103
$1.00

K—4100. Woman's Stylish and Semi-Tailored Blouse. Made of a splendid quality white fancy plaid dimity. This effective style fastens in front with pearl buttons. Neck has a standing military collar and neat revers trimmed with buttons. Sleeves are full-length, finished with double cuff. Plain and very serviceable, and has the appearance of a far more expensive model. 34 to 44 inches bust. 50c.

K—4101. Woman's Dainty Lingerie Blouse. Made of a sheer quality and cool-looking white voile. Excellent in workmanship and style. German Val lace insertion appears down front and on each side is a pretty embroidery panel with inset of handsome lace motifs designed in a beautiful manner. Crystal buttons effect the closing. Stylish collar on this blouse, cut in latest fashion, has a Val lace insertion and picot edging.

Sleeves are full-length with neat hem-stitched organdie cuff. Plain tucked back. This is an especially good Gimbel waist offer, and we wish you to take advantage. 34 to 44 inches bust. 85c.

K—4102. Woman's Serviceable Blouse. Good quality and heavy stock black lawn that is not transparent is used in this good model. Fastens in front. Entire waist is neatly tucked in cluster of uniform pleats. High pleated collar of same material is detachable. The sleeves are full-length and finished with a stylish tucked cuff. An elegant blouse for the low and inexpensive price we offer. 34 to 44 inches bust. $1.00.

K—4103. Woman's Handsome Blouse. Made of pure Irish linen—a material always in great favor—in the Ritz model—careful "Royal" make. An all-around sport's blouse, suitable for the school or college girl. Stylish model fastens high to the neck with pearl buttons. The collar has a

French turnover of self linen and can be worn high or low. Full-length sleeves have cuffs of self material with new flat fastenings. The handkerchief pocket with flap, appearing on left side, adds to the style of the blouse. No smarter waist can be desired or one that is better valued than this exceptional model. 34 to 44 inches bust. $1.00.

K—4104. A Superior Habutai Silk Blouse. Excellent cool model for the hot summer season. At the price mentioned you will hardly be prepared for the wonderful grade of all pure silk Habutai used. White ground with stripes of navy blue or black. The stylish collar, cuff on sleeves and vest are made of organdie with picot edging. Full-length sleeves, set in a deep and comfortable armhole. French band of organdie. Silk waists always appeal, as they are excellent for both dressy and business wear. 34 to 44 inches bust. $1.00.

Gimbels Paris, London and American Style Book

Prices Are Lowered Through Buying for Three Stores

Gimbels have a huge store in each of the cities of New York, Philadelphia and Milwaukee, and most lines of goods are stocked in huge quantities for all three. Naturally, manufacturers' terms are the extremely low ones, for it is a well-known fact that large buying means low prices. Gimbels policy is to pass these extra savings on to the customer.

K-4200
$2.00

K-4201
$2.00

K-4202
$1.00

K-4203
$2.00

K-4204
$1.00

K—4200. Woman's Neat and Beautiful Blouse. Made of a superior quality pure Irish linen in oyster white. Hemstitching on collar, tiny revers and front edge. Revers also trimmed with crochet buttons and buttonholes. The full-length sleeves have a daintily hemstitched double cuff. Front closing is effected by pearl buttons. A very attractive and good-looking model, also an amazing value. Sizes, 34 to 44 bust measure. **$2.00.**

K—4201. The Country Club Blouse for the Athletic Girl. A chic, tailory blouse of pure Irish linen. The stylish deep yoke extends in one piece over the shoulders from back. Stylish collar has a turnover and fastens high to the neck in the Ritz model effect with large pearl buttons. Box pleat on each side extending from the yoke has double pockets which completes the extreme tailor fashion of this model. Full-

length sleeves set into deep armholes are trimmed with French cuffs. A serviceable style, fine material and workmanship. Sizes, 34 to 44 bust measure. **$2.00.**

K—4202. Woman's Stylish Blouse. White dimity in the famous "Royal" make, a blouse noted for its fineness of workmanship and material. This model fastens in front with pearl buttons and is semi-tailored in style. The beautiful and dainty sheer organdie collar has insets of lace with a French band finish. The sleeves are full-length, finished with French cuffs. Decidedly good value at the small price. Sizes, 24 to 44 bust measure. **$1.00.**

K—4203. Woman's Wonderfully Effective Blouse. Washable tub silk of a superior grade. Fastens in front with silk loops and pearl buttons. Plain yet stylish collar neatly flaring. Front edges and cuffs on sleeves are daintily hemstitched. A novel

feature is the fullness in front that falls gracefully from the small yoke effect at shoulders. French back. The sleeves are full-length and set into deep and comfortable armholes. Workmanship and fabric in this model make it the equal of most $3.00 blouses from other houses. Sizes, 34 to 44 bust measure. **$2.00.**

K—4204. Woman's Sheer Lingerie Blouse. Excellent quality white voile in the modish Ritz model. Flaring collar. Panels of filet. shadow Val lace insertion appear down front, on collar and at shoulders and sleeves. Same style insertion suggests a bolero in front. Back has cluster of pleats. Beading joins the long sleeves to waist. Small cuff effect of shadow Val lace insertion and neat frill. Pearl buttons effect the front closing. A handsome model and an extraordinary good value. Sizes, 34 to 44 bust measure. **$1.00.**

New York — Gimbel Brothers — Philadelphia

Blouses Made of Fine Quality Transparent Embroidery

Transparent embroidery has first place in Miladi's favor, and there is nothing more dainty, charming and cool for summer wear. It is also vastly becoming, lying soft and white near the face.
Note that sleeves of these models are all inset with beading in comfortable armholes. Furthermore, their exceptional quality at the prices asked makes them worthy a place in the Gimbel Stores, high as the standard is.

K-4300
$2.00

K-4301
$2.00

K-4302
$2.00

K-4303
$3.00

K-4304
$2.00

K—4300. Woman's Effective Blouse. Made of crisp transparent white French organdie, embroidered in panels in a large, stylish floral pattern. The beautiful collar is of transparent embroidered organdie edged with flat Venise lace. A new feature shows the groups of pleating in the side front and groups of finer pleats in the back. The cool, summery wide three-quarter sleeves trimmed with tucks, embroidered panels and embroidery edge are set into large armholes. An unusually good value for such a low price as we offer. Sizes, 34 to 44 bust measure. **$2.00.**

K—4301. Woman's Handsome Summer Blouse. Made of a fine quality, allover white embroidered voile in a scroll pattern that is most attractive. Blouse can be fastened high to the neck or left open in a graceful turn back. Pretty pearl buttons effect the front closing. Collar, the front and cuffs are edged with beautiful flat Venise lace. Beading trims the shoulders and daintily sets

the full-length sleeves into the deep and comfortable armholes. A gorgeous and dressy blouse, also a good bargain. Sizes, 34 to 44 bust measure. **$2.00.**

K—4302. Woman's Elaborate and Very Hand=some Blouse. Allover white embroidered voile, which is most attractive. The stylish and smart embroidered transparent organ-die collar is a very strong feature of this elegant and charming blouse. The shoulder trimmings of lace and beading add to the attractiveness. Beadings join the shoulders to the elaborate three-quarter sleeves that have an embroidered organdie cuff to match collar. Large armholes. Neat velvet ribbon tie. Low V neck. A rich and tasteful blouse worth much more than the price Gimbels ask. Sizes, 34 to 44 bust measure. **$2.00.**

K—4303. Woman's Dainty Sheer White Voile Blouse. Elaborated with the newest de-signs in embroidery on the front, back and the dainty three-quarter length sleeves.

The beautiful collar with fan pleated sec-tion, standing high in the back, adds grace to this beautiful model. Double revers of transparent fabric hadsomely embroidered to simulate hand work. Neat insertions of filet lace ornament the front panels, shoul-ders and butterfly cuffs. Large armholes. For value and comfort in the hot summer days you could not select anything better than this modish and attractive model. Sizes, 34 to 44 bust measure. **$3.00.**

K—4304. Woman's Pretty and Good Style Blouse. Made of fine and sheer white voile, with panels in the front and collar of transparent embroidered organdie. Pan-els of flat Venise insertion and clusters of pleats further elaborate the front. Pleated shoulders meet a panel of pleats in the full-length sleeves. Back also has clusters of pleats. Cuffs of embroidered organdie. Large armholes. Low V neck. This blouse is exceptionally dainty and is one of our best values. Sizes, 34 to 44 bust measure. **$2.00.**

The Shirtwaist Has Become an American Institution

The women of other lands occasionally wear a shirtwaist—the American woman occasionally wears something else. Her daily apparel is a smart tailored skirt and neat blouse—for better wear a lace or chiffon one. No matter how many pretty frocks she has, an American woman always has a supply of clean blouses at hand.

K—4400 $2.00

K—4401 $2.00

K—4402 $2.00

K—4403 $2.00

K—4404 $2.00

K—4400. Dainty Yet Elaborate Blouse Made of a Sheer Quality of Voile. Panels of embroidered voile and rows of Val. lace alternate over the front of this attractive waist. The shoulders have an embroidered organdie band, and broad pleats show a new and distinctive feature. The collar is of embroidered organdie. The sleeves are full length, tucked and trimmed with cuffs of embroidered organdie and lace frill. Sizes, 34 to 44 inches bust measure. A very beautiful waist and a splendid value—a combination not unusual in the Gimbel stores. $2.00.

K—4401. Exceedingly Smart Blouse Made of Plain White Voile. Panels of embroidered organdie down front and back. Beautiful filet lace inserted along the hemstitched vest. The elaborate collar is of embroidered organdie, edged with Venise lace. Cluster pleats either side of the panels and in the back. Hemstitched shoulders and large armholes. Full length sleeves with organdie cuffs. Sizes, 34 to 44 inches bust measure. The beauty of design, excellence of workmanship, fine quality of materials used, newest mode, and general good value are here most pronounced. This is a garment well worth the moderate price named. $2.00.

K—4402. An Effective Blouse Made of Sheer White Voile Embroidered in Panel Effect Down the Front and Across Top of Back. Flat Venise lace outlines the vest. The collar is in the fashionable fan pleated style, of embroidered organdie, with insertions of flat Venise lace. The vest is likewise embroidered in a pretty pattern. Flat Venise lace joins the shoulders. The full-length sleeves are set in a large armhole with beadings. The cuffs are trimmed in embroidered organdie. Sizes, 34 to 44 inches bust measure. $2.00.

K—4403. Handsome Blouse of Allover Embroidered Voile in a Smart Floral Design. This blouse fastens in front with fancy pearl buttons—always an attractive finish and a most satisfactory closing. The stylish collar stands in the back, and it as well as the revers are of embroidered organdie, edged with flat Venise lace. Beadings join the shoulders and full-length sleeves. The cuffs are of embroidered organdie. Large armholes. Sizes, 34 to 44 inches bust measure. The stamp of distinction is much in evidence in this very dressy waist. Its value is unsurpassed. $2.00.

K—4404. The Season's Most Fashionable Color is used in this stylish blouse of allover embroidered voile in sand color. The embroidery is of white that stands out most distinctly. The lace is of a cream shade that edges the collar. The waist is embroidered all over front, back and sleeves. Finished at the shoulders, sleeves and cuffs with hemstitching. Large armhole. Sizes, 34 to 44 inches bust measure. $2.00.

Wonderful Blouses of Silk and Lace

Paris and London have contributed the genius of their creative originality, and the American manufacturer his wonderful productive aptitude.

Gimbels is the wizard whose magical power has combined the two through their foreign and domestic organizations. These blouses are the very newest and prettiest styles, and prices are most reasonable.

K-4500
$3.95

K-4501
$3.00

K-4502
$3.00

K-4503
$3.00

K-4504
$3.00

K—4500. Woman's Magnificent Crepe de Chine Blouse. Made after an imported model in the fashionable mouchoir or handkerchief style, most becoming to any style of figure. The modish and attractive double handkerchief revers fall gracefully over the front and have deep, hemstitched hems. Particularly becoming and new is the semi-military hemstitched collar standing high in the back. Full-length sleeves inset in large armholes have neat hemstitched cuffs. White, flesh or black. 34 to 44 bust measure. **$3.95.**

K—4501. Woman's Wonderfully Smart Blouse. Made of crepe de chine, a material very fashionable and much in favor. This dainty and beautiful model fastens in front with loops of crepe de chine and large, clear pearl buttons, and displays an open V-shaped neck in front and a standing mili-

tary collar in back. Shirrings form fullness in the front, while the back is in the plain French style. Stylish, full-length sleeves have a dainty double cuff. White or flesh. 34 to 44 bust measure. **$3.00.**

K—4502. Woman's Gorgeous Blouse. A new mode in the fashionable and handsome gold-embroidered net, neatly made over a foundation of soft flesh chiffon. The gold embroidered net falls beautifully and gracefully in a short cape effect, revealing the chiffon foundation below the edge front and back. The smart and very stylish collar is of dainty chiffon and gold color net. Three-quarter sleeves are attractively trimmed with tiny ribbons. 34 to 44 bust measure. **$3.00.**

K—4503. Woman's Gorgeous Blouse. Made of all silk shadow Val lace in soft cream color and flesh colored chiffon alternating

with each other in the overblouse, which falls softly over a lining of flesh chiffon with corsage of flesh colored messaline ribbon. The lace is draped gracefully over the chiffon sleeves that are full length. Effective standing semi-military collar is of satin with the lace falling softly over it. Satin buttons trim the front and shoulders. 34 to 44 bust measure. **$3.00.**

K—4504. Woman's Fashionable and Elegant Blouse. Sand color shadow lace and cream color shadow lace over flesh colored chiffon forms an overblouse which is draped becomingly over a flesh colored chiffon foundation. Neat and coquettish corsage band of flesh silk ribbon appears in the vest. The dainty collar is of handsome ribbon and lace. Three-quarter length kimono sleeves are of the flesh color chiffon with sand lace. 34 to 44 bust measure. **$3.00.**

Specials—Waists On This Page; Sweaters On Opposite Page

The three Gimbel Stores are widely separated, yet managed on the same general lines, the result of over seventy years of merchandise experience. Looking after the customer's interest in the most helpful way by each individual employee has built up the Gimbel house from a modest beginning to a wonderful, mammoth, world-wide organization.

K—4700. Woman's Fine Worsted Sweater Coat. Excellent grade. With collar or V neck. Convenient patch pocket at each side. In all the good spring and summer outing colors. Tan, rose, Delft blue, Harvard, white or navy. Sizes, 34 to 44. **$6.50.** We can take special orders for college girls in their college color in this exceptionally good model.

K—4701. A Serviceable Sweater Coat for Either Girl or Boy. Extraordinarily fine, all wool yarn. Deep shawl collar that can be worn low or fastened high to the neck. Comfortable patch pockets. Wonderful quality at the low price Gimbels are offering. Rose, Copenhagen, Harvard or navy. Sizes, 28 to 34. **$2.50.**

K—4702. Woman's Sweater. Very firm and good-looking garment of all wool. Shawl collar. Roomy patch pockets. Exceptionally fine for out-of-door wear. A good bargain for the price. Good spring colors. Rose, Copenhagen, navy or Harvard. Sizes, 34 to 44. **$3.75.**

K—4703. Child's Sweater Coat. With collar and pockets. All wool. An exceptionally fine grade. It will be a comfort and a joy to the little one who happens to be presented with this style sweater. Navy, cardinal, rose, Copenhagen. Sizes, 26 to 34. **$2.00.**

K—4704. Child's Sweater. Very good quality merino yarn. Shawl collar that can be worn high or low. Patch pocket appearing at each side. A serviceable sweater and one that will be found perfect fitting in the correct size. Navy or cardinal. Sizes, 26 to 34. **$1.50.**

K—4705. The Most Famous Gimbel Norfolk Sweater Coat. Very stylish and well made. Warm collar. White, Harvard, tan, rose, Delft blue, navy or gray. Sizes, 34 to 44. Most stores ask a very high price for this wonderful coat. Gimbels, **$5.00.** Same style sweater can be furnished for college girls in college colors on special orders.

K—4706. Girl's or Miss's Warm Norfolk Sweater Coat. Cut full and very roomy. With collar. A wonderful model for the price. White, tan, rose, Delft blue navy, gray, Harvard. Sizes, 24 to 28. **$3.00.** Sizes, 30 to 34. **$3.50.**

K— 4707. Woman's Sweater. All wool. Fashionable shawl collar. Convenient pockets. Good wearing and sightly garment. White, cardinal or navy. Medium weight. Sizes, 34 to 44. **$2.50.**

K—4707-A. For the college girl or boy, we will furnish a special **Shaker Coat Sweater**, in any college color, at **$6.50.** Have them in stock in white, gray, navy, rose, green, tan or Harvard. Other colors to order special.

All our special Sweaters are full cut in all sizes. Every illustration is an extra value in our new catalogue. Every Sweater is 15 to 25 per cent. under the market for the grades we have catalogued.

In ordering a sweater, be sure to state size, color and give a full explanation of what is wanted, so as to avoid delays in filling the order. Special goods require from ten days to two weeks.

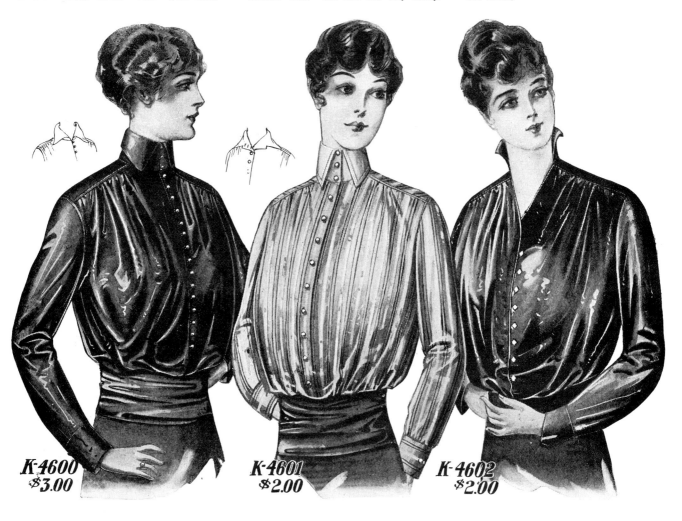

K·4600
$3.00

K·4601
$2.00

K·4602
$2.00

K—4600. Handsome Blouse for Women. Made of a superior quality of black Habutai silk. A practical blouse also suitable for mourning wear. This blouse can be worn fastened high to the neck or opened back in a low collar. Loops of silk and silk-covered buttons fasten the front. The style is semi-tailored with graceful lines. The sleeves are mannish, full length, and have a stylish deep cuff fastened with loops and buttons. Fullness in front from shoulders. Sizes, 34 to 44 inches bust measure. **$3.00.**

K—4601. A Most Stylish Blouse Is This Striped Wash Silk. A Ritz model of the famous Royal make, fastening high at the neck, or it can be left open with a turn-back flare. Fashionable ball buttons give finish. The stripes are of a variety of widths, in either navy, blue, black or lavender, or in all white tub silk. This stylish model has a Ritz collar of white tub silk. Tailored mannish sleeves of full length with a stylish cuff. Sizes, 34 to 44 inches bust measure. **$2.00.**

K—4602. Wonderfully Becoming And Serviceable Blouse for Women. Excellent grade of Habutai silk in black or washable white. Practical and fitting for mourning wear. This blouse has a high standing fashionable military collar, and neck is open in the front in a graceful "V" shape. Loops and smoke pearl buttons elaborate and close the front. The fullness falls gracefully from the corded shoulders. Mannish sleeves are full length with a pointed cuff. Blousy lines without peplum. Sizes, 34 to 44 inches bust measure. **$2.00.**

New York — Gimbel Brothers — Philadelphia

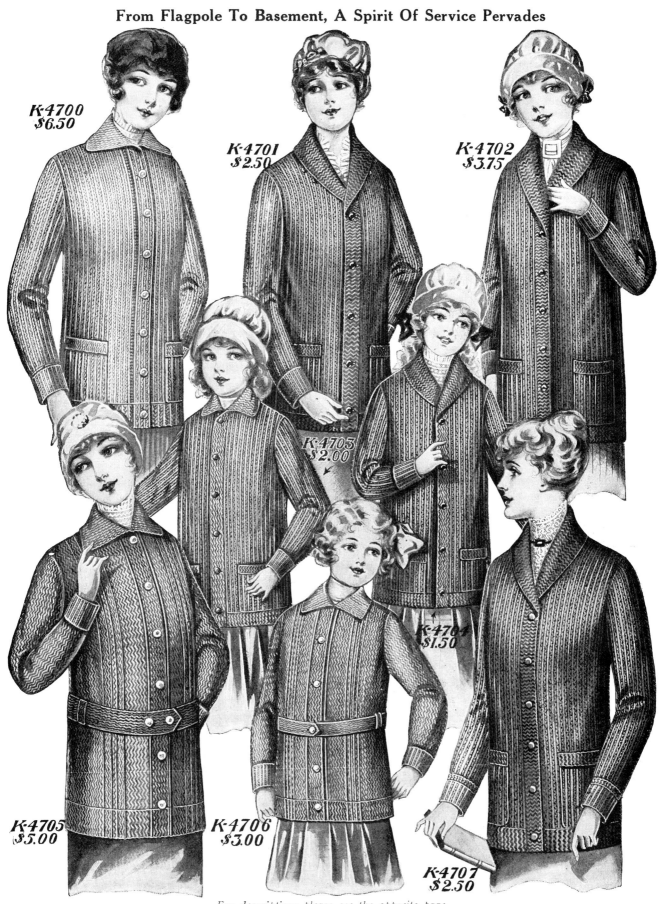

K-4700
$6.50

K-4701
$2.50

K-4702
$3.75

K-4703
$2.00

K-4704
$1.50

K-4705
$5.00

K-4706
$3.00

K-4707
$2.50

For descriptions please see the opposite page.

Gimbels Paris, London and American Style Book

K-4801
$1.95

K-4800
$3.95

K-4802
$1.50

K-4803 $10.75

K-4804 $4.95

Cleverly-Planned Maternity Wear on This and the Opposite Page

On these two pages you will find a group of garments necessary for the prospective mother—each designed to carefully meet with her needs for comfort and entirely without loss of style. In ordering, give normal measurements.

K—4800. Woman's Gown. In this beautiful soft wool albatross gown you see a most comfortable and becoming robe for lounging or general home wear. The full accordion pleated skirt fastens all the way down the front with snap fasteners. The bodice is daintily embroidered with silk polka dots and trimmed with hemstitching, while the edges are finished with fine mercerized scallops. Tailored bows of satin ribbon give a jaunty finish, and the satin covered elastic waistband assures a comfortable and neat set at the waist line. In pink, blue, lavender, rose or navy. **$3.95.**

K—4801. Kimono of Firm Serpentine Crepe. Self-adjusting elastic waistband. Suitable for maternity or invalid wear. Beautifully hand embroidered in a dainty floral spray and scalloped by hand on the deep shawl collar and cuffs. A handsome ornament of self material finishes the waist line. The crepe fabric used washes particularly well and need not be ironed. In pink, blue, French blue or lavender. **$1.95.**

K—4802. Fine Quality Striped Gingham Dress. For house or general wear and especially proportioned for the prospective mother. The self-adjusting elastic waistband is covered with an adjustable tailored belt and a dressy finish is given by the collar, vestee and cuffs of white cordaline, a handsome corded fabric similar to pique. A detachable silk bow completes the neck. In white with stripe in pink, blue, lavender or black. **$1.50.**

K—4803. Maternity Dress. Rich silk finished Poplin, made in a new and most practical manner with snap fasteners holding numerous side pleats and with straight lines carried out by the graduated gores. A novel jabot of self material falls from beneath a rich collar of lace and embroidered batiste. A charming vestee of shadow lace and frill of the same finishes the long sleeves. An adjustable tailored belt covers the waist line. The waist is lined with mull. In navy blue or black. **$10.75.**

K—4804. Petticoat for Maternity Wear. Waist made in two sections with placket and strings on front and back sections on each side. Has properly proportioned gores and ample width. A rich flounce of fine pleatings and ruffles and of ample fullness. Colors, black, navy or any staple color.

In fine Taffeta or Messaline silk........**$4.95**
In Striped Gingham....................**$1.25**
In Sateen **$1.25**

K-4901 $3.00

K-4903 $1.00

K-4900 $3.75

K-4902 $1.50

K-4904 $1.00

K-4905 $5.95

K—4900. Woman's Maternity Skirt. Black or navy serge. A practical garment with correctness of detail. Broad panel in back stitched with a broad tuck edge to a depth of about 15 inches, then opening into pleat fullness. Adjustment is effected by means of clasps at top of panel and along top of skirt to desired requirements, while the bottom edge hangs true. Sides and front have a sloping yoke extending into a loose panel down front, with a loose tuck either side. In ordering give normal waist measurement. **$3.75.**

K—4901. New Maternity Waist. Fine coutille. Made with elastic inserts down each side of clasps. Abdominal belt supports with adjustable lacings, also adjustable lacing at each side to adjust to comfort of wearer. Tempered steel with push back. Sizes, 22 to 30. **$3.00.**

K—4902. Maternity Corset and Waist Combination. Scientifically cut and specially designed for a maternity garment. Lightly boned, adjusted front and lower part of back, with elastic lacers to give comfort to wearer. Can be had in either button or clasp front. Sizes, 22 to 36. **$1.50.** State whether button or clasp front is desired when ordering.

K—4903. Junoform "Wee-Wee" Nursing Shields. Made of finest quality waterproof nainsook. A necessity with nursing mothers. Rustproof fasteners. Elastic webbing back. Medium or large size. **$1.00.**

K—4904. Excellent Corset for Nursing Mothers. Firmly boned. Bust is boned and adjusted by means of snap fasteners. Soft clasps down front. Sizes, 20 to 30. **$1.00.**

K—4904A. Nursing Mother's Corset Waist. (Not illustrated.) Cut on similar lines as K—4904, only very much lighter boned. Sizes, 20 to 30. **$1.00.**

K—4905. Maternity Skirt. We aim to produce a maternity skirt that slenderizes the figure yet gives comfort to the wearer. New circular, wide at foot, with a drop panel front having deep stitched tuck edges. The panel fits perfectly flat. All extension is made in the front by a lacer, under the panel, while the back is as close fitting and neat as a dressy dress. Fitted strap trims the skirt, appearing as a pointed yoke in back and extension belt in front. Buttons trimmed in back. In black or navy blue serge. When ordering, state normal measurements of waistband and length. **$5.95.**

Gimbels Paris, London and American Style Book

K-5000
50¢

K-5001
$1.00

K-5002
$1.00

K-5003
50¢

K-5005
$1.50

K-5008
50¢

K-5006
$2.00

K-5004
$3.00

K-5007
25¢

K-5010
$1.00

K 5011
$3.00

K-5009
$1.50

K-5012
50¢

K-5013
35¢

K-5014
50¢

K-5015
50¢

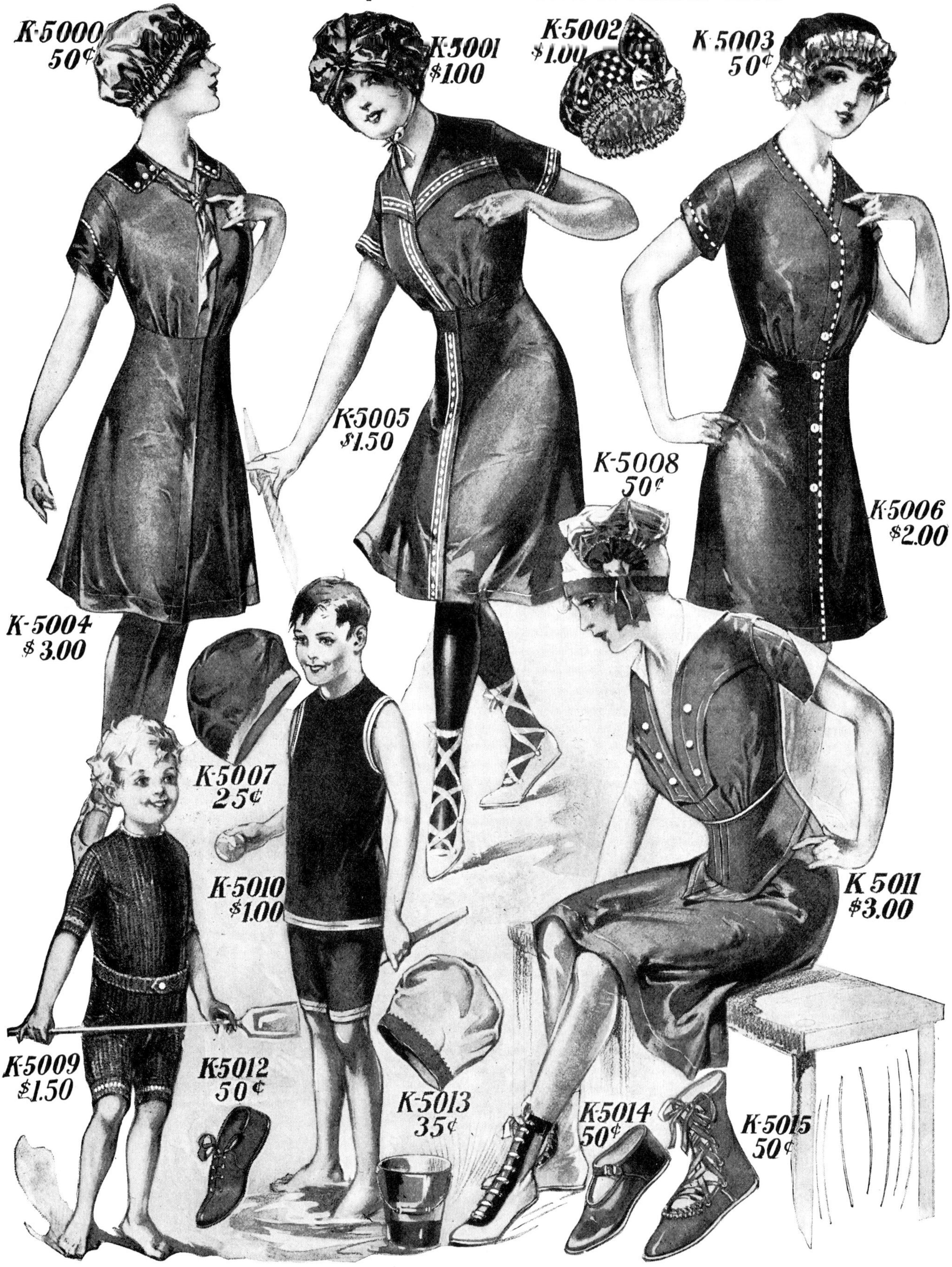

For descriptions see top of opposite page.

New York — Gimbel Brothers — Philadelphia

Gimbels Are Headquarters for All Sorts of Athletic Goods

For Bathing Suits, Caps, Shoes, Combinations, as well as regular sporting equipment, Gimbels are most often consulted. In their huge New York and Philadelphia Stores they have laid out golf courses, where prospective players can seek golf instruction. In the summer, children find amusement playing in the Gimbel sand yards, and using the Gimbel outdoor play apparatus of all kinds.

K—5000. Satin Rubberized Diving Cap. Blue, black, green or red. Close fitting. 50c.

K—5001. Silk Cap. Large bow. Blue with small rose pattern. $1.00.

K—5002. Silk Bathing Cap. Black and white blocks with wing trimmed to contrast. $1.00. Same in white flowered satin with plain green, also black with red or navy. $1.00.

K—5003. Woman's Bathing Cap. All rubber. Very chic. Blue, red, wisteria, black, green or tango. 50c.

K—5004. Woman's or Miss's Mohair Bathing Suit. Sateen collar and cuffs. Black and white piping. Black or navy mohair. Complete with combination. Miss's sizes, 10 to 16 years. Woman's sizes, 34 to 46 inches bust. $3.00.

K—5005. Woman's or Miss's Surf Cloth Bathing Suit. Black and white dotted band, finished with soutache braid trims suit. Complete with bloomers. Navy or black. Woman's sizes, 34 to 46 inches bust. Miss's sizes, 10 to 16 years. $1.50.

K—5006. Woman's or Miss's Bathing Suit. Very nice quality mohair. Black and white sateen pipings. Complete with bloomers. Navy or black. Woman's sizes, 34 to 46 inches bust. Miss's sizes, 10 to 16 years. $2.00.

K—5007. Woman's Diving Cap. Pure gum rubber. Red, black or tan. Tight-fitting. 25c.

K—5008. Woman's Turban Bathing Cap. All rubber. Red, blue, black, wisteria, green, tan, tango, or Bulgarian. 50c.

K—5009. Child's One-Piece Knitted Suit. Sizes, 4 to 10 years. $1.50.

K—5010. Man's or Boy's Bathing Suit. Navy blue trimmed in red or white. Quarter sleeves or sleeveless. Cotton. $1.00 and $1.50. In worsted at $2.50, $3.00, $4.00 and $5.00. Special color combinations to order—no extra cost.

K—5011. Woman's Mohair Bathing Suit. Moire collar and buttons. Short sleeves with lap seam. Pointed cuff of white moire. Piped with white moire at waist. Complete with combination. Sizes, 34 to 46 inches. $3.00.

K—5012. Bathing Oxfords. Heavy soles. Black. 50c. pair.

K—5013. Man's Diving Cap. Pure gum rubber. Red, black or tan. Tight-fitting. 35c.

K—5014. Satin Finish, Heavy Duck Bathing Oxfords. Blue or red. Sizes, 3 to 8. No half sizes. 50c, pair.

K—5015. High Lace Bathing Shoes. Red, blue or black. Heavy soles. 50c pair.

K—5100. Beautiful Striped Silk Bathing Cap. Bow in front trimmed in satin. Red, green, navy or black satin. $1.00.

K—5101. Beautiful Sateen Bathing Cap. Poke shape with wing. Red, green or navy Scotch plaids. Could be sold for $1.00. At Gimbels for 50c.

K—5102. Sateen Bathing Cap. Red, green, navy or black. Special, 25c.

K—5103. Woman's Pure Gum Bathing Cap. Double frill to protect neck and eyes from the sun. Red, blue, black, wisteria, green, tan, tango or Bulgarian. A $1.00 value. 50c.

K—5104. Sateen Bathing Cap. Bow in front. Red, green, navy or black. Tight-fitting. Formerly sold for 50c. Now 25c.

K—5105. Bathing Rubber Rose. 25c. 50c. 75c and $1.00 each. Also corsage bouquet of roses and violets. $1.00.

K—5106. Extra Heavy Sateen Bathing Cap. Roman striped trimmings. State colors. 50c.

K—5107. Woman's Handsome Messaline Bathing Suit. New style skirt with pleats back and front. Pointed belt fastens at side. Stylish flaring collar. Small satin buttons. Two broad simulated pleats are laid in diverging lines down the back. Sizes, 34 to 46 inches bust. $5.00.

K—5108. Woman's Mohair Bathing Suit. Round collar of self material and lapels of silk. Satin buttons down front. Cuff on sleeves. Complete with bloomers. Black trimmed with Copenhagen or white. Navy trimmed with white or navy. 34 to 46 inches bust. $3.00.

K—5109. Woman's Bathing Suit. Navy or black mohair. Collar has straps of material and embroidered dots. Skirt and waist have fancy buttons. Embroidered dots on cuffs. Inverted pleat back and front. Black with black or white dots. Navy with white or green dots. Complete with bloomers. 34 to 46 inches bust. $3.90.

K—5110. Woman's Fine Quality Mohair Bathing Suit. Waist trimmed with striped silk. Round neck finished with tabs and buttons. Skirt is flaring. Suit shows pieces of set-in silk. Navy trimmed in navy and white. Black trimmed in black and white. Complete with combination. 34 to 46 inches bust. $3.90.

K—5111. Woman's Bathing Suit. Very fine quality Sicilian mohair. Black or navy. New flaring collar. Trimmed with braid. Two rows of small satin buttons extend down front. Skirt is made with a yoke. Sleeves especially adapted for swimmers. Panel is in box-pleated effect. Complete with combinations. 34 to 46 inches bust. $6.90. Same style in taffeta. $8.90. In black messaline, $6.90.

K—5112. Heavy Sateen Bathing Pumps. Black and white stripes like picture or plain black, red or blue. 50c, a pair.

K—5113. Bathing Garters. Not illustrated. State color. Plain, 25c, pair; fancy, 50c, pair.

Gimbels Paris, London and American Style Book

K-5200
$3.50 SET

K-5201
$1.00

K-5202
$5.50 SET

K-5203
$2.50 SET

For descriptions see the opposite page.

New York — Gimbel Brothers — Philadelphia

Gimbel Designing and Workmanship Unexcelled

Gimbel designing and workmanship are sure to be an irresistible combination that assures you of most charming effects and also style value that is consistent with the high aim of this organization. If prettiness alone were the object we should have succeeded, but, as in no sense has quality been neglected, you will be gratified in making your choice of these becoming models.

K—5200. Woman's Negligee Of Fine White Swiss. Is made in novel style and has the appearance of a two-piece matinee. Beautifully trimmed with fine Val lace and medallions. Soft ribbon bows are also used to finish, and this negligee is indeed a most beautiful and becoming robe. The cap that is shown in the illustration accompanies this negligee and matches it in style. Complete set, negligee and cap. **$3.50**

K—5201. Woman's Kimono Of White Dotted Swiss. Trimmed with stylish bands of dotted lawn, forming a border down front and finishing the sleeves. This kimono is shirred at the waistline in back and held with sash of self-material. A beautiful and most comfortable kimono. Is in all white with border figured in pink, blue, lavender or black. **$1.00.**

K—5202. Woman's Negligee. Exceedingly soft fine "Seco" silk made into a most graceful Empire model, prettily trimmed with Val laces and silk ribbons. Sleeves are slashed and in an unusually pretty design. There is a soft becomingness about this negligee that will appeal to ladies for dainty lounging attire. Cap to match accompanies this charming negligee and can be had in your choice of pink, blue or white. Complete set, negligee and cap. **$5.50.**

K—5203. Woman's Negligee. Fine white Swiss trimmed in novel manner with frill of shadow lace around collar, down front and bottom, also on the smart slashed sleeves that are a becoming length. Rosettes of silk ribbon are used to trim. A practical negligee that will launder beautifully. Cap to match accompanies this charming negligee. White trimmed with pink, blue or lavender ribbons. Complete set, negligee and cap. **$2.50.**

K—5300. Woman's Dressing Sacque. Fine white dotted Swiss. Effectively trimmed with insertions and edgings of fish-eye lace. Fastens with silk ribbons. The butterfly sleeves are lace trimmed to match. The lovely dotted Swiss used in this dressing sacque is quite the ideal fabric for practical use and will launder perfectly. **$1.50.**

K—5301. Woman's Dressing Sacque. Dotted Swiss. The pretty, square neck and sleeves are trimmed with fish-eye lace and beading run with ribbon. Brought in at waist with belt of Swiss. Dotted Swiss is without doubt the favorite fabric for pretty negligee sacques. It is sheer and fine and the quality used in this model has a modish appearance and will launder beautifully. **$1.00.**

K—5302. Woman's Dressing Sacque. Fine sheer quality lawn, beautifully figured all over in dainty pink, blue or lavender design. Shawl collar and cuff band flatly applied and edged with neat embroidery. The flat stiched belt of self-material is joined to the back of the sacque where it is drawn into neat gathers and crosses over in a comfortable manner to meet the individual requirements. **50c.**

K—5303. Woman's Dressing Sacque. Fine white dotted Swiss trimmed and tucked effectively. Adorned with fine Val lace and Val. medallions to match Pretty ribbon rosettes on sleeves and front. Swiss embroidery at Empire waist drawn with ribbon to match rosettes. The sacque has most graceful lines. and the smart touches of style are shown in many little items which it would be impossible to enumerate in this description. Pink or blue ribbon. **$3.50.**

K—5304. Woman's Dressing Sacque. Fine crepe de chine in a most becoming Empire model. All the dainty frillings are of fine cream shadow lace The Empire waist is defined by a belt of pleated extra fine ribbon and is finished at front with rosettes and streamers. Dainty touches of style are in the pleated kimono sleeves. Deep points on either side. Pink, blue, lavender or white. **$4.50.**

K—5305. Woman's Dressing Sacque. An elaborate Empire model of fine dotted white Swiss, is effectively trimmed with Val lace insertions. Wide Swiss embroidery at waist and is drawn with messaline ribbon. The sleeves are slashed, and also have lace and ribbon trimming to match. Pink or blue ribbons. **$2.50.**

Gimbels Paris, London and American Style Book

Negligee Attire of Superb Comfort and Style

You cannot find a better assortment of styles or more sterling merit anywhere in the country. Our experts are unsurpassed as to knowledge of the markets and as to the needs of our clientele. Sizes, 34 to 44 inches Bust Measure.

The Splendid Negligees and Robes Illustrated on This and the Opposite Page.

K—5500. **Woman's Negligee.** Fine crepe de chine in a very graceful Empire model. The skirt is pleated. The collar and cuffs are of white chiffon with picot edge. Elastic at waist makes this a good style for the corsetless figure. The ornaments which adorn the waist are of self material. Pink, light blue, French blue, rose, navy or black. **$5.95.**

K—5501. **Woman's Bath or Lounging Robe.** Excellent quality jacquard terry cloth, made on the mannish order with roll shawl collar and set-in sleeves, finished with gauntlet cuffs. The trimming is a silk cord on collar, cuffs and pocket. Fastened with cord frogs and bone ball buttons. Girdle with tassel at waist. Pink, blue, lavender or gray. **$4.95.** Bath slippers to match. A pair, **50c.**

K—5502. **Woman's Bath or Lounging Robe.** Jacquard terry cloth in pink, blue, lavender or gray. Square sailor collar and patch pocket. Cord girdle with tassels at waist. **$2.95.** Slippers to match. A pair, **50c.**

K—5503. **Woman's Negligee.** Fine crepe de chine in Empire style. Around the neck, front of waist and sleeves are pleatings of shadow lace. Elastic self-adjusting waistband makes it ideal for the corsetless figure. Can be had in pink, blue, lavender or rose. **$4.95.**

K-5400 $2.95   K-5401 $1.50   K-5402 $1.95   K-5403 $1.00

K—5400. **Woman's Negligee, of Jacquard Crepe.** We call particular attention to the convenient waistband that holds the fullness of this comfortable gown. It is thoroughly practical and is an innovation that will appeal to those who desire comfortable garments of this kind for general wear. Graceful Empire model, prettily trimmed with two rows of dainty frills of pleated net around the neck, and finishing the sleeves. The pleated skirt is joined to the Empire bodice with the convenient elastic described, and we know of no simple negligee of this character that can compare in neatness and style with this inexpensive model. Pink, rose, Copenhagen or lavender. **$2.95.**

K—5401. **Woman's Kimono of Fine Serpentine Crepe.** Don't judge the quality by the price. as you will be agreeably surprised when you see this excellent model which is in popular style, full fashioned and comfortable, and most graceful. Serpentine crepe is a most practical fabric for a lingerie robe, because being a wrinkled fabric, it need not be ironed. This in itself is a wonderful innovation in comfort garments. It is trimmed with a puffing of messaline ribbon around neck, all the way down the front and the pretty slashed sleeve. Fastens toward side with silk frog and button. Pink, blue, rose, navy or lavender, **$1.50.**

K—5402. **Woman's Kimono of Plisse Crepe.** When we say that this kimono is an unusual value, we are fully aware that you will compare it with all other kimonos that you have seen at this price, and we are therefore very conservative in our statement, for it is indeed a most unusual value, and we know you will find it absolutely satisfactory. The shawl collar and sleeves are scalloped and finished with pleatings of net, belts in with a pretty sash of self material, finished to match collar. Pink, blue or lavender. **$1.95.**

K—5403. **Woman's Kimono of Serpentine Crepe.** This model is particularly convenient and serviceable. It is made of excellent quality of serpentine crepe that washes exceptionally well. Need not be ironed, being wrinkled fabric, which makes it an ideal lounging robe. It is made in a neat and altogether attractive Empire style. Satin ribbon trims the neck and sleeves. In blue, pink or lavender. **$1.00.**

New York — Gimbel Brothers — Philadelphia

Bath Robes and Charming Negligees

K-5500
$5.95

K-5501
$4.95

K-5502
$2.95

K-5503
$4.95

For descriptions please see the opposite page

New York — Gimbel Brothers — Philadelphia

K-5600
$2.00

K-5601
$4.50

K-5602
$3.50

K-5603
$3.00

For descriptions please see the opposite page

New York — Gimbel Brothers — Philadelphia

Descriptions of the garments illustrated on the opposite page.

K—5600. Woman's Dress. Fine quality crisp lawn, in a charming new panel effect forming graceful long, slender lines from shoulder to hem. Blouse has set-in sleeves, finished at three-quarter length with crisp turnover cuffs of Swiss embroidery; a dainty flat collar of the same material finishes the neck. The crosswise panel that embellishes the waist is tailor stitched and trimmed with buttons. Around the waist is a soft, flat, pleated girdle of lawn same color as the stripe, and that also appears in the attractive little pipings that are placed here and there with chic effect. Pleated skirt has deep yoke top. White with stripe in blue, lavender or black. Price, $2.00.

K—5601. Woman's Dress. Fine quality solid colored linen. Military coat effect. Front closes over in double-breasted style with large ornamental pearl buttons. The flat belt of velvet

is finished with a tailored bow. Collar and cuffs are of striped basket weave cloth stitched and trimmed with buttons to match the color of the material. The new flare skirt has a deep yoke top as shown, and wide stitched fold near bottom finished with four-inch hem. Shell pink, French blue, lavender, rose or white. $4.50.

K—5602. Woman's Frock. Charming semi-tailored style with soft blouse waist laid in unstitched pleats and outlined with hemstitching in yoke and down the front, forming panel. Blouse also closes slightly to one side with large ornamental buttons. Finishing the neck and sleeves are collar and cuffs of a particularly handsome Swiss embroidery. The raised waistline of the skirt has a medium wide yoke cut in circular style, from below which the skirt hangs in slender lines with double inverted box pleats stitched to knee depth and falling in smart flare at the hem. Excel-

lent quality linen in white, pink, grey, wistaria, Copenhagen or putty. $3.50.

K—5603. Woman's Semi-Tailored Frock. Superior quality gingham—the dainty stripe showing to excellent advantage in the smart military shoulder yoke and also in the skirt yoke, both being in bias effect and giving an attractive bit of contrast The blouse is prettily gathered below the yoke and has a smart vest of basket weave cloth, the same also forming the pointed collar and turn-back cuffs, both of which are embroidered by hand in an artistic pattern. Finishing the neck is a smart slip-knot tie of velvet and the waistline is also emphasized by flat velvet belt and tailored bow. A novel feature of this frock are the black jet buttons that serve to trim and close. The skirt also is cut in the new flaring lines with snug hip line and wide fold above the flat flounce that forms the hem. White with stripe in blue, lavender or black. $3.00.

K-5700
$1.00

K-5701
$2.00

K-5702
$1.50

K-5703
$1.00

K—5700. Morning Dress of Striped Gingham. Though conventional in style, this smart little porch or morning dress is tailored according to the standard demanded by the Gimbel organization for its customers. Properly designed, carefully put together, and fitted and finished that each garment may be absolutely satisfactory. Outlining the neck and forming a wide band down the front is colored gingham to match the stripes, piped with contrasting color. The large buttons that are used to close also serve as a trimming. Skirt is the new flare with hem. May be had with stripes and trimming in blue, lavender or black with white. $1.00.

K—5701. Fine Chambray Dress for Home Wear. Fabric shows a waved hair line that is most effective and shows to excellent advantage in

the shoulder yoke, in the smart tailored belt and on the pocket. Collar is a very pleasing innovation of the conventional notched one with revers and is of excellent quality white pique. Neatly bound and finished with fancy slip-knot tie. The wide cuffs that finish the short sleeves are also of white pique. Attractive skirt has the new flare and has wide overlapping fold about knee depth. In blue and white or black and white French percale. $2.00.

K—5702. Marketing Frock of Fine Blue Chambray. Woman's dress of most practical design. Has tailored shoulder yoke in one piece with back section, below which the blouse is nicely gathered, forming comfortable fullness. The closing is with large pearl buttons that also serve as a trimming. The short sleeves are

wide and finished with cuffs of white cotton corduroy, same also forming the smart little collar with points. Tailored belt is trig and firm, and the new flaring skirt is most practical and becoming. Large housekeeper's pocket is placed at one side. In cadet blue only $1.50.

K—5703. Linene Porch Dress with Embroidered Bands. Woman's house dress in solid color that is sure to be a great favorite. It has the easily fitted waist, neatly gathered into the raised waistline of the skirt. The pretty collar, vestee, sleeves and front of waist is trimmed with bands of embroidered self-material. Flaring skirt is on the new lines and has wide overlapping pleat down the entire front. In excellent quality linene in cadet blue, grey or lavender. $1.00.

Ultra-Fashionable High Effects or Comfortable V-necks

The Gimbel Neckwear stocks are immensely varied, showing clever American originations—inexpensive adaptations of luxurious imported models—and from these myriad hosts there is just the mode to suit any particular type of woman. Every one is immaculately fresh and crisp with newness—has the elusive daintiness of a rare perfume.

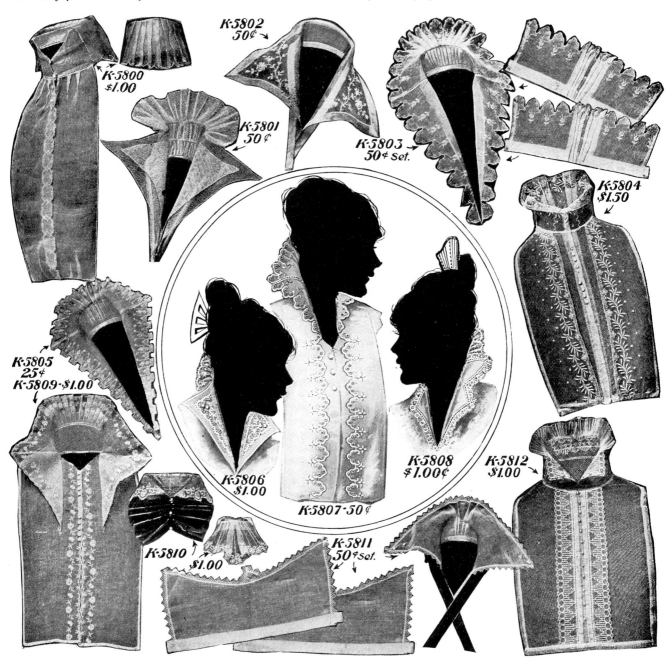

K—5800. Charming Organdie Vestee. New high pleated back. Small pearl buttons finish front closing. This model is beautiful in its simplicity. **$1.00.**

K—5801. Effective Collar of Fine Net. Shirred back. Double rever front is a pleasing novelty. White or cream. 50c.

K—5802. Imported Transparent Embroidered Collar. The close roll collar is adaptable for almost every style blouse and is one that will be much in evidence during the coming season. 50c.

K—5803. Dainty Collar and Cuff Set of Sheer Embroidered Organdie. Back of collar and center of cuffs neatly pleated. A charming finish for the fancy blouse or tailored dress. Specially priced for our Mail Order patrons. 50c a set.

K—5804. Oriental Lace Guimpe. New, high pleated back collar. Neat hemstitched front closing finished with small pearl buttons. Ex-

quisite embroidered design. Cannot be surpassed in daintiness. White or cream. Moderately priced at **$1.50.**

K—5805. Novel Flare Collar. Made up of transparent embroidered organdie. New, pleated collar. You will wonder at the low price when you see this article. Special. 25c.

K—5806. Beautiful Collar of Oriental Lace. One of the season's newest designs. Shirred collar with double rever. Upper rever of Oriental lace finished with tiny buttons. Lower rever of chiffon with corded edge. **$1.00.**

K—5807. Vestee of Embroidery. Fashionable pleated back collar giving graceful flare. Very appropriate for the tailored or afternoon dress. Remarkable value. 50c.

K—5808. Stylish Collar of Chiffon. Neatly edged with Venise lace. Shirred back of Oriental lace. Comfortable and cool for summer wear. You will be delighted with this collar. **$1.00.**

K—5809. Embroidered Vest of Organdie. Popular, pleated back collar. Front closing effected by small buttons. Sheer and beautiful. Gimbels neckwear holds first place in charm and value. Special, **$1.00.**

K—5810. Very Newest Stock. Charming combination of cream Oriental lace and black messaline ribbon. Pleated back. Ribbon front pleated and finished with tiny gilt buttons. **$1.00.**

K—5811. Neat Collar and Cuff Set of Organdie. Dainty and practical. Edged with narrow lace. Pleated back collar finished with velvet ribbon. Will look well with the tailored blouse. Well worth the small amount it will cost you. 50c.

K—5812. New Short Vestee. Charming model of Oriental lace and net. Fastens in back. Stylish Piccadilly collar with fluting of net. Front finished with pearls. Special value. **$1.00.**

New York — Gimbel Brothers — Philadelphia

Oh! Such Fascinating Bits of Lace and Embroidery Are Here

Exquisitely sheer and transparent are the newest creations—dainty as a cobweb—delicate yet really substantial. The minute ramifications of the Gimbel organization cover every field of endeavor, and the newest and best of everything are gathered for Gimbels immense Stores.

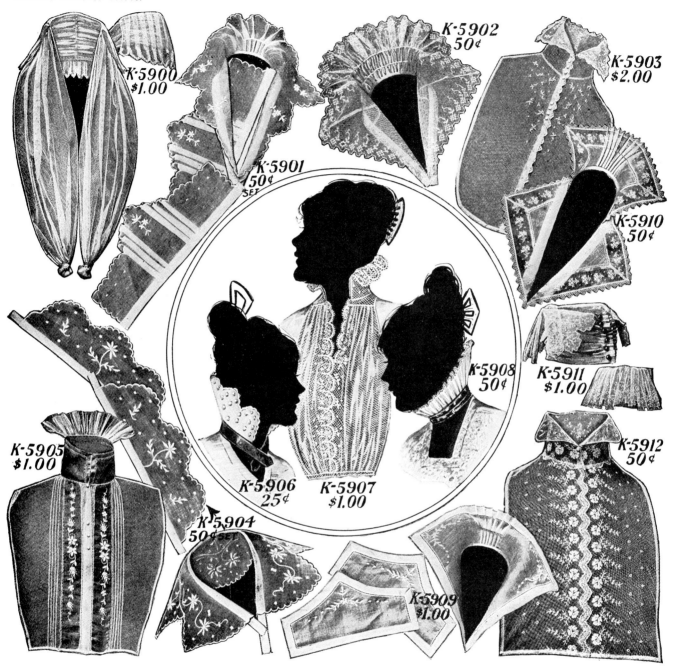

K—5900. Unusually Pretty is this Charming Vestee of Plain Net. Pleated turn-back piece of Oriental lace. **$1.00.**

K—5901. Beautiful and Novel Sheer Lawn Collar and Cuff Set. Pleated. Exquisitely embroidered. Effective flare collar. **50c a set.**

K—5902. Charming Collar of Oriental Lace. Shirred back. Very appropriate as a finish for the dressy blouse. Variety of patterns. White or cream. **50c.**

K—5903. Exquisite Hand Embroidered Net Guimpe. Edged with Irish crochet picot. Closing effected by pearl buttons. Very dainty embroidered design each side of front. A special Gimbel offering at **$2.00.**

K—5904. Dainty Embroidered Collar and Cuff Set of Organdie. This popular material is much in evidence this season for neckwear. Specially offered at **50c a set.**

K—5905. Very Effective Vestee Representing a Combination of Embroidered Organdie and Net. Finely embroidered panel on each side of front. Fastens with small buttons. Collar can be worn militaire or with corners turned down, giving the Piccadilly finish. **$1.00.**

K—5906. This Model Embodies the Latest Style in Collars. Short standing flare collar. Attached to black velvet band. **25c.**

K—5907. Oriental Lace Fashions This Charming Vestee. The novel clover leaf collar will gain many friends this season. Regularly, $1.50. Special for this season, **$1.00.**

K—5908. Dainty in the Extreme is This New Ruche of Fluted Organdie. The fastidious woman could not desire a prettier ruche than this. Finished with black moire ribbon. **50c.**

K—5909. Handsome Collar and Cuff Set of Hand Embroidered Organdie. Neatly hemstitched. Flare collar. Special at **$1.00 a set.**

K—5910. Very Pretty Collar of Sheer Lawn and Embroidery. Finished with dainty lace edge. Pleats in collar afford the charming flare effect. Neat hemstitching is an added feature. **50c.**

K—5911. This Very Novel Stock is Composed of Crushed White Net and Oriental Lace. Tiny black buttons effect front closing. **$1.00.**

K—5912. Fashionable Vestee of Oriental Lace. Short model. Variety of choice patterns. Collar has popular Piccadilly shape. **50c.**

Gimbels Paris, London and American Style Book

Guimpes, Collars, Vestees and Pleatings

"Tuckers" were favored in the Victorian days, and show their influence now in exquisite pleatings and frillings. Then the military tendency influenced the high collars, made charmingly feminine at times by lace and embroidery.

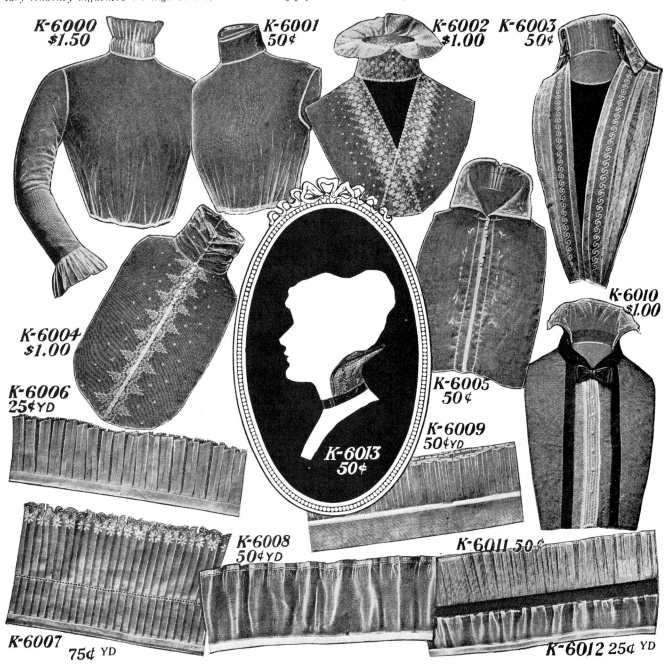

K-6000 $1.50
K-6001 50¢
K-6002 $1.00
K-6003 50¢
K-6004 $1.00
K-6006 25¢ YD
K-6013 50¢
K-6005 50¢
K-6009 50¢YD
K-6010 $1.00
K-6008 50¢YD
K-6011 50¢
K-6007 75¢ YD
K-6012 25¢ YD

—6000. Handsome White Net Guimpe. Fastens in back. A beautiful style at a low price. Sizes, 36, 38, 40. **$1.50.**

K—6001. Neat Sleeveless Guimpe of Good Quality Net. White, cream, ecru or black. A very good offer for 50c.

K—6002. This Beautiful Vestee will certainly delight by its daintiness and style. The high standing collar has a pretty frilling, closes at the neck and has an open V-shaped space below. Exquisite oriental lace and net. Very new and special. **$1.00.**

K—6003. This Charming and Dainty Vestee has a modish pleated collar in back, so much in vogue this season. Of good quality net with a handsome embroidered design appearing on collar and each side of vest. 50c.

K—6004. Here is an Exquisite and Very Fashionable Vestee of Oriental Lace. Has the new crushed collar trimmed with pretty buttons.

A delightful style for the woman who prefers high collars. **$1.00.**

K—6005. Dainty and Handsome Hand Embroidered Organdie Vestee. Collar is neatly hemstitched, pleated in the back and Piccadilly style in front. Vestee trimmed with pretty buttons. An exceptional value for the price. 50c.

K—6006. Chic New Pleating in Box Pleated Style. Of organdie, a material now so fashionable and that appeals to most everyone. White. 2¾ inches wide. 25c a yard.

K—6007. Handsome Pleating. Used for collar and cuffs. Beautiful and dainty sheer embroidery with hemstitching through the center. Width, 5 inches. 75c a yard.

K—6008. French Pleating Organdie with a neat hemstitched end. Will make an exquisite and chic trimming. 3½ inches wide. 50c a yard.

K—6009. Fancy Pleating. Two rows neatly box pleated. Good quality net on a deep band.

A good value for 50c a yard.

K—6010. Modish and Beautiful Vestee. Black net over white, something very new this season. High standing collar is in flare effect and finished with a ribbon band and tie. A black net tuck on each side of vest extends from collar to waistline. Pearl buttons trim vest. **$1.00.**

K—6011. Box Pleated White Net Frilling on Black Velvet Band. 3½ inches wide. A pretty trimming for the neck. 50c a yard.

K—6012. Handsome French Pleated Organdie. Width, 1½ inches. A neat pleating and a good value. 25c a yard.

K—6013. Very fashionable and appealing is this collar. New Flare Collar of dainty lace edged neatly with satin and fastened to a black velvet band. Trimmed on each side of band with small buttons. Comes in all black or cream lace collar with black velvet band. A special offering at 50c.

Quiet Good Taste Is Evident In Gimbel Handkerchiefs

People of refinement prefer Gimbel Handkerchiefs because the fabrics are exquisitely fine and designs are always the favored new ones. Moreover, Gimbel handkerchiefs are of matchless quality at the prices. Our experts know this because of ceaseless comparison with all known makes.

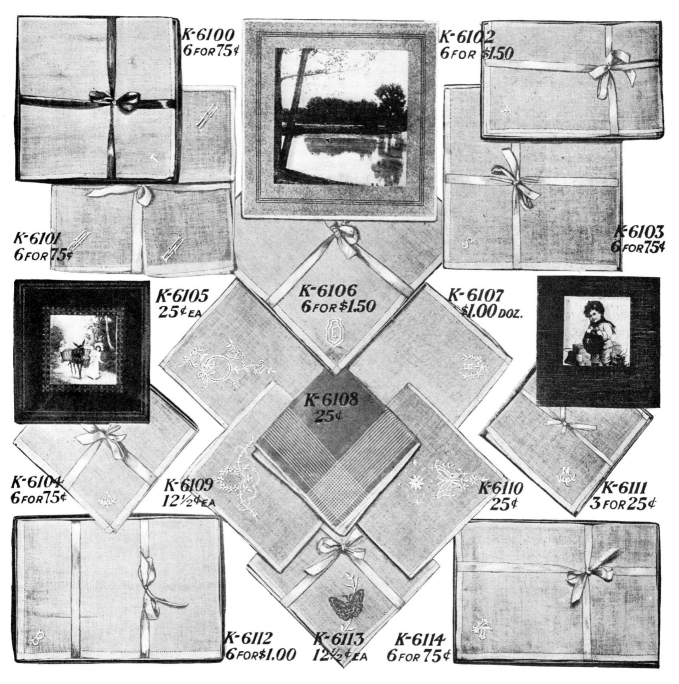

K-6100 6 FOR 75¢
K-6102 6 FOR $1.50
K-6101 6 FOR 75¢
K-6103 6 FOR 75¢
K-6105 25¢ EA
K-6106 6 FOR $1.50
K-6107 $1.00 DOZ.
K-6108 25¢
K-6104 6 FOR 75¢
K-6109 12½¢ EA
K-6110 25¢
K-6111 3 FOR 25¢
K-6112 6 FOR $1.00
K-6113 12½¢ EA
K-6114 6 FOR 75¢

K—6100. Woman's Linen Hemstitched Handkerchiefs. Very narrow hem with neat small block initials. Effective in their simplicity. 6 for 75c.

K—6101. Woman's Sheer Quality Irish Linen Handkerchiefs. Popular semi-elongated colored initials. Three colors, pink, blue and lavender, in each box of six. 6 for 75c.

K—6102. Man's Plain Irish Linen Handkerchiefs. Very neat block initials. Narrow hem. An excellent handkerchief for the price. 25c. 6 for $1.50.

K—6103. Boy's Good Quality Linen Handkerchiefs. Small block initials. Will stand for long wear. 6 for 75c.

K—6104. Child's Hemstitched Linen Handkerchiefs. Pretty floral design with neat initial. Six in attractive picture box. 75c a box.

K—6105. Woman's Fine Sheer Linen Handkerchiefs. Narrow hemstitched hem. Neatly embroidered in one corner in unique designs. Variety of patterns. 25c each.

K—6106. Man's Irish Linen Handkerchiefs. Very dainty shield design with initial. The discriminating man will be well pleased with these. 6 for $1.50.

K—6107. Woman's Linen Handkerchiefs. The block initial is enclosed in wreath design. Cannot be surpassed in quality elsewhere for the price we have placed on it. 6 for 50c; $1.00 a dozen.

K—6108. Woman's Imported Chiffon Handkerchiefs. Have beautiful corded border. Newest novelty. 25c.

K—6109. Woman's Sheer Linen Handkerchiefs. Hemstitched and neatly embroidered in one corner in exquisite designs. Assorted patterns. 12½c each.

K—6110. Woman's Irish Linen Handkerchiefs. Daintily hemstitched. Beautifully embroidered in one corner. Just the handkerchief for the particular woman. 25c each.

K—6111. Child's Linen Handkerchiefs. Narrow hem. Small initial and design. Any child would be pleased with these. 3 for 25c.

K—6112. Man's Good Quality Linen Handkerchiefs. Embroidered block initial. Generous size. The man of refined taste will appreciate this handkerchief. 6 for $1.00.

K—6113. Woman's Linen Handkerchiefs. Very pretty embroidered design in corner in assorted colors. Exceptionally neat with its narrow hem. Variety of patterns. 12½ each.

K—6114. Man's Pure Linen Handkerchiefs. Popular open-work initial. Medium width hem. An excellent value. 6 for 75c.

Gimbels Paris, London and American Style Book

K-6200
25¢ YD.

K-6202
15¢ YD.

K-6203
12¢ YD.

K-6204
18¢ YD.

K-6205
12¢ YD.

K-6206
15¢ YD.

K-6201
75¢ YD.

K-6207
$1.00 YD.

K-6208
38¢ YD.

K-6209
18¢ YD.

K-6210
18¢ YD.

K-6211
12¢ YD.

K-6212
15¢ YD.

K-6213
$1.50 EACH

K-6214
25¢ YD.

K-6215
50¢ YD.

K-6216
$1.25 YD.

K-6217
75¢ YD.

K-6218
38¢ YD.

K-6219
$1.25 YD.

For Descriptions See Opposite Page.

Dainty Edgings, Flouncings, Insertions and Allovers

On this and the opposite page are beautiful patterns for a variety of uses. We prefer not to send samples, the illustrations giving an adequate idea of the designs.

K—6200. Cambric Petticoat Flounce. 12-inch. Beautifully embroidered and eyeleted. Embroidery work is 5 inches deep. Excellent quality. **25c yd.**

K—6201. Embroidered Voile Flounce. 45-inch. Exquisite floral design. Work is 19½ inches deep. Material below for hem. All blind work in imitation of hand embroidery. **75c yd.**

K—6202. Swiss Double Hemstitched Insertion. 1 inch wide. Actual design not quite ½ inch. For infants' and children's dresses. **15c yd.**

K—6203. Swiss Baby Edge. Daintily embroidered. 1½ inches wide. To match the above. Just the trimming for infants' and children's dresses. **12c yd.**

K—6204. Embroidered Swiss Baby Edge. 2½-inch. Completes this lovely set, as it matches the insertion K—6202, and narrow edge, K—6203. **18c yd.**

K—6205. Insertion. 2-inch. Floral design, with double hemstitched finish, to match K—6206. Work is 1 inch deep. **12c yd.**

K—6206. Embroidered Swiss Edge. 5-inch. Work is about 2 inches deep—very lovely floral and eyelet design to match K—6205. **15c yard.**

K—6207. Nainsook Allover Embroidery. 22 inches wide, in English eyelet design. **$1.00 yd.**

K—6208. Embroidered Nainsook Corset Cover Flounce. 18-inch. Beautifully embroidered, with beaded edge. Work about 6 inches deep. This will make practical and serviceable corset covers. **38c yd.**

K—6209. Insertion to Match K—6210. 2 inches wide. Actual work, 1 inch. **18c yd.**

K—6210. English Eyelet Cambric Edge. Work is about 1 inch wide. Very effective design. 4 inches wide. Matches K—6209. **18c yd.**

K—6211. Insertion to Match K—6212. 2¼ inches wide. Swiss lawn. Actual work 1¼ inches wide. **12c yd.**

K—6212. Beautifully Embroidered Nainsook Edge. 6 inches wide. Work is 2¼ inches deep. **15c yd.**

K—6213. Beautifully Embroidered Child's Dress. Almost ready to wear, as it is correctly cut, ready to be sewed, embroidered on soft batiste in close imitation of hand embroidery. 2 to 6 years old. **$1.50 each.**

K—6214. Embroidered Nainsook Corset Cover Flounce. 18-inch, with beaded edge. Excellent quality in very dainty floral and lattice work design. Embroidery work is 5½ inches deep. **25c yd.**

K—6215. Daintily Embroidered Baby Ruffled Flouncing. 27 inches wide. Exquisite for making babies' and children's dresses, also fancy aprons. Embroidery work, including ruffle, 6¼ inches deep. **50c yd.**

K—6216. Dainty Swiss Allover Embroidery. 22 inches wide. Pretty for yokes in babies' and children's dresses, also night dresses. **$1.25 yd.**

K—6217. Fine Batiste Embroidered Flounce. 27-inch. Lovely floral design, effective cut-out lacy edge. Embroidery work is 5½ inches deep. **75c yd.**

K—6218. Soft Sheer Swiss Flounce. 18-inch. Pretty open cut-out lacy pattern. Work about 6 inches deep. **38c yd.**

K—6219. French Batiste Embroidered Flounce. 45-inch. Handsome Japanese embroidered design. Work is about 17 inches deep. Material below for hem. **$1.25 yd.**

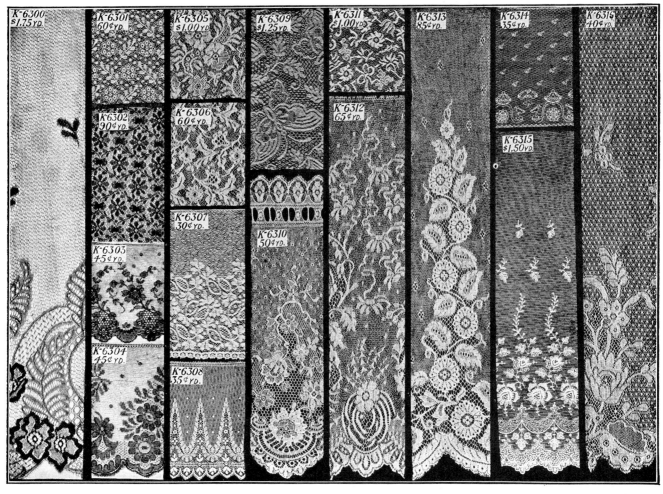

K—6300. Black Shadow Lace Flouncing. 27 inches wide. Work 20 inches deep. Rich black lace that is very elegant for all lace frocks. **$1.75 yd.**

K—6301. White Shadow Allover. 17 inches wide. **60c yd.**

K—6302. Black Shadow Allover. 17 inches wide. Rich allover filmy tracery of trailing vines. **90c yd.**

K—6303. Black Chantilly Lace. 4¼ inches wide. Exquisitely dainty lace. **45c yd.**

K—6304. Black Chantilly Lace. 6 inches wide. Beautiful pattern in floral design. **45c yd.**

K—6305. White or Ecru Shadow Allover. 34 inches wide. Beautiful allover lace of sheer fine mesh. **$1.00 yd.**

K—6306. White Shadow Allover Lace. 21 inches wide. Dainty lace for smart little waists. **60c yd.**

K—6307. White Shadow Val. Lace Edge. 6½ inches wide. **30c yd.**

K—6308. White Shadow Lace Edge. 5 inches wide. Exceedingly beautiful frill width. **35c yd.**

K—6309. White or Ecru Shadow Lace Allover. 42 inches wide. **$1.25 yd.**

K—6310. Shadow Val. Lace with Beading on Top. 13 inches wide. **50c yd.**

K—6311. White Shadow Allover Lace. 20 inches wide. **$1.00 yd.**

K—6312. White Shadow Lace Edge. 17 inches wide. **65c yd.**

K—6313. White Point de Paris Edge. 22 inches wide. **85c yd.**

K—6314. White Shadow Lace. 5¼ inches wide. Very attractive design. **35c yd.**

K—6315. Embroidered Net Top Flounching. 20 inches wide. Work 12 inches deep. **$1.50 yd.**

K—6316. White Shadow Val. Lace Edge. 21 inches wide. Work 16 inches deep. **40c yd.**

New, Beautiful Flounces, Allovers and Top Laces

K-6400 $1.35 YD.

K-6401 $1.50 YD.

K-6402 60¢ YD.

K-6403 $1.00

K-6404 $1.25 YD.

K-6405 50¢ YD.

K-6406 25¢ YD.

K-6407 $1.00 YD.

K-6408 20¢ YD.

K-6409 $1.85 YD.

K-6410 $1.65

K-6411 $2.50

For descriptions please see opposite page

New York — Gimbel Brothers — Philadelphia

New, Beautiful Flounces, Allovers and Top Laces

K—6400. **Embroidered Net Flouncing.** 45 inches wide, work 30 inches deep. Yd., $1.35.
K—6401. **White or Ecru Embroidered Net Allover.** 36 inches wide. A yard, $1.50.
K—6402. **White or Ecru Embroidered Net Top Lace.** 6½ inches wide. A yard, 60c.
K—6403. **White or Ecru Net Top Lace.** 24 inches, work 13 inches deep. Yard, $1.00.

K—6404. **White or Ecru Embroidered Net Allover.** 36 inches wide. A yard, $1.25.
K—6405. **White or Ecru Net Top Lace.** 5½ inches wide. A yard, 50c.
K—6406. **White or Ecru Embroidered Net Top Lace.** 5½ inches wide. A yard, 25c.
K—6407. **Embroidered White Net Lace Allover.** 18 inches wide. A yard, $1.00.

K—6408. **White or Ecru Embroidered Net Top Lace.** 5½ inches wide. A yard, 20c.
K—6409. **White or Ecru Embroidered Net Allover.** 35 inches wide. A yard, $1.85.
K—6410. **Embroidered Net Flouncing.** 45 inches wide, work 23 inches deep. Yd. $1.65.
K—6411. **Black Shadow Lace Flouncing.** 32 inches wide. A yard, $2.50.

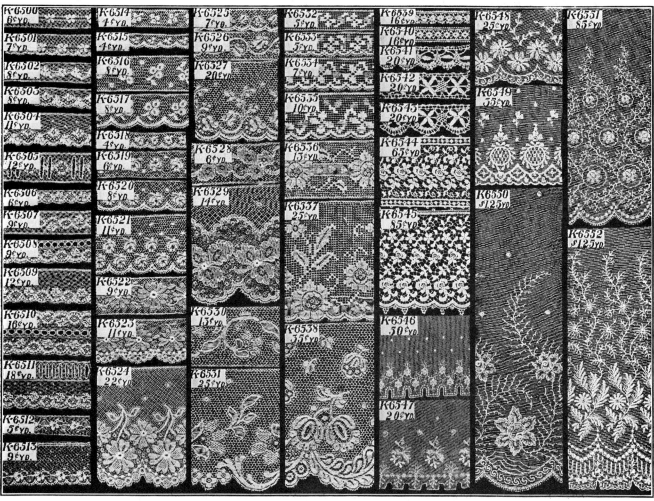

K—6500. **Diamond Mesh Val Insertion.** ¾ inch wide. A yard, 6c; per doz. yards, 65c.
K—6501. **Diamond Mesh Val Edge.** ¾ inch wide. A yard, 7c; per dozen yards, 75c.
K—6502. **Diamond Mesh Val Insertion.** ¾ inch wide. A yard, 8c; dozen yards, 85c.
K—6503. **Diamond Mesh Val Edge.** ¾ inch wide. A yard, 8c; per dozen yards, 85c.
K—6504. **Diamond Mesh Val Edge.** 1¾ inches wide. A yard, 11c; dozen yards, $1.25.
K—6505. **Diamond Mesh Val Beading.** 1¼ inches wide. A yard, 12c; dozen yards, $1.35.
K—6506. **Diamond Mesh Val Edge.** ½ inch wide. A yard, 6c; a dozen yards, 65c.
K—6507. **Diamond Mesh Val Insertion.** 1 inch wide. A yard, 9c; a doz. yards, $1.00.
K—6508. **Diamond Val Edge Beading.** 1 inch wide. A yard, 9c; a dozen yards, $1.00.
K—6509. **Diamond Mesh Val Edge.** 1½ inches wide. A yard, 12c; a doz. yds., $1.35.
K—6510. **Diamond Mesh Double Edge Val Beading.** 1¾ inches wide. A yard, 16c; a dozen yards, $1.85.
K—6511. **Diamond Mesh Val Edge With Beading.** 2 inches wide. A yard, 18c; a dozen yards, $2.10.
K—6512. **Diamond Mesh Val Insertion.** ¾ inch wide. A yard, 5c; a dozen yards, 55c.
K—6513. **Diamond Mesh Val Edge.** 1¾ inches wide. A yard, 9c; a doz. yds., $1.00.
K—6514. **Round Mesh Val Insertion.** ½ inch wide. A yard, 4c; a dozen yards, 45c.
K—6515. **Round Mesh Val Edge.** ½ inch wide. A yard, 4c; a dozen yards, 45c.
K—6516. **Round Mesh Val Insertion.** 1½ inches wide. A yard, 8c; a doz. yds., 85c.

K—6517. **Round Mesh Val Edge.** 1½ inches wide. A yard, 8c; a dozen yards, 85c.
K—6518. **Round Mesh Val Edge.** ½ inch wide. A yard, 4c; a dozen yards, 45c.
K—6519. **Round Mesh Val Insertion.** 1 inch wide. A yard, 6c; a dozen yards, 65c.
K—6520. **Round Mesh Val Edge.** 1½ inches wide. A yard, 8c; a dozen yards, 85c.
K—6521. **Round Mesh Val Edge.** 2¼ inches wide. A yard, 11c; a dozen yards, $1.25.
K—6522. **Point de Paris Val Insertion.** 1½ inches wide. A yard, 9c; a doz. yds., $1.00.
K—6523. **Point de Paris Val Edge.** 1½ inches wide. A yard, 11c; a doz. yds., $1.25.
K—6524. **Point de Paris Val Edge.** 5 inches wide. A yard, 22c.
K—6525. **Round Mesh Val Edge.** ¾ inch wide. A yard, 7c; a dozen yards, 75c.
K—6526. **Round Mesh Val Edge.** 1¼ inches wide. A yard, 9c; a doz. yds., $1.00.
K—6527. **Round Mesh Val Edge.** 3¼ inches wide. A yard, 20c.
K—6528. **Point de Paris Insertion.** 1¾ inches wide. A yard, 6c; a dozen yards, 65c.
K—6529. **Point de Paris Edge.** 5 inches wide. A yard, 14c; a dozen yards, $1.65.
K—6530. **Normandy Val Insertion.** 2½ inches wide. A yard, 13c; a dozen yards, $1.50.
K—6531. **Normandy Val Edge.** 5 inches wide. A yard, 25c.
K—6532. **Square Mesh Val Insertion.** ¾ inch wide. A yard, 5c; a dozen yards, 55c.
K—6533. **Square Mesh Val Edge.** 1 inch wide. A yard, 5c; a dozen yards, 55c.
K—6534. **Square Mesh Val Edge.** 1¼ inches wide. A yard, 7c; a dozen yards, 75c.

K—6535. **Square Mesh Val Edge.** 2 inches wide. A yard, 10c; a dozen yards, $1.10.
K—6536. **Square Mesh Val Insertion.** 2½ inches wide. A yard, 13c; doz. yds., $1.50.
K—6537. **Square Mesh Val Edge.** 5 inches wide. A yard, 25c.
K—6538. **Round Mesh Val Edge.** 7 inches wide. A yard, 35c; 10½ in. wide, yd. 50c.
K—6539. **Linen Burman Cluny Edge.** ½ inch wide. A yard, 16c; a dozen yards, $1.85.
K—6540. **Linen Burman Cluny Insertion.** ½ inch wide. A yard, 16c; doz. yds., $1.85.
K—6541. **Real Cluny Lace Edge.** 1 inch wide. A yard, 20c.
K—6542. **Real Cluny Lace Insertion.** 1 inch wide. A yard, 20c.
K—6543. **Real Cluny Lace Edge.** 1¼ inches wide. A yard, 20c.
K—6544. **White Venise Insertion.** 3 inches wide. A yard, 65c.
K—6545. **White Venise Edge.** 4¼ inches wide. A yard, 85c.
K—6546. **White or Ecru Emb. Net Top Lace.** 6½ inches wide. A yard, 50c.
K—6547. **White Emb. Net Top Lace.** 5 inches wide. A yard, 20c.
K—6548. **White or Ecru Emb. Net Top Lace.** 5 inches wide. A yard, 25c.
K—6549. **White or Ecru Emb. Net Top Lace.** 6½ inches wide. A yard, 35c.
K—6550. **Cream Emb. Net Top Lace.** 21 inches wide; work 13 inches deep. Yd. $1.25.
K—6551. **Cream Emb. Net Top Lace.** 18 inches wide; work 8 inches deep. Yd. 85c.
K—6552. **Cream Emb. Net Top Lace.** 25 inches wide; work 10 inches deep. A yard, $1.25.

Gimbel Trimmers Loop Up Ribbon Into Fascinating Creations

Fresh ribbons improve the worn costume wonderfully, also the clever use of a particular color will bring out the tints in hair or coloring in a most becoming manner. Ribbons are also particularly dainty for underwear. These ribbons, being made to order, are not exchangeable.

K-6600-60¢
K-6601 25¢
K-6602 50¢
K-6603-75¢
K-6605 40¢
K-6604 50¢
K-6606 30¢
K-6607 $1.00
K-6608 35¢ PER SET
K-6609-25¢ EACH 50¢ PER SET
K-6610 75¢
K-6611 75¢
K-6612 75¢
K-6613 75¢
K-6614-35¢

K—6600. Child's Beautiful Hair Band. Finished with bow or self-colored jacquard ribbon in pink, blue or white. A pretty and very becoming finish to the hair. Good value. 60c.

K—6601. Soft Pretty Silk Blossoms with Their Natural Leaves. These come in all colors and can be selected to blend with any colored costume. They give just the finishing touch. And the cost really is insignificant considering the value. 25c each.

K—6602. Handsome Artificial Rose with Rich Velvet Foliage. In pink, cerise or American beauty. A very beautiful ornament to grace the hat or may be worn on any outside garment. Splendid value. 50c.

K—6603. Stylish Belt of Black and White Ribbon. Finished with tailored bow. This can be worn with colors, but is especially beautiful on white. Please state waist measurement when ordering. 75c.

K—6604. Ribbon Coat Hanger. Of plain or fancy ribbon. A much-needed article for the care of the pretty summer dresses and coats. The silk-covered hanger is always desirable and is the greatest convenience. Please state color desired and whether of plain or fancy ribbon. 50c each.

K—6605. Ribbon Blossom Band. Makes a dainty and pretty trimming for lingerie dresses. Very fashionable this season. Comes in all colors. These blossoms show much skill and taste in the making, and are an excellent value. Single blossom, 15c. Set of four, 40c.

K—6606. Rosette Set of Three. Very much used for women's and misses' lingerie, also for children's clothing. Made of satin dotted wash ribbon. Pink, blue or white. They add greatly to the beauty of any garment. 30c set.

K—6607. Hair Band of Handsome Satin Ribbon Lattice, finished with dainty maline bow and rose buds. All colors. A charming hair ornament. Fitting for any dress occasion. $1.00.

K—6608. Child's Pretty Cap Rosettes with Strings. 1½ inch satin jacquard ribbon. Pink or blue. Dainty trimmings which set off the sweet little faces. Very reasonable. 35c set.

K—6609. Knotted Shower Rosette. Made of ¾-inch satin ribbon in all colors. Pretty for children's and infants' dresses. 25c each. 50c set.

K—6610. Roman Stripe Sash. Made of handsome Roman ribbon 4¾ inches wide. Excellent value. 75c.

K—6611. Pleated Ribbon Rosette for Small Hat. Makes a stylish and durable trimming. Grosgrain ribbon in solid colors, including black. 75c.

K—6612. Utility Bag. Made of plain satin and fancy ribbon. A good value. 75c.

K—6613. Ribbon Sash for Summer Frock or Evening Dress. Made of satin ribbon 4¾ inches wide. 75c.

K—6614. Ribbon Neck Bow. Made of messaline ribbon and silk rose buds. All colors. 35c.

For Carriage, Auto or Seashore Wear, A Coat Is Indispensable

A wrap is frequently required, even in midsummer, and its seasonable lightness admits of a fanciful treatment in the design difficult to attain in the heavier winter garments. These coats are chic, dressy and wonderfully stylish. The very latest style points are in evidence, for Gimbels have advance information as to modes.

K-6700
$2.95

K-6701
$7.50

K-6702
$3.95

K-6703
$5.75

K-6704
$7.50

K-6705
$4.75

K—6700. Girl's Stylish Coat. Excellent quality serge in navy, brown or Copenhagen. Wide belt extends from side to front and fastens with two fancy buttons. Detachable lace collar for laundering. Fancy buttons effect front closing. Lined throughout. This is a charming garment and one to which we would call your special attention. Sizes, 6 to 14 years. $2.95.

K—6701. Girl's Dress Coat. Beautiful quality black silk. Shirred belt in Empire effect, now so very fashionable, fastens in centre front with a beautiful ornament. Detachable lace collar for laundering. Odd buttons in a combination of black and white trim revers and effect the front closing. Lined throughout. This garment can hardly be duplicated elsewhere at our low price. Sizes, 6 to 14 years. $7.50.

K—6702. Girl's Coat. Made of a novelty shepherd check. Inlaid silk poplin collar with bands of self material. Wide sectional belt of shirred silk and self material extends from front to back and ends with buckle in front. Inset sleeve has turn back cuff, button trimmed. While this coat is inexpensive you can rely on its merit. Sizes, 6 to 14 years. $2.95.

K—6703. Girl's Attractive Coat. Made of the modish tan covert cloth that will give splendid service. Short waisted effect with belt in the Empire style. Side-pleated front and back trimmed in centre with buttons give ample fullness. Detachable collar of plaid pique. Large and convenient patch pocket. Coat i. cut on the newest shape and is an exceptional value. Sizes, 6 to 14 years. $5.75. Also in navy serge. $5.75.

K—6704. Girl's Fashionable Coat. Popular black and white club check. Pretty black satin collar with contrasting color piping of green, Copenhagen or navy. Coat is cut in the new flare model with a new sash front attached to a belt of self-material. Fancy buttons trim belt and effect the closing. Lined throughout. You could not get a better coat anywhere at the price. Sizes, 6 to 14 years. $7.50.

K—6705. Girl's College Coat. Exceptionally stylish in tan covert cloth. Pleat down either side of back and broad belted effect finished with buttons. Panel stitched at each side to waistline breaking into fullness below. Man tailored front with four large patch pockets. Tailored set-in sleeve with mannish cuff, button-trimmed. Serviceable and very fine value. Sizes, 8 to 14 years. $4.75.

Gimbels Paris, London and American Style Book

67

Intermediate and Junior Girls' Dainty Dresses

Short girls and tall girls of the same age cannot wear the same sizes, therefore the Gimbel Stores have developed the junior girls' sizes for the shorter girl who likes her skirts a trifle below the shoe tops, while the tall girl would look best in misses' "even number" sizes with skirts about to the ankles. The junior styles, too, are more appropriate for these girls than the older sizes.

K-6801
$3.95

K-6802
$4.75

K-6800
$2.50

K-6803
$1.75

K-6804
$2.95

No. 6800. Intermediate and Junior Girl's Stylish Russian Dress. Blue linene with combination of pretty white novelty ratine. Sleeves and collar of ratine edged with white lace. Fastens down front invisibly. Front is trimmed with loops and buttons. Jacket effect is given by a band and wide belt of self-material, piped with white cordeline. Russian overskirt of self-material with fullness at the back. Blue, pink or tan. Sizes, 12 to 16 years. A very attractive, becoming dress, and splendid value. $2.50.

K—6801. Intermediate and Junior Girl's "Miss Muffett" Dress. Combination of plain linon and striped gingham. Waist, sleeves, collar and underskirt of striped gingham. Pointed cuff of the plain linon. Apron effect of plain linon over front and back of waist, fastened on left shoulder. Beautiful silk lacer with tassels at neck. Stylish detachable overskirt of plain linon buttoned to waist with large pearl buttons and buttonholes. The striped gingham skirt is pleated and very full. An ideal dress for the growing girl. Colors, green, pink or blue combination. Sizes, 12 to 16 years. $3.95.

K—6802. Junior Girl's Beautiful White Dress. Made of embroidered voile. Waist has a bolero effect back and front of embroidered voile. Revers of fancy lace edged with pleated net. Dainty vest of plain white voile trimmed with tiny black buttons, black satin band and bow. Sleeves edged with white pleated net and finished with black satin band. Narrow black silk belt forming slight Empire effect. Full pleated skirt with deep fold of self-material and embroidered border Sizes, 13 to 17 years. $4.75.

K—6803. Intermediate and Junior Girl's Nobby Dress. Combination of plain lineen and striped percale. Skirt, sleeves, collar and shield of striped percale, with an overdress of plain linene fastened down front, the straight lines modified by a belt of stripes. Long waist. Sleeves trimmed with a cuff of plain lineen. Colors, cadet or tan with stripes to match. Sizes, 12 to 16 years. This is one of those good serviceable "handy" dresses. $1.75.

K—6804. Junior Girl's Beautiful Dress. Excellent quality linon. Bodice and sleeves of white cordeline with plain linon bolero and bands crossing front and buttoned invisibly at sides. Bolero, collar, cuffs and straps neatly hemstitched. New pleated skirt with pointed yoke. Covered buttons of self-material to match. Colors, blue or tan. Sizes, 13 to 17 years. $2.95

New York — Gimbel Brothers — Philadelphia

The Gimbel Stores Design for All Sizes and Needs

We call attention to "intermediate" girl's sizes, 12, 13, 14 and 15 years, specially designed for the girl "large for her age," who does not yet wear corsets, and who wears short skirts—that is, skirts almost to the shoe tops—between the little girl's and the junior girl's lengths. These styles will appeal to the mother who has had trouble in getting a youthful frock of a good fit, suitable for her large daughter. Gimbels catalogue is one of the very, very few which mention "intermediate" sizes. State bust measure and length in back from neck to hem.

K·6901
$6.75

K·6902
$3.50

K·6903
$10.00

K·6900
$5.75

K·6904
$4.95

K—6900. Very Stylish Dress. For the intermediate girl of 13, 14 and 15 years. This is the girl "large for her age" who wears girls' fashions, with skirts about to the shoe tops. She dresses more girlish than the junior girl. Fine cord white pique forms the skirt and jacket. Flowered or all white voile forms the waist and sleeves. Jacket is hemstitched. The tunic skirt falls over a sham skirt with pique facing. Wide satin girdle. All white or white with blue or pink. **$5.75.**

K—6901. Graduation or Confirmation Dress for Junior Girls. This charming, girlish mode is also suitable for any other dressy occasion. Allover butterfly embroidered white voile forms the dress, and plain voile the short sleeves. High-waisted silk girdle in front overlapped by a pointed jacket effect edged with Val. lace. Wide skirt with three ruffles having hemstitched edges.

V-neck back and front. All white or white with maize, light blue or pink girdle. Sizes, 15 and 17 years. **$6.75.**

K—6902. Junior Girl's Stylish School or Afternoon Dress. Made of an excellent, serviceable linen in the stylish new jacket effect. Embroidered on front panel to simulate handwork, and a clever imitation it is. Crochet buttons fasten tabs of bolero which trim the front. Hemstitched organdie collar and cuffs. New flare skirt—the very newest style idea of the season—with tailored peplum and Peggy pocket on right side, also an innovation. Colors, blue or rose. Sizes, 13, 15 and 17 years. **$3.50.**

K—6903. Junior Girl's Beautiful Graduation Dress. Pin-pleated net frock made on the new Empire lines, which is the accepted mode for this season. Dainty embroidered net yoke and sleeves in guimpe effect.

Shirred at waist and trimmed with beautiful satin rosette, catching a drooping sash which ties low in the back. Skirt made with double tunic effect veiling a satin ribbon band below hips. All white or white with pink or blue ribbon. Exquisitely beautiful and of decided value. Sizes, 15 and 17 years. **$10.00.**

K—6904. Junior Girl's Dainty Dress. Here is a remarkable value offered by the Gimbel Stores. Model shows a combination of plain and allover embroidered voile. Material and making are both excellent. Entire waist and sleeves of embroidered voile neatly trimmed with wide Val. lace edge insertion. Plain voile hemstitched collar and vest. Allover embroidered tunic shirred on at yoke depth over a plain skirt. Finished with soft silk girdle and bow. White with blue, salmon or white girdle. Sizes, 15 and 17 years. **$4.95.**

Gimbels Paris, London and American Style Book

K-7000
$1.95

K-7001
$1.50

K-7003
$1.00

K-7002
$1.00

K-7006
$1.50

K-7004
95¢

K-7005
$2.75

K-7007
$1.00

For descriptions please see the opposite page.

New York — Gimbel Brothers — Philadelphia

The Very Smart Apparel Illustrated on Opposite Page

They discuss their children's requirements and it is their final judgment and preference that selects or eliminates the varied lines or changes the style. And this personal contact brings out the best the stores can achieve. Then having a mail order clientele all over the country also reacts upon stocks, making them diversified to meet all requirements.

K—7000. Girl's Stylish Dress. Imitation flowered challis. Dainty yoke with short strap of embroidery insertion. Collar and cuffs of organdie trimmed to match. Black velvet bow, belt and buttons. Overskirt of self-material. Sizes, 6 to 14 years. **$1.95.**

K—7001. Girl's Jack Tar Middie Blouse Dress. White drill blouse, with regulation sailor collar, cuffs and strap on pocket, also skirt, of navy blue. All white dress with navy blue or red trimmings. Kilt skirt invisibly buttoned on blouse. Sizes, 6 to 14 years. **$1.50.**

K—7002. Girl's Plaid Gingham Dress. Deep bias yoke with white lacer. Overskirt laced at top to match yoke. White rep collar. Set-in short sleeves. Cuffs piped in white. Beautiful assorted plaids. Sizes, 6 to 14 years. **$1.00.**

K—7003. Paul Jones Middie Blouse. Suitable for school, sports or camping Regulation sailor collar and cuffs in navy, red or all white, braid-trimmed. Laced front. Long or short sleeve. Colors are fast. Sizes, 8 to 22 years. **$1.00.**

K—7004. Girl's Dress. Combination of plain chambray and checked gingham. Plain chambray waist with vest of white embroidery. Fancy corsage. Skirt of checked gingham. Set-in sleeves of plain chambray. Collar and cuffs of checked gingham edged with embroidery. Colors, blue, pink or black and white combination. Sizes, 6 to 14 years. **95c.**

K—7005. New and Stylish Dress for Girls. Excellent quality of linon. Loose bolero jacket effect closed with crochet buttons

and loops. White collar, shield and cuffs, machine-scalloped and embroidered to simulate hand-work. Black silk girdle with long ends. New flare skirt with tuck down center front. Colors, rose, blue or green. Sizes, 8 to 15 years. **$2.75.**

K—7006. The New Sports Blouse. White drill or khaki cloth. Belt buttons through flaps of the patch pockets appearing at either side. Three-quarter set-in sleeves. Collar has a new shape buttoned tab. Pearl buttons fasten blouse. Comes with skirt K—7007. Sizes, 8 to 16 years. Blouse, **$1.50.**

K—7007. Girl's New Flare Skirt. Has pointed yoke, finished with new coin pocket on each hip. Panel front, and pleats in back. Length, 20 to 34 inches. White or khaki, also navy drill. Matches blouse, K—7006. **$1.00.**

K-7100 $1.95

K-7101 $4.95

K-7102 $1.50

K-7103 $1.25

K-7104 $3.95

K-7105 $1.00

Dainty Little Dresses for Dainty Girls—Equally Fine for Bigger Girls

K—7100. Girl's Handsome White Eyelet Embroidery Dress. Long waisted effect fastening down back. Skirt has two full pleated embroidery ruffles joined to waist with insertion to match. Embroidery waist and short sleeves are both run with ribbon in pastel shades of pink or blue, also white. Sizes, 6 to 14 years. **$1.95.**

K—7101. Girl's Dainty Net Dancing Frock. Cape bolero of exquisitely embroidered net. Wide girdle of messaline, trimmed with tiny buttons. Net chemisette. Pleated net ruffle at neck. Full short inset sleeves gathered at elbow. Skirt of plain net with an overskirt of embroidered net. Foundation dress of white net. Girdle comes in

pastel shades of pink or blue, also white. Sizes, 6 to 14 years. **$4.95.**

K—7102. Girl's Dress of Beautiful Embroidery Flouncing. Long waisted effect. Short pleated skirt of embroidery. Insertion at waistline. Stylish waist of embroidery with vestee of Val insertion and square neck edged with lace. Short sleeves. Fastens in back. The price emphasizes the great Gimbel values. Sizes, 6 to 14 years. **$1.50.**

K—7103. Dainty Embroidery Frock in the New Long Waisted Effect. Full pleated double skirt. Dutch neck. Embroidery on waist forms vest. Kimono sleeves with tucks and lace edging. Pin tucks at waist

line. Another great bargain. Sizes, 6 to 14 years. **$1.25.**

K—7104. Girl's Lingerie Dress. Exceptional quality of batiste elaborately trimmed with laces, insertions and pretty open embroidery in the newest style. Rich ribbon girdle in pastel shades of pink or blue, also white. Sizes, 6 to 14 years. An unexcelled value. **$3.95.**

K—7105. Beautiful Long Waisted Embroidery Dress. Full pleated skirt of embroidery. Dutch neck is formed by embroidery and two rows to match extend to waistline. Short inset sleeves of embroidery edging. Waist has wide beading threaded with ribbon. Sizes, 6 to 14 years. A grand value. **$1.00.**

Modest Prices and Much Merit Are a Gimbel Combination

Did you know that a corps of Gimbel experts, with many years' experience in their particular field, worked for weeks comparing, eliminating and finally selecting these styles as the very best in the market for design and merit?

Descriptions of the Dresses Illustrated on Opposite Page.

K—7300. Serviceable and Stylish Dress for Girls. Good quality plain colored gingham combined with wide or narrow Roman-striped gingham. Surplice waist with pin tucks to add fullness. White pique collar and vest. Pearl buttons and loops trim waist. New scalloped tunic overskirt. Skirt, belt and cuffs on sleeves of the striped gingham. Cadet or pink effects. Sizes, 6 to 14 years. $2.00.

K—7301. Girl's Stylish New Jacket Dress. Soft sheer white lawn waist, trimmed with embroidery and Val lace. Suspender jacket of rep with all hemstitched edges. New flare circular rep skirt, buttoned in front. Light blue or rose with white. Sizes, 8 to 14 years. $1.75.

K—7302. Dainty Combination Dress for Girls. Checked gingham with white all-over embroidery. Novel vest showing in front and around waist. Bands of plain color with button trimming on the bolero effect. Set-in sleeves. Collar and cuffs plain color. Stylish plain skirt with box-pleated front and back. Waistcoat overskirt is button-trimmed. Pink, brown, blue or black effects. Sizes, 6 to 14 years. $1.00.

K—7303. Girl's Dainty One-Piece Russian Sailor Dress. Good quality linene in white with blue or red percale collar, tie, cuffs and belt. Silk anchor on shield and silk stars in back of collar. Chevron on right sleeve. Watch mark on left sleeve. Sizes, 4 to 12 years. $1.75.

K—7304. Girl's Serviceable Bloomer Dress. Sturdy check gingham strapped with plain colored chambray, also plain colored chambray strapped with striped gingham. Small sailor collar and tie to match trimmings. Pearl buttons. Pink or blue checked gingham or plain blue or green chambray. State style wanted and color. Sizes, 6 to 12 years. $1.55.

K—7305. Girl's Lovely Dress. French linon, resembling good linen. Made in the newest style over-dress. Large sailor collar and cuffs of white drill braided to match dress. Full kilted skirt. Large bone buttons trim pleats. Brown, cadet or rose. Sizes, 6 to 14 years. $1.95.

K-7200 $5.95   K-7201 $3.95   K-7202 $2.00   K-7203 $4.50   K-7204 $3.00   K-7205 $8.75

K—7200. Girl's Exquisite Dress of Sheer White Organdie. Most becomingly made. Long waist has clustered tucks. Embroidery front simulates delicate French work. Flirty skirt with pleated tunic. Val lace and insertion finish edges. Finished with satin rosettes. All white, or pink or light blue. Sizes, 8 to 14 years. $5.95.

K—7201. Girl's Stylish White Dress. Made of the newest fabric of cross bar voile, daintily sheer and pretty, yet serviceable. A beautiful dress with long waist, embroidered, tucked and lace-trimmed. New pleated tunic skirt. Pretty satin girdle run through exquisite embroidery beading, with rosette in front. White with pink or blue trimming. Sizes, 6 to 14 years. $3.95.

K—7202. Girl's Pretty Dress of Sheer White Voile. Inexpensive yet very dressy. Long waist is tucked and lace-trimmed. Full skirt with deep hem finished with cluster tucks. Dainty ribbon girdle. White, with pink or light blue girdle. Sizes, 6 to 12 years. $2.00.

K—7203. Girl's White Dress. A combination of sheer lawn and delicate all-over embroidery lawn flouncing. Separate scalloped tunic and blouse of lawn in one piece with absolute straight lines, and trimmed with Val lace edge and insertion. All-over embroidery sleeves. Finished with satin roses and wide sash. All-over embroidery flounce skirt. White with pink or blue sash. Sizes, 6 to 14 years. $4.50.

K—7204. Girl's Serviceable White Lawn Dress. Long waist with surplice effect front of Val lace insertion and band of Swiss embroidery insertion having eyelets laced with ribbon. Belt to match. Cluster-tucked back. New pleated skirt with cluster-tucked front. White with pink or blue ribbon. Sizes, 6 to 14 years. $3.00.

K—7205. Dainty and Beautiful White Voile Dress for Girls. New long bloused jumper waist and ruffled peplum set on with cord shirrings. Wide satin ribbon girdle. Fronts of waist beautifully hand-embroidered and tucked. Long tunic and wide skirt trimmed with cluster of tucks. All edges finished with Venise lace. All white or white with salmon, nile green or light blue girdle. Especially suitable for the older girls. Sizes, 6 to 14 years. $8.75.

For Confirmation, Processions, Children's Day, also Practical Wear

K-7300
$2.00

K-7301
$1.75

K-7302
$1.00

K-7303
$1.75

K-7304
$1.55

K-7305
$1.95

For descriptions please see the opposite page

New York — Gimbel Brothers — Philadelphia

73

Order from Either Store and Make First and Second Choice

The management of the Gimbel New York and the Gimbel Philadelphia Stores is expert, and at either store your order will receive careful and conscientious attention.   Favor the nearest store with your order, as the merchandise catalogued is carried by both.

K—7400
$6.95

K—7401
$5.00

K—7402
$2.00

K—7403
$3.95

K—7404
$3.00

K—7405
$2.50

K—7400. Little Girl's Newest Empire Coat. Made of good quality serge. Adjustable white satin collar and vestee over a self material notched collar. Dainty new Empire waist with loose pleats below in back and front, girded by a satin sectional belt trimmed with buckles and small buttons. Copenhagen, rose or navy. The dressiest, most stylish coat for girls we have seen this season. The value is indeed remarkable. Sizes, 5 to 12 years. **$6.95.**

K—7401. Girl's Newest and Most Stylish Coat. Made on the swagger cut, with fullness held by a narrow belt all around, giving rather short-waisted line, the new 1915 style point. Belt can be adjusted to suit figure. Slanting side pockets. Sizes, 6 to 15 years. Fancy broken checks in multi-colors, a seasonable fabric. **$5.00.** Same coat in plain navy storm serge or tan covert, **$5.00.** All three materials are being much worn this season, being attractive and serviceable.

K—7402. Girl's Serviceable and Stylish Dress. Fine quality striped gingham forms Russian overdress, and plain colored chambray forms foundation skirt and trimmings. Collar, cuffs and belt of white pique. Pretty ball buttons give stylish finish.   The best dress for the price we could find. Green or blue effects. Sizes, 6 to 14 years. **$2.00.**

K—7403. Very Attractive Dress for the Intermediate or Growing Girl of 13, 14 and 15 years—the girl, "large for her age," who wears short skirts. Made of good quality large plaid Scotch gingham. Strap of embroidered white pique down front, and tucks on sides. Pearl buttons fasten through tab in front. New skirt with wide bias band. Piped white pique belt with beautiful pearl buckle. Dainty embroidered lingerie military collar. Lingerie band on cuff. Assorted plaids in combined colors. **$3.95.**

K—7404. Beautiful Ramie Linen Dress. A linen less prone to crush; serviceable and cool. We have selected a very good quality. Imitation hand embroidery sprigs on front, which is side-pleated. Lingerie collar and cuffs with dainty embroidery edge. New pleated tunic on the skirt. Black velvet belt on the lowered waist. Pink or blue. Sizes, 6 to 14 years. **$3.00.**

K—7405. Girl's New Dress of Large Scotch Plaid. New extremely wide, two-tier belt of bias plaid. Adjustable straps over shoulder. Large fancy pearl buttons. New gored pleated skirt, very pretty and stylish. White lawn guimpe with blind embroidery collar and cuffs. Assorted plaids in combination of colors. The Gimbel Stores here offer a dress at a price unquestionably low for the value given. Sizes, 6 to 14 years. **$2.50.**

New York — Gimbel Brothers — Philadelphia

Boys' Cool Wash Suits for Vacation Days

K-7500 $1.65

K-7501 $2.95

K-7502 $2.00

K-7503 $3.95

K-7504 $2.00

K-7505 $2.85

K-7506 $2.00

K-7507 $1.95

K—7500. **Boy's Middy Suit.** In good quality natural linon. An inexpensive suit of unusual wearing quality. Blouse is the slip-on model with pleated sleeves, trimmed with blue collar and cuffs and wide band at the bottom of blouse. White braid trimming. Black silk tie. White shield with blue band at neck. **$1.65.**

K—7501. **Boy's New Model.** Belted middy suit. This is a trim smart little suit made of first quality white repp, trimmed with absolutely fast colored pink or blue linen. Opened in front to waist and can easily be slipped over head. Has white pearl buttons, white silk tie, and straight knee pants with three white pearl buttons on either side. 2½ to 8 years. **$2.95.**

K—7502. **Boy's Vestee Suit.** Fine quality chambray in blue or brown with white vest and collar. Has two side pockets with flaps. Separate white vest of drill with collar attached. Small pearl buttons on vest. Straight knee pants. 3 to 8 years. **$2.00.**

K—7503. **Boy's Palm Beach Norfolk Suit.** Genuine Palm Beach cloth, in single breasted model with four patch pockets on front, yoke in back from beneath which are four side pleats. Belt is stitched down in back, is loose in front and passes through belt straps. Straight knee pants with two side and patch pockets. Color, tan. 6 to 17 years. **$3.95.**

K—7504. **Attractive Suit For Boys.** The very latest Dickens model. Excellent wearing and fast color chambray in green, blue or brown with white collar, cuffs and belt. Blouse made with double breasted shawl collar, pleated belt and turned-up cuffs of repp. Trimmed and closed with large pearl buttons. Straight knee pants buttoned on to waist. 2½ to 8 years. **$2.00.**

K—7505. **Regulation Middy Suit.** Hydegrade white galatea. Made with slip-on blouse with yoke. Collar and cuffs are of plain blue linen, trimmed with flat white braid. Shield has embroidered anchor in red. Left sleeve has regula-

tion chevron. Pocket is piped with red and red lacers are provided. Long Jack Tar pants. 3 to 10 years. **$2.85.**

K—7506. **Boy's Norfolk Middy Suit.** Kindergarten cloth in blue and white, gray and white, or brown and white stripe. Has white repp collar, cuffs, belt and shield. Blouse made with yoke, two box pleats front and back, and is provided with black silk tie. Knee pants are straight cut. This suit is also made in all white and trimmed with blue. 3 to 8 years. **$2.00.**

K—7507. **Boy's Washable Middy Suit.** This suit is made for comfort. Blouse is made in easy slip-over model with Eton collar, opened at the neck with white silk lacing. Sleeves are pleated and handkerchief pocket is provided. Brown or blue French chambray with white collar. Also in all white with blue collar. This suit is also made with short sleeves with white cuffs. 3 to 8 years. **$1.95.**

New York — Gimbel Brothers — Philadelphia

K-7600
$1.85

K-7601
$1.65

K-7602
$2.00

K-7603
$2.75

K-7604
$2.00

K-7605
$2.85

K-7606
$2.85

K-7607
$2.95

For descriptions see opposite page

New York — Gimbel Brothers — Philadelphia

See this Great Variety in Suits for Little Brother

K—7600. Boy's Crepe Chambray Beach Suit. Middy blouse and wide beach trousers. The collar is of repp trimmed with a band of plain blue and nicely finished with repp straps. Band of the same also finishes the short sleeves, the bottom of the shirt and pockets. A fancy cord tie adds a nobby finish to the soft flat collar. White trimmed with blue. 3 to 8 years. $1.85.

K—7601. Striped Chambray Norfolk Model. Stylish collar, vest, belt and cuffs of plain colored chambray to match the stripe. A fancy cord slip-knot tie finishes the neck and pleated sleeves have neat buttoned cuffs. Straight and full fashioned knickerbockers are substantially made and have complete reinforced button band. Blue or brown. 3 to 8 years. $1.65.

K—7602. Galatea Middy Suit. Detachable vestee. Plain collar in solid color trimmed with neat white bands. Black silk tie. Extra wide knickerbockers are a part of this stunning little middy suit and these are fitted with a substantial buttoning waist band. White with blue. 3 to 10 years. $2.00.

K—7603. Khaki Norfolk Suit. Smart mannish yoke, side pleats, belt and two large pockets. The belt is stitched in back and loose in front. The regulation knee pants have belt loops and a full set of pockets. The stitching throughout is such that it will stand the hardest wear. In strong natural dark tan khaki cloth. 3 to 8 years. $2.75.

K—7604. Boy's Dutch Suit. Plain white repp shirt having fancy collar finished with cord slip-knot tie and tailored cuffs. Trousers made in a novel overall effect and joined to the blouse with large pearl buttons. The collar and cuffs match the pants and these are made of new fancy striped kindergarten cloth, a substantial washable cotton twilled fabric that is of extra weight and very practical. 3 to 8 years. Blue or brown stripe with white. $2.00.

K—7605. Dress Suit. High grade mercerized repp having a rich silky appearance. Elaborate white repp vest with silk lacings and fancy hand embroidered collar and cuffs. Neat handkerchief pocket adorns one side and the soft loose belt is a very popular and effective finish to the blouse. Knickerbockers are fitted with a substantial button band. White, blue or tan. 3 to 8 years. $2.85.

K—7606. "Dixie" Model. Formal suit of substantial repp with separate fancy pointed vest, built on a lining and having adjustable straps in back just like a man's vest. Has collar, fancy turn-back cuffs and neck strap giving an exceedingly dressy finish. Wide knickerbockers are fitted with a substantial button band. White or tan. 3 to 8 years. $2.95.

K—7607. "Dickens Junior Suit." A quaint model that has been very popular during the past season for little boys. It is artistic and unusually practical. Made with white silk blouse of the regulation style with soft Eton collar and slip-knot tie. The wide yet fitting pants are joined to the substantial waist band of the shirt with large fancy buttons, that also afford the trimming. White silk shirt with pants in white or tan. 3 to 8 years. $2.95.

K-7700 $1.00
K-7701 $1.35
K-7703 $1.35
K-7704 $1.35
K-7705 $1.45
K-7702 $1.00
K-7706 $1.00
K-7707 $1.00

K—7700. Boy's Washable Middy Suit. Hyde-grade galatea in neat combinations of navy blue, cadet blue or brown striped blouse material. The collar, cuffs and bottom of blouse are of plain colored material with three rows of flat braid. Trousers of plain color, finished with pearl buttons. 3 to 8 years. $1.00.

K—7701. Boy's Washable Vestee Suit. Extra good quality repp. Collar and cuffs trimmed with three rows of flat braid. Six large white pearl buttons on front. Vest made with military neck band and strap fastened around body. Trousers finished with pearl buttons at side. White trimmed with blue or tan collar and cuffs. 3 to 8 years. $1.35.

K—7702. Boy's Washable Dutch Suit. Hyde-grade galatea in neat combinations of blue striped jacket, plain blue straight trousers and blue collar and cuffs. Brown striped jacket, plain brown trousers, collar and cuffs. Cadet blue striped jacket, plain cadet blue trousers, collar and cuffs. Cuffs have white braid. White cord tie. White pearl buttons. Also plain white. 3 to 8 years. $1.00.

K—7703. Galatea Middy Blouse Suit. One pair long and one pair straight knee pants. These suits are in white only, with blue galatea collar and cuffs trimmed with white flat braid. Blue laced front and blue trimmed pocket on left side. 3 to 8 years. $1.35.

K—7704. Boy's Washable Dickens Suit. Very fine repp. Body of jacket, and full pleated sleeves of white. Trimmed with blue, tan or plain white embroidered collar and cuffs. Straight trousers fastened on jacket with large white pearl buttons and finished at side with three smaller buttons. 3 to 8 years. $1.35.

K—7705. Boy's Regulation Middy Sailor Suit. Hydegrade galatea. Middy blouse and long trousers. The sailor collar and cuffs of blue galatea trimmed with rows of flat white braid. Blue tie and red band on right sleeve. Detachable shield is embroidered with navy emblem. Breast pocket on left side trimmed with blue. Long trousers, either white or blue, buttoned at side. 3 to 8 years. $1.45.

K—7706. Boy's Washable Middy Blouse Suit. Slip-over style. Neat small blue tie. Plain white with blue collar and cuffs with three rows of white braid, and fine blue stripe around the bottom of blouse. Trousers trimmed with buttons. 3 to 8 years. $1.00.

K—7707. Boy's Washable Suits. Hydegrade galatea. White cord tie. Sewed-on belt with two rows of white braid. Navy blue, brown or cadet blue stripes. Also white and navy blue trimmed. 5 to 10 years. $1.00.

Very Proper, Sturdy Clothing for Small Boys

Every mother knows only too well how hard boys are on clothes. Our boys' clothing is made by manufacturers of national reputation from the most durable and lasting materials possible to procure. That is why the purchase of a Gimbel Suit for the boy is such a wise investment and why it will prove least expensive in the end.

K-7800 $4.75
K-7801 $3.50
K-7802 $4.75
K-7803 $3.50
K-7804 $1.85
K-7805 $2.95
K-7806 $5.00
K-7807 $5.00

K—7800. Boy's Vestee Suit. Wool shepherd check or fine quality of blue serge. Edge of coat bound with flat black silk braid, also on cuffs, collar and pockets. Vest made of white pique, opened down the front. Collar attached which turns over collar on coat. Can be worn with or without vest. Silk corded tie at neck. Straight knee trousers. Small pearl buttons trim sleeves and trousers. 3 to 8 years. **$4.75.**

K—7801. Boy's Spring Reefer. Standard double-breasted model of all-wool, black and white shepherd check or blue serge or gray and brown mixtures. Box style back and front. Careful tailoring throughout. Patch pocket on each side. Embroidered chevron on left sleeve. Light in weight and very stylish. 2½ to 10 years. **$3.50.**

K—7802. Boy's New Middy Suit. Exceptionally pretty and well made. New style collar cut square in front and round in back. Wide opening at neck, making it easy to slip over head. Shield of white serge. Patch pocket

at side of blouse. Three rows of silk soutache braid on collar, cuff, pocket, shield and bottom of blouse. Heavy silk sailor tie. Straight knee trousers. Fine quality blue serge, white trimmed. Also made in black and white shepherd check, black trimmed. 3 to 8 years. **$4.75.**

K—7803. Boy's New Model Russian Suit. New because the blouse is cut short with high waisted effect. Opened down front and trimmed with nine small pearl buttons. Detachable white pique collar and cuffs. Straight knee trousers with white pearl buttons on side. A very becoming and dressy suit for small boys. All-wool blue serge or pure worsted black and white shepherd check. 2½ to 8 years **$3.50.**

K—7804. Boy's Dickens Suit. Excellent wearing fabric in plain blue, also gray and brown mixtures. Trimmed with large white pearl buttons. Blouse has Eton collar with silk cord tie. Trousers button outside of blouse

and are straight knee style. A very becoming suit for all-around wear for small boys. 2½ to 8 years. **$1.85.**

K—7805. Boy's Sou'wester Combination. Coat and hat of good heavy tan rubberized material. Plaid back. Buttons up to neck. All seams double stitched. Guaranteed waterproof. Excellent coat to protect the boys going to and from school. 6 to 18 years. **$2.95.**

K—7806. Boy's Balmacaan Reefer. Double breasted. Side pockets and cuffs on sleeve. Made of an unusually fine quality blue serge or of black and white shepherd check, also in gray and brown mixtures. Velvet collar. The stylish and dressy coat lined with alpaca. 3 to 10 years. **$5.00.**

K—7807. New Dickens Model Suit. Wide pointed Byron collar. Extra detachable pique collar. Laced at neck with black silk tie. Trousers button on to blouse in broadfall fashion. Straight at knee. Pure worsted shepherd check or all-wool blue serge. 3 to 8 years. **$5.00.**

New York — Gimbel Brothers — Philadelphia

Boys' Clothing of the Gimbel Standard

The Gimbel standard as applied to Boys' Clothing of the class represented here is the highest attainable. Correct style, finest, all wool fabrics, the most dependable linings and the best tailoring comprise their make-up.

K-7900 $3.50
K-7901 $3.50
K-7902 $4.75
K-7903 $1.85
K-7904 $7.50
K-7905 $4.75
K-7906 $5.00
K-7907 $7.50

K—7900. Boy's Navy Blue Norfolk Suit. The new Bulgarian model—two box plaits in front and two in back. Stitched belt and yoke. Well made and durable. Trousers in knickerbocker style are full cut with reinforced seams. All wool fabric. Sizes, 6 to 17 years. $3.50.

K—7901. Boy's All-Wool Norfolk Suit. Stitched belt, patch pocket style. Two box plaits back and front, made in a wide assortment of mixtures, especially selected for practical wear. Two pairs of full cut knickerbockers. Seams that stay together. 7 to 17. $3.50.

K—7902. Boy's Navy Blue Serge Suit. Splendid quality pure worsted that is fast color. Coat a smart Norfolk model with yoke front and back, four knife plaits from yoke to firmly stitched belt. Two roomy patch pockets. Nicely lined. Knickerbocker trousers lined throughout and with all seams reinforced.

Splendid suit for confirmation. 7 to 18. $4.75.

K—7903. Boy's Norfolk Suit. Made in several serviceable mixtures and put together to stand hard wear. The coat is made with two stitched box plaits front and back, running from yoke to stitched down belt. Full roomy knickerbocker trousers with all seams reinforced. 6 to 16 years. $1.85.

K—7904. Boy's Norfolk Suit. Extra pair of knickerbocker trousers, made in the newest patterns and colorings. Coat has patch pockets, stitched belt in back, detachable in front, six knife plaits in back running from yoke to belt. The materials are absolutely all wool and very durable. Alpaca lined. Full roomy knickerbockers, lined throughout. 7 to 18 years. $7.50.

K—7905. Boy's Knickerbocker Suit. Single breasted plaited model. Brown or gray mixtures of excellent quality all wool fabrics.

Stitched down plaits running from pointed yoke to pocket in front, box plait in back. Stitched on belt, coat lined with alpaca, trousers are full cut with reinforced seams; extra watch pocket. 7 to 18 years. $4.75.

K—7906. Smart Norfolk Suit. Black and white shepherd check of fine quality pure worsted fabric. Single breasted patch pocket model; plaited back, stitched belt. The coat is alpaca lined; knickerbockers full fashion, all seams reinforced. 7 to 18 years. $5.00.

K—7907. Boys' Navy Blue Serge Suit. Norfolk model. Splendid quality serge, guaranteed pure worsted and fast color. The coat a smart new model with patch pockets and flaps that button over, knife-plaited back belt made in three pieces and detachable in front. Large roomy knickerbocker trousers. A smart suit for dress or party wear. 7 to 18 years. $7.50.

Gimbels Paris, London and American Style Book

Solid Gold Jewelry—20-Year Guarantee and Solid Gold Case Watches

The Gimbel Stores have wonderful Jewelry Sections which possess a large clientele. It has been gained through the proven reliability of Gimbel jewelry, also the fact that everything novel and new is first displayed at Gimbels. If you wish package insured, add 5c. extra.

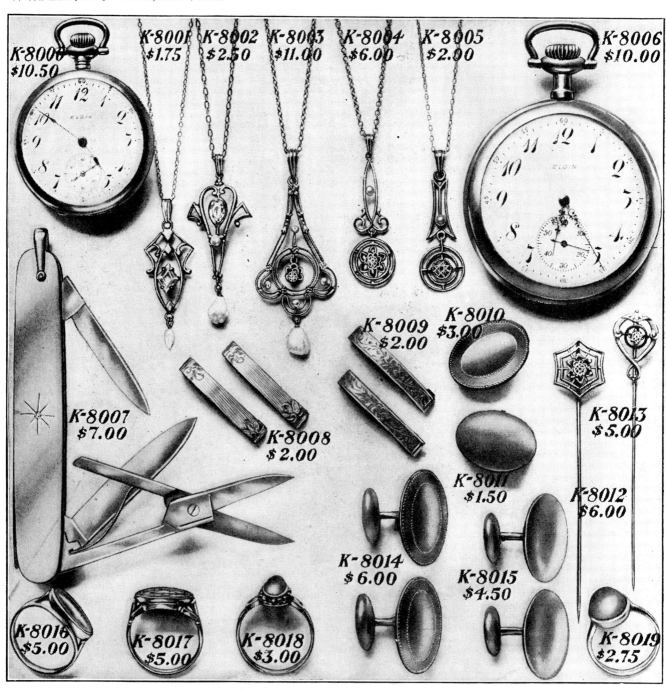

K—8000. **Woman's Watch.** Open face. Twenty year guarantee gold-filled case. Swivel pendant. Elgin or Waltham movement. Thin model. $10.50. Same style, 14-K. solid gold case, $14.50.

K—8001. **La Valliere.** Solid gold. Pearl drop. Amethyst, ruby, garnet, emerald or sapphire center stone. Fine chain. $1.75.

K—8002. **Solid Gold La Valliere.** Baroque pearl drop. Garnet, ruby, amethyst, sapphire or emerald center stone and one small pearl. $2.50.

K—8003. **Solid Gold La Valliere.** Set with four whole pearls. One pendant diamond. Baroque pearl drop. $11.00.

K—8004. **La Valliere.** Solid gold. One diamond and one baroque pearl. $6.00.

K—8005. **La Valliere.** Solid gold. Sapphire, amethyst, garnet, ruby or emerald center stone and one pearl. $2.00.

K—8006. **Man's Watch.** Plain case. Twenty-year guarantee gold-filled case. Thin model, jointed case. Elgin or Waltham movement. $10.00. 14-K. solid gold, same style. $18.00.

K—8007. **Pocket Knife.** Solid gold handles. Diamond setting. Two blades and scissors. Roman finish. $7.00.

K—8008. **Lingerie Pins.** Engine turned design. English finish. $2.00.

K—8009. **Lingerie Pins.** Hand engraved. English finish. $2.00 pair.

K—8010. **Solid Gold Tie Clasp.** Engine turned border. English finish. Solid back. $3.00.

K—8011. **Tie Clasp.** Plain, English or Roman finish. $1.50.

K—8012. **Solid Gold Scarf Pin.** Pierced design. One diamond. English finish. $6.00.

K—8013. **Scarf Pin.,** Solid gold. Black enameled circle with one diamond. English finish. $5.00.

K—8014. **Solid Gold Cuff Buttons.** Heavy back. Engine turned border. English finish. $6.00 pair.

K—8015. **Cuff Buttons.** Solid gold. Plain, English or Roman finish. $4.50 pair.

K—8016. **Woman's Small Finger Ring.** English finish. Amethyst, garnet or topaz stone. $5.00.

K—8017. **Woman's Small Finger Ring.** Pierced shank. English finish. Garnet, amethyst, topaz or imitation sapphire stone. $5.00.

K—8018. **Girl's Finger Ring.** Fancy shank. Bloodstone or sardonyx stone. $3.00.

K—8019. **Boy's Finger Ring.** Plain shank. Sardonyx or bloodstone setting. $2.75.

New York — Gimbel Brothers — Philadelphia

Have You a Penchant for Your Particular Birthstone?

Women's Finger Rings and a few other pieces of Jewelry on pages 80 and 81 can be furnished in any color birthstones except the diamond. If not in stock, two weeks' time may be required.
TABLE OF BIRTHSTONES—January, Garnet; February, Amethyst; March, Bloodstone; April, Diamond; May, Emerald; June, Pearl; July, Ruby; August, Sardonyx; September, Sapphire; October, Opal; November, Topaz; December, Turquoise. Ask for Card for Taking Measurements of Rings. Parcel Post packages may be insured for safe delivery, fee 5 cents extra. Solid gold jewelry we engrave with script letter free of charge.

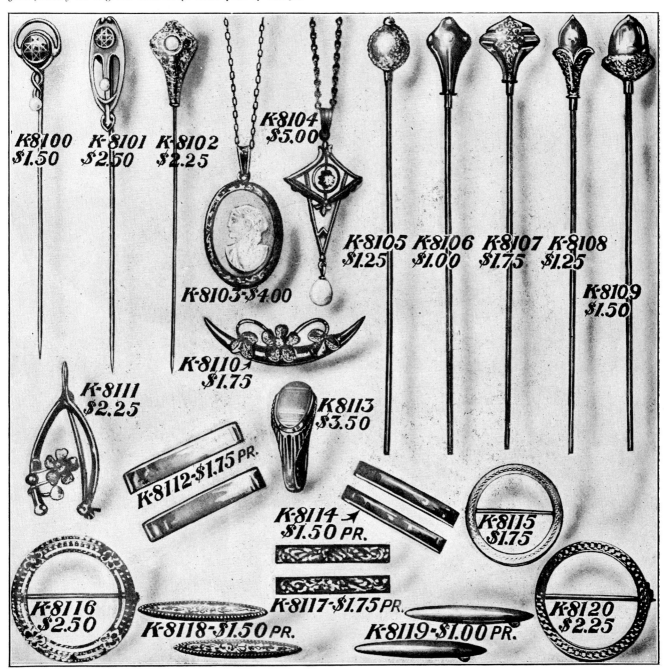

K—8100. Solid Gold Scarf Pin. One garnet and one pearl setting. English finish. **$1.50.**
K—8101. Solid Gold Scarf Pin. Rose gold finish. One sapphire and one pearl setting. **$2.50.**
K—8102. Scarf Pin. Solid gold. Pear shape. Vermicelli design. One pearl setting. **$2.25.**
K—8103. Solid Gold La Valliere. Set with pink cameo, white head. Very artistic. **$4.00.**
K—8104. La Valliere. Solid gold. Pearl drop. One diamond setting. **$5.00.**
K—8105. Solid Gold Hat Pin. Ball shape. Vermicelli design. **$1.25.**
K—8106. Hat Pin. Solid gold. Plain Roman finish. **$1.00.**

K—8107. Solid Gold Hat Pin. Half plain and half vermicelli design. **$1.75.**
K—8108. Solid Gold Hat Pin. Vermicelli design. English finish. **$1.25.**
K—8109. Hat Pin. Solid gold. Vermicelli design. **$1.50.**
K—8110. Solid Gold Brooch. Crescent design. Green leaves and one amethyst setting. **$1.75.**
K—8111. Solid Gold Brooch. Wishbone design. One ruby and one pearl setting. **$2.25.**
K—8112. Lingerie Pins. Plain design. Roman or English finish. **$1.75 pair.**
K—8113. Woman's Small Finger Ring. Fluted shank. Sardonyx, bloodstone, moss agate stone or other color birthstone. **$3.50.**

K—8114. Solid Gold Handy Pins. Plain square English or Roman finish. **$1.50 pair.**
K—8115. Circle Brooch. Solid gold. Engine turned design. English finish. **$1.75.**
K—8116. Circle Brooch. Solid gold. Hand engraved and engine turned design. English finish. **$2.50.**
K—8117. Solid Gold Handy Pins. Square edge. Hand engraved. English finish. **$1.75 pair.**
K—8118. Handy Pins. Solid gold. Hand engraved. English finish. **$1.50 pair.**
K—8119. Solid Gold Handy Pins. Plain English or Roman finish. **$1.00 pair.**
K—8120. Circle Brooch. Solid gold. Engine turned design. English finish. **$2.25.**

Gold-Filled, Gold-Plated, Sterling Pins, Rings, Bracelets, Buttons, Etc.

Small in price, but excellent in quality and most new, novel and pleasing as to styles. Look this page over carefully, for it well and truly represents Gimbels ability to, in Jewelry as well as other goods, serve you best.

K—8200. **Hat Pin.** Gold-filled. Vermicelli design. **$1.00.**

K—8201. **Hat Pins.** Gold-plated with dainty touch of black enamel and imitation pearls. **50c pair.**

K—8202. **Woman's Gold-Plated Ring.** Single stone setting. Pearl, rhinestone, or colored stone. **50c.**

K—8203. **Woman's Finger Ring.** Gold-plated. Amethyst or sapphire setting. **50c.**

K—8204. **Woman's Sterling Ring.** Cabochon stone setting. Various colored stones. **50c.**

K—8205. **Woman's Finger Ring.** Gold-plated jeweled with amethyst, sapphire or ruby. **50c.**

K—8206. **Brooch.** Pierced design. Gold-filled. Real cameo in center with four imitation pearls and lines of black enamel. Very effective. Two fancy leaves. **$1.50.**

K—8207. **Brooch.** Gold-plated. Dainty pierced design jeweled with three colored stones and pearl setting combined with black enamel. **75c.**

K—8208. **Cigarette Case.** Sterling. Engine turned one side, plain on the other. 3 inches long. **$6.00.**

K—8209. **Cuff Links.** Gold front. Engine turning with engraving. **$1.50 pair.**

K—8210. **Cuff Links.** Gold-plated combined with black enamel. Smart looking style. **75c pair.**

K—8211. **Cuff Links.** Gold front. Fancy border. Plain center. **$1.50 pair.**

K—8212. **Sterling Photo Frame.** Plain polished. Square shape. **$1.50.**

K—8213. **Sterling Frame.** Oval cabinet. Extra heavy with ball feet. **$2.00.**

K—8214. **La Valliere.** Gold-filled. Dainty pierced pendant with real cameo setting and three pearls. Pearl drop. **$2.50.**

K—8215. **La Valliere.** Gold-plated. Dainty pierced pendant jeweled with an amethyst or sapphire with pearl drop. **$1.00**

K—8216. **Vanity Case.** Sterling silver. Hand-engraved border with engine turning one side. Fitted with puff, mirror, tablet, pencil and coin compartment. 3½ inches long. **$8.00.**

K—8217. **Dorine Box.** Sterling silver. Plain polished. Fitted with cake of powder, puff and mirror. **$2.00.**

K—8218. **Bangle Bracelet.** Gold-plated. Engine turning with engraving all around. **50c.**

K—8219. **Gold-Filled Bracelet.** Engine turning with engraving. Secret lock. Space for monogram. **$5.75.**

K—8220. **Lingerie Clasps.** Gold-filled. Prettily engraved. **50c pair.**

K—8221. **Circle Collar Pins.** Gold top. Engine turned design. **50c pair.**

K—8222. **Circle Pin.** Gold-plated. Fancy design. **75c.**

K—8223. **Collar Pins.** Oval shape. Black enamel and gold plate. **50c pair.**

There Is Again a Vogue for Hair Ornaments

The new styles are perhaps the daintiest and most graceful worn in years. Gimbels have the cream of the market and quali-ites are exceptionally fine—in appearance and service—giving close to the real shell or amber.

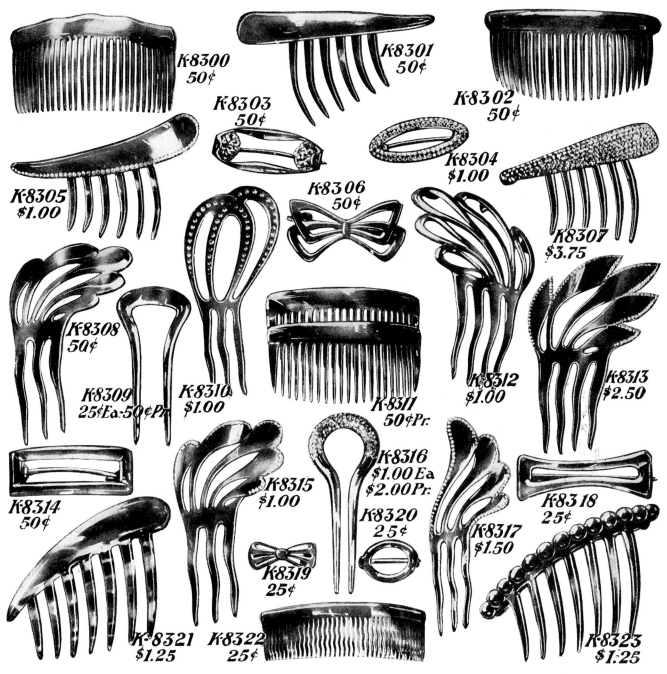

K8300 50¢
K8301 50¢
K8302 50¢
K8303 50¢
K8305 $1.00
K8304 $1.00
K8306 50¢
K8307 $3.75
K8308 50¢
K8309 25¢Ea.50¢Pr
K8310 $1.00
K8311 50¢Pr.
K8312 $1.00
K8313 $2.50
K8314 50¢
K8315 $1.00
K8316 $1.00 Ea $2.00Pr.
K8320 25¢
K8319 25¢
K8317 $1.50
K8318 25¢
K8321 $1.25
K8322 25¢
K8323 $1.25

K—8300. **Chignon Comb.** Waved top. Amber or demi-amber color. **50c.**
K—8301. **La Casque Comb.** Shell, amber or demi-amber color. Medium size. **50c.**
K—8302. **Chignon Comb.** Plain heavy top. Shell, amber or demi-amber color. **50c.**
K—8303. **Barrette.** Oval shape. Carving on each side. Shell, amber or demi-amber color. **50c.**
K—8304. **Barrette.** Jeweled with brilliant rhinestones. Demi-amber color. **$1.00.**
K—8305. **La Casque Comb.** Prettily jeweled with a single row of brilliant rhinestones. Medium size. **$1.00.**
K—8306. **Barrette.** Bow knot design. Shell, amber or demi-amber color. **50c.**
K—8307. **La Casque Comb.** Thickly studded with brilliant rhinestones. **$3.75.**
K—8308. **Sans Gene Comb.** Shell, amber or demi-amber color. **50c.**

K—8309. **Braid Pins.** Plain. Shell, amber or demi-amber color. **25c** each, or **50c** a pair.
K—8310. **Madame Sans Gene Comb.** Demi-amber or amber color. Rhinestone setting. **$1.00.**
K—8311. **Side Combs.** Straight, plain tops. Finely finished and polished. **50c** a pair.
K—8312. **Sans Gene Comb.** Pretty loop design. Demi-amber or shell color. **$1.00**
K—8313. **Madame Sans Gene Comb.** Jeweled with brilliant rhinestones. **$2.50.**
K—8314. **Barrette.** Fits snug to head. Demi-amber or amber color. **50c.**
K—8315. **Madame Sans Gene Comb.** Amber or demi-amber color. Jeweled with rhinestones. **$1.00.**
K—8316. **Braid Pins.** Loop design. Jeweled with rhinestones. Shell or demi-amber color. **$1.00** each, or **$2.00** a pair.

K—8317. **Madame Sans Gene Comb.** Daintily jeweled with rhinestones. Shell, amber or demi-amber color. **$1.50.**
K—8318. **Barrette.** Fancy shape. Demi-amber or amber color. Medium size. **25c.**
K—8319. **Barrette.** Dainty, small, bowknot design. Shell, amber or demi-amber color. Small in size. **25c.**
K—8320. **Barrette.** Oval shape. Small in size and plain. Amber or demi-amber color. **25c.**
K—8321. **La Casque Comb.** Good fitting shape. Shell, amber or demi-amber color. Large size. **$1.25.**
K—8322. **Push Comb.** To be worn on top of head. Waved teeth. Heavy top. **25c.**
K—8323. **La Casque Comb.** Ball top. Demi-amber or amber color. Large size. **$1.25.**

Gimbels Paris, London and American Style Book

Gimbels Advise a Generous Supply of Stylish Gloves

Gloves cleaned by newest and best process. All short lengths, 10c. a pair, and all long lengths, 15c. a pair.
Art gum for cleaning soiled spots on gloves, 10c. a piece.
Glovina for touching up white spots on black gloves, 15c.

K-8400
$1.00

K-8401
$1.00

K-8402
50¢

K-8403
$2.00

K-8404
50¢

K-8405
$1.50

K-8406
65¢

K-8407
$1.00

K-8408
85¢

K-8409
50¢

K-8410
$1.00

K-8411
50¢

K—8400. Man's "Kayser" Made Silk Gloves. Becoming more popular every year with men for spring and summer wear. $1.00 a pair.

K—8401. Woman's "Kayser" Long Silk Gloves. Beautiful quality. 12-button length, 75c and $1.00 a pair. 16-button length, $1.00. $1.25 and $1.50 a pair. 20-button length, $1.50 a pair. The finger tips guaranteed to outwear the glove proper, but the wear must be confined to the patent double tips, otherwise the guarantee becomes void.

K—8402. Man's Chamois Lisle Gloves. A cool comfortable glove that washes nicely. Gray or natural. Self or black back stitching. As only the best materials are used in Gimbel gloves perfect fit and wear are assured. 50c a pair.

K—8403. Woman's 16-Button Length White Glace Lamb Skin Gloves. Generous in arm width. Fully warranted. Practical as well as beautiful. $2.00 a pair.

K—8404. Woman's 16-Button Length White Chamois Lisle Gloves. These gloves are of the Gimbel standard and surprisingly good considering the low price asked. 50c a pair. Better quality, same make, 75c and $1.00 a pair.

K—8405. Woman's Two Clasp Pique or Overseam French Kid Gloves. White with white or black stitching, black with black or white stitching. Our "La Favorite." We feel sure you will appreciate the quality of this dressy glove. $1.50 a pair.

K—8406. Woman's Special 16-Button Length Tricot Silk Gloves. Double-tipped fingers. Three single stichings on back. Black or white. Very serviceable. 65c a pair.

K—8407. Woman's One-Clasp Doeskin Gloves. White. Exceptional quality. Can be washed nicely in lukewarm water and any pure soap, Ivory or castile recommended. $1.00 a pair. Also at $1.25 and $1.50 a pair.

K—8408. Woman's Special 16-Button Milanese Silk Glove. Paris point-stitching on back. Double-tipped fingers. Black or white. A dressy completion of the stylish afternoon or evening costume. 85c a pair.

K—8409. Woman's Two-Clasp "Kayser" Gloves. Chamoisette or leatherette. Both resemble suede leather and wash perfectly. The leatherette must be washed in cold water. Either style, 50c a pair.

K—8410. Woman's "La Mascotte" Gloves. In overseam kid or outseam cape. One of our very popular makes. $1.00 a pair.

K—8411. Woman's Two-Clasp "Kayser" Made Silk Gloves. Black, white, tans or gray. A guarantee in each pair. 50c, 75c and $1.00 a pair.

New York — Gimbel Brothers — Philadelphia

Veils, Veilings, Motor Hoods, Boudoir and Dancing Caps

A Veil adds the completing touch of daintiness to the costume, and if the proper shade is selected, brings out the tints of the complexion most becomingly. A cap or hood is at times necessary. As to a mourning veil, these are absolutely correct and of a soft, draping quality.

K-8500 $3.00 · K-8501 $1.00 · K-8502 25¢ YD · K-8503 $2.25 · K-8504 65¢ · K-8505 25¢ YD · K-8506 50¢ · K-8507 $1.00 · K-8508 $3.00 · K-8509 50¢ YD · K-8510 50¢ YD · K-8511 $1.00 · K-8512 $2.25 · K-8513 $2.00 · K-8514 50¢ · K-8515 $1.50 · K-8516 $1.00 · K-8517 25¢ YD · K-8518 $1.00 · K-8519 $1.00 · K-8520 $2.00 · K-8521 $1.50

K—8500. Stylish Motor Hood. Full crown of satin with straw brim. A veil can be worn with this model, being drawn through the straw bands on hood. Black, brown, green, navy or taupe. $3.00. Veil, extra.

K—8501. Grenadine Mourning Veil. Neatly hemstitched. 1½ yards long, 18 inches wide. $1.00.

K—8502. Octagon Mesh Veiling. Heavy edge. Black or brown. 25c a yard.

K—8503. Black Lace Veil. Very fashionable. Beautiful design. Special at $2.25.

K—8504. Dainty Little Flowered Cap. Trimmed with two rows of shadow lace, ribbon and ribbon bows. 65c.

K—8505. Very Neat Veiling With Square Velvet Dots. Black or brown. 25c a yard.

K—8506. Pretty Boudoir Cap of Net. Lined with chiffon. Pink or blue trimmings. 50c.

K—8507. Dainty Little Boudoir Cap of Net. Trimmed with lace pleating, ribbon and rose buds. Pink, blue or lavender trimmings. $1.00.

K—8508. Dancing Cap. Gold or silver lace. Castle style now so very fashionable. Trimmed with tiny bunch of chiffon rosebuds on left side. $3.00.

K—8509. Filet Mesh Veiling with Fancy Border. Very serviceable. Black or brown. 50c a yard.

K—8510. Small Octagon Mesh Veiling. Fancy edge. Fashionable and practical. Black or brown. 50c a yard.

K—8511. Hexagon Mesh Mourning Veil. Neatly trimmed with one inch band of grosgrain ribbon. $1.00.

K—8512. Beautiful Hemstitched Chiffon Veil. Choice of colors. Black, navy, cerise or red. $2.25.

K—8513. Motor Hood. Trimmed with shirred band of satin and buttons. Black and all fashionable colors. Also tan trimmed with colored band. $2.00.

K—8514. Attractive Boudoir Cap. Made of fine net and lace. Prettily trimmed with flowers. Pink or blue trimmings. 50c.

K—8515. Charming Boudoir Cap of Lace and Net. Pleated lace frill and ribbon finishes edge. Light blue or pink trimmings. $1.50.

K—8516. Very Dainty Shadow Lace Cap. Trimmed with ribbon. An attractive necessity moderately priced. Pink or light blue ribbon. $1.00.

K—8517. Plain Filet Mesh Veiling. Becoming in its simplicity. Black or brown. 25c a yard.

K—8518. Extra Size Chiffon Veil. Neatly hemstitched. Appropriate for evening wear or outdoor sports. All colors. $1.00.

K—8519. Black Lace Veil. Handsome design. Fancy edge. Special at $1.00.

K—8520. Oblong Grenadine Mourning Veil. 48 x 36 inches. Of excellent quality. Specially priced at $2.00.

K—8521. Mourning Veil of Fine Octagon Mesh. Edged with ribbon. Good taste and durability combined. $1.50.

Gimbels Paris, London and American Style Book

Floral Mounts—The Queen of Summer Millinery Trimmings

In every climate dress follows Nature's aspect. When flowers deck the way Miladi's hat bursts into gorgeous bloom. The Gimbel Millinery Salons are fascinating with gorgeous creations in blossoms, and the prices are so little one can gratify any particular whim.

K-8600-50¢

K-8601-50¢

K-8603 50¢

K-8602 25¢

K-8604 35¢

K-8605 65¢

K-8606 50¢

K-8608 25¢

K-8607-25¢

K-8609 50¢

K-8610-75¢

K—8600. Beautiful Wreath of Fascinating and Very Dainty Satin Roses. About 30 inches long. The pretty foliage adds to the attractiveness, the dark color bringing out prettily the tints of the roses. Pink and Jack. A wonderful value. 50c.

K—8601. Enticing Wreath of Small and Chic June Roses. With green foliage. Pink, tea and Jack. An exceptionally dainty and natural-looking wreath, and which will make a very effective trimming. Particularly suitable for the Tipperary turbans. 50c.

K—8602. Pond Lily, with Handsome and Good-Looking Foliage. Pink or white. This attractive trimming will certainly give a smart and neat finish to your summer hat. Also pretty for the corsage. 25c.

K—8603. Cluster of Beautiful and Natural Color Satin Pansies. Pansies have a place all their own in the large flower world, and their saucy and sweet faces have no duplicate. Suitable for all ages. 50c.

K—8604. Spray of One Large and Three Small Shy Roses. Beautiful and natural-looking foliage. Length permits the spray to be placed in various arrangements. Sufficient **trimming for any hat.** Pink, tea or Jack. 35c.

K—8605. Charming Spray of Beautiful Roses. Handsome full-blown roses with an occasional bud in a pretty setting of natural foliage. Pink or Jack. This bunch is exceptionally fine value. 65c.

K—8606. Handsome Spray of American Beauty Roses. Artistic and dainty buds and foliage. This trimming will give to a hat a touch of the chic style of Paris. Pink or Jack. 50c.

K—8607. Pretty Bunch of Three Satin Poppies. With green foliage. An exquisite, petite and exclusive trimming. Suited to both old and young, and is always in good taste. Pink, red, yellow or blue. 25c.

K—8608. Cluster of Natural-Sized Daisies. Either the modest field daisy or the impudent little black-eyed Susan, nodding their independence. Foliage is very graceful. The daisy never loses its popularity as a trimming. 25c.

K—8609. Handsome Floral Wreath of Small and Timid Satin Dahlias. Neat foliage peeping out here and there. 30 inches long. Very graceful and an appropriate trimming for the summer hat. Pink, Jack, blue or dahlia color. 50c.

K—8610. Artistic Wreath of the Always-in-Fashion Satin Roses. Beautiful and dainty satin foliage. Long enough to sufficiently encircle the crown. Pink, tea or Jack. A very good-looking wreath. 75c.

New York — Gimbel Brothers — Philadelphia

86

Beautiful Trimming Fancies and Ostrich Goods at Modest Prices

We will trim hats free of charge if the hat and ribbons or trimmings are purchased from us. Of course, the hat would not then be exchangeable. We tie ribbon bows free of charge as nearly as possible to customer's specifications; but C. O. D. orders not accepted. Lining 15c.

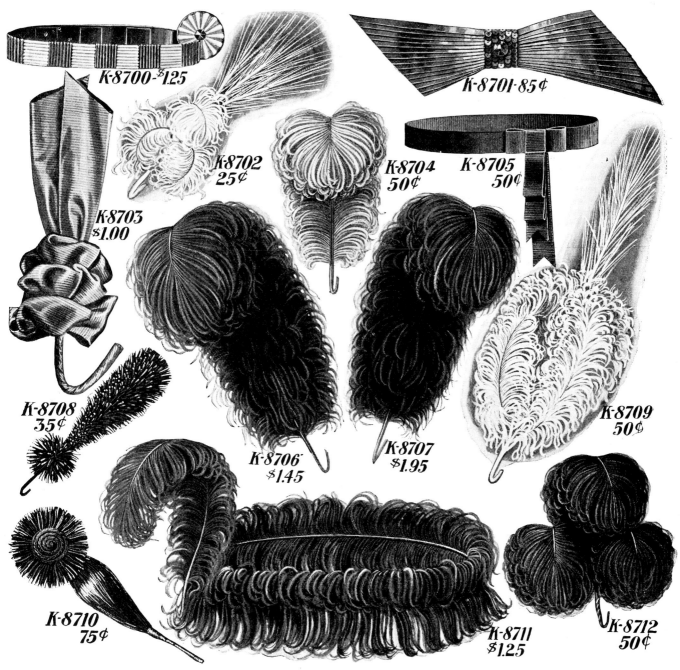

K-8700-$1.25

K-8701-85¢

K-8702 25¢

K-8703 $1.00

K-8704 50¢

K-8705 50¢

K-8708 35¢

K-8706 $1.45

K-8707 $1.95

K-8709 50¢

K-8710 75¢

K-8711 $1.25

K-8712 50¢

K—8700. **Fancy Band and Ornament.** Black and white fluted squares, also all black or brown and tan combination. It completely encircles the crown. Very serviceable. **$1.25.** Band can be sold separately for 85c, and ornament for 50c.

K—8701. **Stylish Jet Effect Bow.** Suitable for any shape hat. Extremely stylish and pretty. Sequin band in center. Black only. **85c.**

K—8702. **Cluster of Three Tips with Large Bunch of Imitation Aigrettes.** 9 inches high. Black or white. A beautiful decoration for any style hat. **25c.**

K—8703. **Handsome Military Ribbon Bow.** Heavy faille ribbon with wired ends. Approximately 12½ inches long. Black and all the newest colors. A most fashionable hat ornament for the spring and summer season. **$1.25.** Same style in moire ribbon. **$1.00.**

K—8704. **Demi Plume.** Very stylish trimming to be placed on brim of hat. 10 inches long.

Black, white and staple colors. Exceptional value for the price. **50c.**

K—8705. **Regimental Hat Band.** Grosgrain ribbon. Piece for around the crown and bow to hang down back. Very fashionable. Black, brown, sand, red or new blue. **50c.** In narrow width, **35c.**

K—8706. **Beautiful Ostrich Plume.** 13½ inches high. Black or white. Best quality flues. A desirable trimming that can be used for several seasons, as it is always fashionable. **$1.45.**

K—8707. **Handsome Ostrich Plume.** French curl. Broad full head. 14½ inches. Black or white. The flues are lustrous and very rich looking. Excellent value at the price. **$1.95.**

K—8708. **Military Pompon.** "Military" says

fashion this season. Very modish and attractive. Black and in all the newest colors. **35c.**

K—8709. **Very Large Curled Ostrich Pompon.** Imitation aigrette finish. A neat and good-looking trimming. 15 inches high. Black or white. **50c.**

K—8710. **Fancy Stick-up.** Made of visca straw. All black, black and white, brown and tan or black and red combination. Beautiful and very delightful ornament. **75c.** Any other color, one week for delivery is required.

K—8711. **Beautiful Soft Feather Band with Plume Trimming.** A complete trimming, as the band encircles the hat and the plume gives the finishing touch. In any staple color. Hard to duplicate elsewhere for the price we ask. **$1.25.**

K—8712. **Cluster of Three Ostrich Tips.** 7 inches long. Black, white, blue or pink. Very smart and stylish, and a real value. **50c.**

The Charm and Style of Accomplished Designing

Have you ever noticed what a difference is made in your appearance by a stylish hat? It doesn't seem possible that so simple a finish to your costume could possibly be the deciding feature as to whether or not you are well dressed. Try it yourself by wearing last year's hat—and going among your friends. Of course you do not need THEM to tell you that you might as well wear last year's suit—in fact, you had better wear last year's suit than last year's hat, so wonderful and radical have been the changes in this department of woman's attire.

K-9000
$3.50

K-9001
$4.50

K-9002
$2.95

K-9004
$3.50

K-9003
$2.50

K—9000. Woman's Basket Straw Sailor. A beautiful, medium-sized hat made of the new lustrous silk, basket straw in the becoming sailor model you see here. Effectively tipped at one side and faced with rich Faille silk, this striking model is very becoming and youthful. Around the upper edge of the medium high crown are placed rich red roses with green foliage. A nobby hat in the best of style and also exceedingly light in weight. Sand, new blue, rose or white. $3.50.

K—9001. Woman's Dressy Feather Hat. A stunning model of medium size with striking height carried out with a trimming of three natural ostrich feather tips and a full, fluffy ostrich feather band around the crown. Made of lustrous silk straw braid smartly turned up in back and gracefully rolled in front. A beautiful rose in natural colorings and deep green foliage is placed at one side. A dressy

hat in all black, black with white, or all navy blue. $4.50.

K—9002. Woman's Medium Size Hat. This smart tailored hat is a modified military toque, hand-made of lustrous fancy silk hemp braid on substantial canvas and wire shape. The braid is put on in the new front to back style and also shows as a wide edge over the facing of rich silk Faille. A snappy little, tailored bow is on the right side and directly in front a military cockade of fancy straw. This hat is thoroughly substantial and is unusually well tailored to harmonize with tailored suits. Colors: grey, straw with navy facing, white with black, sand with black, all navy, all black or all brown. $2.95.

K—9003. Woman's or Miss's Flat Brim Sailor. A captivating hat is this simple, new sailor style with round crown and medium size, flat brim. It is one of the most generally becoming styles that the season has developed and

is made of silk Tagal straw, the crown being soft and the brim firm, to maintain its shape. A wide velvet ribbon with huge flat, double bow and a fascinating wreath of rosebuds with foliage is used to trim. Colors: new blue, sand, white, rose, black, brown or navy, and with black or colored wreaths. $2.50.

K—9004. Woman's Silk Straw Poke. This attractive hat is fashioned after the popular poke bonnet styles that are very youthful and becoming. Made of the new, fancy silk straw braid placed in the popular front to back style and faced with satin. Around the crown is placed a smart, tailored ribbon with small bow in back and with a handsome, trailing vine of flowers and berries. The hat that will attract attention for its effective harmony. Colors: sand with new blue, all white, all new blue, or all rose. May also be had in all black or all brown, the flowers in each instance harmonizing with the color of the hat. $3.50.

New York — Gimbel Brothers — Philadelphia

Conservatively Styled Millinery of Pleasing Lines

Smartly tailored hats are not as easily created as might be expected from their apparent simplicity. It is in their style value that they shine paramount—in the cleverness of their set and in the modish finish they give to your entire attire. Gimbel Hats have Style and Character, and the Quality is such that they can only be compared to all other Gimbel Merchandise that exceeds in Quality-Value that of any other similiar offering. These correctly tailored hats have Style Lines of authentic designing and are very, very low in price.

K-9100 $2.75

K-9101 $2.95

K-9102 $1.90

K-9103 $3.25

K-9104 $1.25

K—9100. Woman's Smart Hat of Medium Size. An unusually fine and cleverly designed model, made by hand of silk straw braid with nicely **rolling brim** prettily turned up at one side and falling in a smart sweep about the face. The **novel bell-shaped crown** is of folded Maline and across the top are two snappy dragon **wings of wired Maline**, forming a stunning **trimming.** Completing this stylish hat are three bunches of flowers in dainty contrast. In all black with colored flowers, all white, all navy, sand or straw color with black Maline. **$2.75.**

K—9101. Woman's Modified Continental Hat. A charming new model of glossy Tagal Braid, made with the new wide, square-topped crown and a very fetching high and dropped setting of the brim. Around the crown are placed two wide ribbon bands finished at one side with a snappy, wired butterfly bow and at the other side a cluster of velvet flowers in lovely colorings. May be had in sand color, the new blue, purple, green or black. **$2.95.**

K—9102. Woman's Close-fitting Mourning Hat. Made in the new, long Toque effect of rich black silk with abruptly upturned brim slightly higher at one side. Around the crown is a soft, folded drape of silk finished with two standing loops properly wired and substantial. This smart hat has the firm, close set that is conservative and correct. A well-made and stylish model. All black. **$1.90.**

K—9103. Woman's Small Hat. A most engaging small hat with handsome high crown of fancy straw braid and side and brim of satin. A facing of white satin gives a dressy finish to the rolling brim that is abruptly raised at one side and droops effectively on the other. Heading the crown in snappy style is a tailored band of Grossgrain ribbon and a fan and buckle ornament. A splendid style in an exceedingly well-tailored hat. Colors: all purple, all grey, all navy blue or all black with white facing. **$3.25.**

K—9104. Woman's Smart Toque. A dressy hat especially well suited for traveling. Has crown and brim of fancy fluted straw braid and is formed in the new long shape that is generally becoming. Around the crown is a soft, folded drape of taffeta silk with folded silk loop firmly wired and substantial. A dressy little tailored hat with excellent lines. In all black. **$1.25.**

Gimbels Paris, London and American Style Book

The Small Hat Is Favored and Flowers Are Much Worn

It is hardly necessary to call attention to the freshness and beauty of the hats illustrated upon this and the opposite page, as it is so apparent. They are the best styles and the best values—matchlessly clever conceptions charmingly produced at most reasonable prices.

Descriptions of Hats and Flowers Illustrated on Opposite Page.

K—9300. Beautiful Wreath of June Roses. The roses are beautifully massed with green foliage in an artistic effect. About 28 inches in length. Pink, tea or Jack. Wreaths will be much worn this season, and this is of excellent value. 85c.

K—9301. Beautiful Hand-made Hat for Girls. Hat is of lustrous silk straw, daintily trimmed with messaline ribbon around crown and finished with large bow with two long loops in back. Clusters of pretty flowers around crown. Over the narrow edge of the brim, which has a shirred messaline silk facing, is an edge of frilled lace. Suitable for child of 6 to 10 years. May be had in all white or

white braid over pink or blue ribbon. $2.95.

K—9302. Smart and Very Stylish Panama Hat. Brim rolls softly high on left side and turns down on right. Around the crown is a faille silk ribbon band with pearl buckle on the front. Very jaunty hat suitable for women and misses. White with band in red, blue or black. An unapproachable value at the Gimbel price. $3.75.

K—9303. Woman's or Miss's Fancy Straw Braid Hat. Beautifully trimmed around crown with ribbon band and garland of flowers. Becoming streamers of ribbon are also a feature. Rich facing of contrasting ribbon is very stylish. The Gimbel millinery experts carefully

compared very many models and feel sure their final choice will more than please you. Colors, sand, rose, navy or white. $2.95.

K—9304. Military Fancy. Made of soft visca straw. These fancies will be much worn on the new regimental turbans and hats. Black, brown, sand or new blue. About 6¼ inches long. 65c.

K—9305. Wreath of Daisies. There is never a season when daisies are not in favor. This wreath is of exceptionally good quality. About 29 inches long. White with yellow centers, yellow with brown centers. 50c.

K-9200 $2.90

K-9202 $3.25

K-9201 $2.25

K-9203 $3.95

K-9204 $2.95

K—9200. Miss's and Woman's Silk Tagal Braid Hat. Trimmed with narrow silk ribbon around crown. Regimental pleated ornament extends out from right side, finished with narrow ribbon bows and two small pompons. Hat is becomingly turned on left side. Colors, old rose with black pompons, new blue with black pompons, black with white pompons, or all white. This stylish hat is a very fine value. $2.90.

K—9201. The Always Popular Panama Hat for Misses and Women. Slightly rolled brim, becoming to so many women. Crown has fancy Roman striped silk band. These hats are good for outing or daily wear in the warm

summer, as they are both cool-looking and serviceable. The bright band suggests the tropics. The price is very little as you will note on examination of the hat. $2.25.

K—9202. Miss's and Woman's Medium-Sized Hat. This is a shape that will be much favored the coming season, and it is very becoming. Slightly mushroom brim and band around crown of silky tagal straw. Top of crown is of satin. A beautiful wreath of foliage around crown, finished with cluster of cherries and velvet forget-me-nots. Colors, all sand, white, rose, black, brown, new blue, or navy with mount in natural colors. $3.25.

K—9203. Miss's or Woman's Dressy Hat. Made of soft, pliable, silk straw in basket weave. Slightly drooped brim suggesting a poke. Trimmed with narrow silk ribbon around crown with smart little bow-knot tied in back. Beautiful wreath is the stylish finish. Silk facing to match shape. Sand with new blue ribbon; black with new blue; all green. A wonderfully dressy little hat. $3.95.

K—9204. Young Woman's Close-Fitting Hat. Made of silk basket straw. Small rolled brim all around. Stylishly trimmed with two-toned ribbon. Small tailored bow with streamers in back. Cluster of silk berries in front. Sand with blue; rose with brown; white with navy; white with black. Excellent quality. $2.95.

K-9300
85¢

K-9301
$2.95

K-9302
$3.75

K-9304
65¢

K-9303
$2.95

K-9305
50¢

For descriptions see top of opposite page

New York — Gimbel Brothers — Philadelphia

K-9402
$1.00

K-9403
$2.95

K-9401
$1.50

K-9406
$3.95

K-9400
$1.95

K-9404
$4.95

K-9405
$1.50

K-9407
$1.50

K-9408
$2.95

K-9410
$2.95

K-9411
$1.50

K-9409
$1.50

For descriptions see opposite page

New York — Gimbel Brothers — Philadelphia

Beautiful New Styles at Gimbels Low Prices

Tailored Skirts and Suits will be more favored than ever the coming season, and they really require a dainty touch of color beneath, preferably in the petticoat, while the silken hose is the only sort now worn for social occasions.

K—9400. Woman's Petticoat. Smart flounce cut with the new circular flare, especially good looking combination of tucks and pleatings. In taffeta, in all messaline or in silk jersey top with messaline flounce. Black, King, navy, Russian, sand or putty. **$1.95.**

K—9401. Woman's Splendid Quality Silk Hose. Black, white and all the new shoe shades now being worn. Excellent shades to match your pretty gown or petticoat. A great value for the price we offer. **$1.50 pair.**

K—9402. Woman's Fine Grade Silk Hose. Black, white and all the street and evening shades for the spring and summer season. Can match the shoes, gown or petticoat. The season of 1915 promises to be the biggest color season ever known. The best value to be had for **$1.00 pair.**

K—9403. Woman's Petticoat. Rich crepe de chine with exquisite flounce of shadow lace overlaid with silk ribbon to match. A new and dainty dancing petticoat or for wear with summer frocks. Pink, blue or white. **$2.95.**

K—9404. Woman's Petticoat. New circular flounce trimmed with pretty pleatings. Well-proportioned gores and superior workmanship. In chiffon taffeta or with silk jersey top with taffeta flounce. Black, King, navy, Russian, sand, putty, or changeable blue and green. **$4.95.**

K—9405. Woman's Silk Hosiery. Good wearing silk in black, white and all the newest shoe shades. Exceptional shades that will match the gown or petticoat. We know you will be pleased with a pair or more of this wonderful quality. **$1.50 pair.**

K—9406. Woman's Petticoat. The new circular flaring flounce effectively trimmed with circular cut folds of self-material. May be had in chiffon taffeta or messaline silk. Black, sand, putty, rose, Belgian blue, navy or Russian. **$3.95.**

K—9407. Silk Stockings. Fine grade of thread-silk is here used. Can be had in all the new shoe shades or to match a gown or petticoat, also in black or white. Exceptional hose for the surprisingly low price quoted. **$1.50 pair.**

K—9408. Woman's Extra Size Petticoat. Fine quality messaline. Rich combination tucked and pleated flounce with dust underlay. May be had in changeable colors or all black. **$2.95.**

K—9409. Woman's Hose. The best $1.50 silk hose to be had. Black, white and all the new shoe shades, also good shades to match the gown or petticoat. **$1.50.**

K—9410. Woman's Petticoat. Particularly well made of all silk taffeta or with silk Jersey top with circular flounce of messaline silk. Has six-inch flounce of messaline. In putty, rose, King, Russian, navy or sand. **$2.95.**

K—9411. Woman's Splendid Quality Silk Hose. Black, white and all the new shoe shades now being worn. Excellent shades to match your pretty gown or petticoat. A great value for the price we offer. **$1.50 pair.**

Special Note.—We can match silk hose to any sample of material that will be sent us for **$2.00 pair.** These will be ordered special and will require four to six days to deliver.

Our 50c silk hose for women are of exceptional quality and wonderful values. These come in black and all the leading colors.

K-9500 $1.00 **K-9501 75¢** **K-9502 $1.50** **K-9503 $1.00** **K-9504 $1.00** **K-9505 50¢**

K—9500. Taffetine Petticoat. New circular flounce effectively trimmed with three two-inch pleatings of self-material, an underlay insuring satisfactory wear. Closes with patent snap fasteners. Black only. **$1.00.**

K—9501. Regular and Extra Size Petticoat. Reliable chambray. Made with deep sectional ruffle and banding of self-material. An underlay insures additional service. Blue, gray or pink stripe. **75c.**

K—9502. Patented Petticoat—The practical "Eppo." This make is the one which seems to serve best the purposes of most women. Petticoat is in a superior quality sateen. The invisible side placket opening and elastic waistband insure perfect fit. Deep sectional ruffle pleated and tucked. Finshed with underlay. Black only. **$1.50.**

K—9503. Shadow Proof Petticoat. Double panel both back and front is a smart innovation. Fine quality, highly finished French sateen with embroidered scalloped edge. White. **$1.00.**

K—9504. Soft Medium Weight Petticoat. All the new spring colors—it is a most satisfactory purchase. Superior quality sateen. New moire ribbon effect adds charm to the deep French pleated flounce. Navy, Russian green, emerald, purple and black. Regular and extra sizes. **$1.00.**

K—9505. Wash Petticoat. A particularly smart well-fashioned model of crinkled, seersucker that requires no ironing. Has embroidered panel and embroidered scalloped bottom. Lavender, blue or gray stripe, also plain white. Special value, **50c.**

Gimbels Paris, London and American Style Book

The Refinement of Night Attire in These Goods

You will readily see by looking at Gimbel undermuslins that they are the result of careful designing, artistic taste in the combination of beautiful laces, and if you have ever purchased any of them before you will know that workmanship is the paramount feature. Furthermore, you will see that Gimbel prices are surprisingly low, and were the home needle woman to make any of these garments herself she would find it barely possible to make up any one of these undermuslins for the price at which she can purchase the materials. Here we offer undermuslins at practically the price of the materials alone.

K-9600 $1.00

K-9604 $1.50

K-9601 50¢

K-9602 $2.00

K-9603 $2.00

K-9605 $1.00

Sizes of Gowns, 34 to 42 inches bust measure.

K—9600. **Woman's Nightgown.** Sheer lingerie nainsook, trimmed with alternating rows of Val and filet lace. Has deep pointed yoke with rich butterfly of net, and princess panel of tucks. Back is also cut in a deep pointed V. A dainty, lacy and beautiful gown of exceptional worth. **$1.00.**

K—9601. **Woman's Nightgown.** In popular Mother Hubbard style with yoke handsomely trimmed with rows of pin-tucks and Swiss embroidery and edged with sheer lawn frill with hemstitched edge. Also has a substantial back yoke. Nicely taped and finished with taped and frilled three-quarter length sleeves. **50c.**

K—9602. **Elaborate Nightgown.** Beautiful front and back Empire bodice composed of sheer Swiss embroidery and rows of wide Val lace inserted to form an elaborate double eight design on front and back. Also run with satin ribbon and finished with fancy knotted bow. Sleeves match the beautiful yoke. **$2.00.**

K—9603. **Woman's Nightgown.** An elaborate trousseau model with rich insertions of Val lace and Swiss embroidery and exquisite butterfly medallions of shadow lace. A princess panel of pin tucks and dainty double bow with satin ribbon adorns the front. Ribbon run beading. Butterfly sleeves are in kimono style. **$2.00.**

K—9604. **Lingerie Nainsook Gown.** In the popular slip-on style with elaborate yoke of Val and shadow lace and with Swiss embroidered medallions forming star shaped yoke. Princess panel of pin tucks on either side and exquisite ribbon run beading at the neck. Set in sleeves are trimmed to match. **$1.50.**

K—9605. **Woman's Nightgown.** An unusually beautiful yoke of Swiss embroidery alternating with rows of Val lace and dainty round neck trimmed with ribbon run beading and edging. The elaborate sleeves are designed to match. Tucks form fullness from beneath the yoke. **$1.00.**

New York — Gimbel Brothers — Philadelphia

Daintiness is the Keynote in These Nightgowns

Daintiest of lingerie nightgowns can be purchased from the great Gimbel Department of muslin underwear at prices that are usually asked for extremely ordinary merchandise. Such quantities of these lovely undermuslins are needed to supply the regular trade of discriminating Gimbel buyers in the Departments of the three great stores in New York, Philadelphia and Milwaukee that we are exceptionally successful in giving values to our mail order patrons that it would be impossible for them to duplicate anywhere else. We cannot say too much in praise of the beauty and wearworthiness of each and every undergarment, even to those smallest in price.

K·9700
50¢

K·9701
$1.50

K·9702
$1.00

K·9703
$2.00

K·9704
85¢

K·9705
$1.00

Sizes, 34 to 42 inches bust measure.

K—9700. Slip=on Nightgown. Excellent quality muslin with neat English eyelet embroidery run with ribbon finishing the medium round neck and sleeves. Prettily gathered on front. As an example of great values at low prices you will have in this wonderful 50c gown, a most agreeable surprise. **50c.**

K—9701. Empire Nightgown. Nainsook with elaborate yoke of Swiss embroidery alternating with Val lace and short sleeves finished with beautiful lace edged frill. Wide band of ribbon run beading across front is finished with bow. **$1.50.**

K—9702. Exquisite Nightgown. Cut in the form of a negligee. Has groups of tucks on either side from shoulder to bust line and also in back. A novel arrangement of revers are trimmed with lace and bow of silk ribbon. Exquisite sleeves are in a novel shape with deep lace trimmed points. **$1.00.**

K—9703. Elaborate Trousseau Nightgown. Deep Empire yoke both front and back, of exquisite shadow lace and wide ribbon run Empire band. Sleeves are also trimmed with large fancy bow. Prettily gathered on front and back. **$2.00.**

K—9704. Slip=on Nightgown. Empire yoke of rich exceptionally beautiful Swiss embroidery. Set in sleeves are edged with Hamburg and has pretty little bow on front. Quite an exceptional gown and one that will please you immensely when you see the beautiful quality of the materials. **85c.**

K—9705. Nainsook Nightgown. Square neck, set in sleeves, finished with tucked and hemstitched lawn band. Entire front has alternating groups of pin tucks run with satin ribbon and finishing with bow. Two additional bows also embellish the front. **$1.00.**

The New Style Lines and Widths in These Petticoats

K-9800 $1.50

K-9804 $1.00

K-9806 $1.50

K-9801 $1.00

K-9807 $2.00

K-9802 $2.00

K-9803 $3.00

K-9805 $1.00

K-9808 $2.00

K—9800. Woman's Petticoat. Of high grade cambric, fitted gores and draw string. Has flounce of Swiss embroidered lawn joined to insertion, hemstitched at either edge, and with wide eyelet beading run with satin ribbon and finished with large bow, also has hemstitched dust ruffle of lawn. $1.50.

K—9801. Woman's Petticoat. Of substantial quality soft finished cambric. Has deep flounce of rows of shadow lace alternating with bands of dotted Swiss and finished with shadow lace edge to match. Beautiful Craquelle lace pattern is used in this delicate edge. $1.00.

K—9802. Woman's Petticoat. Of superior quality cambric with fitted gores and French waist band. Has deep flounce cut in circular fashion of crisp Persian lawn trimmed with rich insertions of embroidered Swiss set in with wide Val lace that also forms a prettily ruffled flat flounce. Smart satin bow with streamers adorns one side. $2.00.

K—9803. Woman's Petticoat. Of superior quality highly finished cambric. Has fitted gores and French waist band. Deep flounce that you see pictured is cut in circular fashion of crisp Persian lawn with novel inserts of Swiss embroidery medallions set in with exquisite Val lace, forming upward points and with deep scalloping. The deep underlay is edged with Val lace and handsome bow of satin ribbon is placed at one side. $3.00.

K—9804. Woman's Petticoat. Of substantial muslin. Has fitted gores and straight line effect and an especially neat flounce of embroidered Swiss in a novel combination of English eyelet with solid embroidery joined to a flat band of hemstitched insertion. An underlay of muslin is also provided. $1.00.

K—9805. Woman's Petticoat. Of cambric with fitted gores and French waist band. Has a novel flat flounce composed of Swiss in a new dotted and banded design joined to wide Val lace insertion with hemstitching and finished with a beautiful frill of Val lace. Smart satin bow is placed at one side and a substantial underlay is also furnished. $1.00.

K—9806. Woman's Petticoat. Of superior quality cambric with elaborate flounce composed of Swiss embroidered oblongs set in between horizontal rows of Val insertion and with an exquisite flat flounce of three rows of Val insertion and lace. The entire flounce is joined to the body of the skirt with an additional row of Val insertion and trimmed with smart satin bow. Also has a dust underlay. $1.50.

K—9807. Woman's Petticoat. Of superior quality lingerie cambric with graduated gores and French waist band. Has elaborate flounce of Swiss embroidery in a novel scalloped design with vertical hemstitching, and joined to a wide band of hemstitched beading run with wide satin ribbon and finished with elaborate double bow and streamers. Finished with a cambric underlay. $2.00.

K—9808. Woman's Petticoat. Of superior quality lingerie cambric with exceptionally dressy flounce formed of two ruffles of wide Val shadow lace mounted on a net ruffle. Each ruffle is headed with Val insertion, underlaid with satin ribbon and finished with fancy bow. This petticoat is essentially one for dressy wear and is a most exquisite dancing model. $2.00.

New York — Gimbel Brothers — Philadelphia

Corset Covers and Drawers of Dainty Style and Perfect Fit

Direct to us from clean, well-conducted factories, where all the conditions are wholesome, come these Corset Covers and Drawers, as fresh, dainty and pretty as represented in the pictures. Corset Covers, sizes 34 to 44—Drawers Lengths, 23 to 27.

K—9900. **Neat Nainsook Corset Cover.** Beautifully trimmed with Val. insertions and rich medallions. Ribbon run beading gathers the low fitted neck. In substantial soft finished cambric. **38c.**

K—9901. **Empire Corset Cover With Sleeves.** Made of soft lingerie nainsook with deep front and back yoke of alternating rows of organdie embroidery and laces, gathered at the low fitted neck with ribbon-run Val. beading. The short sleeves are trimmed to match. The correct corset cover for transparent waists. **$1.00.**

K—9902. **Corset Cover.** With short sleeves. Made of excellent quality nainsook with rich Val. and Swiss embroidery trimming and attractive frill of lace covering the fly. Elastic waistband. **50c.**

K—9903. **Rich Corset Cover.** Deep front and back yoke of alternating rows of Val. lace and Swiss embroidery. Dainty short sleeves are slightly puffed and gathered into fancy frilled band of lace to match. Neck finished with ribbon-run beading. **75c.**

K—9904. **Substantial Corset Cover.** Self finished cambric. Made with medium low neck. Neck and entire shoulder straps of English eyelet embroidery. Ribbon run through Swiss embroidery. **25c.**

K—9905. **Beautiful Corset Cover.** Lingerie nainsook. Richly trimmed front and back yoke of alternating rows of Val. lace and Swiss embroidery. Finished with ribbon-run beading. A well-fitting and dressy cover. **50c.**

K—9906. **Substantial Muslin Drawers.** Well-fitting straight line model with deep flounce trimmed with neat hemstitched tucks, headed with band of tucks. Gored waistline. **25c.**

K—9907. **Sheer Nainsook Drawers.** Elaborately trimmed with flat Swiss embroidery and Val. lace; fitted with French waistband. **75c.**

K—9908. **Excellent Quality Nainsook Drawers.** Slender circular cut lines and French waistband. Trimmed with beautiful quality Swiss embroidery flouncing and joined with hemstitched veining. **50c.**

K—9909. **Substantial Drawers.** Soft finished cambric. Fitted waistline and flat flounce of sheer lawn embroidery, headed with band of tucks. **50c.**

K—9910. **Simple Circular Drawers.** Lingerie cambric. Made with flat flounce of dainty Swiss embroidery. Fitted waistband. **50c.**

K—9911. **Substantial Drawers.** Soft finished muslin. Neat tucks and flounce of English eyelet embroidery. Gore fitted top. **38c.**

The Most Desirable Types of Chemises

Gimbels have a firm foothold in the most important style centers of the world. They have personal and constant representation in Paris, London, Berlin and Lyons. They also have constant representation in Constantinople and Kobe, and all of these connections are maintained that the great Gimbel stores in New York, Philadelphia and Milwaukee may be in constant touch with the best that the world produces. This is why the Gimbel success has been so thorough and so progressive. This will also explain the reason why Gimbel fashions are authentic, and that importation is possible even under the most trying of present conditions.

K-10000
75¢

K-10001
$1.00

K-10002
$1.50

K-10003
$1.00

K-10004
$2.00

K-10005
50¢

Sizes, 36 to 44 inches bust measure.

K—10000. Knee Length Chemise. Lingerie cambric with low round neck edged with handsome English eyelet embroidery finished with beading run with silk ribbon. Firmly taped and also edged at the arm scye with neat Hamburg edging and double stitching. **75c.**

K—10001. Woman's Envelope Chemise. High grade sheer cambric with smart pointed yoke of Swiss embroidery, Val lace and ribbon run beading. Val also edging the arm scye and the bottom of the envelope that buttons over in the practical manner shown in the illustration. A great innovation in women's garments. **$1.00.**

K—10002. Novelty Chemise. Sheer nainsook with elaborate yoke of embroidered organdie medallions set in with Val lace and headed with a deep finish of Val and ribbon run beading. Medallions and Val lace also finish the bottom of the chemise as shown in the handsome illustration. **$1.50.**

K—10003. Empire Chemise. Sheer nainsook with low round neck, finished with Swiss embroidery beading joined with hemstitching and with Hamburg edging the armholes. Empire band of Swiss beading is run with ribbon and emphasizes the high waisted effect. **$1.00.**

K—10004. Novelty Chemise. A most elaborate design. Trimming composed of unique embroidered organdie medallions set in with Val lace and finished with exquisite side yoke of rows of Val. The round low neck is run with ribbon run beading and lace. The bottom of this practical garment is lace-trimmed to match. **$2.00.**

K—10005. Knee Length Chemise. Made of a superior quality of soft finished muslin. It is trimmed with fancy Swiss beading joined with hemstiching and run with ribbon. The arm holes are edged with Swiss embroidery to harmonize. A splendid value in a full fashioned and serviceable chemise. **50c.**

New York — Gimbel Brothers — Philadelphia

Quality Lingerie for Milady of Fashion

PROPERLY FITTING UNDERGARMENTS ARE WITHOUT DOUBT THE FOUNDATION FOR NOT ONLY COR-RECT LINES IN YOUR OUTER ATTIRE, BUT FOR YOUR PERSONAL COMFORT. Unquestionably the "set" of your garments is what will make you feel at ease and thoroughly comfortable. In the designing and cutting of Gimbel combinations, every part has been cut to proportions that are correct, and through which they fit perfectly. There is no need to pull or twist and the outer lines are in harmony with correct and fashionable outline in your outer garments. Buy your undermuslins from Gimbels and feel the difference it will make in your satisfaction.

K-10100
$1.50

K-10101
$1.00

K-10104
$1.50

K-10105
$1.00

K-10102
$2.00

K-10103
$2.00

Sizes of Combinations, 36 to 44 inches bust measure.

K—10100. Sheer Nainsook Combination. Six beautiful medallions of embroidered organdie, set in with Val lace. Wide heading of Val ribbon-run beading and edging entirely around the neck. Swiss ribbon-run beading at the waistline. Drawers are trimmed to match front. Frilled lace over fly. May be had in corset cover and drawers. $1.50.

K—10101. Nainsook Combination. Deep front and back yoke of alternating rows of embroidered organdie and Val lace. Ribbon-run beading gathering the low, round neck and ribbon-run Swiss embroidery at the waistline. Frilled lace over fly. Straight line drawers are edged with Val. May be had in corset cover and drawers. $1.00.

K—10102. Princess Combination. Elaborate yoke with lace shoulder straps and bands of sheer organdie embroidery set in with Val lace, ribbon-run beading and edge finishing the low, round neck. Also trimmed with two smart bows of satin ribbon. Drawers are finished with same beautiful organdie inserts and lace that embellish the back and are also trimmed with bows of satin ribbon. In sheer nainsook. $2.00.

K—10103. Corset Cover and Drawer Combination. Sheer lingerie nainsook with deep yoke of embroidered organdie and rows of Val lace insertion and edge. Ribbon-run Swiss beading at the waistline and straight line drawers embellished with elaborate trimming to match front. Corset cover and drawers. $2.00.

K—10104. Princess Combination. Elaborate yoke of inserts of shadow lace alternating with insertions of sheer Swiss embroidery and Val. The low, round neck is finished with Val embroidered, ribbon-run beading and lace and smart bow trims the frilled fly. The beautiful drawers are trimmed to harmonize. $1.50.

K—10105. Princess Combination. Elaborate empire yoke of Swiss embroidery and Val lace. Dainty round, low neck is edged with lace, ribbon-run beading and edged to match. Val frill trims the fly. Has two smart double bows of silk ribbon. Drawers are trimmed to match front. $1.00.

Gimbels Paris, London and American Style Book

Novelty Crepe Lingerie for Fastidious Taste

Crepe undergarments and nightgowns are growing in favor and they are well worthy the attention of those who launder at home, where timesaving and worksaving is a very important matter. These soft finished Plissé crepe garments are easy to wash and need not be starched or ironed. It is necessary only to gently pull them into shape while drying. Heretofore crepe undergarments have been exceedingly plain, but you will see in these lovely items that they have been trimmed with lace and inserted with medallions after the manner of the handsome lingerie underwear displayed in the Gimbel Stores.

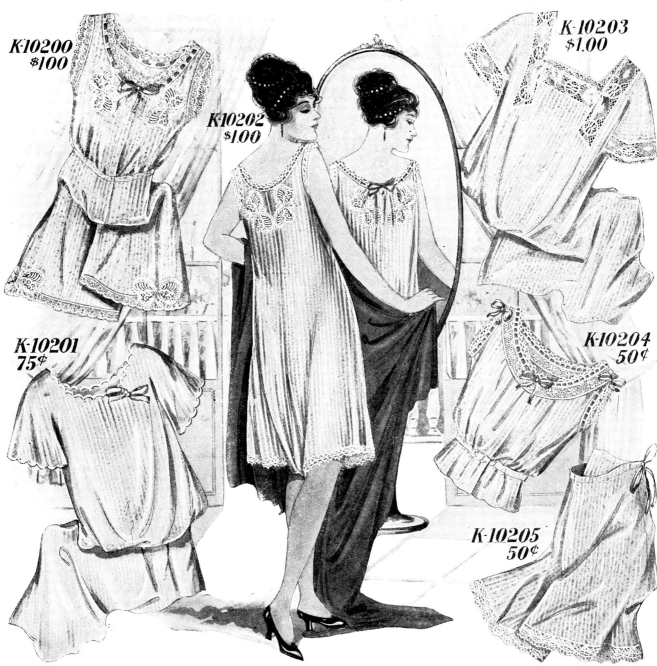

K-10200 $1.00

K-10201 75¢

K-10202 $1.00

K-10203 $1.00

K-10204 50¢

K-10205 50¢

K—10200. **Plisse Crepe Combination.** Richly embellished with shadow lace butterflies and edged with ribbon run beading and edge. An ideal garment. In this combination you will see practically the first attempt to trim and embellish crepe undergarments after the manner of other beautiful lingerie underwear. This does not in any way lessen their practicability for laundering purposes. **$1.00.**

K—10201. **Slip-on Nightgown.** Sheer plissé crepe with firm scalloped edge in blue or pink. Also trimmed with smart satin bow. The convenience in traveling of the crepe nightgown is added to the time saving value. It does not need ironing and can be rolled up into a very small parcel for the traveling bag. The beauty of this gown

is greatly enhanced by the dainty touch of scalloping in color. **75c.**

K—10202. **Envelope Chemise.** Plissé crepe embellished on both back and front with shadow lace butterflies and edged with ribbon run cluny lace. Bottom of the garment crosses under, thus serving the purpose of corset cover and drawers. An innovation in undergarments. **$1.00.**

K—10203. **Plisse Crepe Gown.** Ecru colored cluny lace. Has beautiful square neck outlined with cluny and run with satin ribbon finished with two elaborate bows. Short kimono sleeves are trimmed to match. A beautiful combination of deep ecru color cluny lace with plissé crepe is a novelty that you will admire greatly, and further-

more the substantial cluny lace used is exceptionally strong and has the large popular spider web and wheel pattern. **$1.00.**

K—10204. **Plisse Crepe Corset Cover.** Elaborated with rich band of Val lace and ribbon run cluny. Ribbon run cluny also finishes the armholes. Has complete draw string at the waistline. Even corset covers are now made in this practical plissé crepe and have found great favor, inasmuch as they are soft and follow closely the lines of the figure, and are entirely without any clumsy features. **50c.**

K—10205. **Plisse Crepe French Drawers.** With fitted waistline and circular cut legs. Trimmed with torchon thread lace. **50c.**

New York — Gimbel Brothers — Philadelphia

Beautiful, Rich Crepe de Chine Undergarments

Have you ever enjoyed the luxury of Crepe de Chine Undergarments—their soft silky fineness is most entrancing and becomes a fine habit that you will appreciate when once you try them. At the small prices of the dainty Crepe de Chine undergarments shown on this page there is hardly any difference in price as compared with high-class underwear of cotton fabrics. These garments will launder beautifully and will be of highest satisfaction.

K-10300 $1.00

K-10301 $1.50

K-10302 $2.00

K-10305 $2.95

K-10303 $3.95

K-10304 $3.95

K—10300. Underbodice of Crepe de Chine with White Shadow Lace. Beautifully made in Empire effect with round, low neck edged with Val lace and ribbon-run beading and with Val edging finishing the fly and also the dainty short sleeves that are a special feature of this exquisite bodice. Serves a double purpose of corset cover and bodice for wear under transparent waists. Pink or white crepe de chine. Sizes, 34 to 44. **$1.00.**

K—10301. Crepe de Chine Corset Cover. Made with deep yoke effect entirely around, of a rich and especially beautiful pattern of soft lace run with ribbon. A particularly fine quality of silk crepe de chine in pink or white is used. Waist line is finished with French waistband. Sizes, 34 to 44. **$1.50.**

K—10302. Crepe de Chine Envelope Chemise. A novel innovation in undergarments, as this smart style is thoroughly practical and takes the place of the usual combination, the envelope back passes over and buttons in front in the convenient manner shown in the illustration. Trimmed at neck, armholes and lower edge with superior quality white Val lace. Pink or white. Sizes, 34 to 44. **$2.00.**

K—10303. Crepe de Chine Nightgown. A rich and beautiful model with beautiful cream lace forming deep yoke and finishing the short sleeves. Also trimmed with silk ribbon bows. A beautiful gown that is very rich, and will launder perfectly. Pink or white crepe de chine. Sizes, 34 to 44. **$3.95.**

K—10304. Crepe de Chine Combination. A perfectly tailored garment that is very beautiful and is trimmed with dainty effective, lace to match the beautiful gown K—10303. An excellent quality of pure silk crepe de chine is used and the fit and finish is such as will delight you. Pink or white crepe de chine. Sizes, 34 to 44. **$3.95.**

K—10305. Beautiful Envelope Chemise of Crepe de Chine. Richly trimmed with effective wide lace in most beautiful design. This pattern is cut with V-shaped front and back, and the rich lace passes under the arms, forming a very dressy bodice effect when worn with transparent waists. Four dainty bows are used for trimming. The lower edge of this chemise is trimmed with lace to match, and is made with innovation envelope feature, as shown in the illustration, that buttons over in a convenient manner and thus forms a drawer that is thoroughly practical. Pink or white crepe de chine. Sizes, 34 to 44. **$2.95.**

Misses' and Girls' Dainty Underwear at Matchlessly Low Prices

Again we must explain about the strength and force of the Gimbel Organization in getting the best manufacturers' products and at their lowest prices. Think of the power of three great stores, four buying offices and many foreign and domestic connections! Gimbels have grown to mammoth proportions through their known ability to satisfy and please their clientele. Some kindly comments of our customers will be found on page 7.

K—10400. Miss's Muslin Drawers. Cut on correct lines. Neat ruffle of same material edged with cotton torchon lace. Cluster of tucks above lace. Very dainty and practical at the same time. Sizes, 12 to 16 years. 25c.

K—10401. Girl's Muslin Petticoat. Ruffle of pretty embroidery with cluster of tucks above. Buttonholes on band, so that it can be attached to a drawer waist. Especially convenient for the very small girl. 50c.

K—10402. Miss's Sateen Petticoat. Has accordion-pleated flounce. Colors, black, emerald or King's blue. A good fitting petticoat with sufficient flare below, making this style very desirable for the modish suit or dress. A garment of superior quality. One that will please the particular young lady. Exceptional value at a reasonable price. Lengths, 34 and 36 inches. 50c.

K—10403. Girl's Princess Slip. Lawn ruffle edged with Val lace and insertion to match. Neck finished with lace, insertion and ribbon, giving a very smart touch to this dainty slip. Sizes, 6 to 12 years. $1.00.

K—10404. Miss's Petticoat. Excellent quality muslin. Ruffle of pretty open pattern embroidery with row of insertion above. Draw string at top. A garment that will prove its worth. Attractively priced. Lengths, 34 and 36 inches. 75c.

K—10405. Girl's Muslin Gown. Neck is cut round and low, and has ribbon threaded through. Kimono sleeves are trimmed with neat embroidery edge. What could be more desirable for summer wear than this practical gown of superior quality. Sizes, 4 to 14 years. 50c.

K—10406. Miss's Very Dainty Princess Slip. Made of fine lawn. Skirt has neat ruffle of pretty and good quality embroidery. Neck finished with ribbon-threaded embroidery edge. Armholes with embroidery edge. The serviceable materials make this model very desirable. Altogether an attractive garment that will wear well and give entire satisfaction. Sizes, 8 to 16 years. $1.00.

K—10407. Miss's Princess Slip. Ruffle trimmed with wide embroidery beading and lace edging. Pretty embroidery at neck is hemstitched to the slip and is threaded with narrow ribbon. Lace around armholes. Its appearance will charm and its worth afford lasting satisfaction. A model particularly adapted for wear with the sheer summer dresses. Sizes, 8 to 16 years. $1.50.

New York — Gimbel Brothers — Philadelphia

104

In textiles and many other lines Philadelphia is the leading manufacturing city in the country, and New York is the leading distributing one,—therefore, in these cities, and from the Gimbel Stores, you can always get the best values in muslin underwear.

K—10500. **Child's Princess Petticoat.** Skirt is made with small lawn ruffle trimmed with lace insertion and edge to match. Neck neatly finished with lace and insertion threaded with baby ribbon. Sizes, 2 to 6 years. **50c.**

K—10501. **Child's Princess Petticoat.** Tucked and hemstitched lawn ruffle, edged with small lace trimmed ruffle. Sizes, 2 to 6 years. **25c.**

K—10502. **Child's "Ideal" Drawer Waist.** Made of good quality cambric. Garter attachments. Firmly reinforced. Durable and excellent garment. Sizes, 2 to 14 years. **25c.**

K—10503. **Child's Muslin Drawers.** Ruffle with embroidery and cluster of tucks above. Sizes, 2 to 14 years. **38c.**

K—10504. **Child's Muslin Knickers.** Embroidered ruffle finished with feather edge braid. Sizes, 2 to 8 years. **25c.**

K—10505. **Child's Muslin Gown.** Gathered at neck. Embroidered edge on high neck and long sleeves. Sizes, 6 months to 2 years. **50c.** Same style with semi-low neck and elbow sleeves. Fastens in front. **50c.**

K—10506. **Child's Muslin "Knickers."** Trimmed with neat small blind scallop edge. Sizes, 2 to 8 years. **18c.**

K—10507. **Child's Muslin Drawers.** Neat hem and tucks above. Sizes, 2 to 12 years. **10c.**

K—10508. **Child's Dainty Princess Petticoat.** Neck prettily trimmed with fine embroidered edge and ribbon. Skirt has deep ruffle with two cluster tucks and ruffle of embroidery. Ribbon threaded insertion at top of ruffle. Armholes edged with neat embroidery. Sizes, 2 to 6 years. **$1.00.**

K—10509. **Child's Muslin Night Drawers.** Excellent quality. Sizes, 2 to 8 years. **38c.**

K—10510. **$10.00 Outfit Special for $9.20.** Infant's Layette—Longclothes.

3 Flannel Bands	12c	$0.35
3 Vests.	25c	.75
12 Hemstitched Diapers		1.00
2 Flannel Petticoats..........	50c	1.00
2 Outing Flannel Petticoats...	25c	.50
1 Flannel Petticoat		1.00
2 Nainsook Yoke Slips........	50c	1.00
1 Nainsook Trimmed Slip.....		1.00
3 Plain Slips	25c	.75
2 Nainsook Petticoats........	50c	1.00
1 Nainsook Petticoat		.75
2 Pairs Bootees	12½c	.25
2 Round Nursing Pads........	25c	.50
3 Bibs.	5c	.15
39 pieces.		$10.00

Write for make-up and prices of other outfits.

Gimbel Clothing For Infants Is Scientifically Hygienic

The American mother demands that her Infant's clothes shall be spotlessly clean, and this means frequent trips to the tub. Gimbels have therefore designed dresses that are simple in the extreme and made of serviceable fabrics, yet they are of such a fineness that the dresses are truly exquisite. There is no excess trimmings to annoy the child.

K—10600. Infant's Long Bishop Slip. Soft and good quality nainsook. Long sleeves and round neck edged with lace. 25c. Same style with short sleeves. 25c.

K—10601. Infant's Long Slip. Embroidery yoke in front finished with narrow insertion, lace and small braid. Sleeves trimmed to match. Exceptionally good value for the low price. 85c.

K—10602. Infant's Long Bishop Slip. Rows of shirring and lace edge on neck and sleeves. A surprising value. 50c.

K—10603. Child's White Lawn Dress. Skirt of allover embroidery with beading and ribbon above. Embroidery panel trims front of waist. Semi-low neck and elbow sleeves trimmed with ribbon rosettes and lace. Clusters of tucks back and front. $2.00.

K—10604. Infant's Long Petticoat. Skirt has ruffle of blind scallop embroidery with cluster of tucks above. A fine bargain. 50c.

K—10605. Child's Lawn Dress. Yoke of cluster tucks back and front. Lace on neck, sleeves and skirt. Pleats at center back and front of waist to give ample fullness. An ideal summer garment. Sizes, 1 to 3 years. $1.00.

K—10606. Child's Lawn Dress. Three rows of lace insertion and tucks form front. Lace edged ruffle with insertion above. Ribbon garniture and rosettes are placed on front of dress. Sizes, 6 months to 2 years. $1.00.

K—10607. Child's White Lawn Dress. Skirt of embroidery with embroidered beading and ribbon above. Ribbon bow at back. Insertion and tucks trim waist in front. Neck and sleeves have ribbon and lace. You would pay considerably more elsewhere for a dress of equal value. Sizes, 2 to 5 years. $1.50.

K—10603. Child's Nainsook Dress. Square yoke of embroidery in front, trimmed effectively with briar stiching and knotted rosettes of pink or blue ribbon. Order this dress and we know you will be well pleased. 6 months to 2 years. $1.00.

K—10609. Child's Lawn Dress with French Waist. Skirt edged with blind scallop and dot, and has two tiny tucks above. Neck and sleeves trimmed with embroidery. Insertion belt laced with ribbon and a small bow at right side. 2 to 5 years. $1.00.

K—10610. Child's Short Dress. Semi-low neck trimmed with pretty insertion, cluster tucks and briar stitching, also dainty lace. Back trimmed with cluster of tucks. This model will be sure to give satisfaction. 6 months, 1 and 2 years. $1.00.

New York — Gimbel Brothers — Philadelphia

Reasonably Priced Summer Clothing For Little "Cuties"

The little garments are each "adorable" and worthy the attention of fond relatives who contemplate a gift. You will receive the best of value for your money, for large buying by the big Gimbel Stores means very lowest cost, first to Gimbels, then to you. The Gimbel rule is small profit and to frequently turn their money over by correspondingly increased business.

K-10700 50¢

K-10701 50¢

K-10702 $1.00

K-10704 $1.00

K-10703 $1.00

K-10705 $1.00

K-10706 $2.00

K-10707 $1.00

K-10708 50¢

K-10709 50¢

K—10700. Child's White Lawn French Waist Dress. Skirt neatly gathered and edged with pretty lace. Waist in front has cluster tucks and three rows of lace insertion. Semi-low square neck and short sleeves edged with lace. Sizes, 2 to 6 years. You will wonder how we can sell it for so little. 50c.

K—10701. Baby's Short Dress. An ideally simple little frock. Made of durable quality lawn. Skirt has deep hem. Square neck is edged in front with pretty embroidery laced with ribbon. Sleeves trimmed to match neck. Sizes, 6 months to 2 years. 50c.

K—10702. Baby's Pretty Short Dress. Fine nainsook. Deep hem and tucks above. The dainty little round yoke in front is finished with narrow lace and French knots. Lace edge trims neck and sleeves. 6 months, 1 and 2 year sizes. This dress will attract because of its fineness. $1.00.

K—10703. Child's Very Effective Lawn Waist Dress. Neatly trimmed with lace insertion, cluster tucks and ribbon. You could not find a style daintier for the little "cutie." Sizes, 2 to 5 years. $1.00.

K—10704. Baby's White Lawn Dress. Made in Empire effect. Waist has a full front of embroidery with three panels of work alternating with cluster tucks. Semi-low neck. Waist has embroidery beading belt, threaded with ribbon. Sizes, 1 to 3 years. $1.00.

K—10705. Child's Pretty Washable Dress. Good quality percale in blue, red or tan stripes trimmed with plain color chambray. Piped in white. Long waist. Very stylish and a good value. Sizes, 3 to 6 years. $1.00.

K—10706. Child's Stylish Guimpe Dress. Blue or pink chambray. Trimmed with narrow bands of white. Low belt has two round pockets also with bands. Guimpe of white rep with roll collar and turn-back cuffs. Sizes, 3 to 6 years. $2.00.

K—10707. Oliver Twist Suit. Made of blue chambray with white rep collar and cuffs. Cord at neck. Same style with white blouse. These suits are foremost in favor as they are cool for summer. Sizes, 2 to 5 years. $1.00.

K—10708. Oliver Twist Suit. Tan or blue. Chambray trousers, collar and cuffs with white blouse. Very neat and stylish model. Sizes, 2 to 5 years. A very fine value indeed. 50c.

K—10709. Child's Serviceable Tub Dress. Skirt made of plaid gingham. Waist of plain color chambray trimmed with plaid. Sailor collar. Waist fastens with lacer and eyelets. Same finish on peplum. Blue or pink plaid. Sizes, 3 to 6 years. 50c.

Gimbels Paris, London and American Style Book

107

K-10800
$1.00

K-10801
$2.50

K-10802
$2.95

K-10805
$2.95

K-10803
$1.50

K-10804
$2.95

K-10806
$5.00

For descriptions, Please see the opposite page.

New York — Gimbel Brothers — Philadelphia

A Little Better Than Advertised Is Gimbels Rule

*Style for the little people! Yes, they have their own particular, cunning modes, and they change as frequently as do their Mamma's
Did you ever notice that the little people have a certain amount of vanity, and that they take much pleasure in their little clothes?
Train their taste by always clothing them in the artistic and beautiful.*

K—10800. Child's Useful Tub Pique Coat. Walking or carriage length. Neat collar and cuffs of self material. Made very simple and easy for laundry. Sizes, 1 to 3 years. $1.00.

K—10801. Child's Pretty White Rep Tub Coat. Box-pleated with low belt. Roll collar is neatly scalloped and has embroidered design in each corner. Cuffs on sleeves, also scalloped and trimmed with an embroidery design. Sizes, 1, 2, 3 years. $2.50.

K—10802. Infant's Cream Cashmere Coat. Circular cape attached is neatly scalloped and trimmed with two embroidered flower designs

in center back and on each side. Sleeves have plain deep cuff. Sizes, 6 to 18 months $2.95.

K—10803. Child's Black and White Striped Check Box Coat. Pretty collar with small tabs of Copenhagen mercerized fabric. Fancy buttons trim tabs and effect the front closing. Self fabric cuff on sleeves. Sizes, 2 to 5 years. $1.50.

K—10804. Child's Handsome Coat. Excellent quality navy blue serge in box style with low belt. Back is plain, while front fastens with pretty novelty buttons. Collar and cuffs of scalloped pique. Sizes, 2 to 5 years. $2.95.

K—10805. Infant's Long Cape with Silk-Lined Hood Attached. Cream serge. Prettily scalloped all around. Cord and tassel close the cape at neck. $2.95. Same style in ages 6 months to 2 years. $2.95.

K—10806. Child's Smart Navy Blue Serge Coat. Detachable collar and cuffs of white pique with scalloped ends and embroidery design in center. The slightly full back is laid into pleats at waistline under which a belt extends at sides and front. Pearl buttons. Sizes, 2 to 5 years. $5.00.

K-10900 $1.50 · K-10901 $1.00 · K-10902 $1.00 · K-10903 50¢ · K-10904 $1.50 · K-10905 $1.50 · K-10906 25¢ · K-10907 50¢ · K-10908 50¢ · K-10909 $2.25 · K-10910 25¢ · K-10911 25¢ · K-10912 25¢ · K-10913 $1.00

K—10900. Child's Lawn Hat. High soft crown with two lace insertions in center, ribbon and tiny roses at the side and tailored bow with ends in the back. Two small net frills and lace around face. A beautiful hat that is becoming to any child, and an exceptional offer. Sizes, 2 to 6 years. $1.50.

K—10901. Child's Pique-Poke-Shaped Hat. Button-on crown has embroidered scalloped edge and beautiful embroidered design in center. Two small buttons fasten brim in back. Sizes, 6 months to 2 years. $1.00.

K—10902. Child's White Pique Hat. Poke-shaped. Soft crown. Brim edged with white embroidery. Blue or pink ribbon around crown with bow at side. Sizes, 1 to 6 years. $1.00.

K—10903. Small Boy's Straw Hat. Band of ribbon around crown and tailored bow at side. Red, navy or black. Very serviceable. 50c.

K—10904. Child's Mushroom Shape Straw Hat. Brim, pinched here and there, is decorated

with small rosebuds made of ribbon. Ribbon and tailored bow around crown. Hat comes in navy or white. A pretty model at the price we offer. Sizes, 2 to 6 years. $1.50.

K—10905. Infant's Lawn Bonnet. Puffed crown, Lace shirring and ribbon trimming around face. Wide white ties. When ordering, kindly mention whether pink or blue ribbon is preferred. 13 to 16 inches. $1.50.

K—10906. Lawn Baby Cap. Allover embroidery with lace and wide and narrow ribbon trimming around face edge. Wide ties. Excellent value for the price. 12 to 16 inches. 25c.

K—10907. Infant's Embroidered Lawn Cap. Lace trims face and back piece. Ribbon bow on side. Wide hemstitched ties. 12 to 16 inches. 50c.

K—10908. Child's Serviceable Hat. White pique. Mushroom crown gathered into a band and buttoned to the brim. A good bargain. Sizes, 6 months to 3 years. 50c.

K—10909. Child's White Pique Tailored Hat. Velvet ribbon around the crown with small ends hanging in back and a buckle of white pique at the side. Exceptionally good looking and very fashionable for the spring and summer season. Sizes, 2 to 6 years. $2.25.

K—10910. Child's Hat. White pique trimmed with plain navy or black band around the crown. A knockabout shape for every-day wear. 25c.

K—10911. Child's Sun Bonnet. Blue or pink chambray. Gathered crown and a slightly turned back brim. White ties. Sizes 1 to 6 years. 25c.

K—10912. Child's Crinkled Seersucker Sun Bonnet. Pink, blue or tan striped with white. Turn-back piece around face piped with white. Sizes, 2 to 6 years. 25c.

K—10913 Child's Stylish Straw Hat. High, many cornered crown trimmed with a white band and tailored bow at side. Sizes, 2 to 6 years. $1.00.

Gimbels Paris, London and American Style Book

Here Are Cunning Goods For Very Young Babies

There is no end to the delightful ideas of the designers who create the Gimbel Infants' goods. The Infants' Sections in both stores are very large and overflowing with the most ingenious goods for infants, so reasonably priced as to cause surprise to all who inspect them.

K—11000. Kid Moccasins. Slashed and trimmed with ribbon and feather edge. White kid with pink or blue trimmings or all tan. Softest shoe imaginable. 50c pair.

K—11001. All-Wool Cashmere Hose. Full length. 25c pair.

K—11001-a. Silk and Wool Hose. Extra length. 40c pair.

K—11002. Hand Quilted Bib. Neat embroidery edge. 25c. Plain style, 15c.

K—11003. Lawn Bib. Trimmed with dainty lace and embroidery. Has an invisible quilted pad. 50c.

K—11004. Half Cotton and Half Wool Band. Well woven. Properly fitting. 25c.

K—11005. Half Wool and Half Cotton Shirt. High neck, long sleeves. Infant's size 55c; 6 months, 60c; 1 year, 65c; 2 years, 70c; 3 years, 75c.

K—11005-a. Cotton Lisle Shirt. Not illustrated. High neck and long sleeves or low

neck and short sleeves. Infants' to 3 years, 25c.

K—11006. Hand Painted Safety Pin Holder. White ivory ring trimmed with pink or blue ribbon. Holds large, medium and small gilt safety pins. 50c.

K—11007. One-Strap Leather Sole Slippers. Tailored bow. White, tan or black. 50c.

K—11008. Real Hand Crochet Zephyr Sacque. Fan stitched trimming. White with pink or blue. A beautiful garment for this exceptionally low price. 50c.

K—11009. Zephyr Bootees. Closely hand-knitted in fancy stitch. Your choice of white with pink or blue. 25c.

K—11010. Wool Cashmere Sacque, Crocheted edge and embroidered design in each corner. 50c.

K—11011. Pillow Cover. Good quality lawn trimmed with Swiss embroidery and lace. $1.00.

K—11012. All Wool Crepella Wrapper. Fan

stitched crochet edge and cuffs. Crepella is a soft all-wool fabric that has a smooth finish, crepy surface. $1.00.

K—11013. Lawn Pillow Cover. Embroidered figure in corner with scalloped embroidery ruffle. 50c.

K—11014. Imported Pique Carriage Cover. Daintily embroidered and scalloped. $1.00.

K—11015. White Ivory Toilet Set. Consists of comb, brush, rattle and powder box. Daintily hand painted. $1.00.

K—11016. Comb and Brush Set. White ivory. Hand painted. 50c.

K—11017. Egg Shape Rattle. Novel combination of white ivory with dainty pink or blue. 25c.

K—11018. "Baby's Record" Book. White moire with hand painted floral design in pink or blue and with gold headings for each event in baby's life. 50c.

K—11019. Hand Painted French Ivory Rattle. With movable teething ring. 50c.

New York — Gimbel Brothers — Philadelphia

Aprons, Rompers and Utility Wear Generally

It is in this class of merchandise that Americans excel. The American child at play is certainly the most sensibly dressed child of any land. The American designs for utility wear also are best because they are readily laundered, yet are decidedly smart and attractive and are fanciful up to a certain degree.

K—11100. Handsome Crepe de Chine Boudoir Cap. Trimmed with pretty insertion, lace, ribbon, bow and tiny flowers. Pink or blue. A fascinating little affair. Just what you need to wear when the hair is in curlers. 85c.

K—11101. Maid's Headpiece. Lawn with goffered lace edge fluting. Very smart. A correctly attired maid at the door denotes the well-trained household within. 10c.

K—11102. Maid's Headpiece. Triangle shape with fluted ruffle. A very fine value. Order plenty of them. 5c each or 50c a dozen.

K—11103. Maid's Bow Headpiece. Neatly hemstitched. Can be laundered with little trouble. A most effective headdress. 15c.

K—11104. Maid's Collar and Cuff Set. Dotted Swiss centers and plain hemstitched lawn band. Very dainty for summer wear. 25c.

K—11105. Bungalow Apron. Made of pretty pattern percale trimmed with plain chambray around sleeves, neck and front closing. This garment is a new model. Plain in back.

Open down left side front and is a house dress model with Dutch neck and kimono sleeves. Neatly belted at waistline. When ordering mention whether small, medium or large size is required. 50c.

K—11106. Bungalow Apron. Good quality percale. Made on full lines to cover entire dress. Open down front. Plain in back. Plain chambray trims neck, sleeves, pocket and side closing. Short kimono sleeves and square neck. On the housedress style. Sizes, 36 to 42 bust. 75c.

K—11107. Round Tea Apron. Ruffle with 3 hemstitched tucks and hemstitched hem. Pocket at side. Wide ties. Suitable for sewing and other household uses in addition to tea. 25c.

K—11108. Maid's Apron. Fine lawn. Princess style. Trimmed with two pretty insets of dotted Swiss. Very wide hem at bottom. Wide ties. 50c.

K—11109. Woman's Gingham Apron. Neat bib. Edge, bib and pocket bound neatly with white. 18c.

K—11110. Bungalow Apron. Good quality striped percale. Neck, sleeves and pocket bound with white. Square neck. Short kimono sleeves. 25c.

K—11111. Child's Crinkled Seersucker Romper. Made of all white, blue and white, pink and white or tan and white stripes. Square low neck, trimmed with plain chambray. Sizes, 2 to 6 years. Seersucker needs no ironing, a point worth considering in summer when the laundry is heavy. 50c.

K—11112. Child's Romper. Made of fine pin stripe chambray in tan and white. Belt and yoke back and front are of plain chambray. Neat pearl buttons trim front of yoke. Turkey red piping around pocket, yoke and sleeves. Sizes, 2 to 6 years. 50c.

K—11113. Child's White Linene Romper. Piped neatly with pink or blue chambray around the neck, panel effect, belt, sleeves and pockets. Very pretty and new model, also a very comfortable one on warm days. Sizes, 2 to 6 years. 75c.

K-11200
$1.50

K-11201
$3.00

K-11202
$3.00

K-11203
25¢

K-11204
15¢

K-11205
$1.50

K-11206
$1.50

K-11207
25¢

K-11208
$2.00

K-11209
50¢

K-11210
50¢

K-STAY

TAB

FITTED BELT

RECEPTACLE

K-11211
$1.50

BRACED BACK FLAP

UNWRINKABLE
THIGH-SHIELDS
PREVENT CHAFING

For descriptions, please see the opposite page.

New York — Gimbel Brothers — Philadelphia

Women of Fashion Favor Gimbel Corsets

The modern long corset, with its comfortable low bust, worn with the well-fitting brassiere, make an ideal foundation for the gown of the moment. For the new severe military modes, the corset should be selected with unusual care. The Gimbel Corset Salons display models in the forefront of style.

K—11200. R. & G. New Model Corset. Cut on the new deep bias bust gore lines. Triple hose supporters. Deep embroidery finish at top. Splendid fitting. Sizes, 20 to 30. $1.50.

K—11201. "Smart Set" Corset. Especially adapted to slender or medium figure. Medium bust with deep gores. Back sufficiently high and full to cover and contain flesh around shoulder blades. Long skirt with semi-elastic inserts parallel with and extending far below ends of back steel. Boning is light, but firm. Lace trimming. Six hose supporters. Made of mercerized batiste in white or flesh pink. Sizes, 21 to 30. $5.00.

K—11202. The New Nemo Corset. "Invisible" Self-Reducing with "Visible" Bridge. A series of separate detached tapes compose the new "Invisible" self-reducing straps sewed to inside of corset at hip section, converging fanlike to front steels and hooked thereto with the adjustment. Adjustment draws the lower part snugly to the figure, and throws

out the upper part, assuring full breathing space and freedom from pressure or digging in at waist. For short full figures or tall full figures. Sizes, 22 to 36. Fine white coutil. $3.00

K—11203. Sanitary Elastic Belt. Semi-fitted. Small, medium or large. 25c.

K—11204. Bird's-eye Napkin. Washable. 15c.

K—11205. Sanitary Dress Protector. Made of rubberized muslin with yoke of net. Skirt is divided on either side with one side fastening full length by snap buttons. Give waist measure. $1.50.

K—11206. W. B. Lace-In-Front Corset. A boned tongue in front protects the body from lacers. Hooked at side of lacing. Model shows the new dip bust line, slightly nipped at waist. New insert down back with elastic at end. Sizes, 20 to 30. $1.50.

K—11207. Under Arm Shield. Fine quality waterproofed nainsook. A necessity especially for the higher corset. Lace trimmed. Large size. 25c.

K—11208. C. B. "A La Spirite" Corset. Suitable for stout women. Fine coutil. Heavily boned. Graduated front steels. Deep elastic insert in back. Sizes, 20 to 36. $2.00.

K—11209. Junoform "Wee-Wee" Serviette Bag. Waterproofed cretonne containing two rubber-lined compartments. 50c.

K—11210. Sanitary Absorbent Napkins. Comfortable and antiseptic. Dozen in a neat box. 50c.

K—11211. Dr. Gertrude Rosenthal's Hygienic Sanitary Outfit. It prevents staining clothing, embarrassment, also chafing of limbs. It eliminates use of napkins, their expense and other objectionable features. It prevents diseases and aids in bladder weaknesses most wonderfully. Protector and net-covered sponge can be washed, dried and securely readjusted in a moment. Outfit is soft and lasts for years. Sizes, small, medium or large. $1.50 for complete outfit in "Ideal" brand. $2.00 and upward for "Prudent" brand. For sanitary reasons this garment is not exchangeable.

K—11300. Brassiere. Surplice back with tapes. Perfect fitting. Elaborate embroidery in front and embroidery finishes top. Practical and good style for all around wear. Sizes, 32 to 52. $1.00.

K—11301. Brassiere. Surplice back with tapes. Cut on correct lines. Embroidery yoke back and front. Edging on neck and sleeves. Sizes, 32 to 48. $1.00.

K—11302. "Soutien Gorge" Support Bust. A perfect brassiere. Yoke in front composed of double strips of fine cambric embroidery. One

row in back. Bone support back and front. Embroidery trims armhole. Sizes, 32 to 52. $1.50.

K—11303. Bust Supporter. This model is particularly good for medium or full figures. Reinforced under arm. Embroidery trims front. Sizes, 32 to 48. 50c.

K—11304. Brassiere. Dainty style. Low cut V neck. Five-inch lace trims back and front. Two and one-half inch band of the same lace through waistline. Perfect fitting. Fastens in front. Sizes, 32 to 48. 50c.

K—11305. "Ovida" Brassiere. Style 167. Ideal for bathing and athletics. Medium or large bust. 11-inch bodice. Bust sections of Elastricot. Solid back. No embroidery trimmings. Fastens in front with hooks and eyes and has self-regulating shoulder straps. Scientifically contoured to nature's model, gives a graceful outline either with or without corsets. Sizes, 32 to 52. $3.00. Style 165 same as No. 167 with 8½-inch bodice for medium bust. Sizes, 32 to 40. $3.00. Soak and wash "Ovida" in cold suds. Do not apply hot iron.

Gimbels Paris, London and American Style Book

K-11400
50¢

K-11401
$1.50

K-11402
$1.00

K-11403
95¢

K-11407
50 ¢

K-11404
25¢

K-11405
50 ¢

K-11406
65 ¢

K-11408
$1.00 →

K-11409
50 ¢

For descriptions please see the opposite page.

New York — Gimbel Brothers — Philadelphia

The "La Markette" Corsets On This Page Are Gimbel Productions

Every whisper of coming fashion heard in London or Paris is transmitted immediately by Gimbels foreign organization to the Gimbel Stores. Every creation by clever American designers is displayed for Gimbels inspection. And price at Gimbels are always most reasonable.

K—11400. Gimbel Brothers Special A. A. Corsets. An exceptional value. Graduated front steel. Non-rustible, a fine characteristic for summer. Double supporters attached. Serviceable embroidery edge. Pink or white. Sizes, 19 to 30. The Gimbel Corset Shops pride themselves on the high grade of this inexpensive garment. **50c.**

K—11401. Athletic Corset Waist. A splendid short garment for the athletically inclined woman. Elastic gore in bust to give ease of movement to wearer. Deep lace finish. Sizes, 19 to 30. Is not only comfortable in action, but very durable. **$1.50.**

K—11402. The "American Girl" Corset. Firm coutil. Guimpe edge. Designed especially for the growing girl and young slender woman. Extremely supple and comfortable.

Gives good support. Moderately long skirt. 19 to 26 inches. **$1.00.**

K—11403. G. B. Corset. Gimbels own brand. Invaluable to the stout figure. Reducing tabs across abdomen distribute excess flesh comfortably and give needed support. Triple hose supporters. This corset is made of firm materials to stand the strain the stout figure gives and is everyway an unapproachable value at the price. Sizes, 22 to 36. **95c.**

K—11404. Fine Cambric Embroidery Ruffles. Square shape. Lace-trimmed top. Baby ribbon bow. **25c.** Butterfly shape. Dotted embroidery trimmed. With lace and white satin bow of ribbon. **50c.**

K—11405. Perfect Bust Form. Gives a perfect figure to any woman. Ribs of stiffening distend the form into proper lines for the extremely flat-chested woman. Fine for

shirt waist wear. Sizes, 34, 36, 38 inches bust. **50c.**

K—11406. Lawn Waist With Ruffles. Lace gives finish. Adjusted at neck and waist by means of ribbon. Sizes, 34 to 42. This style is a favorite with many women. **65c.**

K—11407. Ferris Dress Form. Tampico form in a pleated removable cover. Splendid sanitary form. Small, medium or large. **50c.**

K—11408. Shirred Ruffle Form and Corset Cover Combination. Adjustable ruffle inside of form which opens flat for laundering. Gives a graceful, rounded contour. Sizes, 34, 36, 38. **$1.00.**

K—11409. Dress Form. Soft, yielding Dorothy forms in a removable cover of allover embroidery. Very dainty, also very serviceable. **50c.**

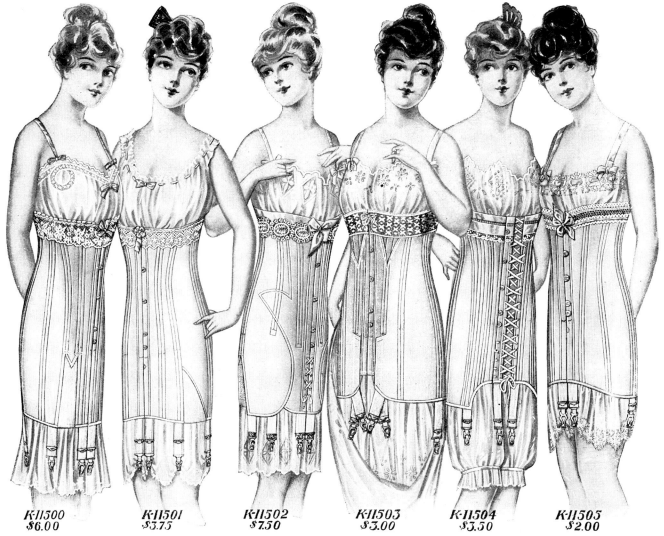

K-11500	K-11501	K-11502	K-11503	K-11504	K-11505
$6.00	$3.75	$7.50	$3.00	$3.50	$2.00

K—11500. "La Markette" Corset. An exceptional model in shape, material and boning. A corset especially for the average full figure. Very firmly boned with walohn, a pliable, yet firm, boning. Coutil of a splendid quality is the fabric. Medium bust. Moderately long skirt with broad elastic insert in front for comfort in sitting. A perfect-fitting corset in every detail, conforming to Fashion's latest decree. Skirt curved at lower edge in back to give smooth lines. Triple hose supporters. 20 to 30 inches. **$6.00.**

K—11501. "La Markette" Model. This corset will beautifully fit the average figure, producing lines to meet the approval of the most exacting dressmaker. Medium high bust. Elastic gore in skirt confines to side of hip for comfort in sitting and to give smoothness. Made of fine white cretonne

cloth. Prettily trimmed with lace. Six hose supporters. Sizes, 20 to 30. Certainly a splendid value. **$3.75.**

K—11502. "La Markette" Corset. This high-grade model shows the extreme fashionable bust line. A nipping in of waist at the front and side follows the latest fashion in corsets. Walohn boning, which is pliable, yet strong. Heavy ventilated elastic give-in curve over hip and adjusts to every movement. Beautiful trimming of lace and satin ribbon. Four pairs hose supporters. Sizes, 23 to 30. **$7.50.**

K—11503. "La Markette" Corset. A splendid model for the woman requiring a shorter skirt. Corset cut full through bust and back, above waist, making an ideal corset for the short full figure. Concealed vents in front each side of steel for ease in sitting. Sizes, 21 to 32. A firm, durable model of

exceptional merit which will give prolonged service and induce more graceful lines than you would think possible. **$3.00.**

K—11504. "La Markette" Corset. Laced in front. Hooks at side of lacing. Perfect fitting, with moderate high bust and medium length skirt. Back is absolutely smooth and has three-quarter inch elastic inserts, which insure close-fitting skirt at back. Beautiful lace and ribbon finish. Sizes, 22 to 32. **$3.50.**

K—11505. "La Markette" Corset. Medium high bust, showing a suggestion of nip-in waist. Firmly boned. Rubber button hose supporters of heavy elastic. Net and lace garniture. A commendable model in every way which will not fail to please. Sizes, 19 to 28. **$2.00.**

Gimbels Paris, London and American Style Book

Women's Stylish and Serviceable Hosiery

The Gimbel Store has every well-known brand of Hosiery that they can thoroughly recommend. For people with tender feet, "Burson" Hosiery is suggested, as it is seamless and well-fitting. Likewise, it is carefully knitted from selected, properly dyed yarns.

K—11600. Woman's Stockings. Good-wearing cotton, in black or tan; specially made for the Gimbel Stores. Exceptional value. Sizes, 8 to 10½. 25c pair.

K—11601. Stockings. Black cotton; split soles. Sizes, 8½ to 10½. 25c pair.

K—11602. Stockings. Black cotton; split-feet. Maco garter-tops. Sizes, 8½ to 10. A Gimbel Special for 12½c pair; 6 pairs, 75c.

K—11603. Boot-silk Stockings. More silk than most makes at the price. Black, white or tan. Cotton top and cotton soles. Full-fashioned. Sizes, 8½ to 10. 50c pair.

K—11604. Stockings. Cotton, in black or tan; lisle thread, in black, tan or white. Extra threads in heels, toes and soles. 8½ to 10. Worth 25c. 18c pair; 6 pairs, $1.00.

K—11605. Stockings. Black cotton; maco feet; full-fashioned; excellent for tender feet. Sizes, 8½ to 10½. 25c pair.

K—11606. Stockings. Heavy thread-silk; black only. Two styles; all silk, or silk with cotton feet. 8 to 10½. $1.50 pair.

K—11607. Stockings. Imported. Mercerized or lisle thread in black, white or tan. Good value for 50c. Sizes, 8½ to 10½. Special at 35c pair; 3 pairs, $1.00.

K—11608. Stockings. Black silk only; extra threads in heel and toe; double garter-tops; cotton soles. 8½ to 10. $1.00 pair.

K—11609. Stockings. Thread-silk; plain black silk, cotton top, cotton sole; black silk top, cotton sole, and black, tan, white, pink or sky blue silk with cotton flare top and cotton sole. Be sure to state style wanted. 8½ to 10. $1.35 pair.

K—11610. Stockings. Mercerized cotton. Recommended by Gimbels. Black, tan or white. Sizes, 8½ to 10. 35c pair; 3 pairs in a box. $1.00.

K—11611. Hosiery. Extra large legs. Black tan or white lisle thread. Black cotton or black with split feet. Full assortment. Be sure to name style wanted. Sizes, 8½ to 10½. 35c pair; 3 pairs. $1.00.

K—11612. Stockings. Special. Lisle thread; double top; extra splicing in heels, toes and soles. Black, tan or white. 8½ to 10½. 50c pair; 6 pairs, $2.75.

K—11613. Special—"Burson" Fine Cotton Stockings. Good wearing; perfect fitting; seamless; black only. 25c grade at 18c pair; 6 pairs, $1.00. Others, cotton or lisle. Regular or out-sizes. 25c pair.

K—11614. Stockings. Thread-silk; black only. Double silk top, cotton or silk soles. Good wearing. Sizes, 8½ to 10. $1.50 pair.

K—11615. Stockings. Out-size silk. Thread-silk top, cotton soles. Sizes, 8½ to 10½. $1.50 pair.

New York — Gimbel Brothers — Philadelphia

116

Misses', Children's and Infants' Stockings

It is the boy or girl who really tests the worth of Gimbel Hosiery. Note how many less Gimbel stockings there are in the darning basket than there are of other makes at the same prices. Gimbel goods are always highest in value. State size of hose or of shoe worn.

K-11700
12½¢

K-11701
25¢

K-11702
18¢

K-11703
25¢

K-11704
25¢

K-11705
35¢

K-11706
35¢

K-11707
25¢

K-11708
35¢ pr.

K-11709
25¢

K-11710
50¢

K-11711
6 Pr. $2.00

K-11712
25¢

K-11713
25¢

K-11716
35¢

K-11714
25¢ pr

K-11715
35¢

K—11700. Child's Stockings. Fine ribbed; seamless; reinforced at points of most wear. Fast-black, tan or white cotton. Sizes, 6 to 10. 12½c. pair.

K—11701. Child's Stockings. Lisle thread. Spliced knee. Reinforced at heel and toe. Black, tan or white. Sizes, 5 to 10. 25c. pair.

K—11702. Child's Stockings. Ribbed cotton. Black or tan; triple knee; reinforced at heel and toe. Sizes, 6 to 10. 18c. pair; 3 pairs, 50c.

K—11703. Miss's Plain Stockings. Black, tan or white cotton; all improvements. Sizes, 7½ to 9½. 25c. pair.

K—11704. Child's Fancy-Top Socks. A great variety of patterns; cotton. Sizes, 4½ to 8½. 25c. pair.

K—11705. Child's Imported Socks. White lisle, with fancy plaid tops. Sizes, 5 to 8. 35c. pair; 3 pairs, $1.00.

K—11706. Child's Imported Socks. White lisle with fancy striped tops. Sizes, 5 to 8. 35c. pair; 3 pairs, $1.00.

K—11707. Child's Socks. White lisle, fancy tops. Sizes, 4½ to 8½. 25c. pair.

K—11708. Infant's Silk-and-Wool Stockings. Black, white, pink or blue. Sizes, 4 to 6½. 35c. pair; 3 pairs, $1.00.

K—11709. Child's Socks. White lisle or cotton. Sizes, 4½ to 9. 25c. pair.

K—11710. Child's Imported Socks. Lisle thread; fancy plaid tops. Sizes, 5 to 8½. 50c. pair.

K—11711. Child's "Holeproof" Stockings. Boy's or girl's. Six pairs guaranteed to wear 6 months without holes. Black cotton. Sizes, 6 to 10. 6 pairs, $2.00.

K—11712. Child's Stockings. Black, tan or white. In fine ribbed lisle or mercerized lisle. Sizes, 5 to 10. 25c pair.

K—11713. Child's Imported Socks. White cotton. Fancy checked tops. Sizes, 5 to 8½. 25c. pair.

K—11714. Infant's Stockings. The "Little Autocrat." Fine ribbed cashmere. Black, tan, red, pink, white or sky-blue. Best for the price. Sizes, 4 to 6½. 25c. pair.

K—11715. Child's Imported Socks. Fancy tops; a variety of patterns; white lisle thread. Sizes, 5 to 8½. 35c. pair; 3 pairs, $1.00.

K—11716. Child's Fine Ribbed Stockings. Black or tan. Lisle or mercerized lisle; excellent grade. Sizes, 6 to 10. 35c. pair; 3 pairs, $1.00.

Men's and Women's Reliable Hosiery

Among the many good makes represented is the "Holeproof" Brand. These wear-resisting Stockings are sold in lots as mentioned, and with each lot you get a block of coupons, dated, which entitles you to new hosiery in case the old wear out within a reasonable time.

K—11800. **Man's Socks.** Fine cotton, in black, tan, slate or navy. Seamless. Sizes, 9½ to 11½. 12½c pair.

K—11801. **Man's Socks.** Fine imported cotton. Black with split soles. Sizes, 9½ to 11½. 25c pair.

K—11802. **Man's "Holeproof" Socks.** Six pairs guaranteed to wear 6 months. Sizes, 9½ to 11½. Medium weight cotton. Six pairs, $1.50. Light weight mercerized. Six pairs, $2.00. Light weight luster mercerized. Six pairs, $3.00.

K—11803. **Man's Socks.** Fine cotton. Black with white soles. 9½ to 11½. Seamless. 12½c pair.

K—11804. **Woman's "Holeproof" Stockings.** Six pairs guaranteed to wear 6 months. Sizes, 8 to 10½. Medium weight cotton. Six pairs,

$2.00. Light weight mercerized. Six pairs, $3.00.

K—11805. **Man's Socks.** Fine lisle. Black, tan, slate or navy. Sizes, 9½ to 11½. Seamless. Value, 25c pair. 18c pair; 3 pairs, 50c.

K—11806. **Man's Socks.** Fine imported little thread embroidered with silk clocks; reinforced at points of most wear. Black, tan, slate or navy. Sizes, 9½ to 11½. 50c pair.

K—11807. **Woman's Stockings.** Fine imported lisle thread. Double garter tops; spliced heels and toes; double soles. Black or tan. Sizes, 8½ to 10. Value, 50c pair. 35c pair; 3 pairs, $1.00.

K—11808. **Man's Socks.** German make; black cotton. Split soles. 9½ to 11½. 35c pair; 3 pairs, $1.00.

K—11809. **Man's Socks.** Imported mercerized

lisle thread. High grade; double heels, soles and toes. Black, tan, lavender, slate, cadet blue or navy, to match neckwear. Strongly recommended. Sizes, 9½ to 11½. 50c pair. 6 pairs, $2.75.

K—11810. **Man's Socks.** Imported gauze lisle thread. Sheer where wanted and reinforced at points of most wear. Black, tan, slate or navy. Sizes, 9½ to 11½. 35c pair; 3 pairs, $1.00.

K—11811. **Man's Socks.** Black cotton with all white feet; good for tender feet. Seamless. Sizes, 9½ to 11½. 12½c pair.

K—11812. **Man's Socks.** French silk, embroidered with self-clocks in all the wanted shades. Stylish. Sizes, 9½ to 11½. $2.00 and $2.50 pair.

K—11813. **Man's Socks.** Thread-silk; in tan. slate, black or navy. Sizes, 9½ to 11½. 50c pair.

New York — Gimbel Brothers — Philadelphia

Men's Underwear—A Peerless Stock

Every well-known brand is here—mostly AMERICAN MADE—so there will be no disappointments or delays in filling orders. Also, American manufacturers, to overcome competition, put every atom of value they can into their product. In putting their name on a brand they take pride in having that brand the best that can be made. For shirts, give chest measure; for drawers, give waist measure.

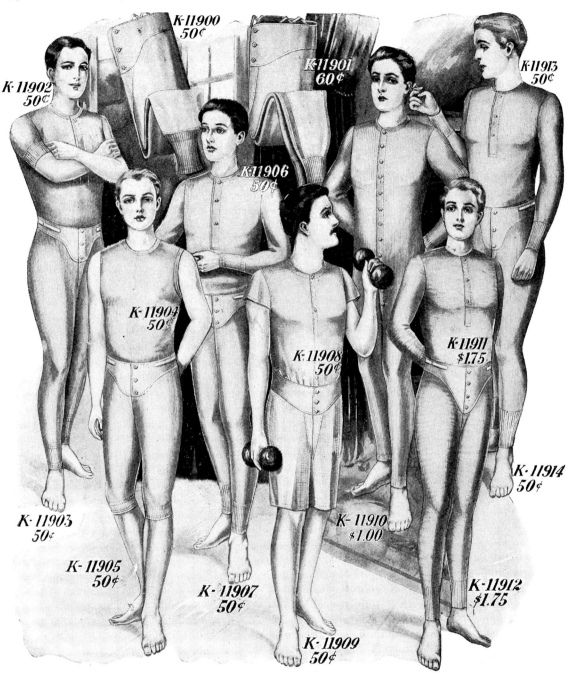

K—11900. **Drawers.** Jean; cut full; banjo seats; ribbed ankles. Sizes, 30 to 50. **50c** a garment.

K—11901. **Drawers.** Jean; elastic seam; ribbed ankles. Sizes, 30 to 44. **60c** a garment.

K—11902. **Shirt.** Balbriggan. High neck; short sleeves. Ecru. Sizes, 34 to 50. **50c.**

K—11903. **Drawers.** Balbriggan. Best make; double seats. Sizes, 30 to 50. **50c** a garment.

K—11904. **Pull-Over Shirt.** Fine cotton; light weight. White or cream. Sizes, 34 to 44. **50c.**

K—11904A. **Pull-Over Shirt.** Fine, light weight; lisle thread. White. Sizes, 34 to 44. **$1.00.**

K—11905. **Knee Drawers.** Fine cotton; light weight. White or cream. Sizes, 30 to 44. **50c** a garment.

K—11905A. **Knee Drawers.** Fine lisle thread. White. Sizes, 30 to 44. **$1.00** a garment.

K—11906. **Medium Weight Shirt.** White or gray cotton; high neck; long sleeves. Sizes, 34 to 50. **50c.**

K—11906A. **Shirt and Drawers.** Light weight, gray merino. Sizes, 30 to 46. **$1.00** a garment. Medium, **$1.00** and **$1.50** a garment.

K—11907. **Drawers.** Cotton; medium weight; white or gray. Sizes, 30 to 50. **50c** a garment.

K—11908. **Coat Shirt.** Nainsook. With or without short sleeves. Sizes, 34 to 44. **50c.**

K—11909. **Knee Drawers.** Nainsook. Sizes, 30 to 44. **50c** a garment.

K—11909A. **Athletic Underwear.** Sizes, 30 to 44. **75c, $1.00, $1.50** a garment.

K—11909B. **Coat Shirt.** Nainsook; sleeveless. Sizes, 34 to 44. **25c.**

K—11909C. **Knee Drawers.** Nainsook. Sizes, 30 to 44. **25c** a garment.

K—11910. **Combination Suit.** Fine ecru or white cotton; high neck; long or short sleeves. Sizes, 34 to 46. **$1.00** a suit. Better grade, **$1.50.**

K—11911. **Shirt.** Fine merino; light weight; natural. Sizes, 34 to 50. **$1.75** and **$2.00** a garment.

K—11912. **Drawers.** Merino; light weight; natural. Sizes, 30 to 50. **$1.75** and **$2.00** a garment.

K—11913. **Shirt.** Fine ecru ribbed cotton yarns; medium weight. Sizes, 30 to 44. **50c.**

K—11914. **Drawers.** Ecru cotton ribbed; medium weight. Sizes, 30 to 44. **50c** a garment.

K—11914A. **Shirt and Drawers.** Fine ecru Egyptian cotton. The best finish. 30 to 44. **$1.00** a garment.

Gimbels Paris, London and American Style Book

Infants' and Children's Underwear, Much Diversified

It is impossible to catalogue our entire line of children's underwear. At each price we have many styles, while perhaps we can show only two or three of them. Write us regarding your favorite style if it is not illustrated. We probably have it in a better quality than you have been getting elsewhere. In ordering Infants' Shirts please state age of baby. Size 2 is for first size; 3, 6 to 9 months; 4, 1 to 1½ years; 5, 2 to 2½ years; 6, 3 to 3½ years; 7, 4 to 4½ years; 8, 5 years.

K—12000. Infant's Shirt. White cotton. Low neck; short sleeves. Sizes, 2 to 6. 25c.

K—12001. Infant's Shirt. White cotton. High neck; short sleeves. Sizes, 2 to 6. 25c.

K—12002. Infant's Shirt. White cotton. High neck; long sleeves. Sizes, 2 to 6. 25c.

K—12003. Child's Waist. White cotton; sleeveless. Light weight for girls. Sizes, 2 to 13 years. 25c.

K—12004. Child's Knee Drawers. White gauze; well made; gusset seat. Sizes, 26 to 34. 35c garment; or 3 for $1.

K—12005. Child's Trunk Drawers. White gauze; gusset seat. Sizes, 26 to 34. 35c garment; or 3 for $1.

K—12006. Infant's Shirt. Merino. High neck; long sleeves. Sizes 2 to 6. 35c for first size; 5c additional for each size larger.

K—12007. Child's Combination Suit. Carters. Fine white cotton; high grade; best finish. Sizes, 2 to 6. 75c suit.

K—12008. Child's Combintion Suit. Carters. Fine white cotton; best make and finish. Sizes, 7 and 8. 90c suit.

K—12007 and K—12008 are made in two ways, viz: High neck; long or short sleeves; knee or ankle length. Be sure to clearly state the style wanted.

K—12009. Child's "Pearl" Waist for Boys and Girls. 2 to 13 years. 25c.

K—12010 and K—12011. Boy's B. V. D. Athletic Underwear. Plaid nainsook coatshirts and knee drawers. Sizes, 26 to 34. 50c garment; $1 suit.

K—12012. Child's Shirt. Gauze. High neck; short sleeves. White. Sizes, 20 to 34. 25c.

K—12013. Child's Pants. Gauze. Knee length. White. Sizes, 18 to 30. 25c.

K—12014. Child's Shirt. Gauze. Fine, white, light-weight cotton. High neck and short sleeves. Sizes, 20 to 34. 35c.

K—12015. Child's Pants. Gauze. Knee length. White. Sizes, 18 to 30. 35c; or 3 for $1.

K—12016. Child's Pull-over Shirt. White gauze. Low neck; short sleeves; very comfortable. Sizes, 20 to 34. 35c garment; or 3 for $1.

Dealing with Gimbels Knit Underwear Sections Is Safe

The Gimbel Stores employ men of long experience to manage their Knit Underwear Sections. You do not have to submit to experimentation—often costly to you. Our experts know the brands thoroughly, and only buy the most reliable goods, made by foremost manufacturers. In ordering be sure to state size wanted, or age of the child.

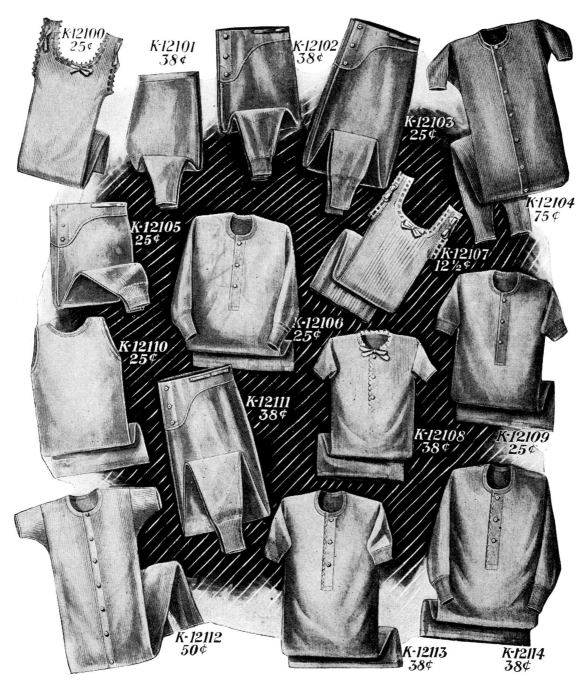

K—12100. **Miss's Vest.** Swiss ribbed; white lisle thread; very fine yarn; well finished. Low neck; sleeveless. 25c.

K—12101. **Child's Pantalets.** Fine white cotton, knee length. Sizes, 18 to 34. 38c garment.

K—12102. **Boy's Knee Drawers.** Fine balbriggan; ecru; double seat. Sizes, 26 to 34. 38c garment.

K—12103. **Boy's Drawers.** Balbriggan; fine combed yarn; ecru; 3 buttons; double seat. Sizes, 26 to 34. 25c garment.

K—12104. **Boy's Combination Suit.** Ribbed; fine cotton; well finished; knee length. Sizes, 6 to 14 years. 75c.

K—12105. **Boy's Knee Drawers.** Balbriggan; fine combed Egyptian yarn; ecru; 3 buttons; double seat. Sizes, 26 to 34. 25c garment.

K—12106. **Boy's Shirt.** Balbriggan; combed Egyptian yarn. Ecru. Sizes, 26 to 34. 25c.

K—12107. **Miss's Vest.** Swiss ribbed; fine cotton; white. 12½c.

K—12108. **Child's Vest.** Ribbed; fine white cotton. Sizes, 20 to 34. 38c.

K—12109. **Boy's Shirt.** Balbriggan; combed Egyptian yarn. Ecru. Sizes, 26 to 34. 25c.

K—12110. **Boy's Athletic Shirt.** Pull over the head and without sleeves. Very cool and comfortable. White cotton. Sizes, 26 to 34. 25c.

K—12111. **Boy's Ankle Drawers.** Fine balbriggan; ecru; double seat. Sizes, 26 to 34. 38c.

K—12112. **Boy's Combination Suit.** Cotton ribbed; sleeveless in white or short sleeved in ecru. Sizes, 8 to 14 years. 50c.

K—12113. **Boy's Shirt.** Fine balbriggan; ecru. Sizes, 26 to 34. 38c.

K—12114. **Boy's Shirt.** Fine balbriggan; ecru. Sizes, 26 to 34. 38c.

Not Illustrated.

Infant's Fine Shirts. 25c. to 90c.

Infant's Fine Bands. 25c. to 50c.

Children's Fine White Gauze Underwear. All styles. 25c. and 35c.

Misses' Combination Suits. According to grade and size. 50c. to 90c.

Boy's Open Mesh Underwear. White shirts and drawers. 25c. each. Combination suits, 50c. suit.

Women's Knitted Vests and Drawers

These garments are evenly woven, carefully made, and finished with fine quality trimmings. You will find them quite superior for the prices asked, both in appearance and service-giving.
Sizes: Vests, 34, 36 and 38, regular sizes; 40, 42 and 44, extra sizes. Drawers, 4, 5 and 6, regular sizes; 7, 8 and 9, extra sizes.

K-12200 12½¢
K-12201 75¢
K-12202 18¢
K-12203 75¢
K-12204 50¢
K-12205 50¢
K-12206 50¢
K-12207 50¢
K-12208 25¢
K-12209 $1.00
K-12210 50¢
K-12211 35¢
K-12212 50¢
K-12213 75¢

K—12200. Cotton Vest. Low neck; sleeveless or short sleeves; well trimmed. White. 12½c.

K—12201. Vest. Fine imported vest with fancy yoke. White. 75c.

K—12202. Cotton Vest. Fine Swiss ribbed; low neck; sleeveless. White. 18c. each, or 3 for 50c.

K—12203. Summer Merino Vest. Ribbed. High neck; long or short sleeves. White. 75c. Knee Drawers. 75c. a garment. Extra sizes, $1.00 a garment.

K—12204. Knee Drawers or Knee Tights. Fine ribbed; French bands. White. Regular sizes, 50c. a garment. Extra sizes, 65c. a garment.

K—12204-A. Vest to Match K—12204 Drawers. High neck; long or short sleeves. White. Regular sizes, 50c. a garment. Extra sizes, 65c. a garment. (Not illustrated.)

K—12205. Umbrella Drawers. White Swiss ribbed; lace trimmed; French bands. Regular sizes, 50c a garment.

K—12206. Vest. Fancy yoke; Swiss ribbed; low neck; sleeveless. White. Many styles. 50c. Also grade at 35c. each, or 3 for $1.00.

K—12207. Vest. Fine Swiss ribbed. Fancy crocheted yoke. White. 50c.

K—12208. Lisle Thread Vest. Low neck; sleeveless or short sleeves. White. Made to our special order. Regular sizes, cut full. 25c.

K—12208-A. Plain Ribbed Vest. Low neck; sleeveless. White. 35c., 50c., 75c.

K—12208-B. Extra Size Vest. Fine grade of yarn; low neck; no sleeves or with short sleeves. White. 35c. each, or 3 for $1.00.

K—12209. Fancy Vest. Fine imported goods with crocheted yoke. White. Many styles. $1.00 a garment.

K—12210. Gauze Vest. Plain fabric. High neck; long or short sleeves. White. Sizes, 30 to 44. 50c. each. Drawers to match, knee or ankle length. 50c. a garment.

K—12211. Swiss Ribbed Vest. Low neck; sleeveless; fancy crocheted yoke. White. 35c. Also grade at 25c.

K—12212. Umbrella Drawers. Lace trimmed; French bands. White. Sizes, 4, 5, 6. 50c. pair. Extra sizes, 65c. pair. Also lower grade. French bands or tight tops. 25c., and superior grades, 75c., and $1.00 a garment.

K—12213. Fancy Vest. Fine imported goods with crocheted yoke. White. Many styles. 75c.

Women's Fine Knitted Combination Suits

Combination Suits are comfortable under the corset, as they are smooth at the waist. In addition, knitted garments are much cooler in summer than fabric ones. Some people also consider it more hygienic not to iron them, which is really unnecessary. Regular sizes are 4, 5 and 6. Extra sizes are 7, 8 and 9.

K-12302
$1.00

K-12301
50¢

K-12300
75¢

K-12303
$1.00

K-12304
$1.00

K-12306
$1.00

K-12305
50¢

K—12300. Combination Suit. Fine lisle thread. Umbrella style. Low neck; sleeveless; lace trimmed at knee. White. Regular sizes. 75c.

K—12301. Combination Suit. Fine, white lisle. Umbrella style; low neck; no sleeves; lace trimmed at knee. Regular sizes, 50c. suit. Extra sizes, 65c. suit. With better lace trimmings, 75c. and $1.00 suit.

K—12302. Combination Suit. Swiss ribbed. Low neck; sleeveless; tight knee. Fine, white lisle. Regular sizes, $1.00 suit. Extra sizes, $1.25 suit. Better grade, regular sizes, $1.50 suit. Extra sizes, $1.75 suit.

K—12303. Combination Suit. Fine, white lisle, Swiss ribbed. Umbrella style; low neck; sleeveless; lace trimmed. Also with fancy yoke. Regular sizes, $1.00.

K—12304. Combination Suit. Fine, white cotton. High neck; short sleeves; knee length. Regular sizes, $1.00 suit. Extra sizes, $1.25 suit.

K—12305. Combination Suit. Fine, white lisle thread. Low neck; no sleeves; knee length. Specially cut and perfect fitting. Regular sizes, 50c. suit. Extra sizes, 65c. suit. Better grade in same style, tight knee, regular sizes, 75c. suit.

K—12306. Combination Suit. Fine, white lisle. Umbrella style. Low neck; sleeveless; cut wide at knee. Deep lace trimming. Regular sizes, $1.00 suit.

12306A. Combination Suit. Extra fine mercerized lisle; umbrella style; with or without lace; also tight knee. White. Regular sizes, $1.50. Extra sizes $1.75.

Specials During the Season.

Low Neck Vests in either regular or special sizes.
Value, 15c....................for 10c.
Value, 18c....................for 12½c.
Value, 25c....................for 18c.
Value, 35c....................for 25c.

Combination Suits. Regular sizes only.
Value, 50c....................for 38c.
Value, 75c....................for 50c.
Value, $1.00.................for 75c.

Women's Plain-trimmed Glove Silk Vests. White. 36 to 42. $1.50 and $2.00 each.

Suit. White lisle. Extra fine gauze. Low neck, sleeveless; umbrella; lace trimmed. 85c.

Combination Suit. White, fine gauze lisle, Low neck; sleeveless. Tight knee or umbrella style, with crochet edge. Regular sizes, $1.50.

Gimbels Paris, London and American Style Book

"Kayser's American Made" Hygienic Silk Underwear

"Kayser's" of Glove fame are producing a particularly fine, dainty and durable silk weave underwear, that is taking the place today of the French and Swiss product. It is woven more carefully, shades are better and the goods are more lasting than the imported ones. The first cost of silk underwear is not even prohibitive to people of even small means and it does not shrink from washing. It is lasting if properly laundered, likewise it is soothing and pleasant to the skin. It is hygienic, as it is a good non-conductor of heat and cold. Also, it is the most luxurious for dress wear.

VEST
K-12405
$1.50

K-12402
$2.00

K-12403
$2.00

K-12401
$3.50

K-12400
$3.00

K-12404
$2.50

K-12406
$2.50

K—12400. "Kayser's American-Made" Fine Silk Combination Suit for Women. Low neck. No sleeves. Crochet edge. White or pink. Sizes, 34 to 42 inches bust measure. $3.00.

K—12401. "Kayser's American-Made" Band-Top Silk Combination Suit for Women. Low neck, sleeveless. Fine grade of silk. Extra value. Pink or white. Sizes, 34 to 42 inches bust measure. $3.50.

K—12402. "Kayser's American-Made" Band-Top Silk Vest for Women. Low neck. Sleeve-less. Great value. Pink or white. Sizes, 34 to 42 inches bust measure. $2.00.

K—12403. "Kayser's American-Made" Dainty Silk Vest for Women. Fine embroidery in a variety of patterns. Crochet edge. Low neck. Sleeveless. White or pink. Sizes, 34 to 44 inches bust measure. $2.00.

K—12404. "Kayser's American-Made" Famous Band Top Vest for Women. Sleeveless. Assortment of styles of embroidery. Pink or white. Sizes, 34 to 44 inches bust measure. $2.50.

K—12405. "Kayser's American-Made" Dainty Silk Vest for Women. Low neck. No sleeves. Plain. Pink or white. Great value. Sizes, 34 to 44 inches bust measure. $1.50.

K—12406. "Kayser's American-Made" Bloomers for Women. Dainty silk. Elastic at waist. Great value. White, pink or black. All sizes up to 40 inches waist measure. $2.50.

The Gimbel Style Books Depict the Newest Modes

Did you ever notice how up-to-date are the styles in the Gimbel Catalogues? These books are not issued as early as many others, as we wait until styles are decided upon before selecting the best for illustrations. We believe our clientele would rather wait a short time in order to be sure of getting authentic, new season styles.

K—12500. **Envelope Purse.** Crepe grain leather. Inside frame and pockets. Strap handle. Black, brown, or tan. 50c.

K—12501. **Hand Bag.** Morocco leather. Novelty frame, flat, welted edges. Large, hanging mirror and purse. Black and colors. $2.95.

K—12502. **Hand Bag.** Crepe grain leather. Polished metal frame. Single handle. Purse, powder box and mirror. Black only. $1.00.

K—12503. **Envelope Bag.** Morocco leather. Novelty shape. Inside frame and pockets. Black, brown, blue, or green. $1.00.

K—12504. **Black Moire Silk Hand Bag.** Self-covered frame. Inside frame and three vanity fittings. Very special. $1.95.

K—12505. **Black Moire Silk Bag.** Metal frame in gilt or nickel finish. Poplin lined. Hanging mirror and purse. $1.00.

K—12506. **Morocco Leather Hand Bag.** Ribbon pleated front. Heavy nickel frame.

handle. Hanging mirror and inside framed pocket. Black only. $1.95 special.

K—12507. **Hand Bag.** Black pin seal leather. Flat, welted bottom. Nickel or gilt frame. Purse and mirror. $2.95.

K—12508. **Morocco Leather Hand Bag.** New "Calling" shape. Inside frame, pockets, purse and mirror. Double strap handle. Black and colors. $2.95.

K—12509. **Party Bag.** Morocco leather. Box bottom. Novelty frame. Single handle. Purse and four vanity fittings. Black. $2.95.

K—12510. **Moire Silk Hand Bag.** Silk lined. Covered frame. Inside frame, hanging mirror and purse. $3.95 value. Special at $2.95.

K—12511. **Hand Bag.** Crepe grain leather. Metal frame. Three vanity fittings and purse. Single handle. Black only. $1.95.

K—12512. **Crepe Grain Leather Hand Bag.** Metal frame in nickel or gilt finish. Single handle. Hanging mirror and purse. $1.00.

K—12513. **Hand Bag.** Pin seal leather. Metal frame in nickel or gilt finish. Silk lined. Mirror and purse. Black. Value, $5.00. Special, $2.95.

K—12514. **Hand Bag.** Crepe grain leather. Metal frame. Purse, mirror, powder box, memo. tablet and three manicure fittings in nickel. Black only. $1.65.

K—12515. **Auto Leather Hand Bag.** Envelope shape with top handle. Silk lined. Inside frame. Extra purse. Nickel or gilt trimmings. $2.95.

K—12516. **Long Grain Leather Hand Bag.** 12 inches long by 8 inches deep. Leather lined. Large pocket and purse. Double handles. Black only. $3.50.

K—12517. **Morocco Leather Hand Bag.** Novelty shape, featuring the new "Turnlock" nickel frame. One turn of the hand-pull locks the bag. Black only. $2.50.

Gimbels Paris, London and American Style Book

The Best and Most Reliable Linings

Only the most reliable linings are carried by us, as is shown by the famous makes and brands listed on this page. Linings are the groundwork of a garment—and the foundation must be good or all else fails. Good linings tend to help in getting a perfect fit and are the greatest factor in a garment's retaining its good shape.

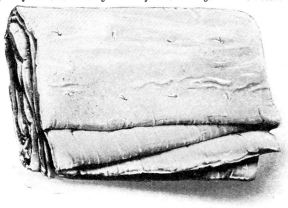

K—12600. Wool-filled Comfort Batts. Cheese cloth covered. Zephyr tied. Filled with long, live fleece lamb's wool, which has been hygienically sterilized. Wool is a perfect non-conductor of heat and cold, therefore is much warmer than cotton in winter and equally cool in summer. A convenient batt for the cotton or silk quilt you may have pieced together, or we will furnish samples of sateens or silk mixtures for covering quilts. Size, 72 x 84 inches. Two-pound weight, **$2.00**; weight, wrapped, 40 ounces. Three-pound weight, **$3.00**; weight wrapped, 56 ounces.

This comes under Gimbels Restricted Delivery Offer, page 4.

"Queen" Bust Forms. They fill out the hollows under the arm, stiffen and pad the front of the coat well down over the bust, and give that tailored appearance as if made by the best man tailor. By using the "Queen" the home dressmaker can tailor her own coat with astonishingly good results.

"Queen" Bust Forms. Made of linen canvas and hair cloth. Collar attached. Sizes, 32 to 44 inches bust measure. **50c** and **$1.00** a pair.

Buckram. 36 inches wide, in black and white. **30c** a yard.

Cambric. Dressmaker's cambric. All colors; 24 inches wide. **6c** a yard.

Crinoline. Black or white. **8c, 10c** and **12½c** a yard.

Tailor Canvas. **25c** and **30c** a yard.

Hair Cloth. Princess Hair Cloth. Black, white or gray. 24 inches wide. **50c** a yard

Lawn Lining. Fine for lining sheer fabrics. 40 inches. **12½c** a yard.

Mercerized Batiste. A sheer lining fabric for inexpensive dresses. Black, white and a good line of colors. 30 inches wide. **15c** yard.

Melba Silk. A sheer silky fabric for slips, dresses, upholstery and many other uses. 36 inches wide. **35c** a yard.

Peau de Cygne. All the wanted lining shades. 35 inches wide. **$1.00** a yard.

Sateen. Mercerized sateen. Fine for draperies, bed sets and fancy work. 36 inches wide. **18c, 25c, 35c** a yard.

Sateen. Mercerized finish, in black, white and colors. 30 inches wide. **12½c** a yard.

Sateen. 27-inch quilted. **50c** a yard.

Skinner's Satin is made to match every cloth shade. We carry a complete line.

$1.35 A YARD

Samples of any color desired sent upon request.

Sateen. "Radiosilk." A highly mercerized sateen for pillows, curtains, upholstery and fancy work, slips, as well as other uses. 36 inches wide. **35c** a yard.

Satin. 23-inch quilted. **75c** a yard.

Satin Brocade. For lining furs and wraps. Pretty designs with two-toned colorings. 36 inches wide. **$2.25** a yard.

Satin Brocade. Pretty designs. Suitable for linings, bed sets, and comfort coverings. Good assortment of colors. 36 inches wide. **$1.75** a yard.

Satin Duchesse. Pure dye. In all the good lining colors. Guaranteed two seasons' wear. 35 inches wide. **$1.50** a yard.

Satin. Tailor's Satin. Cotton back. All the good lining shades. 36 inches wide. **68c** and **85c** a yard.

Silk. Gilt Edge. A pure-dye, soft silk in all the popular colors for linings, petticoats or shirt waists, etc. 36 inches wide. **$1.25** a yard.

Silk. Japanese. Cotton back. 27-inch quilted. **$1.00** a yard.

Silk. Japanese. Wool back. 27-inch quilted. **$1.35** a yard.

Silk. Skinner's No. 404. A pure-dye soft silk for linings, petticoats or shirt waists, etc. 36 inches wide. **$1.50** a yard.

Venetian Cloth. A fine coat lining in black only. 54 inches wide. **85c, $1.10** and **$1.25** a yard.

Venetian Lining. A fine mercerized lining for coats and jackets. Plain or striped in staple colors. 32 inches. **50c** a yard.

Wadding. Lamb's Wool. In sheets. Black or white. **15c** a sheet.

Wadding. Sheet wadding. Black or white. Sheet, **5c**.

K—12602. Lamb's Wool. Carded in one sheet. 72 x 84 inches. Suitable for use as quilt bats, being light weight, cool in summer and warm in winter. Also used in tailoring. **$1.00** a pound.

Lamb's Wool Quilted in Cheese Cloth. 24 inches wide. **40c** a yard.

Cotton Batts. A roll, **9c, 12c, 18c, 20c, 25c** and **30c**.

Cotton Batts. Comfort size. 72 x 84 inches. Made of pure white cotton. Approximately 2 lb. rolls, **55c**; approximately 3 lb. rolls, **80c**; approximately 4 lb. rolls, **$1.10**.

The above four come under Gimbels Restricted Delivery Offer. See page 4.

"BUTTERICK FASHIONS"
A GREAT FASHION BOOK

It is a great fashion book, published quarterly, showing thousands of illustrations of the most up-to-date garments of every kind, for every occasion. It is the one book necessary to the sewing-room, a guide to every stitch, furnishing just the information and help that make your sewing a pleasure. Each issue contains a certificate good for one Butterick Pattern Free, which will be taken in exchange for any 25c pattern you may select at our pattern counters, or order by mail. **Price, INCLUDING THE PATTERN CERTIFICATE, by mail, 35 cents.**

We also take subscriptions to America's foremost fashion monthly, "THE DELINEATOR," 15c. a copy—$1.50 a year, **2 years for $2.00**, charged to your account if you have one and so desire it.

Kleinerts Dress Shields, Hose Supporters and Sanitary Goods

(Continuance of description from page 127.)
K—13021. Kleinert's Seamless Stockinet Dress Shields. Size 1, 16c; 2, 19c; 3, 22c; 4, 25c; 5, 31c pair.
K—13022. Kleinert's Elastic Sanitary Belt. Very small, medium and large. **25c.**
K—13023. Sew-on Hose Supporter. Without tab. Wide with suspender elastic. White. **15c** pair.
K—13024. Satin Pad Hip Supporter. Heavy mercerized suspender elastic. White. **25c** pair.

K—13025. Sew-on Hose Supporter. Without tab. Extra heavy suspender. White. **25c** pair.
K—13026. Satin Pad Hose Supporter. Front sew-on. Heavy mercerized suspender elastic. White. **25c** pair.
K—13027. Sew-on. Without tab supporter. Lisle elastic. White. **15c** pair.
K—13028. Sateen Pad Hose Supporter. Front sew-on. Two straps each side. Heavy suspender elastic. White. **50c** pair

K—13029. Kleinert's "Buster Brown" Hose Supporters. Black or white. Three sizes. Infant's size, 15c pair. Boy's size, 17c pair. Miss's size, 19c pair.
K—13029A. Extra Wide Buster Brown Hose Supporters. Not illustrated. Black or white. Infant's size, 18c pair. Boy's size, 20c pair. Miss's size, 22c pair.
K—13030. Sanitary Skirt Protector. With cambric yoke around hips and rubber sheeting below. Extra size, 75c; smaller size, 50c.

New York — Gimbel Brothers — Philadelphia

Kleinert's Dress Shields, Hose Supporters and Sanitary Goods

Kleinert's goods are the best of their class and most satisfactory in every respect. They easily take the leading place.

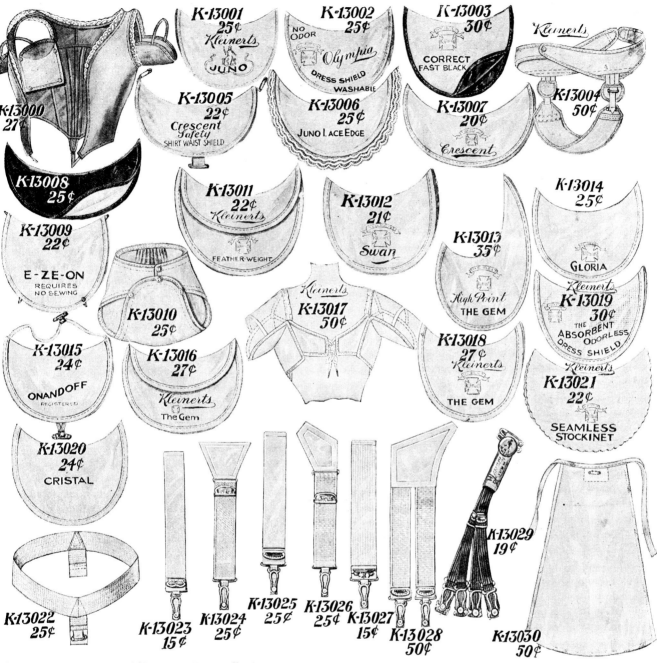

K—13000. Brassiere Dress Shields. Size 3, 27c pair; 4, 30c pair; 5, 36c pair.

K—13001. Kleinert's Juno Dress Shields. Contain no rubber, odorless and may be washed in hot water and ironed when dry. Size 1, 16c pair; 2, 19c pair; 3, 22c pair; 4, 25c pair; 5, 31c pair.

K—13002. Kleinert's Olympia Dress Shields. Washable, odorless. Size 1, 19c; 2, 22c; 3, 25c; 4, 28c; 5, 34c pair.

K—13003. Correct Dress Shields. Inner cover white, outer cover black, for sheer black gowns. Size 2, 27c; 3, 30c; 4, 33c; 5, 39c pair.

K—13004. Kleinert's Sanitary Belt and Shield. State waist measure. 50c.

K—13005. Kleinert's Crescent Safety Shirtwaist Shields. Size 1, 16c; 2, 19c; 3, 22c; 4, 25c; 5, 31c pair.

K—13006. Juno Lace Edge. Contains no rubber. Soft, white, trimmed with lace. Small, medium, large, 25c pair.

K—13007. Kleinert's Crescent Shirtwaist Shields. Size 1, 16c; 2, 18c; 3, 20c; 4, 22c; 5, 26c pair.

K—13008. Coat Shield. For use in outer garments. Gray, light tan, black or white. 25c pair.

K—13009. E-ze-on. Slip the seams of the waist into the slot of the catch attached to the dress shield, securing dress shield to garment without any sewing. Size 2, 19c pair; 3, 22c pair; 4, 25c pair; 5, 34c pair.

K—13010. Baby Pants. Made of rubbered cloth. 25c pair.

K—13011. Kleinert's Featherweight Dress Shields. Nainsook covered. Size 1, 16c; 2, 19c; 3, 22c; 4, 25c; 5, 30c; 6, 35c; 8, 45c; 10, 55c pair. Silk covered. Size 1, 25c; 2, 30c; 3, 35c; 4, 40c; 5, 45c pair.

K—13012. Kleinert's Swan Dress Shields. Size 1, 21c pair; 2, 24c pair; 3, 27c pair; 4, 30c pair; 5, 36c pair.

K—13013. Kleinert's Double Gem High Point Dress Shields. Nainsook. Size 3, 35c; 4, 40c; 5, 45c pair.

K—13014. Gloria. Double covered and interlined, making them highly absorbent. Delicately perfumed. Size 2, 22c; 3, 25c; 4, 30c; 5, 35c pair.

K—13015. Kleinert's Onandoff Dress Shields. Adjustable. Size 1, 19c; 2, 22c; 3, 24c; 4, 28c; 5, 34c pair.

K—13016. Double Gem Opera Dress Shields. Nainsook covered. Size 3, 27c pair; 4, 30c pair; 5, 36c pair.

K—13017. Kleinert's Eton Dress Shields. Worn under the corset. Size 2, for bust measure 28 to 31; 3, for bust measure 32 to 36; 4, for bust measure 37 to 40; 5, for bust measure 40 to 44. 50c pair.

K—13018. Double Gem. Double covered, interlined with pure deodorized rubber, covered with the lightest of cambrics. Soft, white and odorless. Size 1, 21c; 2, 24c; 3, 27c; 4, 30c; 5, 36c; 6, 42c; 8, 54c; 10, 66c pair. Silk covered. Size 1, 42c; 2, 47c; 3, 52c; 4, 57c; 5, 67c.

K—13019. Ideal Double Absorbent. This is specially designed for women who perspire profusely. The covers absorb twice as much moisture as any other dress shield. Size 2, 27c; 3, 30c; 4, 33c; 5, 39c pair.

K—13020. Cristal. As nearly transparent as it is possible to make a dress shield. No rubber, is odorless and hygienic. Size 2, 18c; 3, 21c; 4, 24c; 5, 30c pair.

(Continued on page 126.)

The Very Best in Small Wares

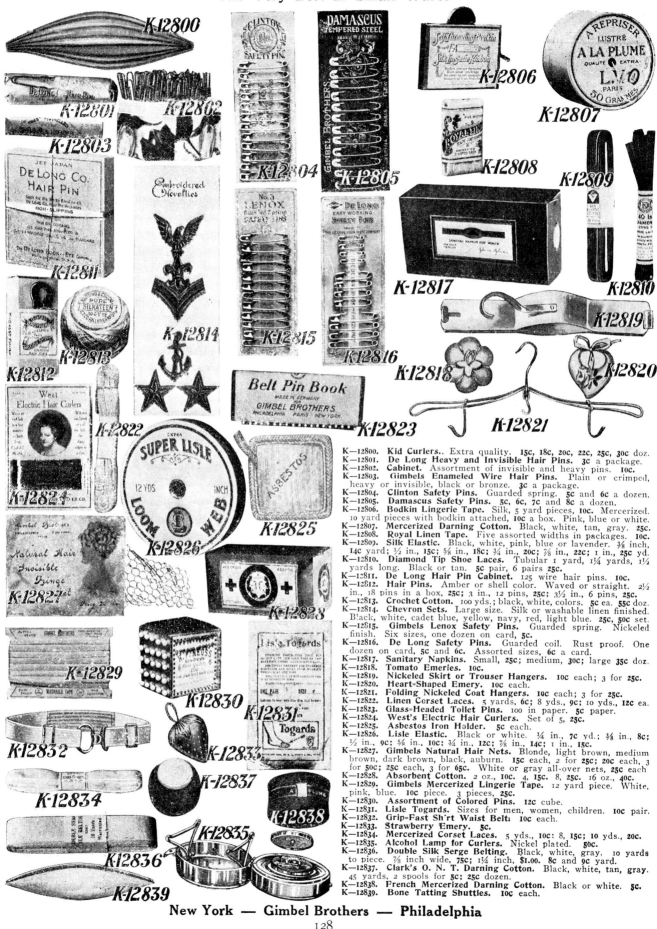

K—12800. **Kid Curlers..** Extra quality. **15c, 18c, 20c, 22c, 25c, 30c** doz.
K—12801. **De Long Heavy and Invisible Hair Pins.** **3c** a package.
K—12802. **Cabinet.** Assortment of invisible and heavy pins. **10c.**
K—12803. **Gimbels Enameled Wire Hair Pins.** Plain or crimped, heavy or invisible, black or bronze. **3c** a package.
K—12804. **Clinton Safety Pins.** Guarded spring. **5c and 6c** a dozen.
K—12805. **Damascus Safety Pins.** **5c, 6c, 7c and 8c** a dozen.
K—12806. **Bodkin Lingerie Tape.** Silk, 5 yard pieces. Mercerized. 10 yard pieces with bodkin attached, **10c** a box. Pink, blue or white.
K—12807. **Mercerized Darning Cotton.** Black, white, tan, gray. **25c.**
K—12808. **Royal Linen Tape.** Five assorted widths in packages. **10c.**
K—12809. **Silk Elastic.** Black, white, pink, blue or lavender. 3/8 inch, **14c** yard; 1/2 in., **15c**; 5/8 in., **18c**; 3/4 in., **20c**; 7/8 in., **22c**; 1 in., **25c** yd.
K—12810. **Diamond Tip Shoe Laces.** Tubular 1 yard, 1 1/4 yards, 1 1/2 yards long. Black or tan. **5c** pair, 6 pairs **25c.**
K—12811. **De Long Hair Pin Cabinet.** 125 wire hair pins. **10c.**
K—12812. **Hair Pins.** Amber or shell color. Waved or straight. 2 1/2 in., 18 pins in a box, **25c**; 3 in., 12 pins, **25c**; 3 1/2 in., 6 pins, **25c.**
K—12813. **Crochet Cotton.** 100 yds.; black, white, colors. **5c** ea. **55c** doz.
K—12814. **Chevron Sets.** Large size. Silk or washable linen finished. Black, white, cadet blue, yellow, navy, red, light blue. **25c, 50c** set.
K—12815. **Gimbels Lenox Safety Pins.** Guarded spring. Nickeled finish. Six sizes, one dozen on card, **5c.**
K—12816. **De Long Safety Pins.** Guarded coil. Rust proof. One dozen on card, **5c and 6c.** Assorted sizes, **6c** a card.
K—12817. **Sanitary Napkins.** Small, **25c**; medium, **30c**; large **35c** doz.
K—12818. **Tomato Emeries.** **10c.**
K—12819. **Nickeled Skirt or Trouser Hangers.** **10c** each; 3 for **25c.**
K—12820. **Heart-Shaped Emery.** **10c** each.
K—12821. **Folding Nickeled Coat Hangers.** **10c** each; 3 for **25c.**
K—12822. **Linen Corset Laces.** 5 yards, **6c**; 8 yds., **9c**; 10 yds., **12c** ea.
K—12823. **Glass-Headed Toilet Pins.** 100 in paper, **5c** paper.
K—12824. **West's Electric Hair Curlers.** Set of 5, **25c.**
K—12825. **Asbestos Iron Holder.** **5c** each.
K—12826. **Lisle Elastic.** Black or white. 1/4 in., **7c** yd.; 3/8 in., **8c**; 1/2 in., **9c**; 5/8 in., **10c**; 3/4 in., **12c**; 7/8 in., **14c**; 1 in., **15c.**
K—12827. **Gimbels Natural Hair Nets.** Blonde, light brown, medium brown, dark brown, black, auburn. **15c** each, 2 for **25c**; **20c** each, 3 for **50c**; **25c** each, 3 for **65c.** White or gray all-over nets, **25c** each.
K—12828. **Absorbent Cotton.** 2 oz., **10c.** 4, **15c.** 8, **25c.** 16 oz., **40c.**
K—12829. **Gimbels Mercerized Lingerie Tape.** 12 yard piece. White, pink, blue. **10c** piece. 3 pieces, **25c.**
K—12830. **Assortment of Colored Pins.** **12c** cube.
K—12831. **Lisle Togards.** Sizes for men, women, children. **10c** pair.
K—12832. **Grip-Fast Sh'rt Waist Belt:** **10c** each.
K—12833. **Strawberry Emery.** **5c.**
K—12834. **Mercerized Corset Laces.** 5 yds., **10c**: 8, **15c**; 10 yds., **20c.**
K—12835. **Alcohol Lamp for Curlers.** Nickel plated. **50c.**
K—12836. **Double Silk Serge Belting.** Black, white, gray. 10 yards to piece. 7/8 inch wide, **75c**; 1 1/4 inch, **$1.00.** **8c** and **9c** yard.
K—12837. **Clark's O. N. T. Darning Cotton.** Black, white, tan, gray. 45 yards, 2 spools for **5c**; **25c** dozen.
K—12838. **French Mercerized Darning Cotton.** Black or white. **5c.**
K—12839. **Bone Tatting Shuttles.** **10c** each.

New York — Gimbel Brothers — Philadelphia

128

Needfuls from the Gimbel Notion Departments

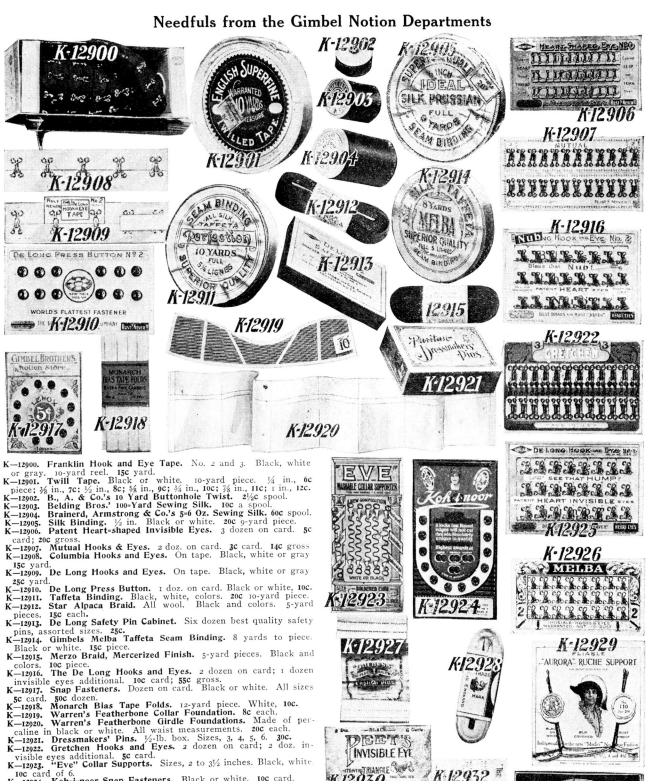

K—12900. **Franklin Hook and Eye Tape.** No. 2 and 3. Black, white or gray. 10-yard reel. **15c** yard.

K—12901. **Twill Tape.** Black or white. 10-yard piece. ¼ in., **6c** piece; ⅜ in., **7c**; ½ in., **8c**; ⅝ in., **9c**; ¾ in., **10c**; ⅞ in., **11c**; 1 in., **12c**.

K—12902. **B., A. & Co.'s 10 Yard Buttonhole Twist.** 2½c spool.

K—12903. **Belding Bros.' 100=Yard Sewing Silk.** 10c a spool.

K—12904. **Brainerd, Armstrong & Co.'s 5=6 Oz. Sewing Silk.** 60c spool.

K—12905. **Silk Binding.** ½ in. Black or white. **20c** 9-yard piece.

K—12906. **Patent Heart=shaped Invisible Eyes.** 3 dozen on card. **5c** card; **20c** gross.

K—12907. **Mutual Hooks & Eyes.** 2 doz. on card. **3c** card. **14c** gross.

K—12908. **Columbia Hooks and Eyes.** On tape. Black, white or gray **15c** yard.

K—12909. **De Long Hooks and Eyes.** On tape. Black, white or gray **25c** yard.

K—12910. **De Long Press Button.** 1 doz. on card. Black or white, **10c**.

K—12911. **Taffeta Binding.** Black, white, colors. **20c** 10-yard piece.

K—12912. **Star Alpaca Braid.** All wool. Black and colors. 5-yard pieces. **15c** each.

K—12913. **De Long Safety Pin Cabinet.** Six dozen best quality safety pins, assorted sizes. **25c**.

K—12914. **Gimbels Melba Taffeta Seam Binding.** 8 yards to piece. Black or white. **15c** piece.

K—12915. **Merzo Braid, Mercerized Finish.** 5-yard pieces. Black and colors. **10c** piece.

K—12916. **The De Long Hooks and Eyes.** 2 dozen on card; 1 dozen invisible eyes additional. **10c** card; **55c** gross.

K—12917. **Snap Fasteners.** Dozen on card. Black or white. All sizes **5c** card. **50c** dozen.

K—12918. **Monarch Bias Tape Folds.** 12-yard piece. White, **10c**.

K—12919. **Warren's Featherbone Collar Foundation.** 8c each.

K—12920. **Warren's Featherbone Girdle Foundations.** Made of percaline in black or white. All waist measurements. **20c** each.

K—12921. **Dressmakers' Pins.** ½-lb. box. Sizes, 3, 4, 5, 6. **30c**.

K—12922. **Gretchen Hooks and Eyes.** 2 dozen on card; 2 doz. invisible eyes additional. **5c** card.

K—12923. **"Eve" Collar Supports.** Sizes, 2 to 3½ inches. Black, white **10c** card of 6.

K—12924. **Koh=i=noor Snap Fasteners.** Black or white. **10c** card.

K—12925. **De Long Invisible Hooks and Eyes.** Two dozen on card. Rust proof. Black or white. **10c** a card; **55c** a gross.

K—12926. **Gimbels Melba Hooks and Invisible Eyes.** Two dozen on card. Black or white. **5c** a card; six sizes, **25c**.

K—12927. **Duchess English Pins.** All brass, solid headed. 300 pins in paper, **5c**; 6 for **25c**.

K—12928. **Dutch Linen Average Tape.** White. Szs., 000 to 10, **10c** pc.

K—12929. **Aurora Ruche Support.** Made of fine silk covered wire. Black or white. **10c** a card; 3 cards, **25c**.

K—12930. **Peet's Invisible Eyes.** 2 dozen in package. **5c**. Peet's Hooks and Invisible Eyes. 2 dozen in package. **10c**.

K—12931. **Warren's W. W. Silk Covered Wire Ruche Support.** 3 yards on card. Black or white. **10c** a card; 3 for **25c**.

K—12932. **Prym's Dress Fastener.** 1 doz. on card. Black or white, **10c**.

K—12933. **Warren's Silk Covered Featherbone.** Black or white. 12 yards to box. **$1.00**.

Gimbels Paris, London and American Style Book

Why We Recommend *Priestley's* English Dress Goods

Because they can be relied upon to give absolute satisfaction to the wearer. They are made from the most excellent materials, the best Australian wool and finest silk being used in their manufacture. The weave is always as firm and durable as the style of fabric permits. The dye is pure, rich unfading black. The prices range from figures to meet modest means to those for the wealthy. There are smooth goods, rough goods, dull fabrics, lustrous fabrics, light cloths and heavy cloths, both in plain and fancy effects, also many of their broché (brocade) and moire weaves which will be popular this season.

Priestley "Cravenette" English Cloths

Every fibre of the yarn is made rain repellent without the use of rubber. Every ounce of yarn used in the weaving of the cloth and every particle of dye used is the best in quality that can be obtained, and the cloth will protect the wearer in a rain or snow storm.

Come in Black and colors, in a variety of mixtures.

This circular registered trade-mark is stamped on the back of every yard of cloth, therefore must appear inside of garments made from them, and a silk Priestley "Cravenette" label is also sewed at the collar or elsewhere on the garment.

Samples gladly sent upon request, only be specific as to color or colors and state about what price you wish to pay so we can submit the right kind of samples.

Buttons, Braids and Dress Trimmings

While we illustrate only Buttons, and of those only the ones in the greatest demand, we have at both the Philadelphia and New York Stores the finest assortments of braids, dress trimmings, buttons, etc., etc.
Write us for anything in these lines wanted, being as definite as possible regarding your requirements, and we will take special pains to serve you.

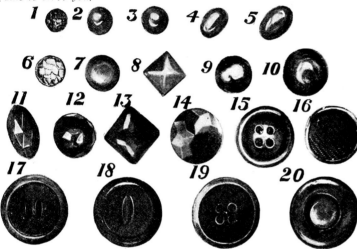

No. 1. Crystal Ball Button. In leading shades. 5/16 inch across. 15c dozen.
No. 2. White Roman Pearl Ball Shape Button. Glass shank. 3/16 inch, 15c. dozen. 5/16 inch, 20c dozen. 7/16 inch, 25c dozen. 1/2 inch, 30c. 5/8 inch, 40c a dozen.
No. 3. Best Quality White Roman Pearl Ball Button. Glass shank. 1/4 inch, 45c. 5/16 inch, 50c. 1/2 inch, 65c dozen.
No. 4. Best Quality White Roman Pearl Button. Olive shape. Glass shank. 7/16 inch, 55c. 1/2 inch, 75c. 9/16 inch, 85c dozen.
No. 5. White Roman Pearl Barrel Button. Glass shank. 3/8 inch, 35c. 7/16 inch, 40c. 1/2 inch, 45c dozen.
No. 6. White Crystal Ball Button. 1/4 inch, 12c. 3/8 inch, 15c. 1/2 inch, 25c. 9/16 inch, 35c dozen.
No 7. Gallalith Ball Button. Black or white. 1/4 inch, 12c. 3/8 inch, 15c. 1/2 inch, 25c. 9/16 inch, 35c. 11/16 inch, 60c. 7/8 inch, 90c dozen.
No. 8. Square Gallalith Button. Black or white. 1/2 inch, 20c. 9/16 inch, 30c. 7/8 inch, 65c. 1 1/16 inch, 85c dozen.
No. 9. Ball-Shape Metal Button. In gun-metal. Bright mat gold or nickel. 5/16 inch, 12c. 3/8 inch, 15c. 9/16 inch, 20c. 3/4 inch, 30c. 7/8 inch, 40c dozen.
No. 10. Half Ball-Shape Ivory Button. Light gray, tan or brown. 5/8 inch, 40c. 1 inch, 75c dozen.
No. 11. Olive-Shape Jet Button. 9/16 inch, 15c. 11/16 inch, 25c. 7/8 inch, 35c. 1 1/16 inch, 45c dozen.
No. 12. Jet Ball Button. 1/2 inch, 20c. 9/16 inch, 30c. 5/8 inch, 40c. 11/16 inch, 50c dozen.
No. 13. Square Jet Button. 9/16 inch, 25c. 11/16 inch, 40c. 7/8 inch, 50c. 1 1/16 inch, 65c dozen.
No. 14. Jet Button. 9/16 inch, 20c. 11/16 inch, 25c. 7/8 inch, 35c. 1 1/16 inch, 40c. 1 1/4 inch, 55c dozen.
No. 15. Tan Horn Button. 4 hole. 5/8 inch, 25c. 3/4 inch, 35c. 7/8 inch, 50c. 1 1/8 inch, 65c. 1 1/4 inch, 85c. 1 1/2 inch, $1.00 dozen.
No. 16. Self-Shank Black Rubber Button. 5/8 inch, 15c. 3/4 inch, 20c. 1 inch, 35c. 1 1/8 inch, 50c. 1 1/4 inch, 65c. 1 1/2 inch, 85c. 1 3/4 inch, $1.10 a dozen.
No. 17. Ivory Button. In black, white, navy, dark green, light or dark grey, tan, medium or dark brown. 5/8 inch, 20c. 3/4 inch, 35c. 7/8 inch, 35c. 1 inch, 45c. 1 1/8 inch, 50c. 1 1/4 inch, 75c a dozen.
No. 18. Fish Eye Black Rubber Button. 1/2 inch, 10c. 5/8 inch, 15c. 3/4 inch, 20c. 7/8 inch, 30c. 1 inch, 35c. 1 1/8 inch, 45c. 1 1/4 inch, 75c a dozen.
No. 19. Black Rubber Button. 1/2 inch, 10c. 5/8 inch, 15c. 3/4 inch, 20c. 7/8 inch, 25c. 1 1/8 inch, 30c. 1 1/4 inch, 50c. 1 1/2 inch, 75c a dozen.
No. 20. Ivory Button. In navy, dark green, light or dark grey, tan, brown. 5/8 inch, 20c. 7/8 inch, 45c. 1 1/8 inch, 60c a dozen.

No. 22. White Pearl Button. Best quality. Shelf shank. 1/8 inch, 18c. 1/4 inch, 25c a dozen.
No. 23. White Pearl Button. Cup shape. 1/8 inch, 14c. 1/4 inch, 22c. 3/8 inch, 25c. 1/2 inch, 30c a dozen.
No. 24. White Fresh Water Pearl Button. 2 or 4 hole. 1/4 inch, 1/2 inch, 5/8 inch across. 5c a dozen.
No. 25. White Ocean Pearl. 4 hole. 1/4 inch across. 10c a dozen.
No. 26. Fancy Pearl Self-Shank Button. 3/16 inch, 20c. 3/8 inch, 30c. 1/2 inch, 40c a dozen.
No. 27. White Pearl Button. Wire shank. 1/2 inch, 35c. 3/8 inch, 55c. 7/8 inch, 85c. 1 inch, $1.10 a dozen.
No. 28. White Pearl Self-Shank Button. 1/2 inch, 50c. 3/4 inch, 75c. 7/8 inch, $1.00. 1 inch, $1.35 a dozen.
No. 29. White Pearl Fish-Eye Button. 1/2 inch, 30c. 3/4 inch, 50c. 7/8 inch, 75c. 1 inch, 95c. 1 1/8 inch, $1.25 a dozen.
No. 30. White Pearl Button. 1/2 inch, 30c. 3/4 inch, 50c. 7/8 inch, 75c. 1 inch, 95c. 1 1/8 inch, $1.35 a dozen.
No. 31. White Cotton Crochet Button. 1/4 inch, 20c. 3/8 inch, 25c. 1/2 inch, 30c. 3/4 inch, 40c. 7/8 inch, 50c a dozen.
No. 32. White Cotton Crochet Ball Button. 3/16 inch, 12c. 1/4 inch, 15c. 3/8 inch, 20c. 1/2 inch, 30c. 5/8 inch, 40c a dozen.
No. 33. White Cotton Crochet Button. 1/4 inch, 15c. 3/8 inch, 20c. 1/2 inch, 25c. 5/8 inch, 30c. 7/8 inch, 50c a dozen.
No. 34. Black Satin Button. 1/4 inch, 6c. 3/8 inch, 7c. 1/2 inch, 8c. 5/8 inch, 10c. 3/4 inch, 15c. 7/8 inch, 20c. 1 inch, 25c a dozen.
No. 35. Silk Crochet Button. Black or white. 1/2 inch, 25c. 1 1/8 inch, 50c a dozen.
No. 36. Satin Ball Button. Black or white. 1/2 inch, 45c. 3/4 inch, 65c. 1 inch, 75c a dozen.

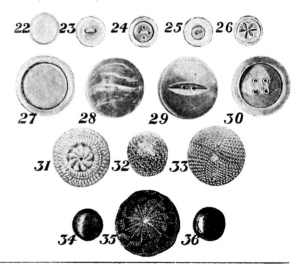

Chiffon Cloth. White, black, pink, light blue, lavender, navy, green, brown and all good colors in season. $1.00 and $1.50 a yard.

Cotton Nets. 72 inches wide. White, 50c, 75c, $1.00 a yard. Black, 90c a yard.
Silk Nets. White or black, 42 inches wide, $1.00 and $1.50 a yard. Black, 72 inches wide, $1.65 and $2.25 a yard.
Silk Net. White. 72 inches wide. $2.50 and $2.75 a yard.

New York — Gimbel Brothers — Philadelphia

The Gimbel Stores Lead in Black Dress Goods

The Gimbel Black Dress Goods are gathered with special care from the leading manufacturers of Europe and America. Nothing but the best is allowed in these stocks, which include all staple and newest weaves. The scientific dyes insure good, lasting black. The prices are so reasonable as to amaze you if you have never before ordered from Gimbels. Samples of all but bordered goods furnished upon request.

Black All-Wool Batiste. Made of fine, all-wool yarns, plain weave, light weight and dull finish. 36 to 42 inches wide. **50c, 75c, $1.00, $1.25 and $1.50 yard.**

Black All-Wool Crepes. Made of fine, soft spun yarns in light weight. Dull finish and deep shade of black. 36 to 42 inches wide. **50c, 75c, $1.00 and $1.25 yard.**

Black Silk and Wool Crepes. Made with silk warp and wool filling. Fine crinkle weave. Light weight and rich dull finish. 40 to 44 inches wide. **$1.25, $1.50 and $2.00 yard.**

Black All-Wool Henriettas. Made of fine all-wool yarns, plain and smooth weaves, medium weight and lustrous finish. 36 to 42 inches wide. **50c, 75c, $1.00, $1.25 and $1.50 yard.**

Black Silk and Wool Henriettas. Made with silk warp and wool filling, plain weave, medium weight, rich lustrous finish. 40 to 44 inches wide. **$1.00, $1.25, $1.50, $2.00 and $2.50 yard.**

Black Silk and Wool Melrose. Made with silk warp and wool filling, fine crepe weave, light weight and rich dull finish. 40 to 42 inches wide. **$1.25, $1.50 and $1.75 yard.**

Black All-Wool Poplins. Made of all-wool yarns, firmly twisted, plain fine cord weave. Dress and tailor weights. Dull finish. 40 to 54 inches wide. **75c, $1.00, $1.25, $1.50 and $2.00 yard.**

Black Silk and Wool Poplins. Made with silk warp and wool filling, fine cord weave, medium weight and lustrous finish. 40 to 42 inches wide. **$1.00, $1.25, $1.50, $2.00 and $2.50 yard.**

Black Tussah Crepes. Made of mohair and wool yarns, fine crepe weave, light weight, lustrous finish. 40 inches wide. **$1.00, $1.25, $1.50 and $2.00 yard.**

Black French Tussah Serges. Made of all-wool yarns, fine twill weave, medium weight, rich dull finish. 36 to 50 inches wide. **50c, 75c, $1.00, $1.25, $1.50, $2.00, $2.50, $2.75, and $3.00 yard.**

Black Worsted Serges. Made of hard twisted all-wool yarns, medium and coarse twill weave, medium weight, dull finish, very serviceable. 36 to 54 inches wide. **50c, 75c, $1.00, $1.25, $1.50, $2.00, $2.50 and $3.00 yard.**

Black Gabardines. Made of all-wool yarns, plain fine twill weave, dress and tailor weights, rich dull finish. 42 to 54 inches wide. **$1.00, $1.50, $2.00, $2.50, $3.00 and $3.50 yard.**

Black Satin Prunellas. Made of all-wool yarns, plain weave, medium weight, lustrous, unspotable finish. 42 to 50 inches wide. **$1.00, $1.25, $1.50 and $2.00 yard.**

Black Satin Soliel. Made of all-wool yarns, plain small cord weave, permanent lustrous finish. 42 to 44 inches wide. **$1.00, $1.25, $1.50 and $2.00 yard.**

Black Broadcloths. Made of fine Australian wool, plain weave, light and medium weights, rich lustrous finish. 50 to 54 inches wide. **$1.00, $1.25, $1.50, $2.00, $2.50, $3.00, $3.50, $4.00, $5.00 and $6.00 yard.**

Black Silk Marquisettes. Made of fine spun, all-silk yarns, plain and stripe weaves, transparent, light weight. 40 to 42 inches wide. **$1.00, $1.25 and $1.50 yard.**

Black Silk Voiles. Made of all-silk yarns, fine plain weave, transparent, light weight. 40 inches wide. **$1.00, $1.25 and $1.50 yard.**

Black Silk Grenadines. Made of all-silk yarns, plain, stripe and figured weaves, transparent, light weight. 40 to 42 inches wide. **50c, 75c, $1.00, $1.25, $1.50, $2.00 and $2.50 yard.**

Black Silk Crepe de Chines. Made of fine grade, all-silk yarns, fine indistinct crepe weave, very rich finish. 40 to 42 inches wide. **$1.25, $1.50, $2.00, $2.50 and $3.00 yard.**

Plain Flannels of Merit

Woven and Wash Flannels. Part wool and cotton; combinations, stripes and embroidered dots of figured effects in grey, tan, pink, sky blue, marine blue, cadet or cream grounds. For waists, kimonos, house gowns and children's wear. 27 to 32 inches. **25c to 50c yard.**

White Skirting Flannels. Part cotton. 27 inches wide, 25c, 30c, 37½c, 40c. All wool, 50c, 60c, 65c. Part cotton, 31 inches, 50c to 75c. All wool, 31 inches, 75c. Part cotton, 36 inches, 50c, 60c, 65c. All wool, 36 inches, 65c, 75c, 90c, $1 yard.

An All-Wool Crepe-Weave Flannel with Silk shirts and babies' wear; thoroughly shrunken. 31 Finish. In cream only. Excellent for waists, inches wide, cream, **$1.00 yard.**

Cream Suiting Flannel. Soft chamois cloth finish. For suits, wraps or coats. 54 inches wide. **$1.00 and $2.00 yard.**

French Twilled Flannels. Medium weight, all wool, soft suede finish; new colorings. For waists, sacques, housegowns, children's wear. 27 inches. **60c yard.**

Silk Warped Flannels. Cream. The best material for infant's skirts, 31 inches wide, 85c yard. 36 inches wide, **$1.50.**

A New Taffeta-Weight Wash Flannel. In light and medium shades, with contrasting stripe and plaids. 32 inches wide. **37½c yard.**

Wash Flannels. Imported English Viyella flannels. Unexcelled as to wear and laundering qualities. Combination stripe and plaids: two and three-toned effects. 31 inches, 68c. Cream, 44 inches, **$1.35 yard.**

Embroidered Flannels

The embroidery work illustrated is on fine quality cream white flannel 33 inches wide or deep, the weight of flannel running according to price. The seams are 1 to 1¼ inches deep. Some of the scalloped edges are worked on the double edge of flannel, forming a narrow hem, making it very durable. It requires 1½ to 1¾ yards of flannel for an infant's petticoat, and from 2 to 2¼ yards for a woman's petticoat.

We do not sample embroidered flannels as statement above tells about them and the illustrations hereon show the pattern and price a yard. Order by number.

Suitings and Coatings

Cream and White Washable Serge. Suitable for suits, dresses and separate skirts; thoroughly shrunken. 36 inches wide. **60c yard.**

Double-faced Eiderdown. For women's, children's and infant's coats. Cream only. 36 inches. **$1.10 and $1.25 a yard.**

Great Eiderdown Coating. An exceptionally fine quality. Striped effects. 52 inches. **$1.75 a yard.**

Cream Eiderdown. Beautiful chinchilla finish. 52 inches. **$2.25 a yard.**

(Illustration diamond with garment samples labeled: K-13100-85c, K-13101-50c, K-13102-75c, K-13103-65c, K-13104-$1.00, K-13105-75c, K-13106-90c, K-13107-$1.00, K-13108-50c)

$16.00 Outfit of Infant's First Short Clothes. Special for $14.75.

3 Vests @ 50c	$1.50
3 Bands @ 50c	1.50
3 Nainsook Morning Dresses @ 50c	1.50
2 Nainsook Dresses @ $1.00	2.00
1 Nainsook Dress	2.25
3 Nainsook Petticoats on waist @ 50c	1.50
2 Nainsook Petticoats @ $1.00	2.00
3 Flannel Petticoats @ 50c	1.50
1 Flannel Petticoat	1.00
3 pair Stockings @ 25c	.75
1 pair Soft Sole Shoes	.50
25 pieces	**$16.00**

$6.70 Outfit, Special for $5.95

2 Vests @ 25c	$0.50
2 Bands @ 12½c	.25
2 Night Slips @ 25c	.50
2 Night Petticoats @ 25c	.50
2 Day Slips @ 50c	1.00
2 Flannel Petticoats @ 50c	1.00
1 Pretty Yoke Slip	.85
1 Nainsook Petticoat	.50
1 Outing Flannel Sacque	.25
2 Bibs @ 5c	.10
1 Nursery Pad	.25
1 Dozen Hemmed Bird's-eye Diapers	1.00
19 pieces	**$6.70**

Colored and Black Silks

The Gimbel Silk Stores maintain a most complete variety of the in-demand silks at all seasons. The vast buying power of our three great stores enables us to practically have first choice of the best silks that Europe and America supply, and the quantity we are able to buy brings lowest prices. Daily adding to the color assortments of plain silks of every description insures our being able to be reasonably sure of supplying all your needs in silks.

In writing for samples you will serve your own interests by specifying as nearly as possible the colors and approximate price you wish, also if plain or fancy. Indefinite requests, such as "Please send samples of your new summer silks" cannot be filled, and only consume time in requiring us to write back for more specific information.

BLACK SILKS.

It is practically certain that black silks will be in vogue for a long time to come.
Black Faille Francaise, 35 inch, $1.50, $2.00 and $3.00 a yard.
Black Satin Duchesse, 35 inch, $1.00, $1.25, $1.50, $2.00, $2.50 and $3.00 a yard.
Black Crepe de Chine, 40 inch, $1.00, $1.35, $1.50, $2.00, $2.50 and $3.00 a yard.
Black Crepe Meteor, 40 to 42 inches, $1.25, $1.50, $2.00, $3.00 and $3.50 a yard.
Black Satin Messaline, 35 and 36 inches, 85c, $1.00, $1.25, $1.50 and $2.00 a yard.
Black Taffetas, 35 to 40 inches, $1.00, $1.25, $1.50, $2.00 and $3.00 a yard.
Black Japanese Silks, 27 inches, 50c to $1.00 a yard; 36 inches, 75c, 85c, $1.00, $1.25 and $1.50 a yard.
Black Peau de Cygne, 35 inches, 85c, $1.00 and $1.25 a yard.
Black Peau de Soie, 35 inches, $1.00, $1.25, $1.50 and $2.00 a yard.

SPECIAL.

Black Bathing Suit Satins and Taffetas.
35-inch Satin, $1.25 a yard.
30-inch Satin, $1.50 and $2.00 a yard.
35-inch Taffeta, $1.50 a yard.

VARIOUS COLORED SILKS.

In the new spring and summer weaves and colors.
Satin Messaline, 35 inches, 85c, $1.00, $1.25 and $1.50 a yard.
Chiffon Taffeta Silks. Plain or changeable. 35 inches. $1.25, $1.50 and $2.00 a yard.
Satin Imperial, 35 inches, $1.50 and $2.00 a yard.
Silk Poplins, 40 inches, $1.00, $1.25, $1.50, $2.00 and $3.00 a yard.
Besides many other plain silk weaves.

CREPE DE CHINES AND CREPE WEAVES.

Some of the most important silk weaves of the season.
36-inch Crepe de Chine, $1.00 a yard.
39-inch Crepe de Chine, $1.25 a yard.
40-inch Crepe de Chine, $1.25, $1.50, $2.00 and $2.50 a yard.
40-inch Crepe Meteor, $1.25, $2.00 and $3.00 a yard.
36-inch Canton Crepe, $1.00 a yard.
40-inch Crinkle Crepe, $1.00 a yard.

SILK CHIFFONS AND SILK VOILES.

Chiffon Cloth, double width, 75 to $1.50 a yard.
Crepe Chiffon, 40 inches, $1.00 and $1.50 a yard. Both in a very great range of colors, also black.
40-inch Flowered Chiffons, white grounds, $1.50 to $2.50 a yard.
40-inch Pekin Striped Chiffons, $1.50 a yard.
Beautiful New Bordered Chiffons and Tinsel Effects. These are not sampled. Prices on application.

WASHABLE OR SHIRTING SILKS.

White grounds with colored stripes. Many in rich contrasting satin stripes.
36-inch Imported Striped Habutai, 50c a yard.
32-inch Striped Tub Silks, 75c, 85c and $1.00 a yard.
32-inch Satin Striped Wash Silks, 85c, $1.00 and $1.25 a yard.
36-inch All White Wash Silks, 50c, 65c, 75c, 85c, $1.00, $1.25, $1.50 and $2.00 a yard. All of these were hand-made in Japan.

FOULARD SILKS.

The favorite American Summer Silks in new styles and colors.
23 inches, in dots and designs, 85c and $1.00 a yard.
40 inches, in many styles and colors, $1.00, $1.50 and $2.00 a yard.
40 inches, Fleur de Soie, $1.00 to $2.50 a yard.

WHITE SILKS.

In addition to the White Japanese Wash Silks mentioned above, and also white crepes, there are:
35-inch White Satins, at $1.00, $1.25 and $1.50 a yard.
35-inch White Satin Irene, at $2.00 a yard.
35 to 40-inch Rich White Italian Satins, $2.50, $3.00 and $4.00 a yard.
35-inch White Brocade Satin, $1.50 to $2.50 a yd.
Besides, practically every silk made in black or colors may also be had in white.

NOVELTY SILKS.

Roman Striped Silk, for trimmings and combinations, at $1.00 to $2.50 a yard.
35-inch Striped Satin Messalines, $1.00 and $1.35 a yard.
35-inch Striped Taffeta Silks, $1.00 and $1.50 a yard.
Printed Crepes in a great variety of styles and prices. Write for prices.

VELVETS—VELVETEENS—CORDUROY.

Full line of Plain or Paon Velvets, also Chiffon Velvets and Pannes, for dress trimming or millinery. We do not cut panne or chiffon velvet on the bias.
18-inch Panne Velvets, new spring shades, $1.25 a yard.
White Washable Corduroy, 27 inches, $1.00 to $2.00 a yard.
Black Velveteens, 23 to 27 inches, $1.00 to $3.00 a yard.

Our Silk Chiefs journey to England, France, Italy and Switzerland in the search for that which is newest in style and best in value. They buy directly from the mills and the silks are shipped in bond straight to us—so we are absolutely first hands after the making.

THE LOWER PRICE SILKS
BLACK SILKS—SUBWAY STORE.

We have never known of such staple qualities of Black Silks at these exceptionally low prices. Mostly all double width.

Duchesse Messaline, 35 inches. Heavy body and high lustre, 75c a yard.
Black Habutai. Good weight. Serviceable quality. 27 and 36 inches. 50c to $1.25 a yard.
Black Peau de Soie. Wonderful wearing qualities. 35 in. 90c to $1.35 a yard.
Black Messaline. Fine weave. Various widths. 38c to $1.00 a yard.
Black Duchesse Satin. One of the best wearing weaves on the market. Quality exceptionally heavy at these prices, 35 to 40 inches. 85c to $1.50 a yard.

COLORED SILKS—SUBWAY STORES.

Chiffon Pongees. Full assortment of colors and black. A nice, soft, draping material, a little cotton with the silk. 26 inches. 25c a yard.
Crepe in a Heavy Weight. Suitable for street and evening wear. Full yard wide. All good colors and black. A little cotton mixed in. 38c a yard.
Striped Shirting Silks. Part cotton. 32 inches. Good patterns and of serviceable quality. 38c a yard.
Messalines. In most any good shade and black. Heavy weight. 18 inches. 38c a yard.
One of the Best Assortments of Striped Shirting Silks to be Found. Durable qualities. 32 and 36 inches. 75c to $1.00.
White Habutais. 36 inches. 38c to $1.25 a yard.
Messalines. Big line of colors. 35 inches. 85c. a yard.
Chiffon Pongee. 36 inches. A little cotton mixed in. 25c a yard.

SILK SPECIALS—SUBWAY STORES.

Black Chion Pongees. Part cotton. 15c a yard. Value, 25c. 24 inches.
Striped Shirting Silks. Part cotton. 38c a yard. Value, 50c. 32 and 36 inches.
Staple Black Silks. 35 inches. 85c for $1.00 black Messaline.
85c for $1.00 Messaline Duchesse. 35 inches.
$1.00 for $1.25 35-inch Satin Duchesse.
$1.35 for $1.75 40-inch Colored Crepe Meteor.

In the American markets we placed big orders for silks when prices dropped to lowest level at commencement of European War believing they would quickly advance, which they did. Our foresight is your gain in buying silks

New York — Gimbel Brothers — Philadelphia

All That Is Fashionable in Dress Goods
for Spring 1915

Oh, yes. We have them, despite war and the other conditions that have a tendency to make poor assortments in the average store. Anticipating the scarcity in foreign dress goods, we placed orders early for staple fabrics, and can promise an excellent variety of weaves and colors at the very low prices which prevailed last season.

Quality is first consideration in Gimbel dress goods, but good qualities must always be backed by the correct style and proper colors. This season plain weaves are most desirable, owing to the change in fashion. All our goods were selected with a complete knowledge of style as well as fabric. Being in constant communication with our European offices and close to all home designers enables us to keep in touch with the latest modes at all times and make best selection of fabrics. Buying dress goods at Gimbels is as safe as Government bonds. Money back for the asking if for any reason we are at fault.

We invite you to write for samples. State fully and clearly what you desire and about the price you wish to pay, also give color idea. Your request will be handled by expert service, making it an easy matter to make selection.

The Most Desirable Fabrics for Street Wear Include:

All Wool French Serges.
   "   "   Imperial Serges.
   "   "   Storm Serges.
   "   "   French Poplin.
   "   "   Satin Prunella.
   "   "   Gabardine.
   "   "   Broadcloth.
   "   "   Nuns' Veiling.
   "   "   Crepe Poplin.
Covert Suitings.
Fancy Checks.
Mixed Suitings.
    For Street and Reception Wear.
Silk and Wool Poplin.
Silk and Wool Crepe.
Other Sheer Silk and Wool Fabrics.
Cream Fabrics will predominate for seashore and summer resorts.
Covert Cloths, Fancy Checks and Mixed Fabrics will also be very fashionable for top coats.

LEADING COLORS FOR SPRING.

Sand, Putty, Reseda, Stone Green, Marine, Navy, Belgium, Blue, Russian Green, Nutmeg, Taupe, Wistaria, Tan, Olive, New Brown, Silver, Gun-metal and combinations of black and white.

AN IDEA OF PRICES ON PLAIN COLOR FABRICS.

All Wool French Serges, 50c, 75c, $1.00 to $1.50 a yard.

All Wool Imperial Serges, $1.00, $1.25, $1.50 to $2.00 a yard.

All Wool Storm Serges, 50c, 75c, $1.00 to $1.50 a yard.

All Wool French Poplin, 75c, $1.00 to $2.00 a yard.

All Wool Satin Prunella, $1.00, $1.25, $1.50 a yard.

All Wool Gabardine, $1.00, $1.25, $1.50 to $2.00 and $3.00 a yard.

All Wool Albatross, 50c and 75c a yard.

All Wool Broadcloth, $1.00, $1.50, $2.00, $2.50 to $3.00 a yard.

All Wool Crepe Poplins, $1.00, $1.25, $1.50 to $2.00 a yard.

SILK AND WOOL FABRICS PREDOMINATE FOR SPRING AND SUMMER.

Like the birds returning after a dreary winter, silk and wool fabrics give us new pleasure each season. Old and new favorites are here in great variety.

Silk and Wool Poplins still hold first place on account of their rich lustrous beauty and good wearing qualities. Shown in the latest colors. 40 to 44 inches. $1.00, $1.25, $1.50 to $2.00 a yard.

Silk and Wool Crepe. Every season brings out new ideas in crepe effects. Always charming and pretty for street and reception wear. Beautiful new shades. 40 to 44 inches. $1.00, $1.25, $1.50 a yard.

Other silk and wool fabrics in great variety at very modest prices.

FANCY SUITINGS FOR WOMEN'S WEAR.

The Gimbel Stores are always noted for their great variety tailored suitings. This season Covert Cloths and Fancy Checks will predominate. Sand and Putty shades prevail in Covert Cloths. 54 inches. $1.25, $1.50, $2.00 and $3.00 a yard.

Check Suitings are to be had in great variety, in black and white and other combinations.

All Wool—42 to 54 inches 75c, $1.00, $1.25, $1.50 to $2.00 a yard.

Part Wool—42 inches, 38c, and 50c a yard.

Mixed Suitings. Various weaves, weights and qualities. 75c, $1.00, $1.25 and $1.50 a yard.

ALL WOOL SERGES.

In buying serges quality is always first consideration. A poor serge is a bad bargain at any price. All our serges are warranted for wear and fast color. Never better qualities or lower prices than this season. Taking advantage of unsettled conditions, we placed quantity orders at rock-bottom prices. Buying for three stores enables us to secure extra concessions. Our customers always receive the benefit. French Twills, Imperial Twills, Men Wear Weaves. All wool—36 inches, 50c a yard; 42 to 50 inches, 75c a yard; 50 to 54 inches, $1.00, $1.25, $1.50 to $2.00 yard.

<hr>

SPECIAL IN SERGE.

50-inch Storm Serge, 50c a yard. Not quite all wool, but excellent heavy quality. Will give splendid service. Suitable for tailored suits, dresses and separate skirts. Colors: Navy, Russian Green, New Brown, Copenhagen Blue. Note the width, 50 inches.

<hr>

CREAM FABRICS.

Cream Fabrics are in greater demand than ever. The style was launched at the Florida Coast resorts in the late winter, and will be continued all through the spring and summer.

A great variety of the leading weaves in the Gimbel stocks.

All Wool Cream Serge, 50c, 75c and $1.00 a yd.

All Wool Nuns' Veiling, 50c, 75c a yard.

All Wool French Serge, 50c, 75c and $1.00 a yd.

All Wool Henrietta, 60c, 75c, and $1.00 a yd.

All Wool Gabardine, $1.00, $1.25 and $1.50 a yd.

All Wool Cream Coatings, $1.00, $1.25, $1.50 to $2.00 a yard.

All Wool Crepe Poplin, $1.00, $1.25, $1.50 a yd.

All Wool Broadcloth, $2.00, $2.50 and $3.00 a yard.

Silk and Wool Poplin, $1.00, $1.25 and $1.50 a yard.

Silk and Wool Crepe, $1.00, $1.25 and $1.50 a yard.

Silk and Wool Lansdowne, $1.25 a yard.

Other new weaves constantly arriving.

ALL WOOL FRENCH PRINTED CHALLIS.

The inspiration of these beautiful printings is taken from the flowers and the fruits. Only the genius and taste of the artist designers could account for their beauty. Purchasing before the war progressed enables us to have an excellent assortment.

Fine for children's wear. Wash beautifully. 50c, 60c and 65c a yard.

Gimbels Paris, London and American Style Book

The Neatest, Prettiest and Best of Wash Dress Fabrics

In the Gimbel Wash Dress Fabric Sections will be found an assortment of foreign and best "American Made" goods for season of 1915. The choice is larger, the materials are prettier than ever before and the prices, too, are very attractive. If you will compare our prices with those quoted by other houses we feel confident that the superiority of our values will be easily recognized. Fashion predicts this season the increased vogue of Voiles, Crepes and fine fancy woven fabrics of sheer, soft, clingy quality.

Samples of anything on these pages, except bordered and embroidered goods, will be furnished upon request, if you are definite as to colors, width and prices.

VOILES

The very best French, English and American makes, in plain shades, silk mixed and figured, printed, also woven stripes; an assortment without any really good thing missing and our prices are unchallenged.

Finest Imported Voiles. Made in England, and an extra fine cloth, the product of thoroughly expert weavers. For charming evening gowns. Plain colors, 40 inches wide. **50c a yard.**

Finest Imported Voile Effleur. In the most beautiful printed effects. Soft wool finish. 40 inches wide, **75c a yard**; 27 inches wide, **50c yard.**

Finest French and English Embroidered Voiles. White or tinted grounds with the most beautiful color combinations. Silk embroidery. **$1.00 to $1.50 a yard.**

Embroidered Swiss Voile. Made in Switzerland, the home of embroideries. White ground with colored embroidered figures. 38 inches wide. **75c to $1.00 a yard.**

Embroidered Costume Voiles. The largest stock to select from. White grounds with pretty colored embroidered figures. 38 inches wide. **75c to $2.00 a yard.**

Best Imported Voile Lisse. Woven colors, not printed. An excellent wearing fabric. 40 inches wide, **45c a yard**; 24 inches wide, **25c a yard.**

Woven Striped Dress Voiles. Various size stripes. Fast colors. 38 inches wide. **25c a yard.**

Black and White Striped Voiles. All size stripes, from whale bone to the awning stripes, so much in demand. 38 inches wide. **18c a yard.**

Printed Shadow Lace Voile. 38 inches wide. In the most beautiful styles. **35c a yard.**

Extra Fine Printed Costume Voiles. 38 inches wide. The largest stock to select from in the most beautiful color combinations. "American Made." Prettier than ever. **25c a yard.**

Fine Embroidered Voiles. Neat figures in dainty colors. 38 inches wide. **50c a yard.**

OTHER COTTON FABRICS

Silk Striped Crepe Dore. Imported. A beautiful fabric, soft and clingy, with silk stripes, in pretty shades for nice costumes. 36 inches wide. **$1.00 a yard.**

Silk and Cotton Crepe A Jour. Imported. The mixture of the silk with the fine cotton makes it a very attractive fabric. 36 to 38 inches. **90c a yard.**

Fine Embroidered Snowflakes and Crepes. 28 inches wide, **45c a yard**; 30 inches wide, **50c a yard.**

Embroidered English Novelties. White ground with colored embroidered dotted figures. 26 inches wide, **30c and 35c a yard.**

Fine Imported Swisses. Embroidered dots on white or tinted grounds. 32 inches wide. **50c to 75c a yard.**

Fine Printed Organdies. Newest designs. 38 inches wide. **28c a yard.**

New Printed Rice Cloth. Copies of the imported; white ground with pretty flower effects. 28 inches wide. **12½c a yard.**

New Empress Plisse. Fine crepy cloth with pretty printed flower effects. Need no ironing or starching. Fast colors. 27 inches wide. **12½c a yard.**

New Printed Dress Batistes. Extra fine quality, every piece fresh and new. Made for this season. A large assortment to select from. 29 inches wide. **12½c a yard.**

Silk and Cotton Chiffons. A mixture of silk with fine cotton. Lustrous as the all silk. In all the fashionable shades. 26 and 27 inches wide. **25c a yard.**

The "Suesine" Silk, also silk and cotton mixed. In prettiest shades made. 27 inches wide. **38c a yard.**

Mercerized Poplins. The yarn being mercerized before woven gives the material a highly silk lustre. Beautiful tints to select from. Street or evening shades. The wearing qualities of a poplin like these are unsurpassed. 27 inches wide. **25c a yard.**

GINGHAMS—SUITINGS

The best imported and the best American makes are represented here. Plain colors, checks, plaids, in the most striking effects. All new, made for season 1915.

D. & J. Anderson are known the world over as the best gingham makers. We carry a large assortment of their goods. 32 inches wide. **40c and 45c a yard.**

Wm. Anderson's Scotch Ginghams and Madrasses. 32 inches wide. **25c a yard.**

Fine American Zephyr Ginghams. 32 inches wide. Excellent styles. **25c a yard.**

Fine American Zephyr Ginghams. 32 inches wide. **15c and 18c a yard.** Called the rival of the 25c Scotch goods. Absolutely fast colors.

Best American Dress Ginghams. Best assortment. Plain stripes, checks and plaids. Fast colors. 27 inches wide. **12½c a yard.**

Apron Ginghams. The best standard makes. All size checks and colors. 27 inches wide. **6½c and 8c a yard.**

Percales. The very best made. The old reliable fabric, only improved in finish and colors. A wonderful assortment to select from. Full yard wide. **12½c a yard.**

Plain Colored Chambrays. In all the wanted shades. 27 and 32 inches wide. **6½c to 18c a yard.**

Crinkle Seersuckers. The very best makes. Good serviceable material for children's rompers and dresses. Need no starching or ironing. Absolutely fast colors. 27 inches wide. **12½c a yard.**

Buster Suiting. An ideal fabric for children's play room, for boy's suits, girl's dresses and house dresses where hard service is required. Made of double-twisted yarn and the colors are absolutely fast. The manufacturer guarantees them to be tub and sun-proof colors. No other fabric made, foreign or domestic, has such a guarantee back of it. This cloth has no equal. 32 inches wide. **18c a yard.**

Long Beach Suiting. White or sand color only. 35 inches wide. **25c a yard.**

Gabardines are among the new offering in Cotton Dress Goods. White, and all the most popular shades. Wool finish. 36 inches wide. **25c to 50c a yard.**

About Dress Linens

Maintaining as we do extensive buying establishments in Paris, London, Lyons and Berlin, our purchases are made direct from the best mills of France, Ireland, England, Belgium, Germany and Russia, the middleman's profit being eliminated. Our orders were placed abroad, before declaration of the war, and we had them shipped weeks ago, ready for our Spring and Summer Sale. There is scarcely anything in Dress Linens that we do not carry. Ramie, French, Irish, Linen Ratines, Russian Crashes, Motor Linens in Oyster, and in all the fashionable shades.

Prices have advanced considerably. We will give our patrons a chance to buy them at the low price.

36 to 45 inches wide....**30c to $1.50 a yard.**

Ramie Weave Linen Suiting. Every thread pure linen. 45 inches wide. **65c a yard.** Comes in the following colors: Belgium blue, Gettisburg gray, pink, navy, tuxedo brown, mulberry, catawba, Newport tan, Oregon green, distaria, heliotrope, light blue, oyster or black.

New York — Gimbel Brothers — Philadelphia

Beautiful Fabrics in White

Many of them delightfully soft and clingy, so especially adapted to the prevailing modes. WHITE will be the predominating fabric this coming season—for that matter, what warm season shall we ever have when dainty, cool white fabrics will not constitute the essential element of good taste and comfort? Crisp, sheer fabrics will have many admirers, but the tendency is now strongly toward the soft, snowy, clingy ones—so they predominate in the Gimbel stock. Most fastidious women like to make their own dainty underwear and that of their children, and to such many of the goods listed upon this page will be a real delight.

Voiles, Crepes, Negeux and Lace Lawns are all clingy fabrics.

In ordering samples mention kind of material, width and about the price you care to pay.

Bordered and Embroidered fabrics we do not sample.

Fine Embroidered Costume Voile. 38 inches wide. With beautiful embroidered figures, all new. From 60c to **$1.50** a yard.

Fine Embroidered Negeux—or Snowflake. These beautiful goods were made in Switzerland and represent the ability of the makers of that country to produce the most charming things in white fabrics. 40 inches wide. **$1.25** to **$1.50** a yard.

Embroidered French Grenadines. Extra fine sheer cloth. Open mesh. 40 inches wide. **$1.25** to **$1.50** a yard.

Embroidered Dress Voiles. The best and most complete stocks and the best French, Swiss and best American makes are represented here. Fine, sheer, clingy cloth, with handsome embroidered figures. 36 to 40 inches wide. **50c** to **$2.50** a yard.

Fine French Fancy Woven Voiles and Fancy Lace Cloths. Plain or embroidered. 38 to 44 inches wide. **75c** to **$2.50** a yard.

Fine Embroidered Voile. With handsome embroidered border. For effective costumes. Not sampled. 40 inches wide. **$1.95** a yard.

Plain Voiles. Fine collection of best foreign and American makes. 38 to 42 inches wide. Prices range from 18c to **$1.00** a yard.

New French Crepons. Those who want a delightful but inexpensive crepon will find it here. 38 to 42 inches wide. Fine goods at 50 and **75c** a yard.

Ratines. They were very scarce last season, in the height of the season, for skirts and very few had such a supply of them as Gimbels. We are equally prepared this year. French and American. 40 to 50 inches wide. **50c** and **$1.00** yard.

Dotted Swisses from Switzerland. Swiss Swisses are always dainty and beautiful and the ones mentioned here are unusually charming in fabric and patterns. 31 inches wide. Prices ranging from 40c to **65c** a yard.

Fine Piques. Big assortment and all fine value. Narrow, medium and wide **cords.** Various widths.

27 inches wide........20c to 60c yard.
36 inches wide......38c to $1.00 yard.

Mercerized Poplins. Made from fine grade mercerized yarn, so possess a fine silky lustre that will be permanent. 27 inches wide. 12½c to **35c** yard.

Suiting Linene. A cleanly bleached, closely woven fabric that makes up nicely. Also used for uniform suitings.

31 inches wide..........12½c a yard.
36 inches wide.............20 a yard.

Percales. The best American and imported goods. 32 inches to 36 inches wide. 12½c to **35c** yard.

Batiste. Pure white bleach. Several qualities. 38 inches wide, 12½c, 15c and 20c a yard. 45 inches wide, 25c to **75c** a yard.

Flaxons. This beautiful fabric is noted for its strength and durability, and is, therefore, in special demand for waists and suits and children's apparel. Possesses the real flax finish. 36 inches wide. 15c, 20c, 25c and **30c** a yard.

Fine Persian Lawn. Always among the most desirable white goods. In light and medium weights. 40 and 45 inches wide. 12½c to **35c** a yard.

Indian Head Linene. So much used for suiting purposes and is very desirable.

32 inches wide..........15c a yard.
36 inches wide..........18c a yard.
45 inches wide..........28c a yard.

Marvel Linon for Uniform Suitings. The nearest to au all linen in thread and finish. 36 inches wide. **15c** a yard.

Shirting Madrasses. A splendid collection, in 32-inch goods. 12½c to **50c** a yard.

Dress and Handkerchief Linens. Pure white and pure flax. We do not carry cotton mixed goods here. Excellent for children's clothes, men's and women's underwear, etc. A truly fine 36-inch handkerchief linen is quoted at **$1.50** a yard and thence down; prices range until they stop at 40c a yard.

In heavier than the handkerchief goods we have a line 45 inches, selling from 65c to **$1.00** a yard.

French Linen, 90 inches wide, **$1.50** a yard.

Belgium Ramie, 45 inches wide, **45c** a yard.
Special Irish Ramie, 36 inches wide, 30c a yd.

Here are a few items, great in value:

Corded Voiles, 38 inch..............25c a yard.
Corded Lace Cloth, 38 inch..........25c "
Petit Pois Voile, 38 inch...........25c "
Snowflake Grenadine, 38 inch.......25c "
Russian Cord Voile, 38 inch........25c "
Shadow Striped Voile, 38 inch......25c "
Embroidered Voile, 38 inch.........38c "
Lace Cloth Novelty, 38 inch........25c "
Cord Voile Raye, 38 inch...........25c "
Cord and Nub Voile, 38 inch........25c "
Fine Seed Voile, 38 inch...........25c "
Snowflake Voile, 38 inch...........25c "
French Organdie, 45 inch...........65c "
American Organdie, 40 inch..18c to 25c "

LONG CLOTHS AND NAINSOOKS BY THE PIECE.

These are made of specially high-count goods, meaning an unusual number of threads woven to the inch, and are "Made in America." In comparing prices, please note whether for 10-yard pieces or 12-yard pieces. Ours are all 12-yard pieces. Gimbel Long Cloths, extra soft finish so very desirable for home sewers.

Gimbel Special. 36-inch, 12-yard piece.....$1.00
No. B. 36-inch, 12-yard piece............ 1.25
No. C. 36-inch, 12-yard piece............ 1.50
No. XX. 36-inch, 12-yard piece........... 1.75
No. EE. 36-inch, 12-yard piece........... 2.00
Liberty Bell. 42-inch, 12-yard piece....... 2.25
No. 600. 42-inch, 12-yard piece........... 2.50

GIMBELS NAINSOOKS

No. H. 36-inch, 12 yards.................$1.50
No. 44. 36-inch, 12 yards................ 1.65
No. G. 36-inch, 12 yards................. 1.75
No. 55. 36-inch, 12 yards................ 2.00
Fine Messaline finish. 44-inch, 12 yards.... 2.50
Fine Sea Island. 42-inch, 12 yards........ 3.25

STAMPED
50¢
FINISHED
$5.50

K-13600

K-13601
$9.00

STAMPED 25¢

K-13602
$3.00

K-13603
STAMPED
50¢
FINISHED
$6.00

K-13604
2 YEAR STAMPED
75¢
4 YEAR STAMPED
85¢
6 YEAR STAMPED
$1.00
FINISHED
$7.00

K-13606
85¢

K-13607
40¢

50¢
STAMPED

K-13605
$5.00

K-13608
25¢

K-13613
$1.00 →

K-13614
$3.00
STAMPED
25¢

K-13609
25¢

K-13612
$1.50

K-13611
$1.50

K-13610
25¢

K-13616
25¢

K-13615
$1.75

Pretty Novelties from The Art Needlework Stores

For the illustrations, see opposite page.

K—13600. Royal Society Package. Containing a stamped and made-up dress of good quality linen finished lawn, including cotton to embroider. (Lace and ribbon not included.) Sizes, 6 months to 1 year. 50c. Finished model as illustrated, $5.50.

K—13601. Royal Society Package. Containing a stamped Princess Knickerbocker of nainsook, made up, with cotton to finish same, but without the lace and ribbon. Sizes 36, 38, 40, 42, $1.00. Finished model as illustrated. $9.00.

K—13602. Royal Society Package. Containing unmade doll's morning attire made of white lawn, chemise, combination, drawers, petticoat, long kimono, boudoir cap and bag, and cotton to finish same. 25c. Ribbon and lace not included. Finished model as illustrated, $3.00.

K—13603. Royal Society Package. Contains infant's stamped lawn dress, unmade. First size with cotton to finish same, 50c. Lace and ribbon not included. Finished model as illustrated, $6.00.

K—13604. Royal Society Package. Containing child's stamped lawn dress, made up with kilted skirt with deep hem, with cotton to finish same. Size, 2 years, 75c; 4 years, 85c; 6 years, $1.00. Finished model as illustrated, $7.00.

K—13605. Royal Society Package. Containing a stamped fine linen finished lawn unmade dressing sacque, with cotton to finish same, but without the trimming. 50c. Finished model as illustrated, $5.00. Matches cap, K—13614.

K—13606. Unmade Stamped Nightgown. On a good quality of nainsook. 85c.

K—13607. Unmade Stamped Corset Cover. On good quality of nainsook. 40c.

K—13608. Stamped All Linen Centerpiece. 18x18 inches. 25c.

K—13609. Stamped All Linen Centerpiece. 18x18 inches. 25c.

K—13610. Stamped All Linen Centerpiece. 18x18 inches. 25c.
The above three also in size 22x22, 35c; 27x27, 65c.

K—13611. Stamped Chemise. Made up of a very pretty silk-finish batiste, in pink, blue or white, with enough Heminway's silk to complete. Ribbon not included. $1.50.

K—13612. Stamped Combination. Unmade, on a very pretty silk finished batiste, in pink, blue or white, with enough Heminway's silk to complete. $1.50.

K—13613. Stamped Dressing Sacque and Boudoir Cap. Unmade on a very pretty French crepe white, with enough Heminway's silk to complete. $1.00 for set of two pieces. Trimmings not included.

K—13614. Royal Society Package. Containing a stamped made-up cap to match sacque K—13605, with cotton to finish same. 25c. Finished model as illustrated, $3.00.

K—13615. Stamped Night Gown. Unmade, on a very pretty silk-finish batiste, in pink, blue or white, with enough Heminways silk to complete. Without the ribbon. $1.75.

K—13616. Stamped All Linen Centerpiece. 18x18 inches. 25c

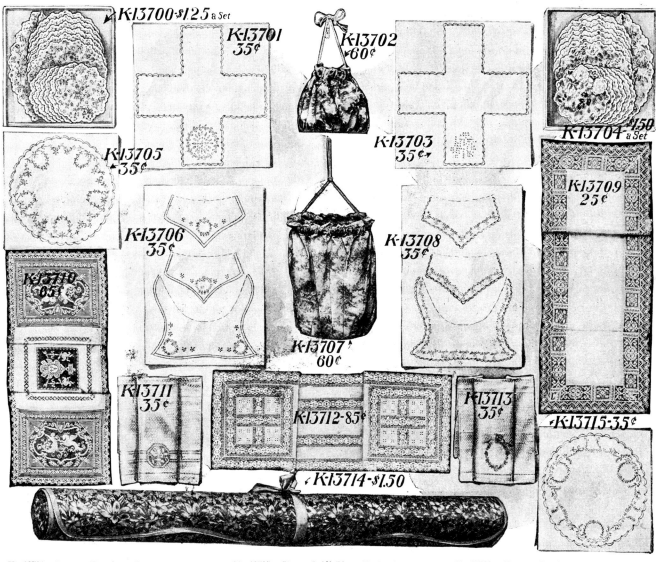

K—13700. Cretonne Luncheon Set. Pink or blue flowers. 13 pieces. Consisting of six 6-inch doilies, six 9-inch doilies and one 20-inch centerpiece. $1.25 a set.

K—13701. Stamped Linen Toast or Napkin Folder. For eyelet work. 35c.

K—13702. Dainty Sewing Bag. Figured cretonne. Top shirred with cord. 60c.

K—13703. Stamped Linen Toast or Napkin Folder. For cross stitch. 35c.

K—13704. Cretonne Luncheon Set. Pink or blue flowers. Consisting of six 6-inch doilies, six 9-inch doilies and one centerpiece, 20 inches. $1.50 a set.

K—13705. Stamped All Linen Centerpiece. For eyelet work. 22x22. 35c.

K—13706. Stamped Lawn Collar and Cuff Set. Assorted designs. 35c.

K—13707. Cretonne Work Bag. With hoop top cord handle. 60c.

K—13708. Stamped Lawn Collar and Cuff Set. Assorted designs. 35c.

K—13709. Lace Trimmed Cotton Scarf. Row of insertion. Size, 19x50 inches. 35c.

K—13710. White Cotton Scarf. Trimmed with filet lace medallion. 18x50 inches. 65c.

K—13711. Stamped Hemstitched Guest Towel. For cross-stitch embroidery. 35c.

K—13712. Bureau Scarf. Embroidery medallions set in between rows of wide cluny lace in filet design, both ends having deep lace inserts. 17x54 inches. 85c.

K—13713. Stamped Hemstitched Guest Towel. For cross-stitch embroidery. 35c.

K—13714. Cretonne Centerpiece Rolls.

18 inches	65c	30 inches	$1.00
24 inches	75c	36 inches	1.50
27 inches	85c	45 inches	1.75

Restricted delivery offer applies to these rolls.

K—13715. Stamped Centerpiece. Beautiful Marie Antoinette wreath. 35c.

K-13802 · $1.00

K-13800
25¢

K-13801
$1.00 DOZ.

K-13806
16¢

K-13803
30¢

K-13804
$1.10 DOZ.

K-13805
$1.65 EACH

K-13807
90¢ DOZ.

K-13808
65¢ yd.

K-13810
12½¢

K-13809
$1.10
EACH

K-13811
$1.25 EACH

K-13812
40¢ yd.

For descriptions please see the opposite page.

New York — Gimbel Brothers — Philadelphia

Part Linen and Cotton Goods as Illustrated Opposite

The goods on this and the opposite page come under Gimbels Restricted Delivery Offer. See page 4.

K—13800. Lace-Trimmed Scarf. Lace insertion and edge. Size, 18 x 50 inches. Linen-finished cotton of good appearance. **25c.**

K—13801. Cotton Huck Towel. Heavy and good quality. Neat red border. Excellent for apartment house or hotel use. Sold by the dozen only. Exceptional bargain for **$1.00 doz.**

K—13802. Three-Piece Renaissance Bureau Scarf. Japanese drawn work in center. Attractive and very good looking. **$1.00.**

K—13803. Hemstitched Mercerized Damask Bureau Scarf. Size, 18 x 50. A good hotel scarf as well as for the home. Glossy and looks like real linen. Special, **30c.**

K—13804. Satin Finish Mercerized Napkin. Very neat pattern. Size, 20 x 20. An exceptionally good napkin to use when finer

ones wished to be saved. Neatly hemmed. Closely woven. **$1.10 a dozen.**

K—13805. Pure German Linen Table Cloth. Silver bleached. Neatly hemstitched edge makes it very attractive. Unique designs. Large enough to seat eight people. **$1.65 ea**

K—13806. Fine Union Huck Towel. Size, 17 x 34. Red or white border. Very substantial and will give good service. A wonderful offering for **16c.**

K—13807. Mercerized Damask Napkins. A large assortment of designs to choose from. Size, 18 x 18. Neatly hemmed. Splendid restaurant napkin or for every day home use. Has the gloss and appearance of damask linen. **90c a dozen.**

K—13808. Heavy Satin Finish Mercerized Damask. 72 inches wide. Assorted designs

Keeps its luster after laundering and looks like a beautifully fine damask. **65c yard.**

K—13809. Round Scalloped Mercerized Table Cloth. Size, 62 x 62. Something new and very pretty. Assorted designs. **$1.10 each.**

K—13810. Hemmed Bleached Turkish Towel. A good absorbent quality. Medium size. **12½c.**

K—13811. Fine Satin Finish Mercerized Table Cloth. Square edges and round designs in a large variety. Sufficiently large to seat eight people. Woven to simulate a high-grade fine damask. Special, **$1.25 each.**

K—13812. Heavy Mercerized Table Damask. 58 inches wide. Beautiful assortment of designs. A good restaurant or hotel damask. **40c. a yard.**

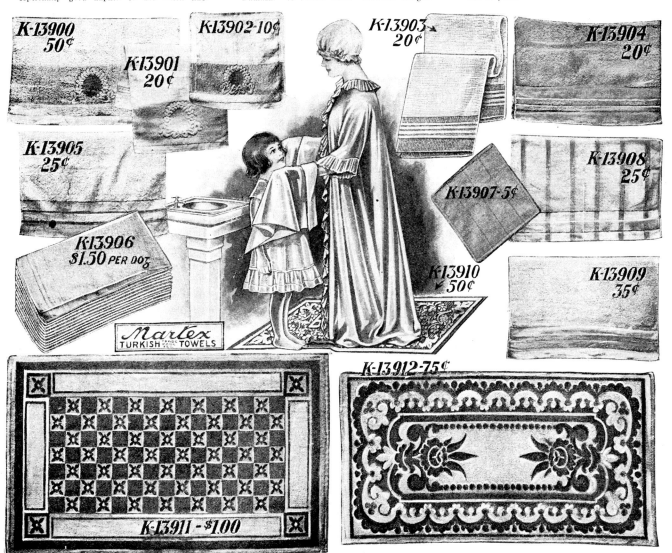

"Martex" Turkish Towels—Made in Philadelphia, U. S. A.

"MARTEX" represents the utmost in Turkish Towel Value. **IT IS TURKISH TOWEL INSURANCE—AN ABSOLUTE GUARANTEE OF QUALITY—A GUARANTEE WITH THE STUFF BEHIND IT—MAKE, FABRIC, ENDURANCE.**

Genuine "MARTEX" TURKISH TOWELS bear the "MARTEX" trade-mark. It is the guarantee tag that they are the best. For 16 years the mill has had the reputation of making the best terry products on the market, and "MARTEX" is the "high water" mark.

NO OTHER TOWEL WILL TAKE THEIR PLACE. The "MARTEX" line is most comprehensive, and embraces everything from a simple wash rag to luxurious bath sets.

K—13900. "Martex" Heavy Absorbent Turkish

Bath Towel. Hemmed ends. Fancy pink or blue border. Neat space for monogram. Very special value and quality. **50c.**

K—13901. Guest Size Turkish "Martex" Towel. Matches towel No. K—13900. **20c.**

K—13902. "Martex" Turkish Wash Cloth. Matches towel K—13900. **10c. each.**

K—13903. "Martex" Turkish Face Towel. Pink or blue border. Medium size. Special, **20c.**

K—13904. Snow White "Martex" Turkish Towel. Hemmed ends. A splendid offering. **20c.**

K—13905. Heavy Double Warp "Martex" Turkish Towel. Neat blue line border or all white. Our special, **25c.** Value. **40c.**

K—13906. Handsome "Martex" Turkish Towel. Snow white. Hemmed ends. **$1.50 a dozen.**

K—13907. "Martex" Turkish Wash Cloth.

Color stitched edge. Hard wearing quality. **5c each. 60c a dozen.** Matches towel K—13908.

K—13308. "Martex" Striped Turkish Towel. Hemmed ends. Blue or pink stripe. **25c.**

K—13309. Durable and Good Quality "Martex" Turkish Towel. Extra heavy. Hemmed ends. All white or white with fancy pink or blue border. Splendid value. **35c.**

K—13910. Embossed "Martex" Turkish Bath Rug. Size, 22 x 40. Pink, blue, tan, red or green. Special, **50c. each.**

K—13911. Splendid Quality "Martex" Turkish Bath Rug. Size, 28 x 46. Good patterns. Blue, pink, drab or red. **$1.00.**

K—13912. "Martex" Turkish Bath Rug. Extra heavy. Size, 25 x 48. Blue, pink, green, drab or red. Effective pattern. **75c.**

Gimbels Paris, London and American Style Book

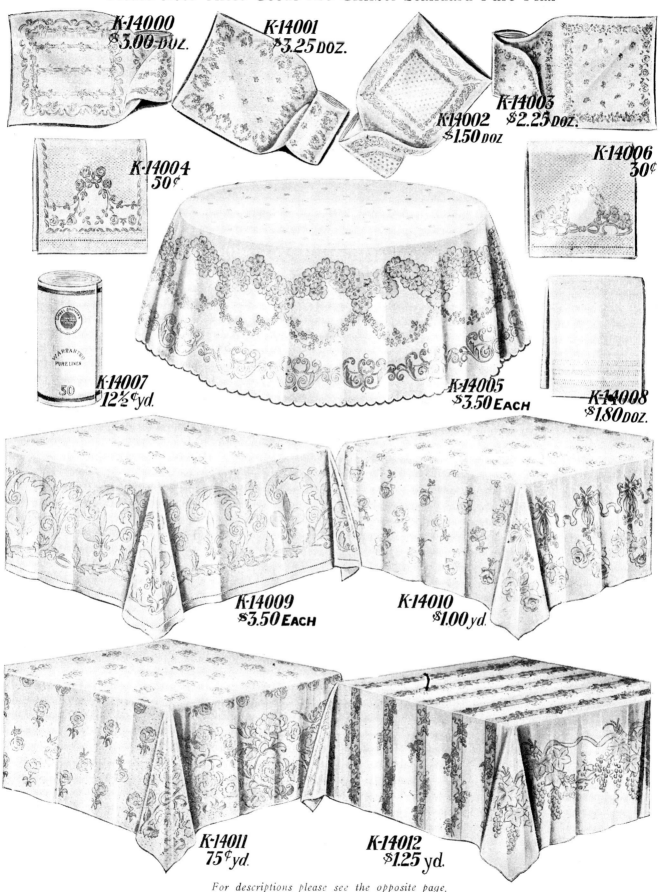

K-14000
$3.00 DOZ.

K-14001
$3.25 DOZ.

K-14002
$1.50 DOZ.

K-14003
$2.25 DOZ.

K-14004
50¢

K-14006
30¢

K-14007
12½¢ yd.

K-14005
$3.50 EACH

K-14008
$1.80 DOZ.

K-14009
$3.50 EACH

K-14010
$1.00 yd.

K-14011
75¢ yd.

K-14012
$1.25 yd.

For descriptions please see the opposite page.

New York — Gimbel Brothers — Philadelphia

Order From Gimbels If You Wish Handsome, Substantial, Genuine Linens

The scarcity of ocean-going ships, the extreme danger of ocean travel, increased marine insurance, and actual detention of goods abroad have caused the foreign linen market to go steadily upward. Gimbels were fortunate to place orders and transport their linens months ago, and now have good, substantial linens at usual

Gimbels Restricted Delivery Offer applies. See page 4.

Gimbels Restricted Delivery Offer applies. See page 4.

K—14000. Bleached Damask Napkins. Size, 21 x 21 inches. A variety of beautiful floral designs. Close weave. A durable, splendid wearing linen and one that will withstand frequent launderings. $3.00 a dozen.

K—14001. Bleached Damask Napkins. Size, 22 x 22 inches. Neat and attractive designs. Will launder beautifully. Make a pleasing and elegant appearance on the dining table. Most appropriate for a gift. $3.25 a dozen.

K—14002. Silver Bleached Irish Damask Napkins. Size, 18 x 18 inches. Spot or other neat designs. Will soon wash white and prove most satisfactory. Linen has good wearing qualities. Special, $1.50 a dozen.

K—14003. Full Bleach Damask Napkins.

Size, 21 x 21 inches. These napkins are carefully made and will launder beautifully. A choice of very pretty patterns is also offered. $2.25 a dozen.

K—14004. Handsome Huck Towel. Large size. Monogram space. Hemstitched hem at ends. 50c.

K—14005. Fine Round Damask Table Cloth. Size, 70 inches diameter. Beautiful round design. Soft M. L. O. finish. $3.50 each.

K—14006. Huck Towel with Damask Border. Monogram space with a dainty design. Hemstitched at ends. These values in huck towels are rare. 30c.

K—14007. Heavy Kitchen Crash Towels. For hand or roller towels. Neat red border.

A firm and substantial weave. Excellent value. 12½c yard.

K—14008. Pure Flax Scotch Huck Towels. Hemmed ends. Sold by the dozen only. $1.80 a dozen.

K—14009. Hemstitched Table Cloth. Size, 70 x 70 inches. Beautiful pattern. Splendid quality. Special M. L. O. finish. $3.50 each.

K—14010. Snow White Irish Table Damask. 70 inches wide. An assortment of patterns. Exceptionally good value. $1.00 yard.

K—14011. Bleached Table Damask. 68 inches wide. Several pretty designs. Good quality. Special, 75c yard.

K—14012. Handsome Satin Table Damask. 72 inches wide. Stripe or floral patterns. Satin finish. Extra fine value. $1.25 a yard.

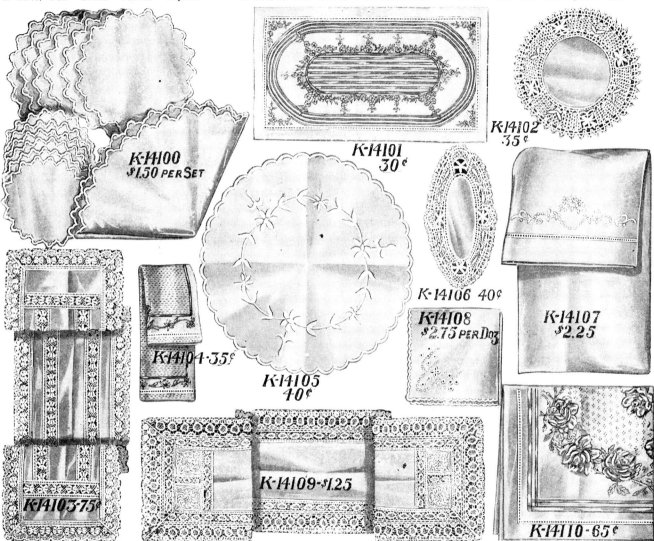

K—14100. Handsome All Linen Lunch Set. Neatly scalloped. Consists of 13 pieces. One 24-inch centerpiece. Six 12-inch plate dollies and six 6-inch glass doilies. Will look well on a finely polished mahogany table. An exceptional value. $1.50 a set.

K—14101. All Linen Damask Tray Cloth. A beautiful piece of damask neatly hemstitched all around. Size, 17 x 26 inches. A useful article at a moderate price. 30c.

K—14102. Pretty Cluny Lace-Trimmed Doily. Fine linen center with beautiful cluny border. Size, 11 x 11 inches. A dainty piece for the well-appointed table. 35c.

K—14103. Handsome Cluny Lace Trimmed Scarf. Linen center with one row of insertion forming panels and finished all around with edging. Bolster and Shams to match. Size, 18 x 35 inches, 75c. Size, 18 x 44 inches,

85c. Size, 18 x 52 inches, $1.00. Size, 27 x 70 inches, $1.50.

K—14104. Fine Huck Guest Towel. Hemstitched ends. Space for monogram, which when embroidered makes a beautiful present. Size, 15 x 24 inches. Special, 35c.

K—14105. Pretty Linen Centerpiece. Wonderfully fine linen. Artistic design beautifully machine embroidered. Scalloped edge. Looks like hand work. Size, 18 x 18 inches. A great value from the great Gimbel store. 40c.

K—14106. Beautiful Oval Bread Tray Doily. Pure linen center, finished with lace edge. Size, 6 x 11 inches. It will be well to take advantage of this fine value. These doilies are ever needed and a few extras, at this reasonable price, will be very acceptable. 40c.

K—14107. Fine "Irish" Linen Pillow Cases.

Beautiful hand-embroidery design and spoke stitching on hem. A linen pillow case is a delight and a possibility when sought at the Gimbel Linen Section. Size, 22 x 36 inches. Special, $2.25 pair.

K—14108. Handsome Linen Tea Doilies. Design in corner beautifully worked by hand and scalloped by machine, around edge, very closely simulating real hand work, make these a much-desired doily. Size, 14 x 14 inches. Exceptional value. $2.75 a dozen.

K—14109. Fine Linen Scarf. Beautiful insertion and edge of cluny form border with panels of embroidered medallions and cluny insertion at each end. Size, 19 x 45 inches, $1.25. Also in size 19 x 54 inches, $1.50.

K—14110. Damask Lunch Cloth. Square. Hemstitched hem. Beautiful round damask patterns. Size, 32 x 32 inches. Splendid value. 65c.

A Fine Lot of Bed Muslins Is the Housewife's Pride

All Sheets, Pillow Cases and Bolster Cases are quoted in the sizes they are before made up. After sewing they measure less the width turned back in hems. They will be found wear resisting and every way satisfactory. Gimbels Restricted Delivery Offer applies. Read page 4.

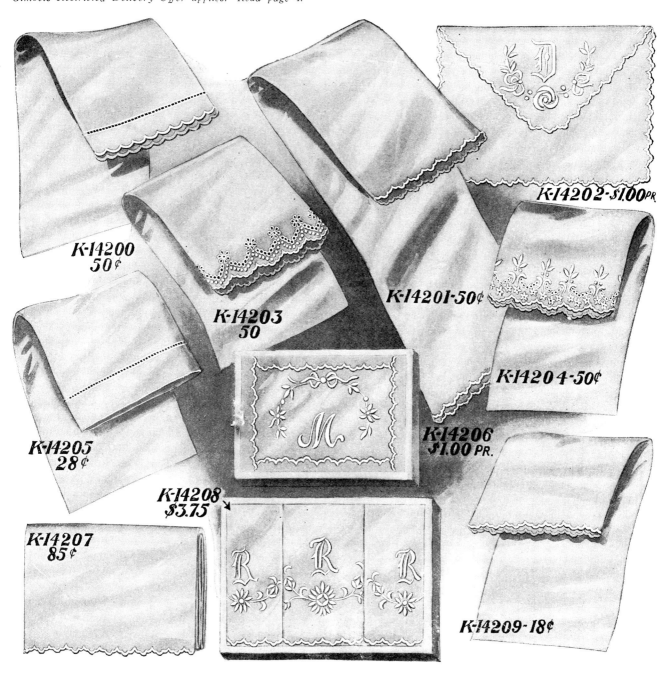

K-14200 50¢

K-14202-$1.00 PR.

K-14203 50

K-14201-50¢

K-14204-50¢

K-14205 28¢

K-14206 $1.00 PR.

K-14208 $3.75

K-14207 85¢

K-14209-18¢

K—14200. Hemstitched and Scalloped Pillow Case. 45 x 38½ inches. 50c. each.

K—14201. Nicely Scalloped Bolster Case. Size, 42 x 72 inches. Matches in quality sheet K—14207. Value, 75c. Special, 50c.

K—14202. New Fancy Envelope Pillow Case. Very popular. Takes the place of shams. Neatly embroidered scallops, initials and spray. Size, 45 x 36 inches. Value, $1.50. Special, $1.00 pair. Sold in pairs only.

K—14203. New Fancy Eyelet Embroidered Pillow Cases. Finished size, 45 x 36 inches. Value, 75c. Special, 50c. each.

K—14204. New Fancy Eyelet Embroidered and Scalloped Pillow Case. Finished size, 45 x 36 inches. Very popular. Value, 75c. each. Special, 50c. each.

K—14205. Spoke Stitched Pillow Case. Made of firm grade, durable "Hudson" muslin. Size

before hemming, 45 x 38½ inches. 28c. each.

K—14206. Initialed Day Pillow Cases. Scalloped all around and beautifully embroidered. Packed two in box. Any initial desired. Value, $1.25. Special, $1.00 pair.

K—14207. Beautiful and Neat Scalloped Sheet. Good quality muslin. Matches in quality, bolster case K—14201. Size, 81 x 90 inches. Regularly $1.00. Special, 85c. each.

K—14208. Embroidered Bed Set. Neatly embroidered initials and spray. Set consists of one sheet, 81 x 99 inches and two pillow cases, 45 x 36 inches. Value, $5.00. Special, $3.75 set.

K—14209. Scalloped Pillow Cases. Size, 45 x 36 inches. Value, 25c. Special, 18c. each.

SPECIALS—(Not Illustrated.)
Durable Brand, Seamless Sheets, made especially for us of a standard serviceable Sheeting

Muslin and priced unusually low; a complete range of sizes:

Size.		Price.
54 x 90	inches	50c.
63 x 90	"	55c.
63 x 99	"	65c.
72 x 90	"	60c.
72 x 99	"	70c.
81 x 90	"	65c.
81 x 99	"	75c.
90 x 99	"	80c.
90 x 108	"	90c.

DURABLE PILLOW CASES.

42 x 36	inches	15c.
45 x 36	"	16c.

DURABLE BOLSTER CASES.

42 x 72	inches	32c.

Bed Spreads, Bed Sets and Piece Goods

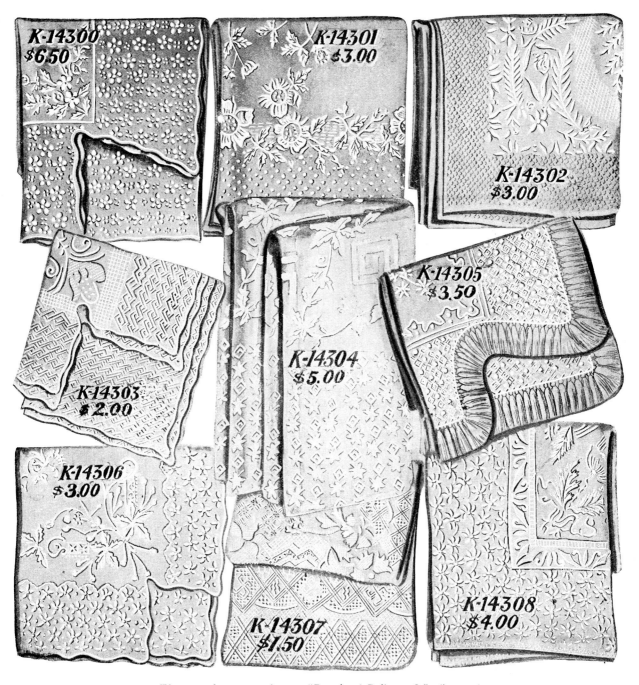

These goods come under our "Restricted Delivery Offer," page 4.

K—14300. Satin-Finished Spread. Scalloped. Cut corners to fit metal bed measuring 4 feet 6 inches. $6.50. Weight, wrapped, 5 lbs. 8 oz.

K—14301. White Satin-Finished Bed Spread. Double bed size. $3.00. Others, $2.00 to $5.00. Weight, wrapped, 5 lbs.

K—14302. Old-Fashioned Marseilles Bed Spread. Double bed size. $3.00. Others at $5.00 and $6.00. Weight, wrapped, 5 lbs.

K—14303. White Crochet Bed Spread. Scalloped. Cut corners to fit metal bed 4 feet 6 inches. $2.00. Weight, wrapped, 4 lbs.

K—14304. Fine Imported English Satin-Finished Bed Spread. Plain hem. Extra size to fit box springs. $5.00. Can be scalloped, cut cornered, for metal beds, for 50c additional. Size, 90x99 inches.

K—14305. Satin-Finished Spread. Fringed or cut corners to fit metal bed 4 feet 6 inches. $3.50, $4.50 and $5.50. Wrapped, 5 lbs.

K—14306. Satin-Finished Bed Spread. Scalloped. Cut corners to fit metal bed measuring 4 feet 6 inches. $3.00. Others at $4.50, $5.50 and $6.50. Weight, wrapped, 5 lbs.

K—14307. White Crochet Bed Spread. Double bed size. $1.50 each. Others at $1.75, $2.00 and $2.25. Weight, wrapped, 4 lbs.

K—14308. White Satin-Finished Bed Spread. Double bed size. Pretty designs. $4.00. Weight, 4 lbs. 12 oz.

NOT ILLUSTRATED.

Bed Sets. Satin-finished bed spread with scalloped edge and cut corners to fit metal bed measuring 4 feet 6 inches; also scalloped bolster roll. $6.00 and $7.50 set. Weight, wrapped, 6 lbs. 6 oz.

White Crochet Crib Spreads. Pretty patterns. 85c and $1.00. Weight, 24 oz.

Satin-Finished Crib Spreads. $1.75, $2.00 and $2.50. Weight, wrapped, 26 oz.

Colored Crochet Bed Spreads. Pretty patterns. pink, light or dark blue or red. $1.75 each. Weight, wrapped, 4 lbs.

Colored Satin-Finished Bed Spreads. Pretty Marseilles patterns. Double bed size. $3.00 each. Weight, wrapped, 4 lbs. 4 oz.

Crochet Bed Spreads for Single Beds. Marseilles patterns. $1.00, $1.25, $1.50 and $1.75. Weight, wrapped, 2 lbs. 12 oz.

Satin-Finished Bed Spreads for Single Beds. $2.25, $2.75, $3.25 and $5.00. Weight, wrapped, 3 lbs. 12 oz.

PIECE GOODS

Samples furnished if request is definite as to price and kind wanted.

Bleached Muslin. 36 inches wide. 8c, 10c, 12½c, 15c and 18c yard. Weight, wrapped, 7 oz. a yard.

Ticking. Old-fashioned blue and white striped. 32 inches wide. 12½c, 15c, 20c, 25c and 40c yard. Weight, wrapped, 11 oz. yard

Fancy Striped or Floral Ticking. 32 inches wide. 30c yard. Weight, wrapped, 11 oz. yard.

The Baggage Smasher Conquered

Damage-resisting, durable, sturdy, too much cannot be said of the strength and durability of the Gimbel offering in the line of trunks. For the home, for storage purposes, for the tourist; in fact, any use to which a trunk may be put, they are peerless. No need to worry; they will stand the rough usage accorded in traveling by rail or steamer.

Many of our customers, when ordering other goods, include a Trunk with directions to pack and ship the goods in the Trunk—this we consider an excellent plan.

These come under Gimbels Restricted Delivery Offer. See page 9.

K—14400. Dress Trunk. Basswood body. Heavy duck canvas covered. Bound and banded with hard, vulcanized fibre. Malleable steel hardware; steel railings. Hardwood slats and heavy straps. Full riveted. Cloth lined and two trays. Sizes: 32, $8.00. 36, $9.00. 40 inches, $10.00.
Steamer Trunk. To match K—14400. Same construction. Sizes: 32, $7.00. 36, $8.00. 40 inches, $9.00.
K—14401. Steamer Trunk. Same construction as Dress Trunk K—14402. Sizes: 32, $9.00. 36, $10.00. 40 inches, $11.00.

K—14402. Dress Trunk. Three-ply veneer body. Covered inside and outside with hard, vulcanized fibre, making the trunk a five-ply. Cold-rolled steel hardware; studded nails all over body. Full riveted and cloth lined. Two trays. Sizes: 32, $10.00. 36, $11.00. 40 inches, $12.00.
K—14403. Genuine "INNOVATION" Wardrobe Trunk. Full size containing 10 arms and hangers. Demi size containing 6 arms and hangers. Petite size containing 5 arms and hangers. All 45 inches high. The prices are according to grade, the size not affecting the price. $25, $35, $50, $65, $85.

K—14404. Steamer Trunk. Same construction as Dress Trunk, K—14405. Sizes: 32, $5.00. 36, $5.50. 40 inches, $6.00.

K—14405. Dress Trunk. Basswood body. Waterproof, painted canvas. Bound and banded with hard, vulcanized fibre binding. Hardwood slats. Strong leather straps. Good hardware. Deep tray. Sizes: 28 and 30 inches long, $5.00. 32 and 34 inches long, $5.50. 36, 38 and 40 inches long, $6.00.

A Hat and Suit From Gimbels Will Please the Little Man

The boy wants to look manly in his clothes, and looks with displeasure at anything not in accordance with his strict code. You will not have any "battles" with your son over his clothes if you procure them from Gimbels. They will meet his entire approval.

K-14500 $1.00
K-14501 $1.50
K-14502 $1.50
K-14503 $2.00
K-14504 $1.00
K-14505 $1.00
K-14506 50¢
K-14507 $1.00
K-14508 50¢
K-14509 50¢
K-14510 $1.00
K-14511 $1.00

K—14500. Boy's Nifty Hat. Blue serge, grey and brown mixture in checks. The newest spring style. Pleasing to the up-to-date little man. Boys from 8 to 12 years. $1.00, $1.50 and $2.00.

K—14501. Small Boy's Hat. Improved Milan straw. Trimmed in velvet. A dressy style for the little chap. Very good-wearing quality. For boys from 3 to 5 years. $1.50 and $2.00.

K—14502. Boy's Rah Rah Hat. In checks, brown and grey tweed effects. For boys from 5 to 8 years. Band of self-material. A good-looking, good-wearing hat. $1.00 and $1.50.

K—14503. Boy's Blue Tam, "Jack Tar" or Sailor Hat. Made of fine blue cloth. Three white pearl buttons on brim, which is laced with small bow on side. Star in center of crown. A jaunty, picturesque style. Will please most boys. Sizes, 5 to 10 years. $1.50 and $2.00.

K—14504. Boy's Rah Rah Style Hat. Improved Milan straw. Jointed crown and turn-down brim. For boys from 5 to 8 years. White band. Sterling quality and good value summer hat. $1.00, $1.50 and $2.00.

K—14505. Boy's Norfolk Hat. In check, grey and brown mixtures. For boys from 6 to 10 years. A good style, thoroughly well-made hat. $1.00 and $1.50.

K—14506. Small Boy's Duck Hat. A fine outing hat for seashore or mountains. In Rah Rah, square or box crown. Blue, blue and white, white and blue, all white or fancy stripes. Very reasonable at 50c.

K—14507. Boy's Straw Hat. Box crown of improved Milan straw with turn-down brim. A high-grade hat in every respect. For ages 6 to 8 years. $1.00, $1.50, $2.00, $2.50 and $3.00.

K—14508. Boy's Rah Rah Shape Hat. Various colors of tweed, blue mixtures or brown and grey mixtures. For boys from 4 to 10 years. 50c and $1.00.

K—14509. Boy's White Duck "Jack Tar" Hat. Appropriate for outing, boating, fishing and all the summer sports. For ages from 8 to 15 years. 50c.

K—14510. Boy's College Hat. Various shades of grey, brown, blue or tweed mixtures. Good materials and a well-made hat for service. 50c and $1.00.

K—14511. Boy's Straw Hat. Improved Milan straw with turn-down brim or one side tilt. A high-grade, good style hat. For boys from 8 to 14 years. $1.00 and $1.50.

Gimbels Paris, London and American Style Book

Men's Bath Robes, Beach Robes and Night-Shirts

Examine the prices. Then note that these garments are substantially made of fine, durable materials that will give good wear even with frequent tubbing, that buttonholes are strongly made and collars set well—items to consider—also that they are comfortable and roomy. These are real bargains.

K—14600
$2.95

K—14602
75¢

K—14603
$1.00

K—14605
50¢

K—14601
$1.00

K—14604
$3.85

K—14600. Man's Bath Robe. Very good quality terry cloth (Turkish toweling) in fancy jacquard patterns. Large and roomy with a cord at neck and girdle at waist. Neat collar and two convenient patch pockets. Will give spendid wear and is an exceptional bargain. Colors: blue, gray, tan or heliotrope combination. Regular $5.00 value. Special at $2.95.

K—14601. Splendid Night-Shirt of Very Fine Quality Cambric in a Good Popular Weight. Surplice neck. Breast pocket appears at left side. Fancy colored braid trimming on neck, front, cuffs and pocket. A most desirable cambric garment, sold elsewhere for $1.25—at Gimbels for $1.00. Sizes, 15 to 20. In muslin or plain white nainsook for summer wear, same style, $1.00.

K—14602. Man's Excellent Quality Muslin Night-Shirt. Full cut. Made with collar or surplice neck. State which style is desired. Neck, cuffs, breast pocket and front are trimmed neatly with white, blue or red fancy braid. This model will give long wear and is without a doubt a regular $1.00 value. 75c. Sizes, 15 to 20. In cambric, same style, 75c.

K—14603. Another Gimbel Special. Muslin Night-Shirt of Extra Fine Quality. Will give lots of wear. Neat collar, down front and cuffs are trimmed with colored braid. Patch pocket on left side is trimmed to match. Very long and amply full. It is practical and will give great comfort to its wearer. Splendid value at $1.00.

K—14604. Man's Beach Robe of the Medium Weight New Cotton Material of the Cheviot Family But Heavier in Weight. The turndown collar, patch pockets and belt of self-material. Splendid for summer wear at home, also when traveling as it takes up very little room in a grip. Black and white, blue and white, tan and white or heliotrope and white. This garment will give exceptional wear and wonderful comfort. It is positively a $6.00 garment, that we offer at $3.85.

K—14605. Man's Good Quality Night-Shirt. Full cut. Surplice neck or collar attached. Neat patch pocket at left side. Fancy braid trimming in white, red or blue on the sleeves, pocket, front and neck. Convenient and cool, and of exceptional worth. Sizes, 15 to 20. Special at 50c.

K—14605a. Special Large Size Night-Shirt, Not Illustrated, for Large Men. Made extra long and extra wide. Plain muslin with surplice neck. Sizes, 15 to 20, $1.00.

Men's Comfortable Night and Lounging Wear

We are very successful in catering to the men's wants, for we know just what pleases them in garments of this kind. Comfort and serviceability are two most desirable qualities and they are to be found in every garment on this page. All these garments are made of exceptionally fine materials.

K-14702
$1.00

K-14701
$4.95

K-14703
$1.50

K-14704
85¢

K-14705
$1.00

K-14700-$4.35

K—14700. Man's Splendid Bath Robe. Good quality terry cloth (Turkish toweling) in the newest colorings that will wash without fading. Comfortable shawl collar. Buttons and buttonholes and a girdle at waist effect the front closing. Ample and useful patch pockets. Very practical and convenient. Regular $6.00 value. Special, **$4.35.**

K—14701. Man's Terry Cloth Bath Robe. Excellent quality and in good weight for summer wear. Coat style with notch collar is fastened in front by buttons and buttonholes. Girdle at waist. Collar, revers, front of robe, pockets and sleeves neatly bound with silk cord. Will give excellent service and is a real bargain. A $7.00 robe for only **$4.95.**

K—14702. Man's Serviceable Pajamas. Fine quality mercerized pongee, the equal of silk

in weight and coolness, in plain colors or white. A very comfortable and well made garment. Silk loops and buttons effect the closing. Surplice neck. Breast pocket. Pants are cut full and well made. An exceptionally good offering for the Gimbels low price. **$1.00.** Others not illustrated, **$1.50** and **$2.00.** Mention size of collar when ordering.

K—14703. Man's Fine Pajamas. These are made of exceptional quality madras, finished in the best possible manner. Comfort and serviceability are both combined in this desirable garment. Large and roomy, yet in fit is excellent. Coat style with surplice neck and loops and buttons. Roomy patch pocket. Novelty shape cuff on sleeves. A most pleasing style and a wonderful value. **$1.50.**

K—14704. Man's Splendid Pajamas of good

quality printed percale in exceptional patterns. Made with surplice neck and fastened by loops and buttons. Convenient breast pocket appearing on side. Pants are very roomy and well made. A most serviceable garment and a bargain at the reasonable price of 85c. Kindly state size of collar when ordering.

K—14705. Man's Practical Pajamas. Made of madras that will give long and satisfactory service. The coat has surplice neck and trimmed with loops and buttons. Deep roomy breast pocket on left side. Pants are cut very full and painstakingly made. Good style and good colorings. We were compelled to purchase a large stock in order to be able to offer our customers this fine quality at such a low figure. **$1.00.** When ordering, mention collar size.

Gimbels Paris, London and American Style Book

K·14801
$1.50

K·14803
50¢

K·14800
$3.50

K·14802
$1.00

K·14806
50¢

K·14805
$1.00

K·14804
$1.00

K·14809
$1.50

K·14807
75¢

K·14808
$1.00

K·14810
50¢

These Well-Made, Roomy Shirts Are Described on Page 149.

Men's Collars and Cuffs. All the wanted styles. Collars 14 to 18 inches. 15c. each, or 2 for 25c. Cuffs, 10 to 11½ inches, 25c. a pair. Boy's Collars, 12 to 14 inches, inclusive, 12½c. each. Cuffs, 8 to 9½ inches, inclusive, 12½c. and 25c. a pair. Sizes of Shirt neck bands, 14 to 17.

K—14800. Man's Silk Shirt. Coat model with soft turn-back cuffs. White ground with blue, black, heliotrope, pink or tan stripe. Most stores get $5.00 for this quality shirt. Gimbels ask $3.50.

K—14801. Pleated Shirt. Percale or printed madras. An endless variety of handsome stripe effects. Value, $2.00. Special, $1.50.

K—14802. Man's White Dress Shirt. Coat style, with attached cuffs. Others with wrist bands. Made open back and front. $1.00. Same style in a finer line, $1.50.

K—14803. Blue Chambray Shirt, with Collar Attached. Best wearing chambray known.

None better on the market for 50c. Sizes, 14 to 17.

K—14804. Good Quality Printed Percale Pleated Shirt. Handsome colorings. Guaranteed for style and fit and is the equal of most $1.50 shirts. $1.00.

K—14805. Gray Flannel Shirt. Special quality. Gray or blue. $1.00. Better quality, not illustrated, at $1.50 and upward to $3.00. Sizes, 14 to 18.

K—14806. Man's Black Sateen Shirt. Excellent quality. Splendid value at 50c. Sizes, 14 to 18.

K—14807. Negligee Shirt. Percale in stripe effects on white grounds. Coat model with

cuffs attached. Price is special. 75c. Sizes, 14 to 17.

K—14808. Man's Negligee Shirt. Mercerized pongee in striped effects on white grounds. Usual $1.50 quality. Special, $1.00. Sizes, 14 to 17.

K—14809. Man's Tennis or Outing Shirt. White, Oxford or mercerized pongee. Exclusive stores ask a high price for this style. Our price. $1.50.

K—14810. Negligee Shirt. Fine count printed percale. Coat model, laundered cuffs attached. In the newest colors. Cannot be duplicated elsewhere at the price asked. 50c.

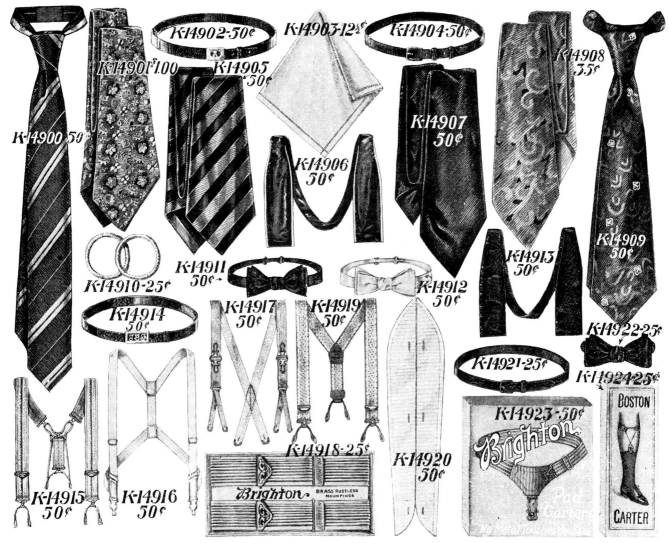

K—14900. Man's Band Teck Tie. Fancy stripes or plain white or black. Excellent quality. 50c.

K—14901. Man's Silk Open-End Four-in-Hand Tie. Made from imported and domestic silks, in all the desirable plain colors, fancy or regimental stripes, or allover effects. Special, $1.00.

K—14902. Man's Leather Belt. Good quality cowhide. With initial buckle. Sizes 30 to 44. 50c.

K—14903. Man's White Handkerchief. Soft finished cambric with one-fourth or one-half-inch hem. 12½ each. In linen, 25c and 50c each.

K—14904. Good Leather Belt. Black or tan. Sizes, 30 to 44. 50c and $1.00.

K—14905. Open-End Four-in-Hand Tie. All the desirable plain colors, fancy stripes or Persian effects. 50c.

K—14906. Newest Dress Bat Wing Tie. For Tuxedo or evening wear. Barathea silk in

white with black piping or black with white. State size of collar. Special, 50c.

K—14907. Plain Colored Open-End Four-in-Hand Tie. Regent or repp silk. Special, 50c.

K—14908. Large Open-End Four-in-Hand Tie. Fine quality silk. Fancy stripe or Persian effects. 35c. Three for $1.00.

K—14909. Shield Teck Tie. In assorted patterns or fancy stripes. 50c.

K—14910. Silk Elastic Arm Band. Plain white, black or light blue. 25c.

K—14911. Black Barathea Band Bow. Good quality silk. Also in fancy stripe or figures. 50c.

K—14912. White Evening Lawn Band Bow. 25c and 50c.

K—14913. Bat Wing Tie. Fancy or plain colors. State size of collar. 50c.

K—14914. Black Leather Belt. With initial buckle. 50c.

K—14915. Well-known "President" Suspenders.

Heavy cotton or lisle elastic. Plain or fancy colors. 50c.

K—14916. Man's Unseen Suspenders. Worn under the top shirt. Durable elastic webbing and trimmings. White only. 50c

K—14917. "Guyot" Suspenders. Made with cantab ends. Elastic in back only. Plain white or fancy. 50c and 65c.

K—14918. "Brighton" Arm Bands. White, light blue, black or lavender. 25c pair.

K—14919. "Police and Firemen" Suspenders. All elastic webbing. Fancy colors. Best style for hard wear. 50c.

K—14920. Vest Edging. Plain white pique. 50c.

K—14921. Black Leather Belt. Excellent quality. Sizes, 34 to 44. 25c.

K—14922. Man's Shield Bow. Black or fancy colors. 25c.

K—14923. New "Brighton" Pad Garters. Plain assorted colors. 25c and 50c.

K—14924. "Boston" Garters. Assorted colors. 25c and 50c.

Personal Belongings for Boys of All Ages

The small boy is the subject of considerable thought on the part of Gimbel people. Shirts, ties and collars must be "just right" or no amount of coaxing will avail to a change of opinion.

K·15000
50¢

K-15001
25¢

K·15002
25¢

K·15003
50¢

K·15004
50¢

K·15005
25¢

K·15006
$1.00

K·15013
50¢

K·15008
25¢

K·15009
50¢

K·15007
75¢

K·15010
$1.00

K·15012
25¢

K·15011
25¢

K·15014
$1.00

Note: All our blouses are made with tapeless bands, which is a big advantage over the old style tape blouse.

K—15000. Boy's Negligee Shirt. Made of fine quality percale—well made and very roomy. effects. Every boy can be pleased. 25c and 50c.

K—15001. Boy's Silk Four-in-Hand Necktie. A wide range of plain colors, stripes or plaid effects. Every boy can be pleased. 25c and 50c.

K—15002. Boy's Silk Windsor Tie. The best made and a large assortment of plain colors, plaids or stripes. Good quality. 25c and 50c.

K—15003. Boy's Samson Suspender Waists. We always have a complete line of this well-known suspender in plain colors or white. No end of wear in these. Ages, 4 to 10 years. 50c. Ages, 12 and 14 years, 65c.

K—15004 Boy's Collar Attached Shirt. Made as well and fit as well as the expensive kinds. Printed percale or woven madras. Splendid styles and unusual value. 12 to 14 inches. 50c.

K—15005. Boys' Underwaist. Made of fine white cotton fabric, in light or heavy weight. Ages, 4 to 12 years. 25c.

K—15006. Boy's Separate Collar Blouse Made of mercerized cotton pongee in good-looking stripes or plain colors. Ages, 5 to 15 years. $1.00.

K—15007. Boy's Soft Collar Attached Mercerized Cotton Pongee Blouse. In handsome stripes or plain colors. All ages. 75c.

K—15008. Boy's Lisle Webbing Elastic Suspenders. In plain colors or stripes. Made with cross backs and leather ends. No end of wearing quality. 25c.

K—15009. Boy's Muslin Night Shirt. Well made and trimmed with white, red or blue braid. Surplice necks. All ages. 50c.

K—15010 Boy's Mercerized Cotton Pongee Shirt. Made with soft, turn-back cuffs. Neckband and separate collar. Plain colors or stripes. Good style for summer. Sizes, 12 to 14 years. $1.00.

K—15011. Boy's Leather Belt. Black or tan. A well-made, durable belt. Sizes, 24 to 30. 25c. A better quality, 50c.

K—15012. Boy's Open-End Four-in-Hand Tie.

In an excellent assortment of stripes, plaids or plain colors. Quality unsurpassed. 25c.

K—15013. Boy's Soft Collar Attached Blouse. Made of fine quality percale in handsome stripes. Well made and plenty of material is used so as to give the full blouse effect. White also. 50c.

K—15014. Boy's Pajamas. Made of mercerized cotton pongee, or printed madras. Fully equal to the $1.50 grade of most stores. Sizes, 4 to 18 years. $1.00.

Not Illustrated.

Boy's Arrow Brand Collars Complete line of this popular collar. All the new shapes.

K—15015. The Arrow soft collar is a great favorite, especially for summer wear. 2 for 25c.

K—15016. The Arrow laundered collar. 2 for 25c.

K—15017. Good line of rubber collars. 25c each.

K—15018. For the little fellows The future Senators and Presidents must have up-to-date garments just as well as daddy. Plain white mercerized cotton pongee shirts. Also striped percale or pongee. Assorted colors. Neckband 12 to 14 inches. $1.50.

New York — Gimbel Brothers — Philadelphia

Women's Perfect Fitting Shoes

This page pictures grades of the less expensive sorts, but strictly solid, honest and shapely to the fullest degree. Our effort is to elevate in quality in every instance. Any shoe purchased from us is found above the usual standard regardless of price.

K-15100 $1.95
K-15101 $1.95
K-15102 $1.95
K-15103 $1.95
K-15104 $1.95
K-15105 $1.95
K-15106 $1.95
K-15107 $1.95
K-15108 $1.95
K-15109 $2.45
K-15110 $2.45
K-15111 $2.25

K—15100. **Woman's Cloth Top Button Shoes.** A very pretty model with patent leather vamps. Plain toe. Black cloth tops. Cuban heels. Flexible stitched soles. Sizes, 2½ to 7. Widths, C, D and E. **$1.95 pair.**

K—15101. **Woman's Low Heel Shoes.** Dull black gun-metal calf vamps. Dull leather tops. Full round toes. Low broad heels. Extension soles. Sizes, 2½ to 7. Widths, C, D and E. **$1.95 pair.**

K—15102. **Growing Girl's Dress Shoes.** Button style of black patent leather with black cloth top. Short vamp. Perforated tip. Round toe. Common sense heel. Medium weight extension sole. Sizes, 2½ to 7. Widths, C, D and E. **$1.95 pair.**

K—15103. **Woman's Kid Lace Shoes.** Soft kid shoe. Neat in appearance and very easy. Glazed kid vamp and top. Flexible sole. Rubber heel. Sizes, 3 to 9. D, E and EE widths. **$1.95 pair.**

K—15104. **An Extremely Neat Shoe.** Made on a comfortable last. Patent leather vamp. Black cloth top. Cuban heel. Flexible sewed soles. Sizes, 2½ to 7. Widths, C, D and E. **$1.95 pair.**

K—15105. **Woman's Lace Shoes.** Black patent leather vamp. Dull black leather top. Perforated tip. Military heel. Medium weight extension soles. Sizes, 2½ to 7. Widths, C, D and E. An exceptional bargain. **$1.95 pair.**

K—15106. **Smart Serviceable Shoes.** Patent leather with dull leather top. Short vamp. Perforated tip. Military heel. Extension sole. Sizes, 2½ to 7. Widths, C, D and E. **$1.95 pair.**

K—15107. **Soft Black Kid Comfort Shoes.** Especially adapted for those troubled with tender feet. Button style of soft glazed kid. Flexible turned soles. Cushion inner sole and rubber heel, making it easy on the feet. Sizes, 2½ to 8. C, D, E and EE widths. **$1.95 pair.**

K—15108. **Woman's Low Heel Kid Shoes.** Broad toe. Glazed kid, button style. Low common sense heel. Flexible sewed sole. Sizes, 2½ to 7. Widths, C, D and E. **$1.95 pair.**

K—15109. **Woman's Gaiter Boots.** Remarkably handsome, their distinctive style assuring a smart appearance. Fine patent leather vamp and heel foxing. Gray cloth top. Leather eyelet straps. Neat military heel. Sizes, 2½ to 6. Widths, C, D and E. **$2.45 pair.**

K—15110. **Woman's Cloth Top Gaiter Boot.** Choice of black or gray cloth top. Patent leather vamp. Cuban heel. Light weight extension soles. Sizes, 2½ to 6. Widths, C, D and E. **$2.45 pair.**

K—15111. **Woman's Button Shoes.** Very fine style at a low price. Patent leather vamp and heel foxing. Black cloth top. High heel, slightly concaved. Sizes, 2½ to 6. C, D and E widths. **$2.25 pair**

Gimbels Are Very Strong On Inexpensive Shoes

Look at the style and up-to-date lines in most of these shoes. Further, leathers are durable and of fine appearance. The shoes are everyway copies of the very expensive models costing sometimes four times as much. The woman who needs to count the pennies should consider Gimbels when buying, for they employ some experts whose sole business is to procure high-grade, low-priced goods.

K—15200. Woman's Colonial Pump. One of this season's new models. Patent leather vamps and heel foxings. Fawn color cloth quarters. Tongue and buckle. Flexible-stitched soles. Concave heels. Sizes, 2½ to 7. C, D and E widths. $1.95 pair.

K—15201. Patent Leather Colonial Pump. Flexible-sewed soles. Concave heel. Narrow toe last. A very pretty model. Sizes, 2½ to 6. Widths, D and E. $1.95 pair.

K—15202. Woman's Oxford. A soft shoe with flexible turned soles. Low heels give comfort to the wearer who is much on her feet. Black kid vamps. Kid quarter lining. Sizes, 2½ to 7. Widths, D and E. $1.75 pair.

K—15203. White Canvas Colonial Pump. Made over our new pump last that hugs the heel. Light turned soles. White canvas vamps and covered heels. Tongue and buckle. Sizes, 2½ to 6. C, D and E widths. $1.95 pair.

K—15204. Woman's White Canvas Oxford. Fine white canvas uppers. Turned soles. Covered wooden heels. Neat pointed toe. A dainty shoe for warm weather. Sizes, 2½ to 7. Widths, C, D and E. $1.95 pair.

K—15205. Woman's Kid Oxford. Soft black kid uppers. Flexible turned soles. Medium height heels. Made on a round toe last. Sizes, 2½ to 7. D and E widths. $1.75 pair.

K—15206. Woman's Juliets. Gypsy cut Princess slippers of soft black kid leather. Comfortable for house wear. Medium round toe. Elastic side gores. "Common Sense" heel. Turned soles. Sizes, 2½ to 8. Widths, D, E and EE. $2.00 pair.

K—15207. Woman's New Tongue Pump. Patent leather vamps and quarter. Tongue and two-strap effect. Kid quarter lining. Flexible-stitched soles. Sizes, 2½ to 6. D and E widths. A real bargain. $1.95 pair.

K—15208. White Canvas Colonial Pump. Fine white canvas with covered buckle, small tongue and covered heels. Turned soles. Sizes, 2½ to 7. Widths, C, D and E. $2.25.

K—15209. Woman's Colonial Pump. White shoes will be very fashionable this season and this Colonial is a bargain. White canvas vamp. Tongue and buckle. White kid quarter lining. Receding toe last. Sizes, 2½ to 6. Widths, C, D and E. $1.50 pair.

K—15210. Woman's Gun-Metal Colonial Pump. Dull gun-metal vamps. Concave heels. Gun-metal buckle. A very stylish shoe at a reasonable price. Sizes, 2½ to 7. Widths, C, D and E. $2.50 pair.

K—15211. Woman's Colonial Pump. A beautiful model and a Gimbel bargain. Patent leather vamp. Fawn color cloth quarter. Concave heel. White kid quarter lining. Pretty tongue and buckle. Sizes, 2½ to 6. D and E widths. $1.95 pair.

New York — Gimbel Brothers — Philadelphia

Dress Shoes for Women

The Gimbel Shoe stocks for women are most comprehensive and complete. Their scope is almost endless in resources and variety—stocks calculated to please and fit every well-gowned woman. We picture a few of the wanted styles of this season, but can fill your order by mail, if not too closely detailed, in whatever you might wish that is not shown below.

K—15300. **Fashionable Stylish Button Shoe.** For dress wear as well as general service. Patent colt with fine black cloth tops. Medium toe and sensible walking heel. Sizes, 2½ to 7. Widths, A to D. $3.50 a pair.

K—15301. **New Petite Pump.** A neat combination of patent leather vamps and heel foxing with grey cloth insert. Small tongue and jet ornament. Concave heels. Welted soles. Sizes, 2½ to 6. Widths, C, D and E. $3.00.

K—15302. **Paris Pump.** A new design of this season. Patent colt or black gun-metal vamps with grey suede tops. A very smart summer shoe at a reasonable price. Sizes, 2½ to 7. Widths, A to D. $3.50 a pair.

K—15303. **Wide Ankle Shoe.** Meets all the requirements for stout women. Soft black kid uppers. Flexible soles and flat heels. Sizes, 3 to 8. Widths, D, E and EE. $3.50 a pair.

K—15304. **Handsome Colonial.** In fine patent

colt or black gun-metal leathers. It is a real bargain. Goodyear welted. New soles can be hand sewed. Sensible heels for the person who does lots of walking. Sizes, 2½ to 7. A to D. $3.00 a pair.

K—15305. **Special Shoe at $5.00.** Why not save a dollar. We know of no shoe as good at $6.00 a pair. Fine patent coltskin with black cloth tops and neat tips. Sizes, 2½ to 8. Widths, AA to D. $5.00 pair.

K—15306. **Smart Dressy Boot.** It's one of the season's most fashionable models. Patent coltskin, plain toe vamps of finest quality. Black cloth tops. Button. Sizes, 2½ to 7. Widths, A to D. $5.00 a pair.

K—15307. **A Smart Oxford for the College Girls.** Made in black gun-metal leather. Broad flat shanks and heels, especially for tramping. Sizes, 2½ to 7. Widths, A to D. $3.50 a pair.

K—15308. **A Shoe That Is Sure to Please You.**

Dressy in appearance and well made. Fine patent coltskin with black cloth tops. High arch to fit feet with high instep. Sizes, 2½ to 7. Widths, A to D. $4.00 a pair.

K—15309. **New Two-Bar Colonial Pump.** One of the spring favorites. Concave heels. Small pointed tongue. Welted oak soles. Sizes, 2½ to 6. Gun-metal calf vamps and quarter. C, D and E widths.....................$3.00
In patent coltskin 3.00
In white Nu-Buck 3.00

K—15310. **White Nu-Buck Colonial.** You could not choose a more dainty or serviceable summer shoe than this, with turn soles and Louis heel. Easy and soft on the feet. Sizes, 2½ to 7. Widths, A to D. $3.50.

K—15311. **Woman's Black Kid Shoe.** Soft glazed kid vamps and tops. Low, sensible heels. Flexible welted soles. Medium round toe. Sizes, 2½ to 8. Widths, D and E. $3.00,

"Designed in America—Made in America"—Shoes

Some very "fetching" shoes are made abroad—Gimbels favorite designers give due consideration to all of them that are artistic—but genuine American shoe originations cannot be excelled. American factory production has been so scientifically improved that wonderfully fine work can be turned out at moderate cost. Naturally, America exports large quantities of shoes

K-15400 $3.00
K-15401 $3.00
K-15402 $3.00
K-15403 $2.50
K-15404 $3.00
K-15405 $3.00
K-15406 $3.00
K-15407 $3.00
K-15408 $3.00
K-15409 $3.00
K-15410 $3.00
K-15411 $3.00

K—15400. The New Paris Pump. Fine patent leather vamps. Quarter of fawn color cloth. Welted soles and neat heels. Widths, C, D and E. Sizes, 2½ to 7. **$3.00** a pair. Same style in black gun-metal calf. **$3.00** a pair.

K—15401. Patent Leather Tongue Pump. Vamps of patent colt skin. Pointed tongue. Two straps and buttons effect. Widths, C, D and E. Sizes, 2½ to 7. **$3.00** a pair.

K—15402. Woman's Gun-Metal Colonial Pump. Gun-metal leather on a new last. Narrow receding toe. Concave heel. Turned soles. Neat buckles and small tongue. Sizes, 2½ to 7. Widths, C, D and E. **$3.00** a pair. Same style in patent colt. **$3.00** a pair.

K—15403. Very Smart Colonial Pump of Black Gun-Metal. New style City last. Gun-metal finish buckle. Medium Cuban heel. Turned soles. Leather quarter lining. Guaranteed counters. Widths, C, D and E. Sizes, 2½ to 7. **$2.50** a pair.

K—15404. Low Heel Colonial Pump. Patent colt skin vamps. Tongue with buckle ornament. Welted oak soles. 1¼-inch heels. Widths, C, D and E. Sizes, 2½ to 6. **$3.00** a pair. Same in black gun-metal leather. **$3.00** a pair.

K—15405. Growing Girl's Boot. Selected patent leather vamps with black cloth tops. Welted oak soles and "Common Sense" heels. Sizes, 2½ to 7. Widths, C, D and E. Price, **$3.00** a pair. Same style with black dull calf vamps, **$3.00** a pair.

K—15406. Fashionable Patent Leather Button Gaiter Boot. Tops of light sand color cloth. Patent colt skin vamps and heel foxings. Welted oak soles. Leather Louis heels. Widths, C, D and E. Sizes, 2½ to 6. **$3.00** a pair.

K—15407. Stylish Dress Model. Made of high-grade patent colt skin vamps. Extra quality black cloth tops. Concave heels and welted soles. Widths, C, D and E. Sizes, 2½ to 7. **$3.00** a pair.

K—15408. Woman's Black Kid Shoe. Low heels and flexible welted soles. Glazed kid vamps and tops. Neat perforated tip. Sizes, 2½ to 7. Widths, C, D and E. **$3.00** a pair. Same in button style, **$3.00** a pair.

K—15409. Woman's Dress Boot. One of the season's favorites. Selected patent colt skin vamps without tips. Fine black cloth tops. Welted oak soles and new Cuban heels. Widths, C, D and E. Sizes, 2½ to 7. **$3.00** a pair.

K—15410. Woman's Gun-Metal Calf Gaiter Boot. Black gun-metal leather vamps and heel foxings. New leather Louis heels. Welted soles. Grey cloth tops. Sizes, 2½ to 7. Widths, C, D and E. **$3.00** a pair.

K—15411. "Last-Minute" Style in Woman's Boots. Patent leather gaiter foxed lace boot. Light fawn color or grey cloth tops. Made over newest City last. Leather Louis heels. Widths, C, D and E. Sizes, 2½ to 6. **$3.00** a pair.

New York — Gimbel Brothers — Philadelphia

Stylish Kid and Satin Slippers, House Shoes, Etc.

These slippers have proven deservedly popular with our patrons. For women who wish broad toe shapes, light weight shoes and plain footwear, our comfortable Home Shoes are most pleasing. Selected leathers of the softest sorts are used—flexible sole leather—and while shapes are broad the lasts are neatly shaped, resulting in unusually good fitting shoes.

K—15500. Woman's Strap Slipper. Soft black leather. One of the most comfortable slippers made. It has a broad toe and low heel. Instep strap. Sizes, 2½ to 8. Widths E and EE. Price $1.00 a pair.

K—15501. Woman's Strap Slippers. A stylish dull black kid, four-strap slipper. Turned soles. Medium heels. Narrow toe last. Sizes, 2½ to 7. Widths D and E. Price $2.50 a pair.

K—15502. Woman's Juliets. Soft black kid. Elastic rubber gores. Flexible soles. Rubber heels. Choice of plain "Common Sense" or tipped toes. Sizes, 3 to 7. Widths E and EE. Price $1.45 a pair.

K—15503. Comfort Shoes. If you have tender feet you will be delighted with these "Comfort Shoes." Soft black kid. Flexible turned soles. Cushion insoles and rubber heels. Sizes, 2½ to 8. Widths C, D and E. Price $2.45 a pair.

K—15504. Woman's Turned Sole Button Shoes. Soft black kid leather. Medium round toe last. Turned soles. Rubber heels. Very soft and comfortable, and will give excellent service. Sizes, 2½ to 9. Widths D, E and EE. Price $2.45 a pair.

K—15505. Black Kid "Comfort Shoes." Ease and comfort at a low price. Broad plain toe. Lace shoe of soft black leather. "Common Sense" heel. Sizes, 3 to 8. Widths E and EE. Price $1.50 a pair.

K—15506. K—15507 and K—15508. Woman's Satin Slippers. Made of black, white, pink or blue satin with satin covered heels. New slipper last that will not slip. Turned soles. White kid lining. Sizes, 2½ to 6. Widths D and E. Price $1.95 a pair.
Chiffon Rosettes to match, 50c a pair extra.

K—15509. Bath Slippers. A useful slipper of Turkish toweling with carpet soles. Sizes for men and women. 35c a pair.

K—15510. Woman's Bathing Slippers. Light in weight and very pretty on the foot. Made of white, navy blue or black canvas. 50c a pair.

K—15511. Woman's Soft Kid Seamless Button Shoes. Made without tips or seams to hurt tender feet. Flexible hand-turned soles. Low flat heels. Sizes, 2½ to 7. Widths D, E and EE. $2.00 a pair.

K—15512. Heel Protectors. 25c a pair.

K—15513. Bunion Protector. Order for right or left. 50c each. $1.00 a pair.

K—15514. Woman's White Kid Slippers. A dainty soft kid slipper with neat ornament and single instep strap. Sizes, 2½ to 7. Widths D and E. $1.50 a pair.

K—15515. Arch Support. "Foot Easer." $2.00 a pair.

K—15516. Arch Support. "Paragon." $1.00 a pair.

Stylish, Sturdy Shoes for Men

Every shoe in the Gimbel Store, whether narrow or broad toe, low or high heel, is built on anatomical lines—comfort combined with fit. Only the best selected stocks are used. We are most particular and accept no shoes not wholly well made.

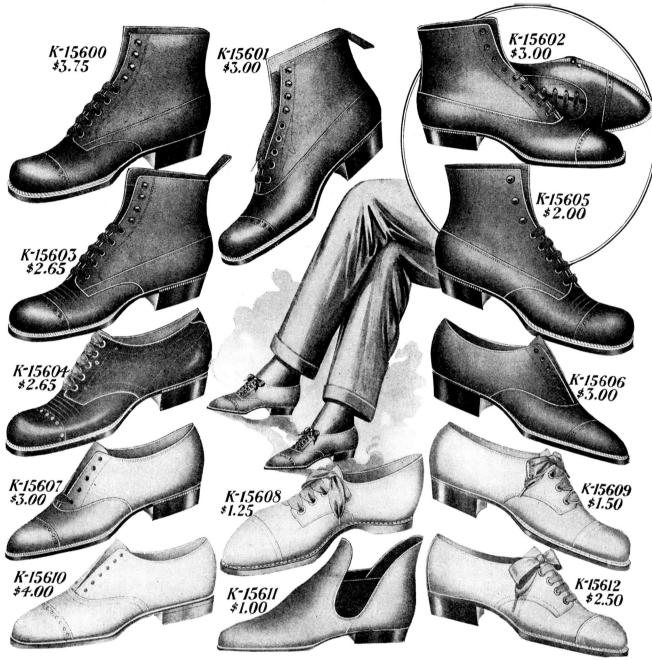

K—15600. **The Gimbel Letter Carrier's Shoes.** Made to stand constant hard wear. Uppers of stout black calf leather. Broad toe last. Double soles welted and viscolized. An all-around shoe of great merit. Sizes, 6 to 12. Widths, E and EE. **$3.75 pair.**

K—15601. **Man's Gun-metal Calf Lace Shoes.** Straight London toe last. Broad low heels. Goodyear sewed oak soles and insoles. May be had also in patent leather or glazed kidskin. Sizes, 6 to 11. C, D, and E widths. **$3.00 pair.**

K—15602. **New Spring Shape for Young Men.** The English last with broad heels and wide shanks. Vamps and uppers of selected dull gun-metal calfskin. Goodyear welted oak soles, heavy leather oak insoles. A shoe it will be hard to find elsewhere at a dollar more than we ask. Sizes, 5 to 10. Widths, C, D and E. **$3.00 pair.**

K—15603. **Man's Blucher Shoes.** Gun-metal calf, broad toe, blucher style. Stout soles, welted. A wonderful shoe for such a low price. Sizes, 6 to 11. Widths, D and E. **$2.65 pair.**

K—15604. **Very Dressy Blucher Low Shoes for Men.** May be had in black patent leather or black gun-metal leather. Made on a new broad toe last and has a welted extension sole and military heels. Sizes, 6 to 11. Widths, D and E. **$2.65 pair.**

K—15605. **Boy's Blucher Shoes.** There is splendid value in this serviceable blucher lace shoe. Made of smooth gun-metal calfskin on a new high toe last with medium low heel and good weight extension soles. Sizes, 1 to 5½. Widths, D and E. **$2.00 pair.**

K—15606. **Man's Gun-metal Oxford.** Very stylish, dressy low shoe of excellent quality. Narrow English last, well liked by young men. Black gun-metal calf uppers. Oak outer soles and insoles. Sizes, 5 to 10. Widths, C, D and E. **$3.00 pair.**

K—15607. **Young Man's Tan Russia Calf Lace Oxfords.** English last. Narrow toe. Broad heels. Welted oak soles, oak insoles. Dark tan vamps (mahogany shade). The newest shade in tan leather. Sizes, 6 to 10. C, D and E widths. **$3.00 pair.**

K—15608. **Man's White Canvas Oxford,** Rubber soles. A shoe suitable for tennis, yachting, country or beach wear. The toe is not extreme, allowing perfect freedom for the foot. Sizes, 6 to 10. Widths, D and E. **$1.25 pair.**

K—15609. **Man's White Canvas Blucher Oxfords.** Stitched rubber soles. Rubber heels. A cool, stylish shoe at a very low price. Sizes, 6 to 10. D and E widths. **$1.50 pair.**

K—15610. **Man's White "Nu-Buck" Lace Oxfords.** Here is a smart, dressy low shoe, one of the newest lasts. Fine white "nu-buck" uppers, white soles and heels. A distinctive model at a reasonable price. Sizes, 6 to 10. Widths, C, D and E. **$4.00 pair.**

K—15611. **Man's Romeo.** This soft, easy house shoe is a great favorite. Tan or black leather. Elastic gores. Flexible leather soles. Low, broad heels. Sizes, 6 to 11. **$1.00 pair.**

K—15612. **Man's White Canvas Blucher Oxfords.** A cool, stylish, serviceable summer shoe of fine, white canvas with welted leather soles, and leather heels. Leather insoles and quarter lining. Sizes, 6 to 10. D or E widths. **$2.50 pair.**

New York — Gimbel Brothers — Philadelphia

Sturdy Shoes for Children, Boys and Men

Our boys' shoes are pleasing to the young fellows—the styles suit them, being same as used by their elders. The shoes are strong, neat and stylish, made in practical shapes, and are built of selected leathers—the kinds best suited to withstand the wear all boys give shoes. Our shoes are all honestly built, and if found lacking we will cheerfully make good.

K-15700
50¢ UP

K-15707
$1.00

K-15708
65¢ UP

K-15701
$2.00

K-15702
$2.00

K-15709
$1.45

K-15704
50¢

K-15703
$2.75

K-15710
$1.50

K-15711
$2.00

K-15705
$2.00 UP

K-15706
$2.00

K-15712
$2.00

K—15700. **Tennis Oxfords.** The boy's and girl's favorite summer shoe for beach wear, tennis and other outdoor sports. Strong canvas uppers. Thick corrugated rubber soles. Excellent quality at a low price. Sizes, boy's and children's, 50c. Men sizes, 6 to 11, 65c pair.

K—15701. **Boy's Blucher Shoes.** Fine, patent coltskin. A neat, stylish shoe of splendid value. Patent coltskin vamps. Dull calf tops. Welted oak soles. Broad toe last. Sizes, 9 to 13½. C, D and E widths. $2.00 pair.

K—15702. **Boy's Button Dress Shoes.** Patent coltskin vamps. Dull calf tops. Welted soles. A mannish shoe on a full, round toe last. Widths, C, D and E. Sizes, 9 to 13½. $2.00 pair. Sizes, 1 to 5½. $2.50 pair.

K—15703. **Boy's Tan Lace Shoes.** Tan Russia calf vamps and tops. New English last with narrow toe. Low heel and broad shank. Welted soles. Sizes, 1 to 5½. Widths, C, D and E. $2.75 pair.

K—15704. **Child's Barefoot Sandal.** Every little tot loves to put on a pair of cool, comfortable sandals when the hot weather comes. Tan leather uppers with two straps and buckles to prevent slipping. Good wearing. Sewed soles. Sizes, from child's 5 to miss's 2. 50c pair.

K—15705. **Scout Shoes for Boys.** Especially constructed to stand the rough usage of boys. Stout tan leather uppers. Stitched soles of chrome tanned elkskin. Sizes, 9 to 13½. $2.00 pair. Sizes, 1 to 5½. $2.50 pair. Men's sizes, 6 to 10. $3.00 pair.

K—15706. **Boy's Blucher Oxfords.** Patent leather vamps and uppers. Broad toes. Perforated tips. Sewed soles. D and E widths. Sizes, 9 to 13½. $2.00 pair. Larger sizes. $2.50 pair.

K—15707. **Man's Everett House Slippers.** A cool, easy slipper of tan or black leather with stitched soles and low heel. Sizes, 6 to 10. $1.00 pair.

K—15708. **High Cut Tennis Shoes for Men and Boys.** White canvas tops cut high to support the ankles. Black rubber soles. Boy's sizes, 9 to 13½. Sizes, 1 to 5½. 75c pair. Men's sizes, 6 to 10. 85c pair.

K—15709. **Boy's Lace Shoes.** A Gimbel bargain. Box calf vamps and uppers. Heavy sole. Flexible stitched, full round toe last. This shoe will give the utmost wear. Sizes, 9 to 13½. $1.45 pair. Sizes, 1 to 5½. Widths, D, E and EE. Black. $1.75 pair.

K—15710. **Child's Blucher Shoe.** This shoe has a protected double toe of stout sole leather which doubles the wearing quality. Gun-metal calf vamps. Dull leather tops. Stitched soles. Sizes, 5 to 12. $1.50 pair.

K—15711. **Scout Shoe.** Upper of stout tan khaki cloth with tan leather vamp trimmings. Low common sense heels. Elkskin stitched soles. This shoe is an exceptionally good value for the price. Small boy's sizes, 10 to 13½. $1.45 pair. Large boy's sizes, 1 to 5½. $2.00 pair.

K—15712. **Boy's Gun-metal Calf Blucher Shoes.** Gun-metal calf vamps and tops. Round toes. Neat, perforated tips. Welted soles. Sizes, 9 to 13½. Widths, D and E. $2.00 pair.

Children's Shoes Illustrated Below Are Anatomical in Shape

K—15900. Child's White Nu-buck Button Shoes. Round toe last. Welted soles. Sizes, 5 to 8, $2.25; 8½ to 11, $2.50; 11½ to 2, $2.75; 2½ to 6, $3.00.

K—15901. Satin Bathing Oxfords. Trimmed with red bow and streamers. Black, blue or red. $1.00.

K—15902. Barefoot Sandals. Tan leather uppers. Leather soles. Child's 5 to miss's 2. 50c.

K—15903. Boy's Scout Shoes. Tan leather uppers and "elk" soles. Sizes, 9 to 13½, $2.00; 1 to 5½, $2.50. Men's sizes, 6 to 10, $3.00.

K—15904. Patent Leather Button Shoes. Fawn cloth tops. Leather Louis heel. Sizes, 2½ to 7. Widths, B, C and D. $6.50.

K—15905. Woman's Colonial Pump. Black patent leather vamp, fawn cloth quarter, concave leather heel. Receding toe and high arch. Sizes, 2½ to 7. Widths, C, D and E. $2.00.

K—15906. White Canvas Colonial Pumps. Light turned soles. Covered heels. Sizes, 2½ to 7. Widths, C, D and E. $1.75.

K—15907. Summer Shoes for $3.50. Patent colt vamps and fawn cloth quarters. Turned soles. Covered heels. Sizes, 2¼ to 7. Widths, B, C and D.

K—15908. Evening Slippers. Patent colt. Turned soles. Louis heels. Sizes, 2½ to 7. Widths, A to D. $4.00.

K—15909. Street or Evening Wear Slippers. Patent leather vamps. White calf quarters. Turned soles. Louis heels. Sizes, 2½ to 6. Widths, A to D. $5.00.

K—15910. Satin Slippers. Bow at vamp. Black, white, pink or blue. $3.00.

K—15911. Man's Traveling Slippers. Red, tan or black kid with padded soles. Made to fold compactly in leather case of color to match. Sizes, 6 to 10. $1.00.

K—15912. White Canvas Oxfords. Four eyelet model with covered Cuban heel. Flexible turned soles. Lambskin sock lining. Sizes, 2½ to 7. Widths, C, D and E. $1.50.

K—15913. Patent Colt Pump. Suede leather quarters. Sizes, 2½ to 6. $3.50.

K—15914. Two-Button Side Colonial Pump. Patent colt vamp. White buck quarters and trimming. Louis heels. Sizes, 2½ to 6. Widths, A to D. $4.50.

K—15915. Boudoir Slippers. Soft lambskin leather with self-color pompon. Flexible leather soles. Light blue, red, pink, tan or black. Sizes, 2½ to 7. $1.00 a pair.

K—15801·$1.50 up

K—15802 $1.25 up

K—15803 $1.25

K—15804 $1.25

K—15800 $1.00

K—15806 95¢ up

K—15807 50¢

K—15808 65¢

K—15805 $1.25

K—15809 $1.25 up

K—15810 $1.25

K—15812 50¢

K—15811 95¢

K—15816 $1.25 up

K—15813 95¢

K—15814 85¢

K—15815 $2.00

K—15817 $1.50

K—15800. Tan Lotus Leather Laced Oxfords. Flexible stitched chrome tanned elk sole. "Nature Shape." Child's 6 to miss's 2. $1.00.

K—15801. Skuffer Shoe for Children. Made on a specially designed last for the growing child's foot. Vamps and uppers of black calf skin. Welted soles. Heavy calf tips neatly perforated. Sizes, 5 to 8, $1.50; 8½ to 11, $1.95; 11½ to 2, $2.25.

K—15802. "Mary Jane" Colonial Pumps. Patent colt skin vamps. Flexible stitched soles. Sizes, 5 to 8, $1.25; 8½ to 11, $1.50; 12½ to 2, $1.75; 2½ to 8, $2.25. Widths, D and E. In black gun-metal calf at same prices.

K—15803. Child's Shoes. Black kid vamps and tops. Flexible sewed extension soles. Widths, D and E. Sizes, 5 to 8, $1.25; 8½ to 11, $1.50; 11½ to 2, $1.75. Young woman's sizes, $1.95.

K—15804. Infant's White Nu-buck Shoes. Light flexible turned soles. 1 to 5, without heels, $1.25; 3 to 6, with wedge heels, $1.50.

K—15805. Child's Shoes. Patent leather vamp. White leather top. Flexible turned soles. Sizes, 1 to 8. $1.25.

K—15806. White Canvas "Mary Jane" Pumps. Leather soles. Silk ribbon bow. Spring heels on the small sizes. Low broad heels on the larger sizes. D and E. 5 to 8, 95c; 8½ to 11, $1.25; 11½ to 2, $1.45.

K—15807. Baby's Moccasins. Blue, pink or white. Sizes, 0 to 3. 50c.

K—15808. Child's Button Shoes. Black glazed kid uppers. Patent leather tips. Flexible turned soles. E widths. Small sizes, without heels, 1 to 5, 65c; 3½ to 7, 85c.

K—45809. Child's Dull Calf Shoes. Black calf skin. Leather extension soles. Reinforced backstay. Widths, D and E. 5 to 8, spring heels, $1.25; 1½ to 11, spring heels, $1.50; 1½ to 2, low heels, $1.75; 2½ to 6, $1.95.

K—15810. Child's Ankle Strap Pumps. Patent leather. Turned soles. Silk ribbon bow. Widths, D and E. Sizes, 2 to 5, without heels, $1.25; 4 to 6, with spring heels, $1.50.

K—15811. Child's Barefoot Sandals. Stout, flexible, sewed soles. Sizes, 5 to 2. 95c.

K—15812. Baby's Soft Sole Button Shoes. Uppers of white, pink or blue kid. Soft turned soles. Sizes, 0 to 3. 50c.

K—15813. Child's Shoes. Patent leather vamps. Cloth or dull kid tops. Flexible turned soles. D or E widths. 5 to 8, without heels, 75c; 3½ to 7, with spring heels, 95c.

K—15814. Infant's White Canvas Button Shoes. Flexible turned soles. Sizes, 1 to 4, without heels, 65c; 3 to 6, with wedge heels, 85c.

K—15815. Child's Genuine White Nu-buck Button Shoes. White welted soles. Perforated tips. Oak soles. Goodyear welted. Widths, C, D and E. 5 to 8, $2.00; 8½ to 11, $2.25; 11½ to 2, $2.75; 2½ to 6, $3.00.

K—15816. Miss's and Child's Shoes. Patent colt skin vamps. Dull calf tops. Flexible sewed extension soles. Broad toe last. Spring heels on smaller sizes. Low heels on miss's sizes, 5 to 8, $1.25; 8½ to 11, $1.50; 11½ to 2, $1.75; 2½ to 6, $2.25. Widths, D and E.

K—15817. Infant's Shoes. Black patent leather vamps. White calf tops. Safety turned soles. Broad toe last. Widths, D and E. Sizes, 1 to 5. $1.50.

New York — Gimbel Brothers — Philadelphia

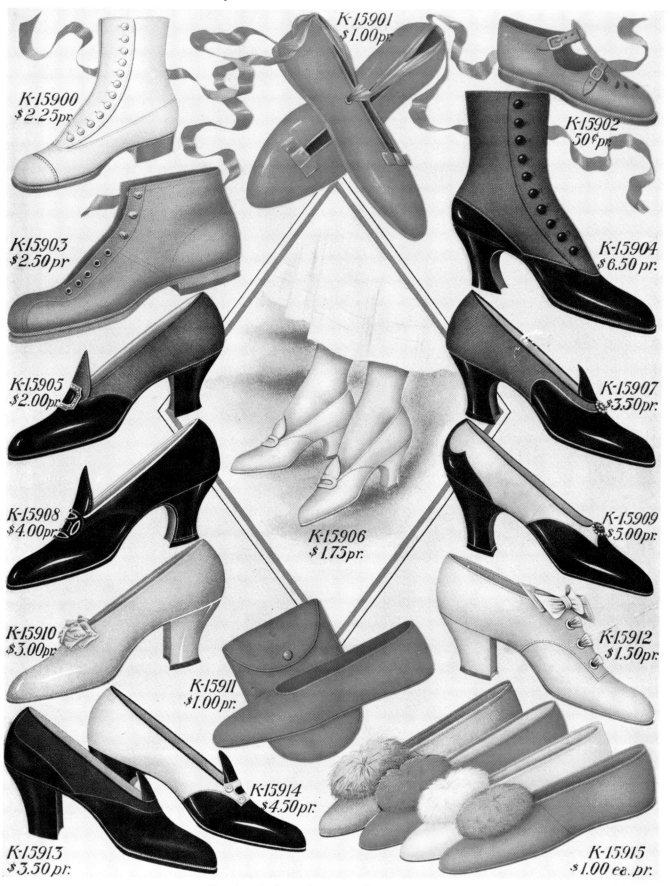

K-15901
$1.00 pr.

K-15900
$2.25 pr.

K-15902
50¢ pr.

K-15903
$2.50 pr.

K-15904
$6.50 pr.

K-15905
$2.00 pr.

K-15907
$3.50 pr.

K-15908
$4.00 pr.

K-15906
$1.75 pr.

K-15909
$5.00 pr.

K-15910
$3.00 pr.

K-15911
$1.00 pr.

K-15912
$1.50 pr.

K-15913
$3.50 pr.

K-15914
$4.50 pr.

K-15915
$1.00 ea. pr.

For descriptions please see the opposite page

New York — Gimbel Brothers — Philadelphia

K-16000 9×12 FT.
$7.00

K-16003
9×12 FT. $9.00

K-16001 9×12 FT.
$8.00

K-16004
$4.95

9×12 FT.

K-16002 9×12 FT.
$28.50

K-16006
55¢ SQ.YD.

K-16008
75¢ SQ
YD

K-16005 9×12 FT.
$11.75

K-16007
75¢ SQ.YD.

K-16009
45¢ SQ.YD.

For descriptions see opposite page
New York — Gimbel Brothers — Philadelphia

"Made In America" Rugs and Linoleums of Quality

For Illustrations See the Opposite Page.

Our floor covering section is in fine shape to take care of your every want, embracing in its stocks all the newest and best that can be found in carpets, rugs, linoleums and mattings.

When ordering floor coverings from us, of any kind, if you will kindly state what room in the house it is for, and coloring desired, we will use our very best judgment in selecting something which we know will please you.

Restricted delivery offer applies to all goods on this page.

K—16000 and K—16001. Genuine Crex Rugs. Made of specially selected wire grass, artistic patterns, very durable, sanitary and perfectly odorless—the most popular summer rug on the market. Made perfectly plain or with stencilled borders in brown, blue, red or green. Remember this is the Genuine Crex rug and not to be confounded with the many imitations now before the public. Sizes and prices as follows:

Size.	Plain. K—16000	Figured. K—16001
18 in. x 36 in.	$0.25	$0.30
24 in. x 48 in.	.50	.55
27 in. x 54 in.	.60	.70
30 in. x 60 in.	.75	.90
36 in. x 72 in.	1.10	1.15
4 ft. 6 in. x 7 ft. 6 in.	2.35	2.65
6 ft. x 9 ft.	3.60	4.15
8 ft. x 10 ft.	5.50	6.00
9 ft. x 12 ft.	7.00	8.00
9 ft. x 15 ft.	9.00	10.50
12 ft. x 15 ft.	13.00	14.50

K—16002. Beauvais Axminster Rugs. A high pile finely finished, beautiful and durable fabric. Gives excellent wear. Made in all the Oriental designs. Copies of such excellent weaves as the Daghestan, Shirvan, Ghorevan, Serapi and Kirman. This rug is made seamless up to the 9 x 15 size. Prices as follows:

Size.	Price.
22½ in. x 36 in.	$1.40
27 in. x 54 in.	2.15
36 in. x 70 in.	3.85
4 ft. 6 in. x 6 ft. 6 in.	7.50
6 ft. x 9 ft.	14.50
8 ft. 3 in. x 10 ft. 6 in.	26.00
9 ft. x 12 ft.	28.50
9 ft. x 15 ft.	36.50
11 ft. 3 in. x 15 ft.	38.50

K—16003. The Artistic Rag Rug. This rug made specially for Gimbel Brothers has been very successful. Made of new rags specially selected and dyed, solid colors, of superior weight and construction in a full range of colorings. White band borders. Just the rug you are looking for, for your bedroom. Sizes and prices as follows:

Size.	Price.
24 in. x 36 in.	$0.65
27 in. x 54 in.	.80
30 in. x 60 in.	1.00
3 ft. x 6 ft.	1.25
4 ft. x 7 ft.	2.65
6 ft. x 9 ft.	5.00
7 ft. 6 in. x 10 ft. 6 in.	7.50
9 ft. x 12 ft.	9.00

K—16004. Special. A genuine 9 x 12 Crex rug at less than wholesale price. Color green with yellow side border and fringed. The regular price of this rug is $7.25—for **$4.95.**

K—16005. Kaba Rug. This most desirable rug is made of fibre and wool. Very heavy and substantial. Hugs the floor and does not turn up at the ends. Its wearing qualities is one of its many virtues. Made in all colors and many designs. There is no rug in the market that will give better satisfaction for the price than the Kaba rug. Slate color. Sizes and prices as follows:

Size.	Price.
36 in. x 72 in.	$1.65
4 ft. x 7 ft.	3.35
6 ft. x 9 ft.	7.35
9 ft. x 12 ft.	11.75
7 ft. 6 in. x 10 ft. 6 in.	10.00

Size.	Price.
9 ft. x 15 ft.	14.00
12 ft. x 15 ft.	18.00

K—16006. Beautiful Tile Effects in Printed Linoleum. Two yards wide, at 55c. sq. yd. Meaning one yard each way.

K—16007. Inlaid Linoleum. Colors run right through to the back and won't wear off. Made in two-yard width, at 75c sq. yd. A square yard is 36 x 36 inches.

K—16008. Inlaid Linoleum. Colors run right through to the back and won't wear off. Made in two-yard width, at 75c sq. yd. A square yard is 36 x 36 inches.

K—16009. A Printed Linoleum. Heavy quality in hardwood effects. Two yards wide. 45c sq. yd. A square yard is 36 x 36 inches.

MATTINGS ARE THE IDEAL SUMMER FLOOR COVERINGS.

Mattings are one of the most popular summer floor coverings and are suitable for any part of the house. They are sanitary and easily taken care of and, judging from the amount of wear a matting will give, they are very inexpensive. Our showing of both China and Japanese matting this season is particularly fine. They are made of all long, fresh new live straw—no short straw mattings will be found in our stock. The China matting is woven on a heavy fibre warp and the Japanese on cotton warp. China mattings are in small checks and stripes and most all colors, are reversible and can be used on either side. The Japanese mattings are in all the popular colorings, in small all over carpet effects, some with white ground, with very pretty inlaid Geometrical figures. Both the China and Japanese mattings are 36 inches wide and 40 yards to the roll, but we will cut from the roll any quantity desired.

China matting range in price from **$6.00** per roll, or 17½c per yard, to **$18.00** per roll, or 47½c per yard.

Japanese matting range in price from **$7.50** per roll, or 22½c per yard, to **$22.50** per roll, or 60c per yard.

Some Most Interesting Pillow Specials

K—16100. Feather Pillow. Made of carefully selected feathers scientifically treated. Choice of fancy ticks. Size, 22 x 28 inches. Regularly, $3.00. Special, $2.25.

K—16101. Feather Pillow. Standard quality, absolutely hygienic. Choice of fancy ticks. Size, 22 x 28 inches. Regularly, $4.75. Special, $3.25.

K—16102. Feather Pillow. The same care is given to all these pillows in the selection of feathers and their scientific treatment. Choice of fancy ticks. Size, 22 x 28 inches. Regularly, $4.00. Special, $3.00.

K—16103. Feather Pillow. Best selection of feathers and scientific treatment. Choice of fancy ticks. Size, 22 x 28 inches. Regularly, $5.00. Special, $3.50.

New York — Gimbel Brothers — Philadelphia

Rich Cut and Light Blown Glassware Attractively Priced

The Rosemary pattern created for, and to be had only from, Gimbel Brothers, is illustrated and described on this page. All pieces entirely hand-cut and finished and, of course, made to match.
The beautiful Cosmos pattern is particularly well executed on the best light blown blanks, and is also here described and illustrated in many ornamental and useful articles. Gimbels Restricted Delivery Offer Applies. See page 4.

K—16200. Rich Cut Glass 6-inch Handled Bon Bon or Olive Dish. Rosemary pattern. Makes a beautiful and inexpensive gift. Especially appreciated by the young housekeeper. **$1.25.**

K—16201. Rich Cut Glass 8-inch Fruit or Salad Bowl. Rosemary pattern. This handsome cut glass bowl, so useful in the coming berry and fruit season, is a great value at **$3.75.**

K—16202. Richly Cut, 6½-inch Glass Spoon Tray, in the Rosemary pattern, is a beautiful ornament to the table. A splendid value. **$1.75.**

K—16203. Rich Cut Glass 3-pint Water Jug. Rosemary pattern. Matches water tumblers No. K—16208. A useful as well as beautiful set. Jug alone 3-pint size, **$3.50,** 4-pint size, **$5.00.**

K—16204. Whiskey Tumblers. Cosmos pattern. 20c. each.

K—16205. Dainty Cut Glass Iced Tea or Lemonade Tumblers. Cosmos pattern. Always seasonable. The draught is so much more inviting when received from a thin, daintily cut tumbler. Best value. 25c. each.

K—16206. Handsome Rich Cut Glass 10-inch Flower Vase, in the Rosemary pattern. This is a magnificent vase and a fitting receptacle for the finest bouquet of flowers nature has to offer. A real Gimbel value. **$5.00.**

K—16207. Beautiful Sparkling, Daintily Cut Mineral Water or Grape Juice Glass. In the popular Cosmos pattern. Very reasonable at the low price. 25c each.

K—16208. Rich Cut Glass Water Tumblers. Rosemary pattern. Match No. K—16203 Water Jug. This set of six tumblers is a remarkably fine value at **$5.00** the set.

K—16209. Cut Glass Tankard Jug for Water, Claret or Lemonade. Beautifully cut in the dainty Cosmos pattern. A clear, sparkling glass. 4-pint size. Similar in style and design to K—16205. A fine water jug and an unusual value. **$1.75.**

K—16210. Rich Cut Glass Tall Oil Bottle. In the Rosemary pattern. Conical shape. 9 inches high, with cut stopper. A slender, graceful bottle for the table. Has a good, firm stand. Best value. **$2.25.**

K—16211. Dainty Sparkling Sherbet or Sundae Glass. In the Cosmos pattern Suitable for all iced desserts. Splendid value. 35c each.

K—16212. Beautifully Cut, Dainty Sparkling Water Tumblers. The popular Cosmos pattern. For a good high-grade water tumbler these cannot be surpassed in value. 25c each.

K—16213. Beautiful, Daintily Cut Glass Water Goblet. In the Cosmos pattern. A pretty, graceful design. Very good value. 35c each.

K—16214. Rich Cut Glass Sugar and Cream Set. In the beautiful Rosemary pattern. A handsome, useful set. Substantial, rich and elegant. A real Gimbel value. **$3.75** the set.

K—16215. Beautiful Sparkling Handled Lemonade or Iced Tea Glass. Cut in the Cosmos pattern. Where a handled glass is preferred this graceful design will certainly please. Best value. 50c each.

K—16216. Rich Cut Glass Tall 7-inch Footed Compote. Rosemary pattern A handsome, ornamental and useful piece for the table, moderately priced **$2.50** each.

Special orders taken and prices quoted on any other items not herein noted at the same low prices. Workmanship on all articles the very best.

New York — Gimbel Brothers — Philadelphia

162

China Is the Expression of the Life of a Nation

The history of a nation's progress is baked into its crockery. Folk songs, romance, festivals, influence the patterns. Gimbels Restricted Delivery Offer applies. Please see page 4.

K–16300. **English Porcelain Dinner Set.** 100 pieces. Oriental border on a vivid blue band. Illustration shows covered dish, tea and saucer and dinner plate. Complete set, **$12.75.**

K–16301. **American Porcelain Dinner Set.** 100 pieces. An attractive yet delicate floral spray design. Illustration shows casserole, tea and saucer and dinner plate. It can be had in open stock and we will gladly quote prices of each piece. Complete set, **$8.75.**

K–16302. **Limoges China Dinner Service.** 107 pieces, including bread and butter plates and all the necessary pieces for twelve persons. Illustration shows casserole, tea and saucer and dinner plate. Charming festoon border decoration. This is an open stock set and pieces can be procured at any time. Prices on request. Complete set, **$28.50.**

K–16303 to K–16306. **Thin Dainty China.** The "Howo" (Bird of Paradise) pattern in blue and white.

K–16303. **Teapots.** 50c each.
K–16304. **Cream and Sugar.** 50c set.
K–16305. **Tea Size Plates.** 7¼ inches. 15c each.
K–16306. **Meat Dishes or Platters.** 14 inches, $1.50 each. 12½ inches, 95c each. 17 inches, $2.75 each.
    "Howo" Pieces Not illustrated.
K–16306-a. **Teas and Saucers.** 15c pair.
K–16306-b. **Chocolate Pots.** 95c each.
H–16306-c. **Chocolate Cup and Saucer.** 20c ea.

K–16306-d. **Ice or Butter Tubs.** 6 in. 50c each.
K–16306-e. **Double Eggs.** 10c each.
K–16306-f. **Jelly Jars.** 75c each.
K–16306-g. **Custard Cups.** 6c each.
K–16306-h. **Salad Bowls.** 10 in. 95c each.
K–16306-i. **Bouillons and Saucers.** 25c pair.
K–16306-j. **After Dinner Cups and Saucers.** 12c pair.
K–16306-k. **Five O'Clock Tea Cups and Saucers.** 15c pair.
K–16306-m. **Hot Milk Pot.** Covered. 5½ inches high. 35c each.
K–16306-n. **Bread and Butter Plates.** 10c each.
K–16306-o. **Breakfast Plates.** 35c each. Dinner Plates. 45c each.
K–16306-p. **Uncovered Vegetable Dishes.** 9½ inches. 75c each. 8¼ inches, 50c each. 7¼ inches, 30c each.
K–16306-q. **Covered Vegetable Dishes.** 5½ inches, 75c each. 6½ inches, $1.00 each.
K–16306-r. **Coupe (round) Soup Plates.** 35c ea.
K–16306-s. **Oatmeal Dishes.** 15c each.
K–16306-t. **Ramekins, with Plates.** 18c pair.
K–16306-u. **Fruit Saucers.** 10c each.
K–16306-v. **Tea Strainers.** 35c each.
K–16306-w. **Teapot Tiles.** 35c each.
K–16306-x. **Mustard Pots with Ladles.** 35c pr.
K–16306-y. **Hot Muffin Dishes.** $1.00 each.
K–16306-z. **Cracker Jars.** 85c each.
K–16307. **Imported China Flower Holder.** Fitted with wire net for short stemmed

flowers and buds. An attractive table decoration. 6 inches high. 7 inches diam. $2.00 ea.
K–16308 to K–16314. **A Classic in English Earthenware for the Summer Table.** Copeland's celebrated "Chelsea" bird design.
K–16308. **Covered Dishes.** $3.50 each.
K–16309. **Square Salads.** $2.75 each.
K–16310. **Teas and Saucers.** $4.75 dozen.
K–16311. **Meat Dishes.** 16 inches, $3.50 each. 12 inches, $2.00 each. 14 inches, $2.75 each. 18 inches, $5.50 each.
K–16312. **Dinner Plates.** $5.00 dozen.
K–16313. **Meat Dishes.** 10 inches. $1.25 each.
K–16314. **Cake Plates.** $1.25 each.
K–16314-a. **Breakfast Plates,** $4.50 dozen. Tea Plates, $3.75 dozen. Bread and Butter Plates. $3.00 dozen.
K–16314-b. **Soup Plates.** $3.75 dozen.
K–16314-c. **Fruit Saucers.** $2.75 dozen.
K–16314-d. **Sauce Boats.** $2.25 each.
K–16314-e. **After Dinner Cups and Saucers.** $4.50 dozen.
K–16314-f. **Cake Plates.** $1.25 each.
K–16314-g. **Covered Muffin Dishes.** $2.75 each.
K–16314-h. **Double Egg Cups.** $5.00 dozen.
K–16314-i. **Covered Butter Dishes.** $3.00 each.
K–16314-j. **Teapots.** $2.25 each.
K–16314-k. **Sugar Bowls.** $2.00 each.
K–16314-m. **Cream Jugs.** $1.35 each.
K–16314-n. **Cereal Dishes.** $3.25 dozen.
K–16314-o. **Bouillon Cups and Saucers.** $6.00 dozen.
K–16314-p. **Open Vegetable Dishes.** $1.50 ea.

Sterling Silver and Reliable Plated Ware

It is not always convenient to purchase a silver chest or dresser set outright. Why not build one up by procuring, piece by piece, articles in the pattern you like best so they will all match?

Gimbels Restricted Delivery Offer applies. See page 4. If package is to go by Insured Parcel Post, add 5c. extra.

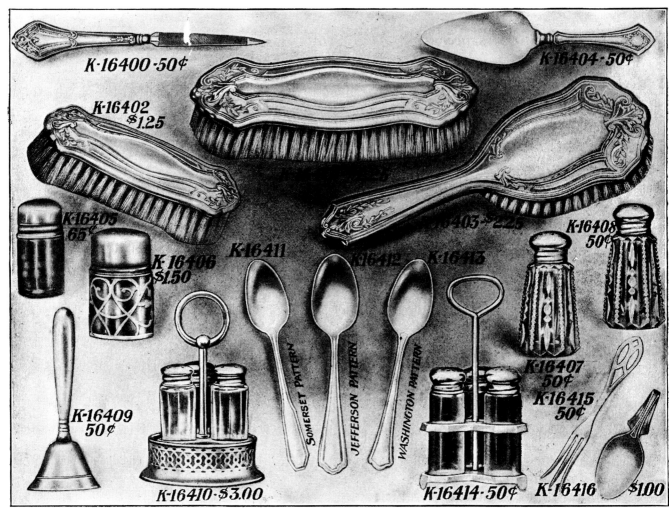

K-16400 - 50¢
K-16402 $1.25
K-16405 65¢
K-16406 $1.50
K-16411
K-16412
K-16413
K-16404 - 50¢
K-16403 - $2.25
K-16408 50¢
K-16407 50¢
K-16415 50¢
K-16409 50¢
K-16410 - $3.00
SOMERSET PATTERN
JEFFERSON PATTERN
WASHINGTON PATTERN
K-16414 - 50¢
K-16416 $1.00

K—16400. Sterling Nail File. 50c.

K—16400A. Sterling Cuticle, Shoe Horn and Button Hook to match. (Not illustrated.) 50c each.

K—16401. Sterling Cloth Brush. $2.25.

K—16402. Sterling Hat Brush. $1.25

K—16403. Sterling Hair Brush. $2.25.

K—16403-A. Sterling Mirror to Match Brush. (Not illustrated.) $4.50.

K—16403-B. Woman's or Man's Sterling Comb. (Not illustrated.) 75c.

K—16403-C. Puff Box, sterling top. (Not illustrated.) $2.25.

K—16403-D. Hair Receiver, sterling top. (Not illustrated.) $2.25.

K—16403-E. Military Brushes. (Not illustrated.) $3.50 pair.

K—16403-F. Salve Jar, sterling top. (Not illustrated.) 50c and 75c each.

K—16403-G. Nail Polisher. (Not illustrated.) 50c and $1.00.

K—16404. Sterling Cheese Spade. 50c.

K—16405. Salts Bottle. Sterling silver top. 65c.

K—16406. Smelling Salts Bottle Sterling silver. Filigree base, 7x5¾. $1.50.

K—16407. Sterling Salt Shaker. 50c.

K—16408. Sterling Pepper Shaker. 50c.

K—16409. Sterling Dinner Bell. 50c.

K—16410. Sterling Castor. $3.00.

K—16411 Sterling Silver Service. "Somerset" pattern. Prices according to weight.

	Each.
Tea Spoons, $9.50, $11.75 and $14.00 dozen................$1.00, $1.25 and	$1.50
Dessert Spoons, $19.00 and $26.25 dozen ....$1.75 and	2.25
Table Spoons, $24.00 and $28.00 dozen ....$2.25 and	2.50
Soup Spoons, round bowls, $21.00 dozen	2 00
Dessert Forks, $19.00 and $23.50 dozen ....$1.75 and	2.25
Dinner Forks, $24.00 and $28.00 dozen ....$2.25 and	2.50
Dessert Knives, hollow handles, silver plated blades, $20.00 dozen..........	2.00
Dinner Knives, hollow handles, silver plated blades, $23.00 dozen..........	2.25
Bouillon Spoons, round bowls, $13.50 dozen	1.25
Coffee Spoons, $5.75 dozen.............	$0.75
Oyster Forks, $10.75 dozen.............	1.00
Butter Spreaders, $14.00 dozen.........	1.25
Berry Spoon	5.00
Bon-bon Spoon	1.00
Jelly Spoon	2 50
Sugar Spoon	1.50
Cold Meat Fork.......................	3.75
Butter Knife.........................	2.00
Cake Server, hollow handle, plated blade	2.50
Gravy Ladle	4.00

Prices of other articles upon request.

K—16412. "Jefferson" Pattern Service. Sectional Plated.

Meat Fork .... .65

	Each.
Berry Spoon	1.00
Tomato Server	1.00
Gravy Ladle	.85
Pie Server	1.50
Cream Ladle	.75
Oyster Ladle	1.50
Medium Soup Ladle...................	2.25
Tea Spoons ....dozen	2.25
Dessert Spoons ....dozen	4.00
Table Spoons ....dozen	4.50
Dessert Forks ....dozen	4.00
Medium Forks ....dozen	4.50
Sugar Shell	.50
Butter Knife.........................	.50
Oyster Forks ....dozen	2.50
Butter Spreaders ....dozen	4.00
Orange Spoons ....dozen	3.00
Individual Salad Forks.........dozen	4.00
Bouillon Spoons ....dozen	4.00
Coffee Spoons ....dozen	2.25
Soup Spoons ....dozen	4.50

Triple Plated.

	Each.
Tea Spoons ....dozen	3.00
Dessert Spoons ....dozen	5.00
Table Spoons ....dozen	$6.00
Dessert Forks ....dozen	5.00
Medium Forks ....dozen	6.00
Soup Spoons ....dozen	6.00
Medium Knives, hollow handles...dozen	8.50
Dessert Knives, hollow handles...dozen	8.00
Flat Handle Medium Knives......dozen	4.00

Remaining descriptions continued on opposite page.

Reliable Plated Ware in Artistic Designs

Gimbels Restricted Delivery Offer on page 4 applies to these goods. If package is to go by Insured Parcel Post, add 5 cents extra. Silverware of $1.00 value and upwards we engrave free of charge with one, two or three initials in script.

K16412. "Jefferson" Pattern Service—Continued from page 164.

	Each.
Flat Handle Dessert Knives......dozen	$8.75
Flat Handle Fruit Knives........dozen	3.25

K—16413. Sterling Silver Service. "Washington" pattern. Prices according to weight.

		Each.
Tea Spoons, $9.50, $11.75 and $14.00 dozen............$1.00, $1.25 and	$1.50	
Dessert Spoons, $19.00 and $21.00 dozen................$1.75 and	2.00	
Table Spoons, $26.25 and $28.00 dozen................$2.25 and	2.50	
Soup Spoons, round bowls, $21.75 dozen	2.00	

		Each.
Dessert Forks, $19.00 and $21.00 dozen.....................$1.75 and	2.00	
Dinner Forks, $24.00 and $26.25 dozen ....$2.25 and	2.50	
Dessert Knives, hollow handles, silver plated blades, $21.50 dozen...........	2.00	
Dinner Knives, hollow handles, silver plated blades, $24.00 dozen...........	2.25	
Bouillon Spoons, round bowls, $16.00 dozen	1.50	
Coffee Spoons, $7.50 dozen.............	.75	
Oyster Forks, $11.50 dozen.............	1.00	
Butter Spreaders, $12.75 dozen........	1 25	
Berry Spoon	5.50	
Bon-bon Spoon	2.00	
Jelly Spoon	3.50	

	Each.
Sugar Spoon	2.00
Cold Meat Fork......................	4.50
Butter Knife	2.50
Cake Server, hollow handle, plated blade	2.75
Cheese Server, hollow handle, plated blade	1.75
Tomato Server	$5.00
Gravy Ladle	5 00
Mayonnaise Ladle	2.50
Sugar Tongs	1.75
Steak Set, two pieces.................	5.25

Prices of other articles to match upon request.

K—16414. Plated Bottle Castor. Three bottles, 50c.
K—16415. Sterling Lemon Fork. 50c.
K—16416 Sterling Baby Spoon. $1.00.

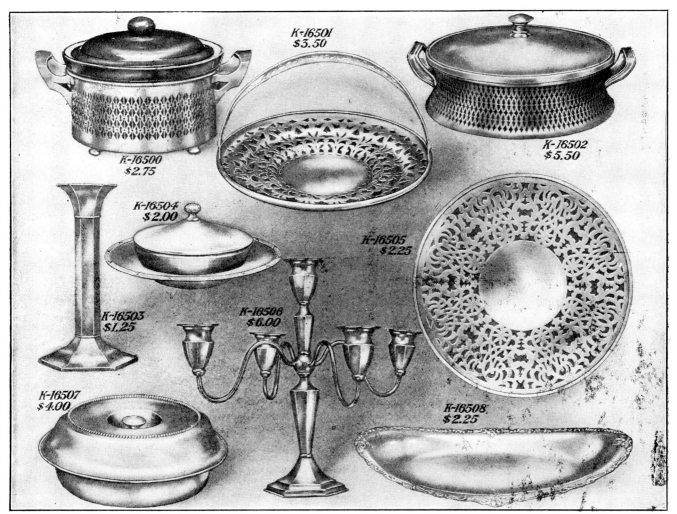

K—16500. Casserole Dish. Quadruple silver plated on hard white metal. Round. 7½ inches in diameter. 4 inches high. $2.75.

K—16501. Cake Basket. Quadruple silver plated on hard white metal. Pierced design. 9½ inches in diameter. $3.50.

K—16502. Bake Dish. Quadruple silver plated on hard white metal. 2½ inches high 9 inches in diameter. $5.50.

K—16503. Candlestick. Quadruple silver plated on hard white metal. Colonial style. 8 inches high. $1.25.

K—16504. Butter Dish. Quadruple silver plated on hard white metal. Glass lining. Round. 7 inches in diameter. Capacity, 3 pints. $2.00.

K—16505. Sandwich Plate. Quadruple silver plated on hard white metal. Pierced design. 9¾ inches in diameter. $2.25.

K—16506. Candelabra. Quadruple silver plated on hard white metal. Five lights. Plain burnished. 11½ inches high. $6.00.

K—16507. Vegetable Dish. Quadruple silver plated on hard white metal. 7½ inches in diameter. $4.00.

K—16508. Bread Tray. Quadruple silver plated on hard white metal. Fancy border. 11¾ inches long. $2.25.

(Not illustrated.)

K—16509. Sterling Silver Child's Cups. $2.75, $3.50, $4.50, $5.75 and $6.50 each.

K—16510. Sterling Silver. Baby Military Brushes. $2.00, $2.75, $3.50 and $3.75 pair.

K—16511. Sterling Silver Baby Rattles. 75c, $1.00, $1.25 and $1.50.

K—16512. Sterling Silver Baby Spoons. 85c, $1.00, $1.25 and $1.50 each.

K—16513. Sterling Silver Child's Fork, Spoon and Food Pusher. $3.25 and $3.50 each.

K—16514. Sterling Silver Pencils. 25c to $2.00 each.

K—16515. Sterling Silver Bud Vases. $1.00 to $5.00 each.

K—16516. Sterling Silver Cheese Servers. 50c to $1.50 each.

K—16517. Sterling Silver Pie and Cake Servers. $1.25 and $1.50.

K—16518. Sterling Silver Tumble Coaster. Glass with sterling mounting. 50c and 75c each.

K—16519. Sterling Silver Individual Castors. Two bottles, $2.25. Three bottles, $2.75 and $3.00.

K—16520. Sterling Silver Corn Holders. 50c pair.

K—16521. Alarm Clocks. Guaranteed movements. 65c to $2.50 each.

New York — Gimbel Brothers — Philadelphia

Tasty, Artistic Marquisette and Dutch Curtains

Some people residing in the country, and which is really the ideal life, have the idea that city houses try to work off old or inferior goods on them. Some houses may attempt this, but they are few in number and small in size. For ourselves, we make the greatest effort to catalogue the latest style, freshest goods and the best values.

Why not apply to one of the Gimbels stores for a charge account. It greatly facilitates shopping by mail or in person. We gladly open such accounts with all people making their responsibility known by references or otherwise.

K-16600
$5.00 Pr.

K-16601
$3.50 Pr.

K-16602
$1.75 complete

K-16603
$2.85 Pr.

K-16604
$4.00 Pr.

K—16600. **White Marquisette Curtains.** An exquisite filet design of decorative merit. Adaptable for dining room or the various living rooms of the home. Its purchase carries every assurance of successful and artistic effect and extended satisfactory service. Length, 2½ yards; width, 36 inches. **$5.00** a pair.

K—16601. **White Marquisette Curtains.** To those looking for unusual treatments in design this popular filet lace effect should appeal. Possesses unusual character. 2½ yards long, 38 inches wide. **$3.50** a pair.

K—16602. **Scrim Dutch Curtains and Valance.** Cluny lace edge appliqued on quality voile scrim. Curtains 2½ yards long. Curtains and valance have a one-inch casing and heading ready to hang. White or Arabian. **$1.75** a set.

K—16603. **Marquisette Curtains** with Cluny insertion and edge. 34 inches wide by 2½ yards long. White or Arabian. **$2.85** a pair.

K—16604. **Artistic Marquisette Curtains.** A charming style that possesses unusual merit. Will add to the furnishings of any room. An attractive quality cambric appliqued on mercerized marquisette. Launders well and hangs gracefully. Length, 2⅓ yards; width, 36 inches. White, ivory or Arabian. **$4.00** a pair.

Charming Novelty Net and Other Curtains

These curtains are positively great values—and give added strength to this splendid catalogue. We have provided big quantities of each number in anticipation of the recognition such bargains will receive from our patrons. See you get your share of them.

K-16700
$2.00 Pr.

K-16701
$1.00 Pr.

K-16703
$1.75 Pr.

K-16704
$3.00 Pr.

K-16702
$2.00 complete

K—16700. Charming Novelty Net Curtain. An exquisite border of linen braid interspersed with Bonaz braid stitching appliqued on quality cable net. Reinforced net edge. 32 inches wide. White or Arabian. $2.00 a pair.

K—16701. Novelty Net Curtains. The continued increasing sales prove the worth. The simplicity of design and excellent quality instantly appeal to one. Renaissance braid border, enhanced with effective Bonaz trimmed corner motif appliqued on French cable net.

White or Arabian. 27 inches wide. 2¼ yards long. $1.00 a pair. 36 inches wide. 3 yards long. $1.75 a pair.

K—16702. White Scrim Dutch Curtains. One of the season's newest styles. By reason of its distinct decorative merit is very desirable. An artistic border of Filet lace effect finished with dainty picquet edge. Valance to match. 16 x 23 inches. White or ivory. Curtains 2¼ yards by 38 inches. $2.00 complete.

K—16703. Handsome Net Curtains. Linen

Cluny lace edge appliqued on French cable net. The extreme simplicity indicates refinement and good taste. White, ivory or Arabian. 36 inches wide. 2½ yards long. $1.75 a pair.

K—16704. Baurman Lace Curtains. Value most unusual at the price. Wearing qualities are unsurpassed. Inside edge and insertion of double cable net. The lace edge and insertion appliqued on French cable net. Well shrunk so as to insure perfect hang. White, ivory or Arabian. Length, 2½ yards. Width, 36 inches. $3.00 a pair.

Gimbels Are Well and Favorably Known to the Trade

Gimbels have furnished vast quantities of goods to the United States Government; a great number of the very largest and most prominent palace hotels; have furnished many big ocean steamers; are listed for supplies with the largest hospitals and public institutions, and their foreign resident establishments buy for a number of the foremost stores in the United States. When shrewd business men who are employed solely to buy economically favor Gimbels, it is the supreme acknowledgment of their merchandise supremacy.

K-16800 $3.50 PR

K-16801 $1.00 PR.

K-16802 $1.25 PR.

K-16803 $1.25 PR

K-16804 $1.75 PR

K-16805 85¢ PR

K—16800. Stencilled Crash Curtains. Equally appropriate for windows, as an overhanging or between doors. Natural color crash with stencilled border in rich blended colorings of green and red, brown and green, or black and green. 2¾ yards long, 40 inches wide. **$3.50 a pair.**

K—16800-a. Couch Cover. 2¾ yards long, 60 inches wide, to match the above (not illustrated). **$3.00 each.** 2¾ yards long, 50 inches wide (not illustrated). **$2.50 each.**

K—16800-b. Table Cover to match the above (not illustrated). 40 inches long, 40 inches wide. **75c each.**

K—16800-c. Table Scarf (not illustrated) to match K—16800. 50x18 inches. **75c each.**

K—16801. Scotch Madras Curtains. 36 inches wide by 2½ yards long. Ivory. Use two to a window. **$1.00 a pair.**

K—16802. Marquisette Curtains. 34 inches wide by 2½ yards long. Effective, two-inch hemstitched hem. White or Arabian. **$1.25 a pair.**

K—16803. Scrim Curtains. Border of French antique lace effect. Hemstitched double hem. Inside insertion makes a beautiful appearance. Quality throughout is one of the Gimbel standards. White or ivory. Length, 2¼ yards; width, 34 inches. **$1.25 a pair.**

K—16804. Organdie Curtains. Pretty band border in a rose design, in combinations of pink and green, yellow and green or blue and green. Appliqued on good quality white dotted Swiss. Charmingly effective. 2½ yards long, 37 inches wide. **$1.75 a pair.** Bed sets to match, having deep ruffle. Bolster piece. For single or full size beds. Not illustrated. **$4.00 a set.**

K—16805. Dainty Swiss Curtains. Floral border. A straight applique of colored swiss in rich shades of pink and green, gold and green or blue. Will give lasting service. Length, 2½ yards; width, 36 inches. **85c a pair.** Bed sets to match with bolster piece. Have deep ruffle. Not illustrated. **$3.50 a set.**

Muslin Curtains Are Essentially Cottage Furnishings

Because of their matchless serviceability, inexpensiveness and extreme daintiness, Muslin Curtains are best suited for cottages and bungalows, bathrooms and kitchens. The Gimbel Muslin Curtains are extra fine value for the money, as comparison will show.

K—16900. Beautiful White Ruffled Swiss Curtains. Nicely finished with dainty-fluted ruffle, inside band and hemstitched border of fine tucks. They make an ideal bedroom curtain. Easily laundered, and for that reason can always be kept fresh and clean—an important item in bedroom furnishings. The quality throughout is excellent, to the extent that the curtain will give satisfaction as long as it lasts. 2½ yards long. 32 inches wide. $1.00 a pair.

K—16901. Pretty White Ruffled Swiss Curtain. One of the ever-popular kind. Popular, because it is practical. It meets the every-day requirements of the ordinary, busy and economical housewife, who must be recognized as belonging to the majority. This curtain has a neat border of tucks and effective hemstitched fluted ruffle around the edge. Will

launder well. It is here offered at a very reasonable price. Length, 2⅜ yards. Width, 30 inches. 75c a pair.

K—16902. Neat White Ruffled Swiss Curtains. Attractive border of tucks with pretty hemstitched ruffle finishing the edge. Our stock would not be complete without this popular style. It is a thoroughly practical curtain, in quality, beauty, durability and price. You could not expect to get elsewhere the good value shown here for the moderate amount asked. What an addition to a window a clean, spotlessly white, soft, prettily draped curtain makes. 2⅜ yards long. 30 inches wide. 50c a pair.

K—16903. Attractive White Filet Effect Swiss Curtains. This style has our hearty endorsement. The lace insertion has been reproduced from the higher priced filet laces, and is a

near copy. The design is dainty, artistic and beautiful in the extreme. It is a distinctively high-grade effect curtain. The Swiss is of the heavier grade closely resembling scrim. Length, 2¼ yards. Width, 33 inches. $1.00 a pair.

K—16904. White Ruffled Swiss Curtains. Effective striped center. Gathered ruffle. Pretty and pleasing to the eye in bedrooms or summer cottages. Very serviceable. 2 1-6 yards long, 20 inches wide. An attractive and inexpensive curtain. 25c a pair.

K—16905. White Dotted Swiss Curtains. Sheer quality dotted Swiss. Dainty fluted ruffle of like quality. Hemstitched hem border. Always a satisfactory curtain. Its purchase will surely please. Length, 2½ yards. Width, 36 inches. $1.25 a pair.

Door Panel, Sash and Window Curtains

Some of the excellent curtains shown on this page are needed somewhere in your house. Think it over! It's wonderful how curtains that are new and crisp tone up the appearance of a room and give the best home spirit.

K—17000. Bris Bise Curtaining. Of quality. Nottingham lace. Decidedly new. Makes an effective sash curtain. Much taste exhibited in this delightful pattern. Loops at top for rod ready to hang. White, cream, or Arabian. 36 inches deep. 50c a yard.

K—17001. Renaissance Door Panel. An exquisite center motif of Renaissance and Bonaz braid appliqued on quality French cable net. Makes a very handsome door panel, a panel we can highly recommend. White, cream or Arabian. 54 inches long by 36 inches wide. $1.00 each.

K—17002. Nottingham Lace Sash Curtain. A distinctive style which is very much in demand. Nicely finished casing at top ready to hang. White or Arabian. Size, 35 inches deep by 38 inches wide. A curtain of worth. Each 20c.

K—17003. Nottingham Sash Net. Allover plaid with squares of filet net to form stripe effect. Makes a very attractive sash curtain. Border on both sides. 30 inches wide. White, cream, or Arabian. 30c a yard.

K—17004. Fish Net in Newest Effect. Splendid wearing qualities in tiny block design. 45 inches wide. White, cream or Arabian. 25c a yard.

K—17005. Colonial Design. Well adapted to curtain material. The pretty border is the same on both sides. Overlocked edge. Has wonderful wearing qualities and makes an effective sash curtain. Represents good goods at a low cost. 30 inches wide. White, cream or Arabian. 30c a yard.

K—17006. Colored Double Bordered Voile. On white and cream grounds, in pink, blue, and blue and green dainty effects. 40 inches wide at 20c a yard.

K—17007. Pretty White Scotch Thread Lace Sash Curtains. This is one of our choicest patterns of this popular style. Its purchase will surely please. Our recommendation for quality and style. Loops at top for rod ready to hang. 36 inches deep by 39 inches wide. 50c each.

K—17008. Colored Double Bordered Voile. In dainty color combinations of pink and green, blues, yellow and green and lavender, and green on white and cream ground. Two-inch hemstitched edges. 40 inches wide. 28c a yard.

The Gimbel Stores Are Headquarters for Curtains and Housefurnishings

These Curtains are positively great values—and give added strength to this splendid book. We have provided good quantities of each number in anticipation of the recognition such bargains will receive from our patrons. See you get your share of them. They will look well in your home and make fine wedding or anniversary presents.

K—17100. High Grade Cable Net Lace Curtains. Wide Cluny lace insertion effect. Lace motif design in center. This has proven a most satisfactory style. Good taste reflected in its neat appearance. White or Arabian. Length, 3 yards; widths, 46 inches. **$2.00 a pair.**

K—17101. "Italian" Filet Effect Panel Lace Curtains. An exceedingly attractive style. Rich in appearance. Its wearing qualities are unexcelled. Made of quality Egyptian yarn, firmly woven. White, rich mellow ivory or dark ecru. 2½ yards long. 33 inches wide, **$1.25 each.** 2½ yards long, 45 inches wide, **$1.75 each.**

K—17102. "Italian" Filet Lace Curtains. A design that has character, reproduced from the high-grade, hand-made kind. Refinement and good taste embodied in these curtains. A pleasing effect certain to be achieved by the use of this style. White or ivory. Length, 2½ yards. Width, 43 inches. **$3.25 a pair.**

K—17103. Excellent Quality Nottingham Lace Curtains. An exquisite border of Cluny lace effect. Unusually attractive and has splendid wearing qualities. Made of English thread, firmly woven. Overlocked edge insures durability. A very high grade for the low price we have placed on it. White or Arabian. 3 yards long. 50 inches wide. **$1.00 a pair.**

K—17104. Charming Lace Panel Curtains. Made of fine quality English thread. An effective design reproduced from the hand-made filet and Cluny lace ones which are to be had only at much higher prices. Its durability is unexcelled. An adornment that will add immeasurably to the appearance of the room. White or Arabian. 50 inches wide. 2½ yards long. **75c each.**

K—17105. Nottingham Lace Curtains. A style that shows character and taste. Same careful finish as in the higher priced curtains. Effectively screens the window, but does not debar the light. One of the Gimbel standard. Length, 2½ yards. Width, 33 inches. **55c a pair.** White or Abrabian.

Matting and Cedar Boxes, Folding Screens, Etc.

The Gimbel Stores Outbid Competitors. The Gimbel Stores have bid on, and furnished complete, including interior decorations, rugs, carpets, kitchenware, etc., the very largest hotels; showing that Gimbels prices are the lowest and Gimbels merchandise the best. Hotel men, who are good judges of quality, know this and patronize Gimbels.

Restricted Delivery Offer Applies.

K-17200 · $3.75

K-17201 - $1.25

K-17203 $1.50

K-17204 $1.75

K-17202 $1.95

K-17205 $8.00

K-17206 50¢

DECORATIVE AND DRAUGHT FOLDING SCREENS.

K—17200. 3 Fold Fumed Oak Frame, filled with green or brown burlap, 5 ft. 8 in. high..	$3.75
K—17201. 3 Fold Golden Oak Frame, filled with green silkoline, 5 ft. high..	1.25
4 Fold Fumed Oak Frame, filled with green or brown burlap, 5 ft. 8 in. high...	5.00
3 Fold Fumed Oak Frame, double burlap, green, brown or blue, 5 ft. 8 in. high...	5.00
4 Fold Fumed Oak Frame, double burlap, green, brown or blue, 5 ft. 8 in. high...	6.75
3 Fold Fumed Oak Frame, burlap with upper panels of tapestry, 5 ft. 8 in. high...	8.00
4 Fold Fumed Oak Frame, burlap with upper panels of tapestry, 5 ft. 8 in. high...	10.50
3 Fold White Enamel Frame, cretonne filled, 5 ft. 8 in. high......	10.00
3 Fold White Enamel Frame, cretonne filled, 5 ft. 8 in. high......	13.50
3 Fold Solid Mahogany Frame, filled with foliage tapestry, 5 ft. 8 in. high...	17.50
3 Fold Gold Leaf Frame Louis XVI—bevel glass panels—brocade filled, 5 ft. 8 in. high.......................................	90.00

45	"	"	20	"	"	22	"	"	.... 20.00
50	"	"	24	"	"	26	"	"	.... 25.00

K—17202. SHIRT WAIST BOXES.

Covered with best quality white matting.

29 inches long,	16 inches wide,	15½ inches high....	$1.95
33 "	" 17 "	" 15½ " "	3.00
35 "	" 18½ "	" 14 " "	4.50
38 "	" 19 "	" 17 " "	6.50
46 "	" 20 "	" 19 " "	8.00
48 "	" 20 "	" 20 " "	9.00

K—17202b. "BED" BOXES. Roll Under the Bed.

A most convenient wardrobe box. Covered with best white matting.

38 inches long,	20 inches wide,	8 inches high........	$4.50
42 "	" 21 "	" 8 " "	6.50
48 "	" 24 "	" 8 " "	7.50

K—17203. Solid Mahogany Candlestick. 12 inches high. $1.50.

K—17204. Tabourette. 19 inches high. Fumed oak or mahogany finish. $1.75 each.

K—17205. **CEDAR CHESTS.** Made of genuine red cedar. Moth proof and dust proof. Outer surfaces polished in the natural color of the wood.

38 inches long,	19 inches wide,	18 inches high........	$8.00
37 "	" 20 "	" 16 " "	14.00

K—17206. Foot Stool. 8 inches high, 9 inches wide and 12 inches long. Rattan top. Oak or mahogany finish. 50c. each.

New York — Gimbel Brothers — Philadelphia

The Most Serviceable Screens for Porches and Verandas

Any porch or veranda can be made cool, shady and comfortable with these screens, also they give a privacy that is often much wanted. Gimbels recommend using the New "Aerolux" Wooden-Slat Screens, "Colonial" Sun-Proof Painted Bamboo Screens or Bamboo Screens in dyed or natural color. These goods come under Gimbels Restricted Delivery Offer. See page 4.

K-17300
$14.50

K-17303
$16.00

K-17301
$5.75

K-17302
$8.00

K-17304
$15.00

AEROLUX SCREENS

The best screen for your porch is the "AEROLUX." It is most effective for shutting out the glare of the sun, while permitting proper ventilation. A special feature is the guide rope attachment, which holds screen securely in position and prevents swaying.

Aerolux Screens are constructed of uniform strips of specially treated linden wood, bound or woven together with strongest seine twine, assuring durability.

"Aerolux" Veranda Screens. 7/8 in. slats. Color: green, olive or brown and olive combined.

4 ft. wide x 7 ft. 6 in. drop	$2.50
6 ft. wide x 7 ft. 6 in. drop	3.50
8 ft. wide x 7 ft. 6 in. drop	4.50
10 ft. wide x 7 ft. 6 in. drop	5.75

The "Veranda" Grade can be ordered in any width or drop in excess of stock sizes. Send measurements for estimate, and we will quote prices.

"Aerolux" Bungalow Screens. 1 1/8 in. slats. Green only.

4 ft. wide x 6 1/2 ft. drop	$1.80
6 ft. wide x 6 1/2 ft. drop	2.65
8 ft. wide x 6 1/2 ft. drop	3.25
10 ft. wide x 6 1/2 ft. drop	4.25

COLONIAL SCREENS

"Colonial" Sun-Proof Screens. (Inside split of the bamboo) painted dark olive green. Complete with American ropes, iron pulleys and hooks.

4 ft. wide x 8 ft. drop	$1.20
6 ft. wide x 8 ft. drop	2.00
8 ft. wide x 8 ft. drop	2.50
10 ft. wide x 8 ft. drop	3.00
12 ft. wide x 8 ft. drop	3.50

INEXPENSIVE BAMBOO SCREENS

Bamboo Screens. Natural outside bark.

4 ft. wide x 8 ft. drop	$0.65
6 ft. wide x 8 ft. drop	.95
8 ft. wide x 8 ft. drop	1.25
10 ft. wide. x 8 ft. drop	1.60
12 ft. wide x 8 ft. drop	1.90

SUMMER FURNITURE

K—17300. Chaise Lounge. Seat, 22 x 44 inches. Height from seat, 30 inches. Regularly, $18.00. Special, $14.50. Staining, $2.25 extra.

K—17301. Table. 30 inches in diameter. Regularly, $8.00. Special, $5.75. 24 inches, $4.25. 27 inches, $4.75. 33 inches, $6.50. 36 inches, $7.25. 42 inches, $9.50.

K—17302. Side Chair. Brown or green stain finish. Regularly, $12.00. Special, $8.00.

K—17303. Tea Cart. 18 x 28 inches. 28 inches high. Regularly, $20.00. Special, $16.00. Staining, $1.50 extra.

K—17304. Arm Rocker. Regularly, $20.00. Special, $15.00.

New York — Gimbel Brothers — Philadelphia

Engraved Calling Cards, Stamped Stationery, Etc.

All orders for engravings promptly attended to, but a reasonable time is required to execute them—usually from a week to ten days. Plates and dies will be carefully registered and retained subject to customers order. We cannot accept C. O. D. orders for engraving or printing. Gimbels Restricted Delivery Offer applies to Stationery. See page 4.

MONOGRAM DIES.

Numbers—200, 201, 208, 304, 306, 309, 311, 402, 405.

HAND ENGRAVED VISITING CARDS.

A1 to A6. Script Style. Plate and 50 cards. Name only, **$1.00.** Each additional line, **50c.**

B1. Black Old English. Plate and 50 cards. Name only, **$1.75.** Each additional line, **$1.25.**

B2. Shaded Old English. Plate and 50 cards. Name only, **$2.50.** Each additional line, **$2.00.**

C1. Roman. Plate and 50 cards. Name only, **$2.00.** Each additional line, **$1.50.**

C2. Shaded Roman. Plate and 50 cards. Name only, **$2.50.** Each additional line, **$2.00.**

D1 and D2. Block Styles. Plate and 50 cards. Name only, **$1.75.** Each additional line, **$1.25.**

E1. Black Caxton. Plate and 50 cards. Name only, **$2.25.** Each additional line, **$1.75.**

E2. Shaded Caxton. Plate and 50 cards. Name only, **$3.00.** Each additional line, **$2.50.**

PLATE PRINTING.

After plate is made. Prices include the cards.

50 cards from plate	45c
100 cards from plate	75c
100 business cards from plate	90c

PLATE PRINTING ADDITIONAL COST FOR MOURNING BORDERS.

Order Mourning Borders by Number.
See illustrations 9 to 13.

If mourning border is desired, in any width illustrated, the additional cost of each card will be 1c, making 50 cards from plate **95c,** and 100 cards from plate **$1.75.**

CARD ENVELOPES.

Envelopes to match and fit cards, packages of 25	10c
Envelopes to match and fit cards (with mourning border)	25c

COST OF CUTTING MONOGRAM DIES.

Cost of cutting dies in styles illustrated.

No. 200 .... $1.50	No. 304 .... $2.00	No. 311 .... $2.00
No. 201 .... 1.50	No. 306 .... 2.00	No. 402 .... 3.00
No. 208 .... 1.50	No. 309 .... 2.00	No. 405 .... 3.00

CUTTING ADDRESS DIES.

Numbers 312, 313 and other styles.

$1.50 for the first line.

$1.00 for each additional line.

PRICES FOR STAMPING PAPER AFTER DIE IS MADE OR FURNISHED.

Plain color or plain embossing	10c per quire
Gold, silver or white ink	20c per quire
Illuminating in two colors	50c per quire

HAND ENGRAVED INVITATIONS AND ANNOUNCEMENTS.

Prices include inside and outside envelopes with sheets inserted ready for mailing and are for script.

Invitations. $8.00, $9.00 and **$12.00** for first 100 sets or less.

Announcements. $6.00, $8.00 and **$9.00** for first 100 sets. Each extra set of 100 or less, **$2.50, $3.00** and **$4.00.**

Reception, Breakfast, or At Home Cards. Usually three lines. First 100, **$2.75.** Extra, per 100, **$1.50.** Ceremony Church Cards, first 100, **$1.50.** Extra, per 100, **$1.00.**

Prices on Invitations and Announcements in Old English, plain or shaded, will be furnished when amount of matter is ascertained.

MENU AND GUEST CARDS.

Designed and made for all occasions, our stock at all times comprising more than four hundred varieties, many of them exclusive with us. Prices range from **15c** to **$3.00** a dozen.

We do not send samples, but if you are reasonably definite as to your ideas we shall use good judgment in choosing.

BUSINESS AND PROFESSIONAL STATIONERY.

Personal and Professional Cards, Note Heads, Bill Heads, Appointment Cards, etc., engraved or printed at rates below usual.
Samples and estimates on request.

New York — Gimbel Brothers — Philadelphia

Gimbels Fine Papeteries for Polite Correspondence

The productions of the best makers are always in stock in every desirable shade and size as approved by people of refinement and taste. More than 400 different shades and sizes. Gimbels Restricted Delivery Offer applies. See page 4.

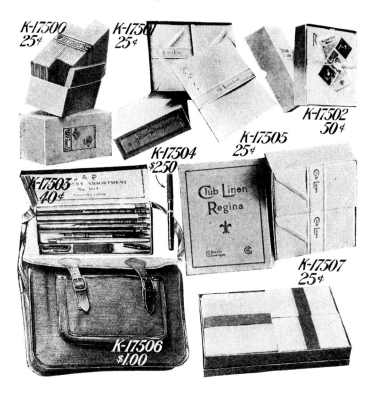

K—17500. Highland Linen Correspondence Cards. Blue, white, pink, grey, acorn or violet. 24 cards and 24 envelopes. **25c.**

K—17501. Beautiful Rose=Bud Die=Stamped Initial Stationery. Initial stamped in blue with a dainty rose spray prettily tinted. 24 sheets of white paper with initial and 24 plain white envelopes. **25c.**

K—17502. Highland Linen Stationery. Gold initial. 24 white sheets with initial and 24 plain envelopes. **50c.**

K—17503. Fancy Pencil Set. Consists of an assortment of pencils, pens and an eraser. In various fancy box tops. **40c box.**

K—17504. Waterman's Ideal Fountain Pen. 14K. gold point. Guaranteed. Choice of fine, medium or stub points. **$2.50 to $10.00.**

K—17505. Club Linen Stationery. 60 sheets of white paper and 50 envelopes to match. **25c.**

K—17506. School Bag. A very fine quality, heavy grey mixed canvas. Has a very large outside pocket. This bag is all bound with tan leather and has shoulder strap of same. Commodious, strong and very good looking. Any school boy will be pleased to own one. Gimbel value. **$1.00.**

K—17507. Stationery. This box contains 48 sheets of excellent quality linen paper and 48 envelopes to match. Can be had in white or blue. **25c. a box.**

K—17508. Children's Writing Paper. 24 sheets of decorated paper and 24 plain white envelopes. **25c.**

K—17509. London Club Lawn. 84 sheets of white paper. Neatly boxed. **35c.** Envelopes to match, 100 in a box. **35c.** Or by package of 25. **10c.**

K—17510. Rosepoint Die=Stamped Initial Correspondence Cards. 24 white cards with blue initial and a dainty rose spray prettily tinted and 24 plain white envelopes. **25c box.**

K—17511. Highland Linen Correspondence Cards. Die-stamped gold initial. 24 white cards with initial and 24 plain white envelopes. **50c.**

K—17512. Highland Linen ·Stationery. White, pink, grey, acorn or violet. 24 sheets of paper and 24 envelopes to match. **25c.**

K—17513. Crane's Lawn Stationery. 48 sheets of all linen paper and 48 envelopes to match. White only. The envelopes are the long narrow effect, now the newest and most popular style. Artistically boxed. **$1.00.**

K—17514. Highland Linen Pad. Contains 50 sheets. White only. It can be had in three sizes at **15c, 20c** and **25c** each. The one illustrated is **20c.**

PLAYING CARDS AND ACCES= SORIES

A large stock of the most popular makes — Steamboat, Fauntleroy, Pinochle, Whist, Congress, Rambler, etc. **10c to 75c** a pack.

Chips, Counters, Score Cards, etc. Prices on request.

Special prices on above to clubs buying quantities.

TALLY CARDS

A great variety designed for all occasions, from **10c to 75c** a dozen.

Die=Stamped Gold Initial Stationery. 24 sheets of plain white paper with a gold initial and 24 plain white envelopes to match. **30c a box.**

Die=Stamped Gold Initial Correspondence Cards. Box of 24 cards with gold letter and 24 plain white envelopes. **30c a box.**

Lenox Linen Stationery. 96 sheets to a package. **15c a package.**

Lenox Linen Envelopes. 100 envelopes in a box. **20c a box.**

Carlton Cambric Writing Paper. 84 sheets of plain white paper neatly boxed. **25c a box.**

Carlton Cambric Envelopes. 25c a box of 100.

Willington Bond Typewriter Paper. Size, 8½ x 11 inches. 500 sheets to a package. **50c a ream.**

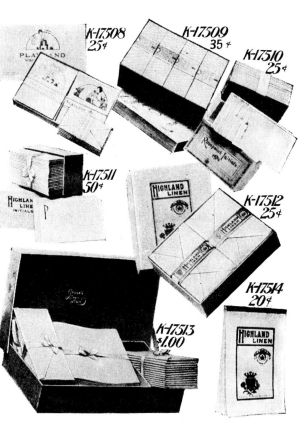

Just Think of $2.75 Buying This
Thoroughly Well-Made
HANDSOME ROCKER 🖙

It's Really Grand Value at $3.75, which is the Usual Price

Restricted Delivery Offer Applies

There is a chief of high reputation as furniture buyer for each of the great Gimbel stores, and it is the Gimbel policy that buyers of all lines shall as much as possible—as much as is consistent with the local requirements of each store—*buy together.*

The combined orders and *the associated thought* of the buyers mean big savings to us and in turn to you. In the case of these chairs the Catalogue Man was not even content to let the joint buying go in the usual way, fine as the arrangement is, but went to each buyer separately and asked him as a personal favor, inasmuch as there were to be but nine pages of furniture in this book, to make them unusually strong—to illustrate some things most in demand for Spring and Summer requirements and to have them of unusual

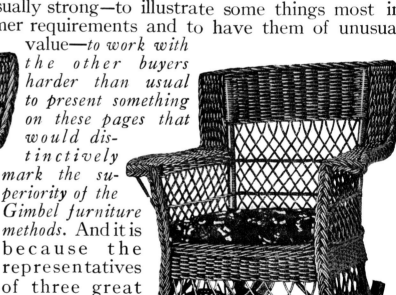

K—17600. **Handsome Reed Rocker.** Extremely well made. High back with closely woven roll all around back and arms and extending down to bottom of front legs. The back is 28 inches high and the seat is 21 inches, making it roomy and very comfortable. Finished in brown, green or shellac. Is appropriate for the porch, sitting room, bedroom or elsewhere in the house. Regular price $3.75. Offered through the catalogue, special at $2.75.

value—*to work with the other buyers harder than usual to present something on these pages that would distinctively mark the superiority of the Gimbel furniture methods.* And it is because the representatives of three great stores in three different cities pulled together that three especially fine bargains are presented to you here.

$5.50

K—17601. **Beautiful Reed Arm Chair.** Fine quality reed, large and roomy. The comfortable broad arms well braced underneath and the chair throughout is both sightly and strong—a chair that diffuses the home feeling if placed on the porch or any room in the house. The height of the back from seat is 21 inches while the seat is 20 inches broad.

In green, brown or shellac finishes. Regular price $7.00. Special price through this catalogue $5.50. Seat cushion covered with fancy cretonne 75c or seat and small pad in back $1.50 extra—or $7.00 complete.

$5.50

K—17602. **Attractive Reed Rocker.** Matches arm chair K—17601. Also of sturdy reed. 21 inches high from seat, with 20 inch breadth of seat.

Thoroughly strongly made and well finished in brown, green or shellac. Regular price $7.00. Special $5.50. Neat cushion covered with fancy cretonne 75c extra, or with seat and small pad in back $1.50 extra —or $7.00 for the chair complete.

New York — Gimbel Brothers — Philadelphia

The Gimbel Furniture Sections Are Stores of Proved Reliability

There are two kinds of furniture that appear much alike at the e are most particular that every piece of furniture entering or made simply to sell—the other to wear and give satisfaction. W start, but vastly different after a little while. The one kind is leaving our salesrooms or warehouses shall be honest—as good underneath as it appears on the surface. You take no chance if you buy your furniture here.

Gimbels liberal restricted delivery offer applies, see page 4.

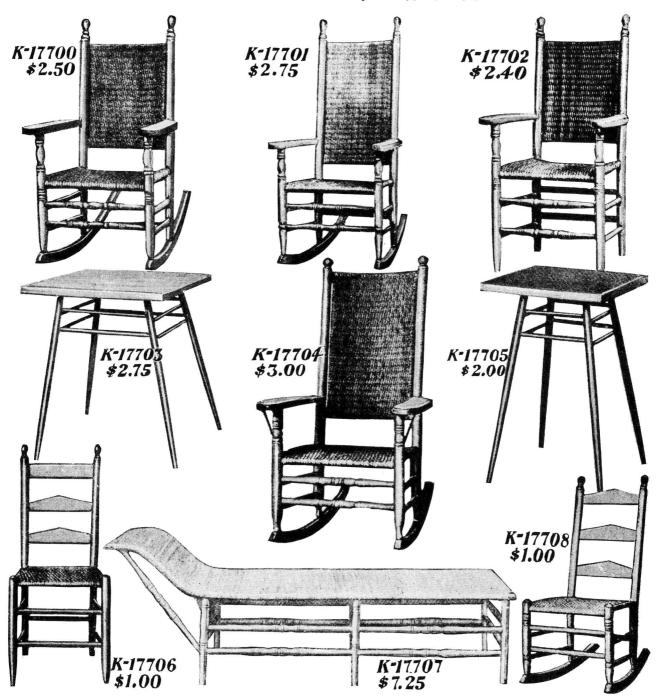

K-17700 $2.50

K-17701 $2.75

K-17702 $2.40

K-17703 $2.75

K-17704 $3.00

K-17705 $2.00

K-17706 $1.00

K-17707 $7.25

K-17708 $1.00

K—17700. **Arm Rocker.** Made of white maple, finished in natural shellac or green. Broad arms, double woven reed seat and back. Handsomely turned front posts. **$2.50.**

K—17701. **Arm Rocker.** Medium sized frame of white maple. Double woven reed seat and back. Flat arms, high back. **$2.75.**

K—17702. **Arm Chair.** Frame of white maple, finished in natural shellac or green. Broad arms, double woven reed seat and back. Handsomely turned front posts. **$2.40.**

K—17703. **Table.** In white maple, square top. Round legs. **$2.75.**

K—17704. **Arm Rocker.** Frame of white maple, finished in natural shellac. Broad arms supported by metal arm braces with double woven reed seat and back. This is the most comfortable chair in the entire collection. **$3.00.**

K—17705. **Table.** Frame of white maple, finished in natural shellac. Square top and round legs. This is a slightly smaller table than K—17703. **$2.00.**

K—17706. **Side Chair.** Frame of white maple, finished in natural shellac. Double woven reed seat and flat back. **$1.00.**

K—17707. **Couch.** Top of split reed and strong substantial frame and white maple. Finished in natural shellac or green. **$7.25.**

K—17708. **Side Rocker.** Frame of white maple, finished in natural shellac. Double woven reed seat and flat back. Matches K—17706 chair. **$1.00.**

Gimbels Paris, London and American Style Book

Improved Chinese Grass Furniture—Durable and Attractive

At 25% and upwards Less Than is Usually Asked for Similar Furniture of Other Materials. This new Grass Furniture, imported directly for us, is manufactured in Hong Kong, China, under American supervision, and is therefore made in the best American designs for practicability and attractiveness. Restricted Delivery Offer applies. See Page 4.

K-17800 $6.00

K-17801 $4.85

K-17802 $6.00

K-17803 $7.50 EACH

K-17804 $6.75

Guaranteed points of superiority of this new Grass Furniture over all similar makes:

It is sea grass, gathered from the China Sea along the Yang-tse Kiang River, cured, dried and hand-woven into a cord which is then woven through the strands of reed to form a complete, compact article. As this grass grows in the ocean it naturally offers the greatest resistance to the effects of moisture and is almost waterproof.

This grass, being thoroughly impregnated with salt and other mineral substances, absorbed while growing, does not burn readily and eliminates the danger always present in articles manufactured from land grass or similar substances.

As a base, the best quality Malacca cane is used—the strongest and most elastic rattan known. To the frame work a fabric of the best grade of reed is woven. No bamboo is used in the construction of this furniture.

At the seat the frame is bound together with the strands of peel cane, which adds further strength at the point of heaviest strain. In addition a support of the same material is woven underneath the seat to prevent sagging. This combination of raw materials produces a resiliency and elasticity impossible to obtain from a rigid wooden frame and therefore these goods offer the highest degree of comfort attainable in this class of furniture.

The only wood used in the manufacture of these chairs is the runners on the rockers.

No shellac or other finish is needed; the goods are ready for use in their natural state. Can be cleaned by scrubbing with brush and water, though care should be taken to remove all dust before wetting.

K—17800. Grass Chair or Rocker. Broad braced arms. Closely woven seat and back. **$6.00.** Matches K—17803.

K—17801. Celebrated Peel Cane Hour Glass Chair. The largest and strongest chair made. Known as the three stick chair because of its extra braces in front. **$4.85.** By careful comparison it will be noted that the price quoted is from $2.15 to $3.15 less than prices quoted elsewhere for a similar chair. This chair is not of the grass described at top of this page.

K—17802. Grass Table. Top 24 inches in diameter, 30 inches high. Shelf underneath. well braced top. **$6.00.**

K—17803. Grass Chair or Rocker. Large broad seat and back. Closely woven seat and apron around bottom. **$7.50 each.** Matches K—17800. Similar chair made in reed, rattan or willow cannot be purchased for less than $12.00.

K—17804. Celebrated Grass India or China Reclining Chair. Full size. High back and extension foot rest. **$6.75.** Similar chair in reed, rattan or willow cannot be purchased for less than $20.00.

These Fine Chairs Are All Special Values

Too much poor furniture upon the market—no doubt about that. Too much furniture made merely to sell. The poor, miserable stuff that drops apart looks as good in a picture as the best. Judged at first sight the furniture itself seems fine, but there is soon keen disappointment. Don't buy that kind. Buy the quality kind as presented here. Restricted Delivery Offer applies. Please see page 4.

K-17900
$14.00

K-17902
$18.75

K-17901
$18.75

K-17903
$15.00

K-17904
$25.00

K—17900. Mahogany High Back Rocker. Upholstered Spring seat covered in tapestry. 19 inches broad in front, 18 inches deep. Cane panel back, flat arms. Back is 26 inches high from seat. **$14.00.**

K—17901. Adam Model Mahogany Rocker. Cane seat, cane panel back. Seat is 19 inches broad in front and 18 inches deep. Back is 25 inches high from seat. **$18.75.**

K—17902. Adam Model Mahogany Arm Chair. To match K—17901 Mahogany Rocker. Same dimensions. **$18.75.**

K—17903. Wing Chair. Upholstered in cretonne or denim, legs may be had in mahogany or white enamel. Spring seat and back. Roll arms. Wings are well padded and exceedingly soft. Seat 19 inches broad at front and 18 inches deep. Back 25 inches high from seat. The back and wing are so shaped as to conform to the body. Very comfortable. $15.00.

K—17904. Fireside Arm Chair. Upholstered in Tapestry. Claw feet of Mahogany. Spring seat and back, filled with hair and moss, seat 19 inches broad at front and 18 inches deep. The chair is very roomy and comfortable just the thing to lounge in. Back 25 inches high from seat. $25.00.
Arm Rockers to match, $25.00.

New York — Gimbel Brothers — Philadelphia

179

UPHOLSTERING OF NEW FURNITURE—FREE

Gimbels Restricted Delivery Offer Applies. See page 4.

A departure that is new and striking—something that permits of wide choosing of shapes and materials and a truly fine saving to you in addition. Take your choice from many styles, select your material and without any charge for labor whatsoever, we do the additional upholstering.

You only pay for the materials—the frame, the springs, the filling and the fabric—and we do the work of upholstery, of putting on the materials that you have selected in the store or from samples we have submitted you by mail—tapestry, damask, plush, velour, or whatsoever it is—without charge for the labor which we do in our own workrooms; and do it skillfully.

The styles illustrated on this page are upholstered with best hair and moss in black and brown striped Bedford Furniture Denim.

When asking for samples by mail, select the style chair or davenport from shapes shown in this book, then kindly give us an idea as to what your room scheme is—the kind of fabric you wish for the covering, the color or colors, etc., and we will send samples and quote you the total cost.

The prices quoted are for pieces wholly completed, upholstered with best hair and moss, in brown and black striped Bedford Furniture Denim that is very sightly, in excellent taste and that wears finely. Understand fully at the prices quoted, no charge has been made for doing the work—no charge for the labor of upholstery—that goes to you at the prices absolutely free. If the denim is not wanted, prices will of course change according to the value of the material used for covering.

K-18000 $32.50   K-18001 $14.75   K-18002 $23 50

K—18000. Fireside Wing Chair. Upholstered as stated at top. $32.50.

K—18001. Woman's Arm Chair. Mahogany finish legs. Spring edge. $14.75.

K—18002. Wing Fireside Arm Chair. Solid mahogany legs, spring edge and back. $23.50.

K-18003 $62.50   K-18004 $69.50

K—18003. Davenport. Spring seat, arms and back. $62.50.

K—18004. Davenport. Spring seat, arms and back. $69.50.

K-18005 $60.00   K-18006 $56.00

K—18005. Two-Piece Chaise Longue. Spring back, arms, seat and foot rest. $60.00.

K—18006. Chaise Longue. Springs throughout. Comfortable day bed or lounge. Tufted seat and back. $56.00.

New York — Gimbel Brothers — Philadelphia

Seeking Substantial, Inexpensive, Fine-Looking Furniture?

Gimbels were the largest buyers of Furniture this season, having to stock three mammoth stores, and naturally they obtained the utmost price concessions that huge buying makes. So, whether you want a modest cottage piece, or a splendid, hand carved specimen of the cabinetmaker's art, Gimbels prices will be lowest of any store. These goods come under Gimbels Restricted Delivery Offer. See page 4.

K-18100
$25.00

K-18101
$25.00

K-18102
$13.50

K-18103
$15.75

K-18104
$16.50

K-18105
$16.50

K-18106
$8.75

K—18100. **Colonial Model Dresser.** Dust-proof construction, a modern idea. Heavy plank top, 42 x 22 inches. Good quality French bevel plate mirror, 30 x 24 inches. All drawers fitted with wood knobs, lock and key. Substantially made and a decidedly fine value. May be had in Circassian walnut or mahogany. **$25.00.**

K—18101. **Colonial Model Chiffonnier.** Matches Bureau No. K—18100. Same substantial construction throughout and a fine piece of furnishing. Heavy plank top, 34 x 20 inches. French plate mirror, 22 x 16 inches. All drawers fitted with wood knobs, lock and key. May be had in Circassian walnut or mahogany. **$25.00.**

K—18102. **Good-Looking, Inexpensive Chiffonnier.** Fine for the summer cottage. Straight front top is 32 x 19 inches. Plain French plate mirror, 16 x 20 inches. All drawers are fitted with wood knobs and lock and key. Tasteful and durable. May be had in white enamel or golden ash. **$13.50.**

K—18103. **Cottage Style Dresser.** Matches Chiffonnier No. K—18102. Straight front top is 38 x 20 inches. Plain French plate mirror, 22 x 28 inches. All drawers fitted with wood knobs, lock and key. Well and durably made. May be had in white enamel or golden ash. **$15.75.**

K—18104. **Chiffonnier.** Matches Bureau No. K—18105. Serpentine front. Top is 32 x 19 inches. French bevel plate mirror, 16 x 20 inches. All drawers fitted with wood knobs, lock and key. May be had in tuna mahogany, bird's-eye maple, Circassian walnut or mahogany. **$16.50.**

K—18105. **Dresser.** Serpentine front. Top is 42 x 21 inches. Fine quality French plate mirror, 22 x 28 inches. Graceful scroll standards. All drawers fitted with wood knobs, lock and key. May be had in tuna mahogany, bird's-eye maple, Circassian walnut or mahogany. A handsome dresser at the price. **$16.50.**

K—18106. **Combination Wash Stand and Dresser.** Called "Toilet Wash Stand." Swell front top, 32 x 19 inches. Plain French plate mirror, 16 x 20 inches. Rack below mirror for towels. Dresser part has three drawers fitted with wood knobs. Fine for the small room. Made in golden oak or white enamel. **$8.75.**

This Is an Interesting Page as to Goods and Values

In good reliable Furniture, beyond doubt we can serve you best. Compare prices with what you can get elsewhere, and keep the reliability of our goods in mind. Write us for full information on anything you may want.

K-18200
$15.00

K-18202
$6.75

K-18201
$7.50

K-18203
$3.75

K-18205
$12.00

K-18204
$12.00

K-18207
$5.00

K-18206
$14.50

K-18209
$4.25

K-18208
$5.75

For full descriptions see opposite page.

New York — Gimbel Brothers — Philadelphia

182

This Is an Interesting Page as to Goods and Values

Comfort, Wear, Economy make this page a most interesting one. It depicts goods of high standard at the lowest consistent prices. Gimbels Restricted Delivery Offer applies. See page 4.

K—18200. Englander Couch Bed. Made of heavy durable steel angles throughout, braced with best steel tie rods. Spring supported by tempered steel helicals. Ball-bearing socket castors, steel wheels. All parts finished in finest quality gold bronze. Mattress has a roll edge and is filled with good white cotton covered with heavy grade plain green denim on the outside and good quality bed ticking on the inside. Prices include mattress. Shown as a full size bed measuring 54 inches wide by 6 ft. 3 in. long. When closed measures 30 in. wide by 6 ft. 3 in. long.
With Woven Wire fabric. Special. **18.00**
With National fabric. Special....**$15.00**

K—18201. Foldaway Chair Cot. Takes up very little space and goes readily into any part of a room where an easy chair will go. Opens with one movement to make a comfortable bed.

Thoroughly durable in construction, well finished throughout. Heavy canvas duck bottom, supported by steel helicals. Resilient, comfortable and durable. **$7.50.**

K—18202. Wit-Edge Wire Spring. Made in all sizes to fit iron or brass beds at the same price. Single and double weave wire fabric with woven wire wit-edge side guard. 1¼-inch steel supports under fabric. Fabric supported by steel helicals. **$6.75.**

K—18203. White Enamel Bed. In "Porslanlyke" finish. Continuous post with four filling rods. Very strong in construction. Just the thing for bungalows. **$3.75.**

K—18204. Brass Beds. Continuous post design. Two-inch continuous post, five one-inch filling rods with ball connection. Bright or satin finish. All sizes. **$12.00.**

K—18205. Brass Bed. Colonial model. Two-inch post. Colonial caps, five one-inch fillers in panel effect and one-inch top rod. Bright or satin finish. All sizes. **$12.00.**

K—18206. Brass Bed. Continuous post model. Massive in design, attractive in appearance, bright or satin finish. Two-inch continuous posts. Two-inch fillers and ball connections. All sizes. **$14.50.**

K—18207. White Enamel Bed. Steel bed in "Porslanlyke" enamel finish. One-inch continuous post; ⅜-inch fillers. Artistic panel effect. May be had in 3/0, 3/6, 4/0 and 4/6 sizes. **$5.00.**

K—18208. Brass Bed. Two-inch posts of simple design and very strongly constructed. Has five filling rods. Bright or satin finish. May be had in all sizes. **$5.75.**

K—18209. White Enamel Bed. Steel bed finished in white "Porslanlyke" enamel. One-inch continuous posts; 5⅜-inch fillers. In attractive design. May be had in 3/0, 3/6, 4/0 and 4/6 sizes. **$4.25.**

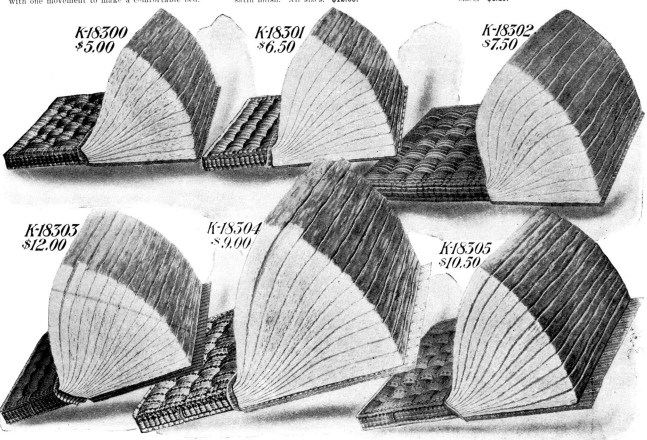

K-18300 $5.00   K-18301 $6.50   K-18302 $7.50
K-18303 $12.00   K-18304 $9.00   K-18305 $10.50

The Best Make of Cotton Felt Mattresses

The mattresses illustrated above are guaranteed to be made of strictly sanitary 100 per cent. pure cotton felt, and of all new material. They are made by a firm that produces the highest quality of cotton felt mattresses manufactured in this country and are mattresses that have the luxury and comfort-giving qualities which are so necessary for restful slumber. The great cotton crop of 1914 and Europe's inability to take its usual share is accountable for the very low prices that follow—for as you know the price of Cotton is low.

K—18300. A Real Cotton Felt Mattress. Built up of layers of clean, new, unbleached felt. Covered with a good quality floral art pattern ticking. Firmly stitched edges and regular biscuit tufting. Full 45-lb. weight, in full size, with a 4-inch border. Value, $7.50. Special, **$5.00.**

K—18301. Cotton Felt Mattress. Made with five pounds more clean, new, sanitary cotton felt than is used in the average mattress. In strong, striped ticking with a 5-inch border. Round corners and an Imperial Stitched Roll Edge. Weight, 50 lbs. for the full size. Special, **$6.50.**

K—18302. A Splendid Mattress. Made from specially selected felted cotton, built up layer upon layer. Covered in a durable twill effect, striped ticking, with Imperial Stitched Roll Edge and 5-inch boxing. Firmly biscuit tufted throughout with white cotton tufts, which prevent bunching or shifting of the stock. 50-lb. weight, in full size. Special, **$7.50.**

K—18303. Mattress. The layers of felt, light, downy, clean and pure as sunshine, are built up one upon another, fifteen in all, and encased in the finest quality 8 oz. sateen finish ticking.
The Three-Row French Imperial Edge and round corners. The Imperial Edge is closely and firmly stitched all around the outer edges on top and bottom, while an extra row of stitches is placed through the border between the rolls, thus making the most durable and firmest edge possible. The round corners allow extra room for tucking the bed covers in, which is a very necessary feature on a well-draped bed. It has strong biscuit tufting, nothing but first quality white cotton tufts and tested tufting twine being used; also side handles for convenience in turning and handling. Weight in full size, 50 lbs. With an occasional sun bath, this mattress should last indefinitely. Value, $15.00. Special, **$12.00.**

K—18304. Solid Comfort Mattress. Pure, new, wholesome cotton, woven into layers of light, resilient, absolutely sanitary elastic cotton felt. Know what solid comfort means when you sleep on one of these 50-lb. beds, covered in beautiful French art pattern sateen ticking. Imperial Stitched Roll Edge, with extra row of stitching all around the border between the roll to make a firmer edge. Made with side handles for convenience in handling and turning. Value, $12.50. Special, **$9.00.**

K—18305. An Extra Fine Mattress. Filled with a beautiful, pure, white bleached cotton felt which has been treated by a special chemical process which makes it absolutely non-absorbent and vermin proof—very desirable features in any bedding. French art pattern ticking, extra heavy and closely woven; three-row Imperial Edge; perfect tufting; 5-inch border; round corners; side handles; 50-lb. weight in the full size. Special, **$10.50.**

Gimbel Go-Carts and Coaches Are Built for Utility, Style and Comfort

The Gimbel Go-Carts and Coaches are built along the newest approved scientific lines for the comfort, ease and safety of the baby. Each is built to safeguard the baby's back, the spine the head and the limbs—no matter how the baby squirms and moves about, its tender bones will find a restful position in a Gimbel vehicle. Each has the hearty endorsement of every physician, nurse or other person interested in the development of the baby.

Restricted Delivery Offer. See page 4.

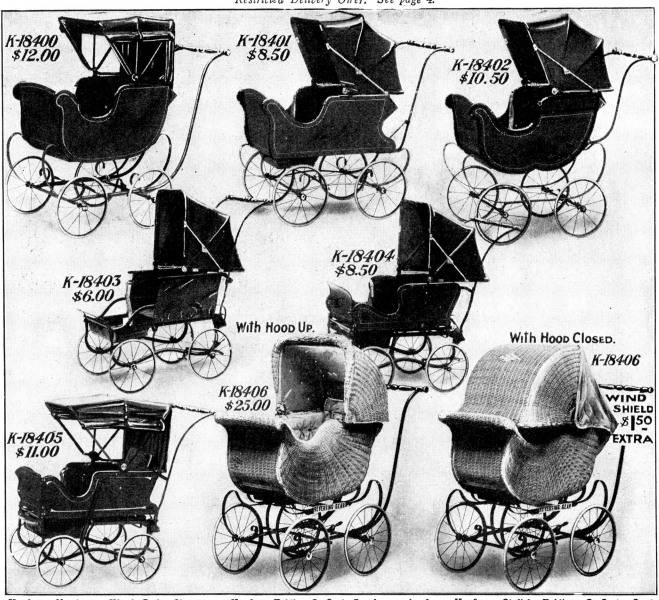

K-18400 $12.00
K-18401 $8.50
K-18402 $10.50
K-18403 $6.00
K-18404 $8.50
With Hood Up.
K-18405 $11.00
K-18406 $25.00
With Hood Closed. K-18406
WIND SHIELD $1.50 EXTRA

K—18400. Handsome Wood Body Sleeper. Leatherette auto hood equipped with back and side curtains to prevent draughts, thus affording complete protection to the child within. Reclining adjustable back. If one position becomes tiresome, it can very easily be changed to another and comfort to the little one thereby assured. Deep footwell. Serviceable tubular gear. 12-inch wheels with ½-inch rubber tires. This sleeper is one of the best in the market, and combines comfort, quality and beauty at a moderate price. **$12.00.**

K—18401. Small Sized Wood Body Roadster. Leatherette hood. Seat and back are upholstered. Adjustable back rest. 12-inch wheels with ½-inch rubber tires. This well designed and very attractively priced roadster will give the best satisfaction. Durability, ease and safety are here combined. **$8.50.**

K—18402. Stylish Wood Body Sleeper. Beautifully painted and striped. Has a fine leatherette hood. Reclining, adjustable back and footwell. 12-inch wheels with ½-inch rubber tires. A finely finished sleeper and one that will give long and satisfactory service. **$10.50.**

K—18403. Folding Go=Cart. Leatherette hood and sides. Back is upholstered. Steel tubing gear. This is a light, easy-running cart, easy to push and equally easy and comfortable to the rider—a cart that will be sure to please, and represents one of our best values. In fact, one that would be hard to duplicate elsewhere. The go-cart is especially in demand during the summer months, when there are many outings and trips planned, as it takes up small space when folded. This particular cart folds with one motion. It is also equipped with a break. **$6.00.**

K—18404. Handsome Folding Go=Cart. Steel sides and dasher. Finished in black enamel. Leather cloth hood. Upholstered seat and back. Steel tubing gear. Equipped with brake and self-adjustable elliptic spring. We cannot recommend too highly this self-adjusting elliptic spring; it does away with all troublesome screws and clamps. It is always ready and in order and, regardless of either light or heavy weight, remains a flexible spring. A fine, comfortable, durable cart very reasonably priced at **$8.50.**

K—18405. Stylish Folding Go=Cart. Steel sides and dasher. Finished in handsome, glossy black enamel. Leatherette auto hood with side and back curtains to prevent draught. A splendid protection to the baby on a blustery day. Tubular gear. Equipped with brake. 10-inch wheel, ½-inch rubber tire. One of the finest finished, best-looking and best-value carts we have to offer. **$11.00.**

K—18406. Reed Pullman Coach. Made of best grade, half-round reed. Reclining, adjustable back and deep footwell. The footwell is also adjustable, and can be open or closed, depending upon desired position for child. Reversible gear. It is desirable and convenient at times to reverse the coach, as in this way the baby can see the mother. Also to avoid wind or sun sometimes the coach is reversed. ⅝-inch rubber tires. Break. **$25.00.**

K—18406=a. Wind Shield. Attached to K—18406 will fit most any other style. The wind shield is very useful, as it furnishes complete protection to the child from draughts. It will also keep out the noise, to an extent, if baby is sleeping. Colors, white, brown, gray or drab corduroy. **$1.50.**

New York — Gimbel Brothers — Philadelphia

Scientific Construction Is Apparent in Gimbel Vehicles

The vehicles on these two pages have that most essential feature—an easy-riding, running gear, with plenty of spring and resiliency. The entire cart rests on the gear, and upon it depends the absence from jolting of the baby, and the ease with which the coach can be pushed. The upholstering is sanitary throughout and in strict compliance with enacted laws. For elegance of appearance, beauty and grace of design, smartness of finish and upholstering, the Gimbel vehicles stand supreme. These goods come under Gimbels Restricted Delivery Offer. See page 4.

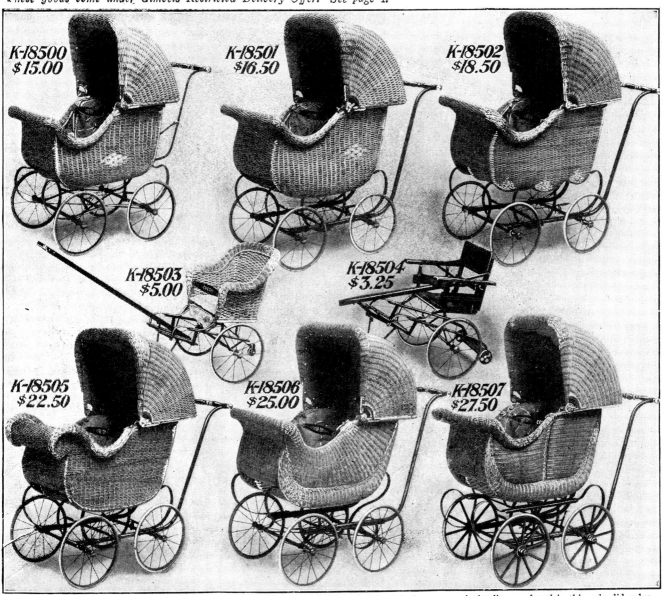

K-18500 $15.00   K-18501 $16.50   K-18502 $18.50   K-18503 $5.00   K-18504 $3.25   K-18505 $22.50   K-18506 $25.00   K-18507 $27.50

K—18500. Runabout Pullman Coach. Made of half-round reed, with extra roll of reed on hood and body. Finished in natural color or brown. Upholstered with best grade corduroy. Wheels are 12 inches and have ½-inch rubber tires. Length of body reclined, 34 inches. Width, 15½ inches. Has a reclining, adjustable back and deep footwell. A well constructed coach, having all the essentials that go for comfort, beauty and service. Exceptional value. **$15.00.** Weight, 60 lbs.

K—18501. Pony Pullman Coach. Made of flat reed with roll of half-round reed on hood and body. Finished in natural or brown. Best grade upholstering. 12-inch wheels with ½-inch rubber tires. Length of body reclining, 36 inches. Width, 15½ inches. Reclining, adjustable back and deep footwell. A good-sized coach, fully equipped with everything of the best at a reasonable price. **$16.50.** Weight, 75 lbs.

K—18502. Pony Pullman Coach. Made of half-round reed. A roll of reed on hood and body. Upholstered in the best grade corduroy with lining in hood to match the body. Finished in natural or brown. Wheels are 12 inches with ½-inch rubber

tires. Length of body reclining, 36 inches. Width, 15½ inches. A handsome coach, light running, serviceable, and splendid value at **$18.50.**

K—18503. Reed Sidewalk Sulky. Made of flat reed with a roll of fine reed on the edge. Splendid tempered steel spring. Wheels in back to lessen shock when going over curbs. Upholstered in leather cloth. 12-inch wheels with ½-inch rubber tires. A good-looking, convenient little cart. Well constructed, of the best materials. A durable and excellent-value article. **$5.00.**

K—18504. Sidewalk Sulky. Built of good, strong oak wood. Tempered steel springs. Steel axles with 14-inch wheels. ½-inch rubber tires. Two wheels in back to prevent jar when passing over a rough surface. A well-made, strong, durable cart at a most attractive price. **$3.25.**

K—18505. Handsome Pullman Coach. Full size. Made of half-round reed. Finished in natural or brown. Best grade of upholstering, hood lined to match. Wheels are 14 inches with ⅝-inch rubber tires. Reclining back, deep footwell. Length of body reclining, 38 inches. Width, 16 inches. All the best known features in this par-

ticular line are found in this splendid-value coach. **$22.50.** Weight, 80 lbs.

K—18506. High Grade Pullman Coach. Full size. Made of all-round reed with the popular shell shape side. Very pretty in design. Finished in natural or brown. Body upholstered in best grade corduroy cushions. Hood lined with corduroy to match body. Wheels, 14 inches. ⅝-inch rubber tires. Length of body reclining, 38 inches. Width, 16 inches. Style, elegance and comfort are combined in this fine coach. **$25.00.**

K—18507. Handsome Pullman Coach. Full size. Made of best grade, all-round reed. Extra roll of reed on hood and body. Upholstered in A. grade corduroy cushions. Has 14-inch, wood artillery wheels. ⅝-inch rubber tires. Reversible gear, so that the coach can be turned to have the child facing the mother. The reversing is done by simply pressing the foot on a lever and turning the coach around. Length of body reclining, 38 inches. Width, 16 inches. Reclining back and deep footwell. This is a high grade coach throughout and a fine value at **$27.50.**

Wagons. Hand Cars. Automobiles. Of Most Substantial Construction

The American "Small Boy" is as near perpetual motion as can be imagined. Locomotion in all forms is appealing to him, and outdoor exercise lays the foundation for physical strength. A hand car, express wagon, tricycle, bicycle or automobile will furnish the incentive for sturdy muscle. Also will provide healthy recreation and amusement. Gimbels Restricted Delivery Offer applies to these goods. See page 4.

K-18600 A. 35¢

K-18600 $2.00

K-18604 $4.50

K-18603 $7.50

K-18601 $5.00

K-18605 $4.50

K-18606 $2.00

K-18602 $7.50

K-18607 $3.75

K—18600. **Express Wagon.** A good-looking, well-built wagon for the boy. Body has locked corners. Steel axles and boxes with improved steel rocker plates. Seat not included.

28 x 13 inch body, varnished. 11 x 16½ inch wheels	$2.00
26 x 13 inch body, varnished. 10 x 15 inch wheels	1.25
26 x 13 inch body, painted red. 10 x 15 inch wheels	1.50
30 x 15 inch body, varnished. 11 x 10½ inch wheels. Shaved spokes	2.50
31 x 15 inch body, varnished. 12 x 18 inch wheels. Shaved spokes	3.00
32 x 16 inch body, varnished. 12 x 18 inch wheels. Shaved spokes	3.50

K—18600A. **Seat.** To fit small-sized wagons, K—18600, 35c. To fit large sizes, 50c.

K—18601. **Automobile.** For boy or girl. Adjustable seat. Nicely painted and striped. In the following sizes:

Front Wheel.	Rear Wheel.	Tires.	Price.
8 inches	14 inches	25-64 inch	$4.50
10 inches	16 inches	25-64 inch	5.00
12 inches	18 inches	½ inch	6.00

K—18602. **Frame Wagon.** These are just the thing for hauling small loads, and can be taken in places where it would be hard for an ordinary light wagon to travel. The sides and ends can be taken down and packed closely. Shaved, spoked wheels. Welded tires. Hub caps. Built strongly to withstand **a lot of** wear and tear. Body, 36 x 18 inches. Wheels, 15 x 21 inches. Seat included. A splendid value at the price. **$7.50.**

K—18602A. (Not illustrated.) Shafts to fit K—18602. The tongue can be taken off and replaced with a pair of shafts for large dogs, goats or small ponies. Small size, $1.50 pair.

K—18603. **Auto.** Well equipped, light running, nicely finished Auto for the ambitious boy. Front wheels, 12 inches. Rear wheels, 18 inches. Tool box under seat. Wheels fitted with ½-inch rubber tires. Equipment includes license tag, starting crank and large wooden steering wheel. Seat is upholstered in black leatherette. This is one of our best values. **$7.50.**

K—18604. **Wagon.** Comes in three sizes and is a very popular wagon. For a less expensive vehicle it is the best of its kind to be found anywhere. Finished with side boards and dasher. Hardwood sills and body braces. Locked corners. Square steel axles and turned bearings. Mortised hubs, shaved spokes, heavy welded tires and hub caps. A fine wagon at a reasonable price. Sizes as follows:

36 x 15 inch body. 12 x 18 inch wheels		$4.50
36 x 15 inch body. 15 x 21 inch wheels		5.25
Without frame body, but with sides and dasher. 32 x 16 inch body. 12 x 18 inch wheels		4.00

K—18605. **Hand Car.** Frame and handle of thoroughly seasoned hardwood, attractively finished in red, gold and black. Gear drive construction. All gears covered. $4.50. Same style, but fitted with a coaster brake attachment controlled from side of frame. $5.25.

K—18606. **Daisy Wagon.** A very nice, light-running wagon. Body has locked corners. Steel axles and boxes. Iron tongue draw with improved pressed steel rocker plates. Whip and socket—an attractive addition for the small boy. Size of body, 26 x 13 inches. Wheels, 11 x 16½ inches, with oval tires and hub caps. Seat included. $2.00.

K—18607. **Hand Car.** Attractively enameled in colors. Light yet strongly constructed. Steel frame reinforced at all points subject to any strain. Gear drive construction makes propelling easy. In the following sizes:

Front Wheels.	Rear Wheels.	Length.	Shipping Weight.	Price.
7 in.	9 in.	28½ in.	35 lbs.	$3.00
9 in.	12 in.	36 in.	40 lbs.	3.75

To Promote Vigor and Stimulate the Imagination

The sane "Boy Scouts" and "Camp Fire Girls" movements have influenced the very small kiddies towards a love for the Indian, as the circus once inspired hatred. And then what boy has not longed to be a policeman or a fireman, and, in his mind, to achieve heroic deeds. These thoughts are good for the child.

These goods come under Gimbels Restricted Delivery Offer. See Page 4.

K-18700
$1.50

K-18701
$1.50

K-18702
$1.00

K-18703
$1.00

K-18704
$1.75

K-18705
$2.00

K-18706
$1.00

K-18707
$1.00

K-18708
$2.00

K—18700. **Boy's Indian Play Suit.** Made of good grade khaki drill, elaborately trimmed with red fringe. Outfit consists of blouse, trousers and dandy feathered head-piece. Sizes, 4 to 14 years. $1.50. Weight, wrapped, 30 ounces.

K—18701. **Girl's Indian Play Suit.** Made of good grade of khaki drill, nicely trimmed with red fringe. Outfit consists of blouse, skirt and feathered head-piece. Sizes, 4 to 14 years. $1.50. Weight, wrapped, 30 ounces.

K—18702. **Boy's Cowboy Suit.** Good grade khaki drill. Trousers trimmed with leatherette fringe. Outfit consists of blouse, trousers, hat, bandana handkerchief and lariat. Sizes, 4 to 14 years. $1.00. Weight, wrapped, 30 ounces.

K—18703. **Girl's Indian Play Suit.** Made of good grade khaki drill and nicely trimmed with col-

ored fringe. Outfit consists of blouse, skirt and feathered head-band. Sizes, 4 to 14 years. $1.00. Weight, wrapped, 30 ounces.

K—18704. **Boy's Cowboy Play Suit.** Fine grade tan khaki drill, elaborately trimmed with leatherette. Outfit consists of blouse, trousers, hat, bandana handkerchief, lariat and leatherette belt with holster. Sizes, 4 to 14 years. $1.75. Made with skirt for a girl. $1.75. Weight, wrapped, 30 ounces.

K—18705. **Fireman's Play Outfit.** Trousers made of good grade khaki drill in dark blue. Blouse made of light red flannel. Outfit consists of hat, blouse, belt and trousers. Trumpet not included. Sizes, 4 to 14 years. $2.00. Weight, wrapped, 55 ounces.

K—18706. **Girl's Broncho Suit.** Made of good

grade khaki drill. Skirt trimmed with leatherette fringe. Outfit consists of blouse, hat, skirt, bandana handkerchief and lariat. Sizes, 4 to 14 years. $1.00. Same in better grade khaki, entire suit elaborately trimmed with leatherette, with leatherette belt. Sizes, 4 to 14 years. $1.75. Weight, wrapped, 30 ounces.

K—18707. **Boy's Indian Play Suit.** Made of good grade khaki drill, elaborately trimmed with colored fringe. Outfit consists of blouse, trousers and a dandy feathered head-piece. Sizes, 4 to 14 years. $1.00. Weight, wrapped, 30 ounces.

K—18708. **Policeman Play Suit.** Made of good grade of khaki in dark blue. Outfit consists of jacket, trousers, hat, belt, club and badge. Sizes, 4 to 14 years. $2.00. Weight, wrapped, 55 ounces.

New York — Gimbel Brothers — Philadelphia

Now Comes the Call of the Great Out-Doors

It is strong—it is insistent—it is irresistible. To some it comes from stream and lake and woods; to others the ballfield and tennis court make strong appeal. But no matter what may be your favorite recreation, it is important that your equipment be the best and most dependable if your pleasure is to be complete and unmarred—that is to say, it should come from Gimbels. Your equipment will also be lowest in price for equal grade if purchased at Gimbels. These goods come under Gimbels Restricted Delivery Offer. See page 4.

K-18809 $3.00
NET ALONE K-18800 $2.00
CENTER STRAP $1.00
POSTS $20.00 PAIR.
K-18802
K-18801 $3.50
K-18803 $3.00
K-18804 $3.00
K-18805 $5.25
K-18806 $7.50
K-18807 $4.50
K-18808 $3.00

K—18800. Tennis Nets. 15 thread. 42 feet long. Tape bound. Strong and serviceable. **$2.00.** Other styles, $1.50, $3.00, $4.00.

K—18800-a. Center Piece of Net K—18800 is called Center Strap. **$1.00** extra.

K—18800-b. Spalding Iron Posts with hooks to hook into the ground are **$20.00** a pair. Plain posts, $1.00, $1.50 and $2.00 a pair.

K—18801. Golf Bag. An ideal bag for women. Special white duck. 6 inches in diameter. Black leather trimmings. Real reed straps covered with canvas. Leather bottom with stud. **$3.50.** Others $2.00, $2.50, $4.50 and upward to $12.50.

K—18802. Golf Clubs. Spalding gold medal clubs. Have specially prepared calf grips made from the finest dogwood and persimmon. All guaranteed. **$3.00.** Irons, $2.50.

K—18803. Croquet Set. Eight-ball set with 6-inch mallets. Made of selected wood, fancy painted and fine varnish finish. Fancy turned stakes. Large wickets. **$3.00.** Others $1.50, $2.00, $2.50 and upward to $7.00.

K—18804. Beach Umbrella. Ideal for seashore use. Seven-foot pointed handle is easily thrust into sand. Strong and attractive. Blue and white, red and white, or green and white stripes. **$3.00.**

K—18805. Girl's Tricycle. Frame finished in black enamel, and wheels in red. Side rails of seat brightly tin-plated. Adjustable seat, controlled by thumbscrews, is comfortably upholstered in maroon leatherette. Handle has black enameled grips with brass ferrule. Wheels have one-half inch rubber tires.

Front Wheels.	Rear Wheels.	For child of	Shipping Weight.	Price.
10 in.	18 in.	3 to 4 yrs.	50 lbs.	$5.25
12 in.	20 in.	4 to 6 yrs.	65 lbs.	5.75
12 in.	24 in.	5 to 8 yrs.	75 lbs.	8.25

K—18806. Girl's Tricycle. Patented seat, adjustment controlled by thumbscrew, is comfortably upholstered in maroon leatherette. Side rails brightly tinned. Wheels have three-quarter inch rubber tires and fenders. Curved steering handle with leather-wrapped bicycle grips. Spring steel seat post absorbs the jar over rough spots. Guards on wheels.

Front Wheels.	Rear Wheels.	For child of	Shipping Weight.	Price.
10 in.	18 in.	3 to 4 yrs.	50 lbs.	$5.75
12 in.	20 in.	4 to 6 yrs.	65 lbs.	7.50
12 in.	24 in.	5 to 8 yrs.	70 lbs	9.00

K—18807. Heavy Rubber Tired Velocipede. Frames and wheels finished in red enamel, striped in gold. Wheels fitted with five-eighth inch rubber tires. The adjustable handle bars are heavily nickel-plated and fitted with best quality leather wrapped grips. Juvenile bicycle saddle is well padded, adjustable, and has a coil spring.

Front Wheels.	Rear Wheels.	For child of	Shipping Weight.	Price.
14 in.	10 in.	3 to 4 yrs.	30 lbs.	$4.00
16 in.	12 in.	4 to 6 yrs.	40 lbs.	4.50
20 in.	14 in.	6 to 8 yrs.	45 lbs.	5.00
24 in.	16 in.	8 to 12 yrs.	50 lbs.	5.50

K—18808. Rubber Tired Velocipede. Frame enameled black, wheels red. Front wheels fitted with one-half inch rubber tires, rear wheels with three-eighth inch tires. Handle bar is adjustable and fitted with black enameled grips with brass ferrule. Saddle also adjustable with coil spring.

Front Wheels.	Rear Wheels.	For child of	Shipping Weight.	Price.
16 in.	12 in.	3 to 4 yrs.	25 lbs.	$3.00
20 in.	14 in.	4 to 6 yrs.	35 lbs.	3.25
24 in.	16 in.	6 to 8 yrs.	40 lbs.	3.50

K—18809. Tennis Racket. Lakeside frame of fine, selected white ash. Highly polished. With combed cedar handle. Leather capped. **$3.00.** Others at $1.50, $2.00, $2.50, $3.50 and upward to $8.00.

New York — Gimbel Brothers — Philadelphia

These Are The Goods We Like To See Around The Home

What a homelike air these goods give to the lawn—you expect to see a child come romping into view. Each piece is splendidly made and finished of selected wood. Any one of them will help to keep the child healthy and happy. Gimbels Restricted Delivery Offer applies. See page 4.

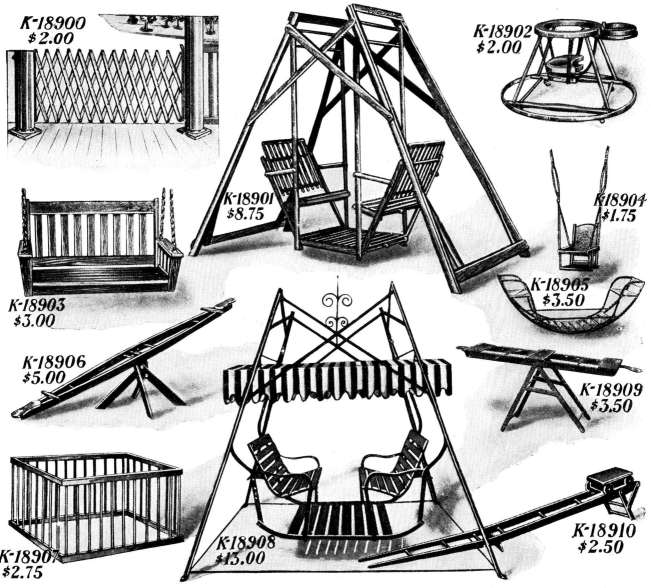

K-18900
$2.00

K-18902
$2.00

K-18901
$8.75

K-18904
$1.75

K-18903
$3.00

K-18905
$3.50

K-18906
$5.00

K-18909
$3.50

K-18907
$2.75

K-18908
$13.00

K-18910
$2.50

K—18900. **A Porch Gate** is essential on every porch where there are young children. Made of smooth, tough oak strips, carefully riveted at each point, and yet elastic enough not to injure the child when it falls against the gate. Will fit any entrance. Opens to 6 feet; closes to 15 inches. Height, 33 inches. $2.00. For stair or hallway. Opens to 3 feet, closes to 8 inches. Height, 31 inches. $1.50.

K—18901. **Keystone Lawn Swing.** Four passenger. Reinforced sides. Frame painted red. Swinging parts natural finish. $8.75.

Two passenger.................... $6.00
Four passenger (not reinforced).. 7.25

Also Paris Lawn Swings.

Six foot......................... 4.50
Eight foot, two passenger....... 6 75
Ten foot, four passenger....... 10.00

K—18902. **Hygienic Baby Walker.** Constructed along scientific lines, giving absolute security against injury to the child. Equipped with four coil springs between top and bottom base of seat. Leather suspension straps and soft webbing in front, which adjusts itself to the child's conformation. Tray for toys. $2.00. The famous Glassock Baby Walker (not pictured) steel springs. $3.25.

K—18903. **Mission Porch Swing.** Flat weathered oak. Held together with bolts and wing nuts. Length 40 inches. Depth of seat 18 inches. Height to top of back, 23 inches.

Equipped with heavy chains; 7½-foot length. $3.00. Another at $4.00.

K—18904. **Baby Swing for Doorway or Porch.** Strongly made. Adjustable to any height. Finished in dark oak. $1.75. Same made in natural wood without springs, $1.00.

K—18905. **Double Rocker.** Can easily be carried from the room to the porch or lawn. Seats are 13 inches wide. Rockers, 6 feet long across from end to end. Braced iron rods. Made substantially to hold children up to 16 years of age. Seats, 7 inches high; 12 inches deep. $3.50.

K—18906. **Merry Whirl Seesaw.** Ten feet long. It is a seesaw on a carriage, which revolves on a stand, giving it a seesaw. merry-go-round motion. Iron bearings. The swing part has adjustments, which will permit persons of unequal weight to form a balance. The varnish will stand the weather. Seats are 18 inches long. Stand is 28 inches high. Weight of complete seesaw, 40 pounds. Crated, 55 pounds. Boxed, 75 pounds. $5.00.

K—18907. **Folding Baby Yards.** Canvas bottom securely attached. Can be detached and washed. Size, 38 x 38 inches. 21 inches high. Folds to 39 x 21 x 4 inches.

Plain spindles, varnished........ $2 75
Fancy spindles, varnished........ 3.50

K—18908. **Steel Lawn Swing.** Accommodates four passengers. Frame of high carbon steel,

finished in green. The slats are made of selected hardwood. Backs adjustable so as to be used as a swing, reclining chair or couch. $13.00.

K—18909. **Adjustable Seesaw.** Designed for the young folks. Great care is taken in selecting the wood used in manufacture to avoid possible injury by eliminating chance of breaking. Can be easily adjusted to suit small or large children by a simple arrangement of bolts. For indoor or out. Length, 6 feet. Width, 21 inches. $3.50.

K—18910. **The Shoot-the-Chutes** has proven one of the most popular of outdoor toys. Has deep groove running down the middle of two long wooden slides to prevent the possibility of the car leaving the tracks. No trouble to store during the winter months, as it can be easily folded into a small package. The wheels on car are solid discs drilled to allow for screw axles. Made for land use only. 12 feet long. $2.50.

Not Illustrated.

K—18811. Child's High Chairs in Golden Oak. $1.25, $2.00, $2.50, $3.00, $3.50 and $4.00.

K—18812. Combination High Chairs, Golden Oak finish. $3.50, $4 50, $6.00 and $6.75.

K—18813. Child's Wooden Nursery Chairs or Commodes, Golden oak finish. In a variety of prices and styles. $1.00, $1.25, $1.50, $2.00 and $2.50.

Write Gimbels Regarding the Article You Need

Gimbels furnish upon request the following catalogues and circulars of general interest:
Kenyon's handsomely illustrated catalogues of Take Down Canvas Houses and Furniture for same; various catalogues and circulars of Canoes and Motor Boats; catalogues and leaflets of Music; catalogues of Dressmakers' Forms; catalogues of Kodaks and Cameras; catalogues of Baby Carriages, Go-Carts and Sidewalk Sulkies.
Restricted Delivery Offer applies to all but K—19007.

K—19000. **Stationary Settee.** For porch or lawn. Frame of channel steel, reinforced on both edges with metal cross braces. Color of slats is green. Length, 48 inches. A good, serviceable settee, well constructed, and of the best materials. Is a great value at the exceptional price. **$4.50.**

K—19001. **Folding Lawn Settee.** Made in hardwood with beveled edge slats. Frame painted red or green. Slats natural finish. 45 inches long. One of the advantages of the folding settee is the small space it occupies when not in use. This is a fine, strong settee at a very small expenditure. Note the price. **$1.75.**

K—19002. **Folding Chair With Arms.** Three slats in back. Veneered seat. Light finish. Very comfortable. Of the greatest convenience in a large lawn, also suitable for porch. They suggest restfulness, pleasure and comfort. Easily moved about to accommodate the different locations desired. Always appreciated by young or old. Best value at a moderate cost. **$1.50.**

K—19003. **Folding Camp Chair.** Handy for the picknicker or camper, as it is easy to carry. Also useful out boating, on the lawn or porch—or wherever a comfortable seat is desired. Has arms and khaki canvas seat. Light-weight, comfortable size and altogether a wonderful convenience. The real value is quite beyond that implied in the price quoted. **$1.50.**

K—19004. **Steamer Chair.** Finished in light oak. Strong and durable cane back and foot rest. With the prospective trips to Panama as the time approaches for the opening of the Great Panama Exposition, there will be an unusual demand for these articles. Therefore, be provident and procure your steamer chair at an early date. Fine also for porches. We have a number to select from at accommodating prices. The one illustrated and described is an excellent value at **$3.50.** Others at **$2.50, $5.00 to $7.50.**

K—19005. **Folding Camp Stool.** Suitable for any use. Very light and durable. Hardwood frame. Carpet seat. Several of these could easily be tucked away in the outing luggage, and would be thoroughly appreciated when needed. Very special. **50c.**

K—19006. **Sand Chair.** Something novel for use on the sand. No more backaches sitting down on the beach when one of these is at hand. A reclining chair without legs —because they are not needed. Rests perfectly flat on the sand. Can be adjusted to any angle, and thus permit of many shifting positions. Canvas seat. One of our best values. **$1.00.**

K—19007. **"Kenyon Take Down House."** Two-roomed bungalow. 9 x 15 feet. 6-foot ceiling. These houses are comfortable, easy to erect and readily moved from place to place. They are recommended by leading physicians. They offer the best method of out-door sleeping. Thorough protection is afforded, as they are waterproof, fireproof and fungus growth proof. **$110.00.** In other sizes as follows:

7 x 9, one room	$62.50
10 x 22, three rooms	155.00
12 x 24, five rooms	195.00
18 x 30, five rooms	325.00

All quotations K—19007 F. O. B. Waukesha, Wis.

New York — Gimbel Brothers — Philadelphia

To While Away the Golden Summer Hours

A hammock is really a necessary luxury—the invalid's best aid to health—the tired housewife's best recreation. Every household should have a hammock. A hammock is fine, too, for the camper, for whom we have listed goods especially for camp use. Prices are the extreme lowest at which high-grade goods can be procured. Gimbels Restricted Delivery Offer applies to this page. See page 4 for details of it.

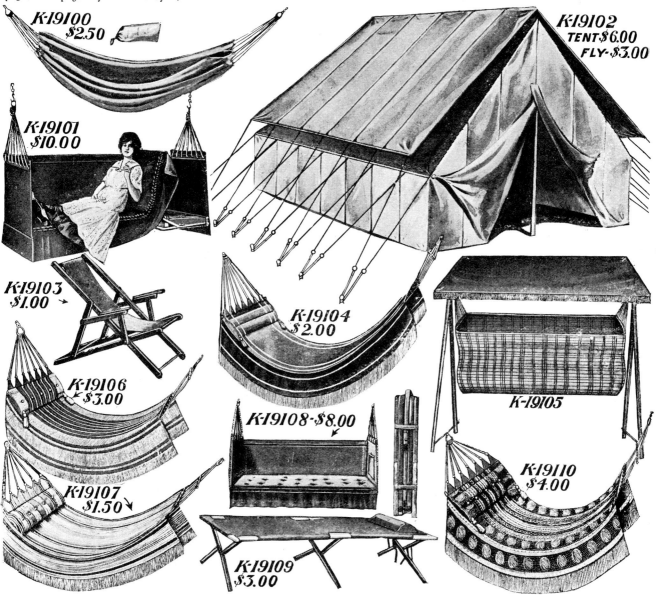

K—19100. Improved Picnic Hammock. Made of stout canvas cloth with extra heavy end cords. Can be washed when soiled. Ideal for scouting, camping or picnic use. A thoroughly well made hammock. Will give satisfactory and endless service. Very reasonable. Can be put in bag, as illustrated. Complete with bag. $2.50.

K—19101. Couch Hammock. Steel frame with adjustable head-rest in combination with the wind shield back-rest. This is the most comfortable hammock made. The best materials are used throughout. A safe and delightfully comfortable hammock. $10.00.

K—19102. Wall Tent. The most useful tent for camping purposes. Complete with pole and stakes.

7 x 7 feet, 8 oz. white duck	$6.00
7 x 7 feet, 10 oz. white duck	7.00
7 x 9 feet, 8 oz. white duck	7.00
7 x 9 feet, 10 oz. white duck	8.00
9 x 9 feet, 10 oz. white duck	9.50
9½ x 12 feet, 10 oz. white duck	12.00

K—19102-a. Boy Scout Tent. 5 x 7 feet, 8 oz. white duck. $4.50.
Fly is one-half price of the tent.

K—19103. Folding Hammock Chairs. Something serviceable for porch use. Made of hardwood, finished natural color. Covered with heavy khaki color canvas. Can be adjusted to any position. Has arms. $1.00.
With arms and foot-rest. $1.25.

K—19104. Hammock. Very attractive and woven entirely of canvas. Large, comfortable throwback pillow. Various stripes add to its beauty and a pretty valance edged with fringe at sides gives it a fancy finish. Concealed head spreader. Three extra supporting cords. Strong and durable. Size, 36 x 86 inches. $2.00.

K—19105. Baby Hammock. A health builder. Well made and popular. Has comfortable, tufted mattress. Made of woven cord with steel frame in bottom, to keep sides from collapsing when in use. When not in use, hammock and stand collapse into a small bundle, and it is therefore easy to carry from place to place. The baby will thrive and grow strong by sleeping out in the open air in this comfortable hammock. 36 inches long.

In Khaki.		In White.	
Hammock	$2.00	Hammock	$2.00
Stand	1.50	Stand	1.75
Canopy	1.25	Canopy	1.25
	$4.75		**$5.00**

K—19106. Hammock. Close canvas twill weave. The colorings are soft and rich in artistically grouped stripes. Large, comfortable throwback pillow with tassels on end. Valance edged with deep fringe on sides. Improved continuous center stringing. This is one of our best and most popular hammocks. Size, 39 x 88 inches. Splendid value. $3.00.

K—19107. Hammock. Made of close canvas damask weave. Richly colored in the popular stripe design, and made of best hard-spun yarn. Reinforced casting at spreader ends. Deep valance edged with fringe on sides finishes this remarkably good-value hammock. Size, 36 x 84 inches. $1.50.

K—19108. Couch Hammock. The While-Away. Well made and popular. Has tufted mattress, patent adjustable wind shield and pockets for books and paper. Chain hung. $8.00.

K—19109. Kenyon Cot. Folding Cot. Reinforced at points susceptible to breakage. Stands firmly on the floor. The frame is rock elm, air-dried and stained. Folds into a compact bundle with canvas strap as handle. Easy to carry. Just the thing for the camper. 28 inches by 6 feet 6 inches. $3.00.

K—19.09-a. Kenyon Cot No. 29. Well made. Light in weight. Especially recommended for light service. Folds less compactly than K—19109. Splendid value. $1.50.

K—19110. Hammock. Beautiful design. Closely woven and of sterling quality. Comfortable throw-back pillow with fancy tassel trimmings, wide drapery trimmed with fringe. Ideal for comfort. Size, 39 x 88. $4.00.

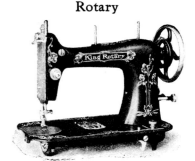

King "Sit-Rite" Central Needle Sewing Machines

OLD WAY

SIT WRONG

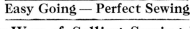

Easy Going — Perfect Sewing

The New Way of Selling Sewing Machines

The old days of buying sewing machines from agents, paying fancy prices, to enable them to draw liberal commissions, which are included in the prices of the machines, are past. You now deal with a responsible store that stands back of every sale and every promise made.

NEW WAY

"SIT-RITE"

Meritorious Features of The King Machines

Superior Beauty of the Entire Machine.
High Quality of Materials.
Perfection of Design.
Ball Bearing.
Automatic Lift.
Accurate Tensions.
Positive Feed.
Self Adjusting Needle.
Automatic Tension Release.

On account of the natural and hygienic position assumed by the operator, the King Central Needle "Sit-Rite" Machines have attracted favorable attention of manual training instructors in charge of sewing classes throughout the country, and are highly recommended by physicians.

4 Drawers.
Central Needle.
Drop Head Automatic Lift.
Ball Bearing Stand.
Selected High Grade Quarter Sawed Oak.

No. 405 (Vibrator) $33.00

No. 406 (Rotary) $35.00

Either cash or on our famous club plan.

Satisfaction First
Thirty Days' Trial
Satisfaction Always

"New Willard Colonial"
only $24.00

Either cash or on our famous club plan of $2.00 first payment and $4.00 monthly. $35.00 to $50.00 is the agent's price for this quality and type of Vibrator Shuttle Sewing Machine.

No. 351

4 Drawers.
Drop Head Automatic Lift.
Ball Bearing Stand.
Colonial Style — Quarter Sawed Oak.

Satisfaction First
Thirty Days' Trial
Satisfaction Always

Special Sewing Machine Catalog, illustrating Parlor and Library Fully Enclosed Cabinets, also many other styles, will be sent you upon request.

Guaranteed for 20 Years

The Mechanical Construction of the **"New Willard Colonial"** is on such perfect lines that it assures Durability, Quiet and Easy Running. All up-to-date improvements, such as Automatic Tension Release, Ball Bearing Stand, Automatic Lift, that works with ease and precision are features found only in High-Grade Modern Sewing Machines.

The Colonial Style Quarter Sawed Oak Cabinet, specially designed for the "New Willard," is very attractive and substantial. Attachments consisting of Tucker, Ruffler with Shirring Plate, four Hemmers, Binder, Braider, Foot Hemmer, and Feller, Quilter, and all accessories furnished free.

Restricted Delivery Offer Applies.

New York — Gimbel Brothers — Philadelphia

The Best and Most Helpful Dress Forms
Restricted Delivery Offer Applies

L. & M.

ALL PACKED IN THIS BOX

$4.50 Collapsible but Non-Adjustable Form, as illustrated above is Very Special at $3.00

A necessity for home dressmaking.

Thousands of women have been disappointed in their attempts at dress making because of the fitting problem. A dress form will overcome this difficulty and will represent you in your fitting, making over or repairing a dress.

The KUMPACKT ACME DRESS FORM is the latest invented dress form on the market. It is an ingenious patented arrangement which enables the user to fold up the skirt to one-half its size, making it fit nicely in a box 28 inches high and 14 inches square.

The figure is the newest 1915 model and graceful in appearance, substantial in construction: The bust is made out of superior papier mache, with jersey cloth covering. The skirt is made of the best flexible steel, highly finished, and with ordinary care will last a lifetime. It does all the work of a high-priced form. It is packed in a strong fiber container. Copper oxidized base and comes in sizes 32, 34, 36, 38, 40 and 42.

The $8.50 Kumpackt Acme Adjustable, Collapsible Dress Form at $6.50

Pneumatic Dress Forms Are Helpful

Just put your own fitted waist lining on the form and blow it up, and there is a perfect representation of your own figure. With a Pneumatic form at hand, the making, fitting and remodeling of waists and dresses at home become a pastime instead of a dreaded time. It is particularly fine for the fitting and draping of skirts. Pneumatic form is the only invention that shows you what you are. The entire outfit can be packed in the little box, base dimensions of which are 12 x 14 x 4. Comes in six sizes, 34, 38, 42, 46, 50, at $14.00. Size 54 is $18.00. The whole thing only weighs 10 lbs., stand and bust complete.

A Regular $8.50 Adjustable Dress Form for $5.00. No. 119, the One Being Draped

This is the latest 1915 model of the Gimbel Acme Adjustable Dress Form that is known country-wide and sold for $8.50. You will get one sooner or later if you ever expect to have the best inexpensive Adjustable Dress Form on the market. $5.00 instead of $8.50.

The Adjustable Dress Form in the sewing room is as indispensable as the sewing machine. To the dressmaker it will do the work and take the place of over one dozen non-adjustable forms, and no home sewer can afford to be without one.

The following adjustments can be easily made:
1. Neck larger or smaller.
2. Bust larger or smaller.
3. Waist larger or smaller.
4. Hips larger or smaller.

Comes in two sizes, 32 adjustable to 42-inch bust and 36 adjustable to 46-inch bust.

The Gimbel Acme Dress Form No. 112,
Shown in Small Illustration, Made in Twelve Sections.

The standard price country-wide is $15.00. Our price, $10.00.

We know of no woman's figure to which this form cannot be adjusted. The waist can be made larger or smaller, and can be lengthened or shortened. The bust increased or diminished.

The hips can be made larger or smaller.

The shoulders can be made higher or lower.

The shoulders can be enlarged without changing the neck measurement. The bust made broader without changing the neck.

Skirt can be made fuller or scantier.

Form raised or lowered on its extension stand.

Style A, when closed, is 32 and extends to 44-inch bust. Style B, when closed, is 36 inches bust measure and extends to 48-inch bust.

New York — Gimbel Brothers — Philadelphia

NO KITCHEN IS PROPERLY EQUIPPED WITHOUT ONE OF THESE CABINETS

$18.50

(Gimbels Restricted Delivery Offer Applies.)

THIS FINELY PLANNED OAK KITCHEN CABINET is white enameled inside and fitted with all the best ideas including cutting bars, tilted flour bin, sugar bins, glass cereal jars, rolling pin rack, wire dish holders, wire sliding shelf, etc. It is a Cabinet that most stores ask $30 for, and one that will give fine satisfaction. While the picture shows it nicely you really couldn't resist buying if you actually saw the Cabinet. It's a most wonderful value.

It is 71 inches high, 43 inches wide.

ONLY $18.50

THESE STEEL CABINETS ARE FINE—AND BUT $29.85

It is Gimbels for splendid values at all times—for dependable goods always, and for matchless bargains in items like this.

The sightly, space economizing Kitchen Cabinet depicted here is ALL STEEL, finished with a hard wear resisting white enamel that has been thoroughly and skillfully baked on. The 37 x 39 inch top, Nickeloid Covered Table inside is most handy and further emphasizes the economy of space for which this splendid All Steel Cabinet is famous. The table pulls out 14½ inches beyond the front of the lower portion of the cabinet.

Some of the other equipments of the Cabinet, and it is sure some equipment to brag about, consist of a strictly sanitary, dust proof flour bin, glass sugar bin of 12 lbs. holding capacity, cutlery or linen drawers, ventilated bread or cake box, cutting board and a seven piece crystal glass spice set.

THE CABINET—All steel, remember, and rust proof, dust proof, fly proof, vermin proof —is finished with nickel trimmings, and we trust we are making it clear that the very finest gloss white enamel is employed inside and outside. This is the opportunity to buy if you haven't a good Cabinet in your kitchen, and fairly no kitchen has reached the proper degree of "efficiency" or safety without one.

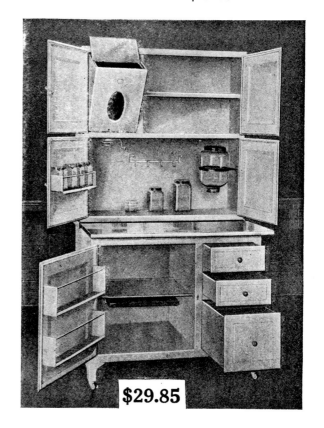

$29.85

Gimbel Refrigerators and Ice Chests Conserve Ice

A refrigerator or ice chest should do more than keep food cold—it should prevent the odor of one food being absorbed by another food, also should do this with the least amount of ice for the size. The construction of the refrigerators and chests carried by Gimbels are the most perfect that science and skill have so far devised, and will keep food and save ice. Gimbels Restricted Delivery Offer applies. See page 4.

K-19600 K-19601 K-19602 K-19603

K-19604 K-19605 K-19606

K—19600. Star Apartment House Style Refrigerator. Hardwood. Baked enamel, lined provision chamber. Removable drain pipe and trap. Dry-air circulation.

Outside Dimensions.

Width. Inch.	Depth. Inch.	Height. Inch.	Ice Cap. Lbs.	Shipping Weight Lbs.	Price.
22	18½	50	70	150	$16.00
25¼	20	53½	100	190	19.75
28½	20¾	58	140	220	23.75
32	21¾	60¾	170	285	27.75

K—19601. The Alaska Refrigerator Company's High Grade Refrigerators. These refrigerators are made of hard wood, packed with pebbled cork. Extra heavy hardware, nickel-plated. Removable drain pipe and trap.

Apartment House Style. Outside Dimensions.

Width. Inch.	Depth. Inch.	Height. Inch.	Ice Cap. Lbs.	Shipping Weight Lbs.	Price
22	18½	50	70	160	$19.00
25¼	20	54	100	195	22.50
28½	21	58	140	220	26.50
32	21¾	61	170	285	30.50

K—19602. Majestic Refrigerator. Made of hardwood, zinc lined. Woven wire shelves. Removable drain pipe and trap. Porcelain lined water tank is extra. Dry-air circulation.

Width Inch.	Depth Inch.	Height Inch.	Ice Cap. Lbs.	Price.
22	15	38	30	$7.50
24	16¾	41	45	9.25
25½	17¾	43½	60	11.50

K—19603. Star Refrigerator. Made of hardwood. Baked enameled lined provision chamber. Removable drain pipe and trap. Woven wire shelves. Porcelain lined. Water tank is extra.

Width Inch.	Depth Inch.	Height Inch.	Ice Cap. Lbs.	Price.
22	15	38	30	$9.00
25½	17¾	43½	60	15.00
30½	19¾	47	90	20.50

K—19604. Alaska Refrigerator. Made of hardwood. Baked enameled lined. Pebble cork packed. Woven wire shelves. Removable drain pipe and trap. Porcelain lined; water tank is extra.

Width Inch.	Depth Inch.	Height Inch.	Ice Cap. Lbs.	Price.
22	15	38	30	$11.25
25½	17¾	43½	60	18.50
30½	19¾	47	90	25.50

K—19605. Alaska Ice Chest. Hardwood. Galvanized iron lined and galvanized iron shelves.

Width Inch.	Depth Inch.	Height Inch.	Ice Cap. Lbs.	Price.
24	16	25	25	$6.50
27	19	27	40	9.00
32	22	31	75	11.00

K—19606. The Alaska Ice Chest. Suitable for country homes or grocery stores. Hardwood Galvanized iron lined and galvanized iron shelves.

Width Inch.	Depth Inch.	Height Inch.	Ice Cap. Lbs.	Price.
38	24	34	100	$14.50
44	26	35¼	150	18.00
54	30	37	225	24.00

Gimbels Offer the Newest Ideas in Housefurnishings

The Gimbel Stores have tremendous Sections devoted to Housefurnishings, with men of long experience to look after them. Their constant search of the markets culls out the best, and you can have the most up-to-date goods at most reasonable prices. Gimbels Restricted Delivery, given on page 4, applies to these goods.

K—19701—$1.25

K—19702

K—19703

K—19700

K—19704—$1.30

K—19705—$3.00

K—19706—$2.75

K—19710—$7.50

K—19707—$12.00

K—19711

K—19708

K—19709

K—19700. "Hall" Hardwood Refrigerator. One piece porcelain lined provision chamber. Woven wire shelves. Removable drain pipe and trap.

No.	Width in.	Depth in.	Height in.	Ice Cap. lbs.	Price.
119	32	20½	43½	65	$33.50
122	39	23½	49½	130	44.75

K—19701. Water Coolers. Nickel-plated faucet and metal side handles, galvanized reservoir.

2 gallon	$1.25
3 gallon	1.50
4 gallon	2.00
6 gallon	2.50
8 gallon	3.50
10 gallon	4.25

K—19702. Nursery Refrigerator. Japanned case. Galvanized lined. Galvanized iron shelf. and nickel faucet.

No.	Width.	Depth.	Height	Price.
1	17 inch	11½ inch	12 inch	$2.25
2½	23 inch	13 inch		3.50

K—19703. Nursery Refrigerator. White finish and nickel faucet.

No.	Width.	Depth.	Height.	Price.
1	17 inch	11½ inch	12 inch	$2.75
2	19 inch	13 inch	13¾ inch	3.25
2½	23 inch	13 inch	13¾ inch	4.00

K—19704. Ice Cream Freezers. Two of the best and most widely known makes.

	Gem.	White Mountain.
1 quart	$1.50	$1.30
2 quart	1.80	1.75
3 quart	2.20	2.10
4 quart	2.65	2.55
6 quart	3.35	3.25
8 quart	4.35	4.50
10 quart	5.75	5.75
12 quart	6.75	7.75
15 quart	7.75	8.50

K—19705. Gimbel Clothes Wringer, 10-inch roll. One year guarantee. We thoroughly tested this wringer before branding with the Gimbel name. It is absolutely reliable. The rubber is of high grade and wear-resisting, and all parts are thoroughly made and fitted. $3.00.

K—19706. "Bissell" Ball-Bearing Carpet Sweeper. The very best make at the price, every way reliable and a labor-saver. Note the very fair prices that Gimbels are able to put on this sweeper. Japan finish, $2.75; nickel finish, $3.25.

K—19707. "Michigan" Motor Washer. Saves time and clothes, and makes washing an easy task. Extra heavy tubs. Stave legs. Strong and thoroughly well made. $12.00.

K—19708. "Hall" Soft Wood Chest. Zinc lined. Double lids. Slate shelves. Lock key.

No.	Width.	Depth.	Height.	Ice Cap.	Price.
1	24½ in.	18 in.	28 in.	35 lbs.	$ 7.00
3	32½ in.	20 in.	30 in.	60 lbs.	10.00
5	36½ in.	22 in.	32 in.	100 lbs.	13.50

K—19709. "Hall" Soft Wood Chest. Zinc lined. Double lids. Slate shelves. Lock key.

No.	Width.	Depth.	Height.	Ice Cap.	Price.
6	38½ in.	23 in.	33 in.	125 lbs.	$15.00
7	42½ in.	24 in.	34 in.	155 lbs.	16.75
8	46½ in.	26 in.	35 in.	210 lbs.	20.00
9	55 in.	26 in.	37 in.	265 lbs.	24.50

K—19710. Over-Head Shower. Complete with curtain, tubing and pins. Can be fastened to the wall very easily. $7.50.

K—19710-a. Bath Spray. Not illustrated. To fasten on any faucet. With three-inch spray head. 5 ft. long. $1.50.

K—19711. Nursery Refrigerator. Extra heavy tin. White finish.

No.	Width.	Depth.	Height.	Price.
1	16 inch	11½ inch	11½ inch	$3.00
2	19 inch	13 inch	13 inch	3.50
3	22 inch	16 inch	16½ inch	4.50

New York — Gimbel Brothers — Philadelphia

Screen Doors, Poultry Wire, Lawn Mowers, Etc.

Get your needed supplies in time. Don't wait until the lawn grass is of unsightly height, or the house is full of flies, before you procure your mower or screens. The "ounce of prevention" is here the part of wisdom, and with the low prices that Gimbels quote from the very beginning of the season there is no occasion for any delay. Gimbels Restricted Delivery Offer applies to these Goods. See page 4.

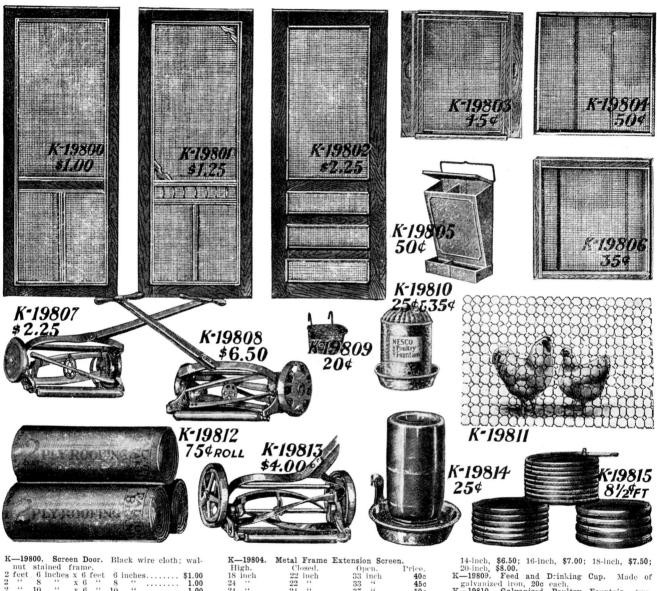

K—19800. Screen Door. Black wire cloth; walnut stained frame.

2 feet 6 inches x 6 feet 6 inches........	$1.00
2 " 8 " x 6 " 8 "	1.00
2 " 10 " x 6 " 10 "	1.00
3 " 10 " x 7 " 10 "	1.00

K—19801. Screen Door. Black wire cloth. Wood natural finish.

2 feet 6 inches x 6 feet 6 inches........	$1.25
2 " 8 " x 6 " 8 "	1.25
2 " 10 " x 6 " 10 "	1.25
3 " 10 " x 7 " 10 "	1.25

K—19802. Screen Door. Four-inch frames; 1⅛-inch thick. Made of selected pine lumber. Finished in natural wood color. Black wire cloth.

2 feet 6 inches x 6 feet 6 inches........	$2.25
2 " 8 " x 6 " 8 "	2.25
2 " 10 " x 6 " 10 "	2.25
3 " 10 " x 7 " 10 "	2.25

K—19503. Adjustable Wing End Window Screen. Wooden frames.

High.	Closed.	Open.	Price.
20 inch	26 inch	32 inch	33c
24 "	22 "	28 "	35c
24 "	26 "	32 "	38c
24 "	30 "	36 "	42c
28 "	26 "	32 "	45c
28 "	30 "	36 "	50c
28 "	34 "	40 "	55c
28 "	38 "	44 "	60c
28 "	42 "	48 "	65c
28 "	48 "	54 "	75c
28 "	54 "	60 "	85c

K—19804. Metal Frame Extension Screen.

High.	Closed.	Open.	Price.
18 inch	22 inch	33 inch	40c
24 "	22 "	33 "	45c
24 "	24 "	37 "	50c
30 "	24 "	37 "	60c
30 "	26 "	43 "	75c

K—19805. Nesco Dry Food Hopper. Self-feeding. The large compartment is intended for dry mash. It will hold a goodly supply, which is always clean and ready. The small compartment holds an ample quantity of beef scrap for an average pen. Size, 8¾x4¼x12, 50c each.

K—19806. Extension Window Screens. Wooden frames.

High.	Closed.	Open.	Price.
15 inch	21 inch	33 inch	25c
18 "	21 "	33 "	28c
22 "	21 "	33 "	30c
24 "	21 "	33 "	35c
24 "	23 "	37 "	40c
24 "	26 "	41 "	45c
28 "	23 "	37 "	45c
28 "	26 "	41 "	50c
30 "	21 "	33 "	40c
30 "	23 "	37 "	50c
36 "	26 "	45 "	60c

K—19807. Gimbel Plain Bearing Lawn Mowers. Easy running, three blades, geared on both sides: 10-inch, $2.25; 12-inch, $2.50; 14-inch, $2.75; 16-inch, $3.00; 18-inch, $3.25.

K—19808. Philadelphia Lawn Mower. Style K; 10-inch wheels, 5 blades; geared on both sides:

14-inch, $6.50; 16-inch, $7.00; 18-inch, $7.50; 20-inch, $8.00.

K—19809. Feed and Drinking Cup. Made of galvanized iron, 20c each.

K—19810. Galvanized Poultry Fountain, two-quart capacity, 25c each; four-quart capacity, 35c each.

K—19811. Poultry Wire. Galvanized steel netting. The cleanest and finest netting on the market. It is made of tough steel wire, thoroughly galvanized after weaving. Will not rust. 150 lineal feet to roll.

2-inch mesh.		1-inch mesh.	
12 inches wide, $.65 roll	12 inches, $1.80 roll
18 " " 1.25 "	18 " 2.60 "
24 " " 1.65 "	24 " 3.40 "
30 " " 2.00 "	30 " 4.20 "
36 " " 2.40 "	36 " 5.00 "
42 " " 2.85 "	42 " 5.50 "
48 " " 3.15 "	48 " 6.50 "
60 " " 4.00 "	60 " 8.00 "
72 " " 4.50 "	72 " 9.50 "

K—19812. 2-Ply Tar Roofing Paper. 108 square feet to roll: 75c roll.

K—19813. Gimbel Ball-Bearing Lawn Mower: 14-inch, $4.00; 16-inch, $4.50; 18-inch, $5.00.

K—19814. Poultry Fountain. With hook for hanging on the wall or post, as illustrated. 25c each. Fruit Jar not included.

K—19815. Garden Hose. Coupled in 25 or 50-foot lengths at 8½c, 10c, 12c, 15c and 18c per foot. All ¾ inches in diameter. We do not recommend anything cheaper than 8½c. It will not wear. Highest grade; most economical.

Kitchen, Bathroom and Garden Goods at Lowest Prices

Owing to the purchasing power of the three Gimbel Stores when buying in unison, Gimbels can sell at all times at lowest prices of any dealer. It will pay you to make up an order with your friends and have goods forwarded by freight, under the terms of Gimbels Restricted Delivery Offer on page 4.

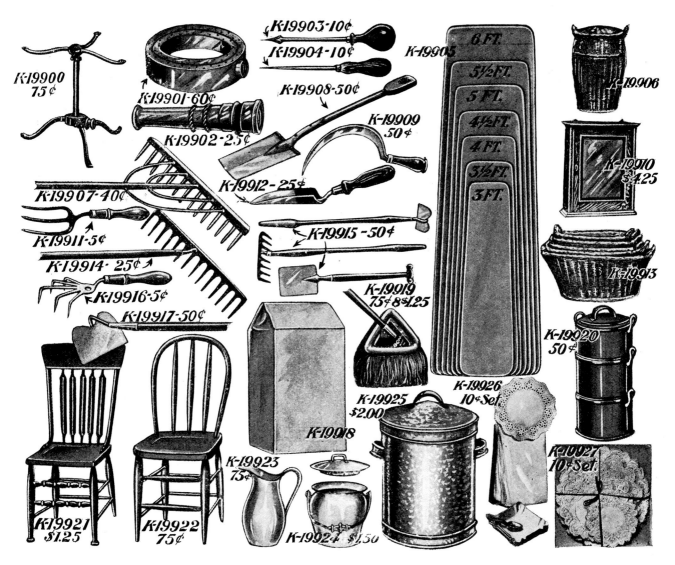

K—19900. **Lawn Sprinkler.** Malleable Iron. Three arms. 12 inches high. Polish brass. 75c.

K—19901. **Round Lawn Sprinkler.** Made of sheet brass. 8 inches in diameter. 60c.

K—19902. **Acme Hose Nozzle.** Suitable for ¾-inch hose. 25c.

K—19903. **Ice Pick.** Steel blade. Stained handle. 10c.

K—19904. **Ice Pick.** Fine tempered steel awl. 5½ inches long. Taper needle point. Hardwood handle. 10c.

K—19905. **Ironing Boards.** Made of clear poplar wood, less liable to warp than many other woods. Legless, for table use. 3 feet, 40c; 3½ feet, 45c; 4 feet, 55c; 4½ feet, 65c; 5 feet, 75c; 5½ feet, 85c; 6 feet, 95c.

K—19906. **White Willow Round Clothes Hamper.** Is more sightly than the open baskets, and takes up less room. 23 inches high, $1.25; 26 inches, $1.50; 28 inches, $1.75.

K—19907. **Wood Hay Rake.** 12 plain teeth. 40c.

K—19908. **Spade..** Steel blade. Riveted back. D handle. 50c.

K—19909. **Acme Grass Hook.** Riveted tang. tempered. Steel blade, full polished. **Black** enameled handle. 50c.

K—19910. **Oak Medicine Cabinet.** 25 inches high, 17 inches wide, 7 inches deep. Commodious shelves. French plate mirror in door. A well-filled medicine cabinet may prevent many a doctor bill. **$4.25.**

K—19911. **Spading Fork.** Extra heavy iron. Varnished handle. 5c.

K—19912. **Garden Trowel.** 6 inch. Crucible forged steel blade and solid shank. Riveted ferrule. Fully warranted. 25c.

K—19913. **Oval White Willow Clothes Baskets.** 26 to 32 inches. 50c, 75c, 85c, 90c, $1.10 and $1.25 each.

K—19914. **Malleable Iron Rake.** Painted blue. 8-tooth, 16c; 10-tooth, 18c; 12-tooth, 20c; 14-tooth, 23c; 16-tooth rake, 25c.

K—19915. **Garden Set.** One spade with steel, size 5½ x 4 inches, and 30-inch varnished handle. One hoe with a bright steel, 5¼ x 3⅛ inch. One malleable rake, 7 teeth, tinned. 50c the set.

K—19916. **Weeding Hook.** Malleable tinned iron. Enameled wood. 5c.

K—19917. **Garden Hose Shank Riveted Hoe.** Steel blade in assorted shapes. 50c.

K—19918. **Manahan's or White Tar Moth-Proof Tar Bag.**

Business Suit size, 30 in. by 37 in.. 50c
Ulster size, 33 in. by 60 in........ 75c
Overcoat size, 30 in. by 50 in.... 60c
Auto Coat size, 30 in. by 64 in.... 90c

K—19918-a. **Tar Sheets.** (Not illustrated.) 40 x 48 inches. 4c each; 35c a dozen. **Tar Balls,** 6c lb. **Flake Camphor,** 6c lb. **Gum Camphor,** 75c lb.

K—19919. **Triangle O-Cedar Polishing Mop.** The newest and best mop on the market. Two sizes, 75c and $1.25.

K—19920. **Steam Cooker.** Heavy tin with copper bottom; three 4-quart compartments for cooking three articles over one burner; 50c.

K—19921. **Hardwood Kitchen Chair.** Golden oak finish. Strongly made. $1.25.

K—19922. **Hardwood Kitchen Chair,** 75c.

K—19923. **White Enameled Pitcher,** 3-quart. 75c.

K—19924. **White Enameled Combinette.** $1.50.

K—19925. **Heavy Galvanized Garbage Can.** Tight-fitting lid. Carefully made. Will not leak. Good quality. The only sanitary kind, as the lid keeps flies away and may be cleaned with boiling water and disinfectants. Approved by all health authorities. 14 inches wide and 16 inches deep. $2.00.

K—19926. **Berry Set.** Consisting of 30 pieces. 10 spoons, 10 paper saucers and 10 napkins. 10c a set.

K—19927. **Lace Paper Doilies.** In assorted sizes. 75 to a set. 10c a set.

"Duplex" Fireless Cookers, Oil Stoves, Gas Stoves, Etc.

"Duplex" Fireless Cooker. No home should be without one of these cookers. It does away with all the inconveniences of cooking over a hot stove during the summer months and saves gas or oil. The "Duplex" Fireless Cooker actually cooks the entire meal. Fruits and vegetables cooked in these cookers retain all their flavor, making them very digestible. You can cook your dinner without danger of fires while off to church, and come back to find everything perfectly "done." They are equipped with the well-known "Wearever" Aluminum Cooking Utensils. Gimbels Restricted Delivery Offer applies. See page 4.

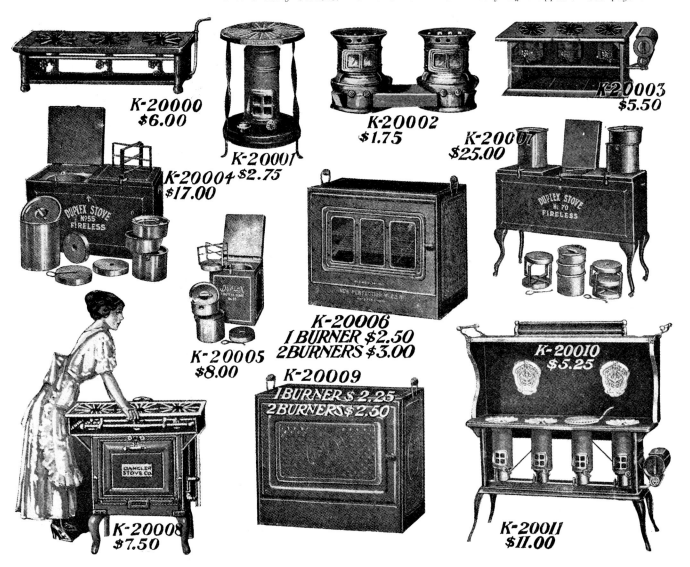

K-20000 $6.00

K-20001 $2.75

K-20002 $1.75

K-20003 $5.50

K-20004 $17.00

K-20007 $25.00

K-20005 $8.00

K-20006 1 BURNER $2.50 2 BURNERS $3.00

K-20009 1 BURNER $2.25 2 BURNERS $2.50

K-20008 $7.50

K-20010 $5.25

K-20011 $11.00

K—20000. Gasoline Stove. One of the best and safest on the market; easily cleaned and regulated; will not leak, perhaps a point most impressive to the housewife. Two burners. $4.00; three burners, $6.00.

K—20001. Special One Burner Perfection Oil Stove. With blue enamel chimney. Diameter of top, 12 inches. Has a glass top through which the oil level may be readily seen. The top is of non-breakable pressed steel. Fine for tents and outing use. $2.75.

K—20002. Double Oil Stove. Made entirely of sheet steel. Each stove has two burners, with 3½-inch wicks; $1.75.

K—20003. Wickless Blue Flame Oil Stove. Very convenient; simple to operate; gives good heat where wanted under the pots, but does not heat up the kitchen. Guaranteed not to smoke or smell, and to give satisfaction in every way; comes in two sizes; two burners, $4.50; three burners, $5.50.

K—20004. "Duplex" Fireless Cooker. Aluminum lined. The best made. Perfectly sanitary and easily kept clean. Has a 20-quart cooking capacity. This cooker is equipped with 4 aluminum cooking vessels. One 12-quart, two 2-quart and one 4-quart deep vessels. Three large aluminum banded baking and roasting disks. One disk lifter. One folding baking rack. One aluminum mat. One "Duplex" Cooking Book included. $17.00.

K—20005. "Duplex" Fireless Cooker. Consists of two aluminum vessels, one 6-quart and one 3-quart capacity. Two large aluminum banded baking disks. One disk lifter. One folding baking rack. One aluminum mat. One "Duplex" Cooking Book. $8.00.

K—20006. The New "Perfection" Steel Oven. With glass doors. Fine for summer baking. One-burner glass door, $2.50. Two-burner glass doors, $3.00.

K—20007. "Duplex" Fireless Cooker. Aluminum lined. Equipped with six aluminum cooking utensils. One 12-quart, one 8-quart, one 4-quart shallow, one 4-quart deep and two 2-quart vessels. Five aluminum banded large baking and roasting disks. One disk lifter. Two folding baking racks. One aluminum mat. One "Duplex" Cooking Book. Complete with a set of four extra heavy cast iron legs. $25.00. Same style stove without legs, $24.00.

K—20008. "Dangler" Gas Stove. Without Broiler. If a steamer is used less burners are required, which saves gas. Three-burner top; size of oven, 16x14x15. $7.50. Value $11.00.

K—20009. The New "Perfection" Steel Oven. A scientific baking apparatus which will bake biscuits, bread, cake, pie and roast meats to the entire satisfaction of the most exacting cook. Two burner, swing door, size 17⅝ inches high, 12¾ inches deep, 21½ inches wide. $2.50. One burner, swing door, size, 17⅝ inches high, 12½ inches deep, 13¾ inches wide. $2.25.

K—20010. Cabinet for the "New Perfection" Blue Flame Oil Cooking Stove K—20011. Protects wall from oily vapors and has convenient shelf for dishes. Comes in three sizes. Cabinet for two-burner stove, $4.25. Cabinet for three-burner stove, $4.75. Cabinet for four-burner stove, $5.25.

K—20011. The "New Perfection" Blue Flame Oil Cooking Stove. Most economical, cleanest and convenient. Will do everything that any kitchen range will, and throws out less heat than any other make. Also makes cooking in the hot summer months a pleasure. With one-hole cooking capacity, size of top, 14 x 19½ inches, $5.50. Two-hole cooking capacity, size of top, 14 x 27½ inches, $7.25. Three-hole cooking capacity, size of top, 14 x 37½ inches, $8.50. Four-hole cooking capacity, size of top, 14 x 48, $11.00.

Electric and Alcohol Grills, Bathroom Goods, Etc.

Many are the appliances devised for the quick camp or roadside luncheon, and Gimbels have stocked the most convenient and useful of them. Our hardware and bathroom supplies departments are complete with all needfuls for the permanent and summer homes. Gimbels Restricted Delivery Offer applies. See page 4.

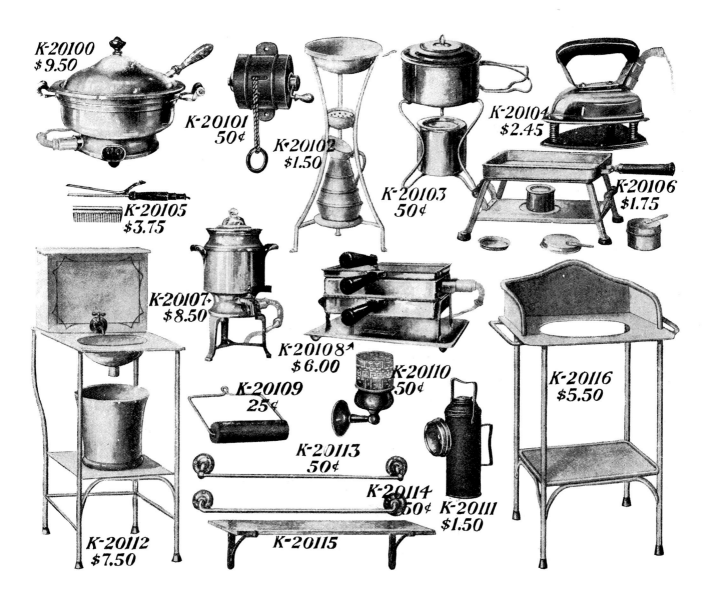

K—20100. Chafing Dish. Nickel-plated or polished copper finish. Ebonwood handles. Equipped with fuse, plugs and safety devices. Guaranteed against any possible blow-out or burn-out. $9.50.

K—20101. "Ever-ready" Dustless Clothes Line Reel. Especially adapted for indoor use. 50c.

K—20102. White Enameled Toilet Set. Consists of stand, basin, soap dish and pitcher. $1.50.

K—20103. Solid Alcohol Stove. Heats water in a jiffy for drinking, shaving, warming baby bottles or for sterilizing instruments. It will also cook coffee, cereals and boil any food. The stand, can of alcohol and metal base are all packed into the stove which goes readily into a traveling bag. 50c.

K—20104. Electric Iron. 4 or 6 pound size. Guaranteed against all possible chances of burning. Complete with 8-foot cord and socket. $2.45.

K—20105. Electric Curling Iron. Something that has been wanted for years to give good service. Has a comb attachment for drying the hair. Ebenwood handle. Heavily nickel-plated. Complete with 6-foot silk finished flexible cord. $3.75.

K—20106. Solid Alcohol Grill. Makes it unnecessary to eat cold food. A hot luncheon can be cooked in a hall room, public school, laboratory or by the roadside. It will heat soup, make toast, Johnny cake, scramble eggs, fry potatoes and pan chops and beefsteak deliciously without losing any of the juice. $1.75.

K—20107. Electric Coffee Machine. Mission pattern. Nickel or copper plated. 4 cup size, $8.50. 5 cup size, $9.50. 9 cup size, $10.50.

K—20108. Electric Grill. One of the handiest and most complete item for summer cooking. Can be used in any current. Will broil, bake, fry and toast. Complete with all attachments. $6.00.

K—20109. Nickel-Plated Toilet Paper Holder. 25c and 50c.

K—20110. Nickel-Plated Tumbler Holder. Prevents glasses from making a ring on the shelf; also, if there is no specific place for them, glasses are apt to be carried away. 50c.

K—20111. Battery Lantern. Always ready. A most convenient article for using around automobiles, boats, camp or the home. Japan finish, $1.50. Nickel or brass finish, $2.00. With ordinary care and use, these lamps will last from one to three months. Extra batteries, 25c each.

K—20112. White Enameled Toilet Stand. Complete with reservoir for water. $7.50.

K—20113. Nickel-Plated Towel Bar. Square ends with ball finish. Many towels are a necessity in the summer. 24 inches, 50c.

K—20114. Nickel-Plated Towel Bar. Curved ends. Adds to the attractiveness of the bathroom. 18 inches, 50c.

K—20115. Bathroom Glass Shelf. Nickel bracket. The most sanitary, the most sightly, the most easily cleaned bathroom shelf made. Furnish the bathroom carefully, for it is the index to the house. This is the best shelf you could get. 18 inches, 75c; 24 inches, $1.00; 30 inches, $1.50.

K—20116. White Enameled Toilet Stand. $5.50.

Dainty Requirements for the Toilet Table

So many toilet preparations on the market are not up to the standard in quality that we feel it necessary to offer for sale only such articles as we can endorse. In order to do this we conduct in New York our own laboratory and put up in our own name a line of toilet requisites which are unsurpassed for quality and purity. In addition, we list only the most widely known of other makes. For transportation, see opposite page.

K-20200 95¢
K-20201 50¢
K-20208 $1.00
K-20202 $5.00
K-20203 15¢
K-20204 8¢
K-20206 35¢
K-20205 10¢
K-20207 32¢
K-20209 25¢
K-20210 39¢
K-20211 25¢
K-20212 25¢
K-20213 20¢
K-20214 20¢
K-20215 60¢
K-20216 15¢
K-20217 25¢
K-20218 22¢
K-20219 K-20220 2 for 25¢

K—20200. **Tourists' Case.** Persian silk, rubber lined. Has pockets for toilet accessories. Large size. 95c.

K—20201. **Bath Brush.** With detachable handle. Very convenient. Large size. 50c.

K—20202. **Handsome Ivory Pyralin Toilet Set.** Three pieces, consisting of bevelled plate mirror, comb and splendid brush with eleven rows of bristles. In flat-lined box. Engraved with your favorite monogram. Bargain for $5.00.

K—20203. **Gimbels Imported Castile Soap.** An absolutely pure castile wrapped in tinfoil. Cake, 15c. Dozen cakes, $1.50.

K—20204. **Kirk's Jap Rose Transparent Glycerine Soap.** Bubb'y bath soap. Square cake. Cake, 8c. Dozen cakes, 95c.

K—20205. **Swiss Violet Glycerine Soap.** Odor of violets. Large cake, 10c. Doz. cakes, $1.00.

K—20205=a. **Gimbels Swiss Verbena Bath Soap.** Not illustrated. A large size cake of pure milled soap. Scented with the true

Verbena odor. Sold elsewhere for 25c cake. At Gimbels, 10c cake. Dz. cakes, $1.00.

K—20206. **Gimbels Vanity Box Rouge.** Very handy to carry in hand. Light, medium or dark colors. Box with puff, 35c.

K—20207. **Gimbel Brothers Theatrical Cold Cream.** A cold cream made from the finest of ingredients. ½ lb. can, 32c. 1 lb., 50c.

K—20208. **Pullman Apron for Traveling.** All rubber lined. Large pockets for holding toilet articles. $1.00.

K—20209. **Rubber Gloves.** Allow two sizes larger, when ordering than street gloves. Value, 50c. Special, 25c. pair.

K—20210. **Melorose Beauty Cream.** A pure cold cream, daintily perfumed. 50c box at 39c. Other Melorose preparations not illustrated. Melorose powder, 39c for a 50c box; and Melorose rouge 50c box at 39c.

K—20211. **Gimbel Brothers Brilliantine.** Excellent for softening and beautifying the hair. In assorted odors. 25c.

K—20212. **Combination Offer.** A 25c open-

back tooth brush and a 15c can of Gimbels tooth powder. The two for only 25c.

K—20213. **Gimbels Benzoin, Rose Water and Glycerine Lotion.** For softening the hands, for use after shaving. ½ pint, 20c. Pint, 35c.

K—20214. **Gimbels Pure Extract of Witch Hazel.** U. S. P. Strength. Pint, 20c. Quart, 35c.

K—20215. **Gimbel Brothers Imported Bay Rum.** For the toilet and bath. Pint size, 60c.

K—20216. **Gimbels Violet Scented Pure Witch Hazel.** ½ pint, 15c. Special, 25c. pair.

K—20217. **Gimbels Violet or Corylopsis Talcum Powder.** Perfumed. 1 lb. can, 25c.

K—20218. **Cutex Cuticle Remover.** Softens and removes ragged and superfluous cuticle without cutting. 22c.

K—20219 and K—20220. **Combination Offer at 25c.** A 25c jar of Erwin's Arbutus Talcum and 25c jar of Erwin's Arbutus Rice Powder. The two special for 25c.

New York — Gimbel Brothers — Philadelphia

Well-known Brands of Drugs and Patent Medicines

The Drugs and Patent Medicines Departments of the Gimbel Stores are complete in every detail. Moreover Gimbel low prices prevail. All the well-known brands of proprietary articles are carried and sold by us very generally at "Cut Sale Prices."
The goods on this and the opposite page come under Gimbels Restricted Delivery Offer on page 4. Liquids of a pint or less can be sent by Parcel Post, but at customer's risk, and expense for retainer. Express is preferable.

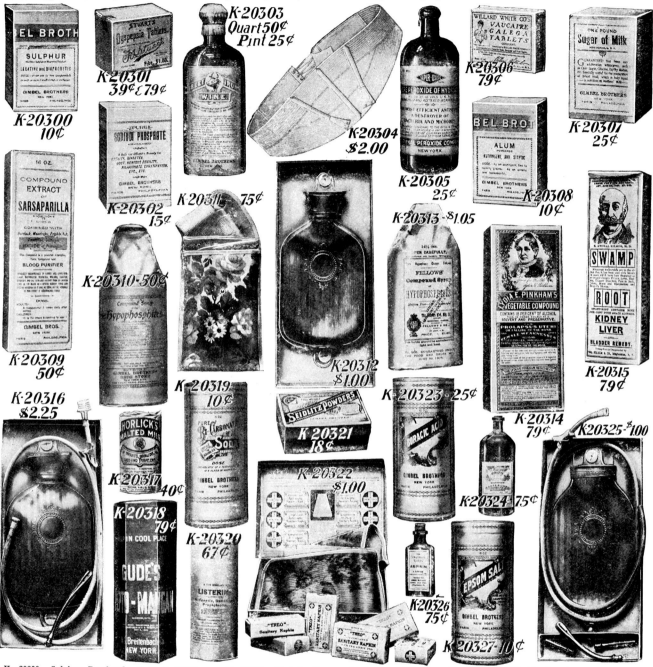

K—20300. Sulphur, Powdered. U. S. P. Grade. 10c a **lb.**

K—20301. Stuart's Dyspepsia Tablets. The 50c size, 39c. $1.00 size, **79c.**

K—20302. Sodium Phosphate Granular. 15c lb.

K—20303. Gimbels Beef, Iron and Wine. Excellent as a body builder. U. S. P. Grade. Quart size, 50c. Pint size, 25c.

K—20304. Abdominal Supporting and Reducing Belt. All elastic. Very comfortable, giving needed support. Regularly $3.50. Now $2.00.

K—20305. Peroxide of Hydrogen. An efficient antiseptic. 16-ounce bottle, 25c.

K—20306. Vaucaire Galega Tablets. Bust and chest developer. A fine tonic and nerve builder. Regular price, $1.00. Special, 79c.

K—20307. Sugar of Milk. U. S. P. Grade. 25c lb.

K—20308. Alum, Powdered. U. S. P. Grade. 10c a lb.

K—20309. Gimbels Syrup of Sarsaparilla Compound. A blood purifier. Regularly, $1.00. Now, 50c.

K—20310. Gimbels Syrup of Hypophosphites Compound. $1.00 bottle, 50c.

K—20311. Sanitary Apron and Elastic Belt. In cretonne case. Compact and convenient. 75c.

K—20312. Seamless Moulded Hot Water Bottle. Red rubber. Guaranteed one year. 2-qt. $1.00.

K—20313. Fellows' Syrup of Hypophosphites Compound. $1.05. Regular, $1.50.

K—20314. Lydia Pinkham's Compound. Regular price, $1.00. Special, 79c.

K—20315. Kilmer's Swamp Root. $1.00 bottle, special 79c.

K—20316. Full 2-qt. Moulded Combination Hot Water Bottle and Fountain Syringe. Best red rubber. Seamless. Guaranteed. $2.25.

K—20317. Hospital Size Horlick's Malted Milk. $3.75 size, $3.00. $1.00 size, 80c. 50c size, 40c.

K—20318. Gude's Pepto-Mangan. Regular price, $1.00. Our price, 79c.

K—20319. Bicarbonate of Soda U. S. P. Grade. Finest quality. 10c a lb.

K—20320. Lambert's Listerine. Regularly. $1.00. Special, 67c.

K—20321. Seidlitz Powder. Box of 12 packages. Regular price, 25c. Now, 18c.

K—20322. Traveling Sanitary Outfits. Apron, belt and six compressed towels. Rubber lined, cretonne case. $1.00.

K—20323. Boric Acid. U. S. P. Grade. 25c lb.

K—20324. Kress Owen's Glyco Thymoline. $1.00 bottle for 75c

K—20325. Red Rubber Fountain Syringe. Seamless. Guaranteed for one year. Complete with all attachments. Two-quart size, $1.00.

K—20326. Aspirin Tablets. Five-grain tablets. Regularly, $1.00. Now, 75c.

K—30327. Epsom Salts. U. S. P. Grade. 10c lb.

NOT ILLUSTRATED.

K—20328. "Pyralin" Ivory Toilet Goods. A full line always on hand. Hair Brushes, $1.25, $2.50, $3.25. Mirrors, $2.50, $4.00. Cloth Brushes, $1.50, $2.75. Hat Brushes, 75c, $1.25. Manicure Pieces, 50c each. Buffers, 50c, 75c. $1.00. Powder Boxes, 50c. $1.00, $1.50.

New York — Gimbel Brothers — Philadelphia

Summer Reading for Boys and Girls

Restricted Delivery offer applies

ALTEMUS' 20th CENTURY BOOKS, 25c a Volume

Publishers' Price, 50c.

FOR BOYS AND GIRLS

THE PONY RIDER BOY SERIES
By Frank Gee Patchin

The Pony Rider Boys in the Rockies.
The Pony Rider Boys in Texas.
The Pony Rider Boys in Montana.
The Pony Rider Boys in the Ozarks.
The Pony Rider Boys in the Alkali.
The Pony Rider Boys in New Mexico.
The Pony Rider Boys in the Grand Canyon.

THE BATTLESHIP BOYS SERIES
By Frank Gee Patchin

The Battleship Boys at Sea.
The Battleship Boys' First Step Upward.

THE HIGH SCHOOL BOYS SERIES
By H. Irving Hancock

The High School Freshmen.
The High School Pitcher.
The High School Left End.
The High School Captain of the Team.

THE AUTOMOBILE GIRLS SERIES
By Laura Dent Crane

The Automobile Girls at Newport.
The Automobile Girls in the Berkshires.
The Automobile Girls Along the Hudson.
The Automobile Girls at Chicago.
The Automobile Girls at Palm Beach.
The Automobile Girls at Washington.

The Battleship Boys in Foreign Service.
The Battleship Boys in the Tropics.

THE GRAMMAR SCHOOL BOYS SERIES
By H. Irving Hancock

The Grammar School Boys of Gridley.
The Grammar School Boys Snowbound.
The Grammar School Boys in the Woods.
The Grammar School Boys in Summer Athletics.

THE HIGH SCHOOL GIRLS SERIES
By Jessie Graham Flower, A.M.

Grace Harlowe's Plebe Year at High School.
Grace Harlowe's Sophomore Year at High School.
Grace Harlowe's Junior Year at High School.
Grace Harlowe's Senior Year at High School.

THE COLLEGE GIRLS SERIES
By Jessie Graham Flower, A.M.

Grace Harlowe's First Year at Overton College.
Grace Harlowe's Second Year at Overton College.
Grace Harlowe's Third Year at Overton College.
Grace Harlowe's Fourth Year at Overton College.

The Bobbsey Twins Books

25c. each

By Laura Lee Hope.

1. The Bobbsey Twins.
2. The Bobbsey Twins in the Country.
3. The Bobbsey Twins at the Seashore.
4. The Bobbsey Twins at School.
5. The Bobbsey Twins at Snow Lodge.

The Little Wonder Books

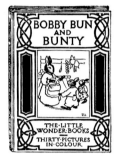

25c each.

1. Bobby Bun and Bunty.
2. The Brownie's Birthday.
3. Apple Tree Villa.
4. Tim Tubby Toes.
5. Tick, Tack and Tock.
6. Mother Goose.
7. Bully Boy.
8. Robbie and Dobbie.
9. A Little Sailor.
10. A Little Soldier.

The Famous Frank Merriwell Stories

25c Each

BURT L. STANDISH.

No modern series of tales for boys and youths has met with anything like the cordial reception and popularity accorded to the Frank Merriwell Stories. There must be a reason for this, and there is. Frank Merriwell, as portrayed by the author, is a jolly, whole-souled, honest, courageous American lad, who appeals to the hearts of the boys. He has no bad habits, and his manliness inculcates the idea that it is not necessary for a boy to indulge in petty vices to be a hero. Frank Merriwell's example is a shining light for every ambitious lad to follow. Twenty-four volumes now ready: Frank Merriwell's School Days. Frank Merriwell's Chums. Frank Merriwell's Foes. Frank Merriwell's Trip West. Frank Merriwell Down South. Frank Merriwell's Bravery. Frank Merriwell's Hunting Tour. Frank Merriwell's Races. Frank Merriwell's Sports Afield. Frank Merriwell at Yale. Frank Merriwell's Courage. Frank Merriwell's Daring. Frank Mer-

riwell's Skill. Frank Merriwell's Champions. Frank Merriwell's Return to Yale. Frank Merriwell's Secret. Frank Merriwell's Loyalty. Frank Merriwell's Reward. Frank Merriwell's Faith. Frank Merriwell's Victories. Frank Merriwell's Power. Frank Merriwell's Set-Back. Frank Merriwell's False Friend. Frank Merriwell's Brother.

The Little People's Series—25c Each

Cloth binding. Illustrated. Well-written stories for children of from 7 to 12 years of age.

Andy. By Lucile Lovell.
Bockers. By Margaret Compton.
The Boynton Pluck. By Helen Ward Banks.
Dearie, Dot, and the Dog. By Julie M. Lippmann.
Dolly's Doings. By Alice George.
Dreamland. By Julie M. Lippmann.
The Green Door. By Margaret Compton.
His Lordship's Puppy. By Theodora C. Elmslie.

Mistress Moppett. By Annie M. Barnes.
The Outdoor Chums. By Alice Turner Curtis.
A Regular Tomboy. By Mary E. Mumford.

A Rose of Holly Court. By Elizabeth Lincoln Gould.
Sweet P'S. By Julie M. Lippmann.
Uncle Tom, the Burglar. By Mabel E. Wotton.
The Walcott Twins. By Lucile Lovell.

The Famous Rover Boys Series

45c Each
By Arthur M. Winfield.

1. The Rover Boys at School.
2. The Rover Boys on the Ocean.
3. The Rover Boys in the Jungle.
4. The Rover Boys Out West.
5. The Rover Boys on the Great Lakes.
6. The Rover Boys in the Mountains.
7. The Rover Boys on Land and Sea.
8. The Rover Boys in Camp.
9. The Rover Boys on the River.
10. The Rover Boys on the Plains.
11. The Rover Boys in Southern Waters.
12. The Rover Boys on the Farm.
13. The Rover Boys on Treasure Isle.
14. The Rover Boys at College.
15. The Rover Boys Down East.
16. The Rover Boys in the Air.
17. The Rover Boys in New York.
18. The Rover Boys in Alaska

The Tom Swift Series—25c Each

By Victor Appleton.

1. Tom Swift and His Motor-Cycle.
2. Tom Swift and His Motor-Boat.
3. Tom Swift and His Airship.
4. Tom Swift and His Submarine Boat.
5. Tom Swift and His Electric Runabout.
6. Tom Swift and His Wireless Message.
7. Tom Swift Among the Diamond Makers.
8. Tom Swift in the Caves of Ice.
9. Tom Swift and His Sky Racer.

10. Tom Swift and His Electric Rifle.
11. Tom Swift in the City of Gold.
12. Tom Swift and His Air Glider.
13. Tom Swift in Captivity.
14. Tom Swift and His Wizard Camera.
15. Tom Swift and His Great Searchlight.
16. Tom Swift and His Giant Cannon.
17. Tom Swift and His Photo Telephone

The Motor Boys Series—45c Each

By Clarence Young.

Each Volume Handsomely Illustrated.

Bound in Cloth, stamped in Color.

1. The Motor Boys.
2. The Motor Boys Overland.
3. The Motor Boys in Mexico.
4. The Motor Boys Across the Plains.
5. The Motor Boys Afloat.
6. The Motor Boys on the Atlantic.
7. The Motor Boys in Strange Waters.
8. The Motor Boys on the Pacific.
9. The Motor Boys in the Clouds.
10. The Motor Boys Over the Rockies.
11. The Motor Boys Over the Ocean.
12. The Motor Boys on the Wing.
13. The Motor Boys After a Fortune.
14. The Motor Boys on the Border.
15. The Motor Boys Under the Sea.
16. The Motor Boys on Road and River.

The Big League Series

45c Each
Bound in Cloth.
Large 12 Mo.

Lefty o' the Bush.
Lefty o' the Big League.
Lefty o' the Blue Stockings.
Lefty o' the Training Camp.
Brick King, Backstop.
The Making of a Big Leaguer.
Courtney of the Center Garden.
Covering the Look-in Corner.

The Big War Series

45c Each

Cloth. Large 12 Mo.
The Search for the Spy.
The Air Scout.
Dodging the North Sea Mines.
With Joffre on the Battle Lines.

Spring and Summer Reading at 25c a Volume

Well-Known Cloth Bound Novels at a Most Unusual Price. Our Restricted Delivery Offer Applies. See Page 4.

PINKERTON, ALLAN

Bank Robbers
Bucholz and the Detectives
Burglar's Fate, The   Claude Melnotte
Criminal Reminiscences
Double Life, A
Expressman and Detectives, The
Gypsies and Detectives, The
Mississippi Outlaws, The
Model Town and Detectives, The
Mollie Maguires, The
Professional Thieves
Railroad Forger, The
Somnambulist, The
Spiritualists and Detectives, The
Spy of the Rebellion, The
Strikers. Communists, etc.
Thirty Years a Detective

HUME, FERGUS

Claude Duval of '95   Peacock of Jewels, The
Coin of Edward VII, A   Rainbow Feather, The
Disappearing Eye. The   Red Money
Green Mummy, The   Red Window, The
Lost Parchment, The   Sacred Herb, The
Mandarin's Fan, The   Sealed Message, The
Mystery of a Hansom Cab. Secret Passage, The
The   Solitary Farm, The
Mystery Queen, The   Steel Crown, The
Opal Serpent, The   Yellow Holly, The
Pagan's Cup, The

MARY J. HOLMES

The Only Complete Edition

ROSS, ALBERT

Black Adonis, A   Garston Bigamy, The
Her Husband's Friend
His Foster Sister
His Private Character
In Stella's Shadow
Love at Seventy   Love Gone Astray
Moulding a Maiden
Naked Truth, The
New Sensation, A   Original Sinner, An
Out of Wedlock
Speaking of Ellen
Stranger Than Fiction
Sugar Princess, A
That Gay Deceiver
Their Marriage Bond
Thou Shalt Not
Thy Neighbor's Wife
Why I'm Single
Young Fawcett's Mabe   Young Miss Giddy

Abandoned Farm, The   Kitty Craig
Bessie's Fortune   Lena Rivers
Cameron Pride, The   Madeline
Chateau D'Or   Maggie Miller
Connie's Mistake   Marguerite
Cousin Maude   Marian Grey
Cromptons, The   Meadow Brook
Daisy Thornton   Merivale Banks, The
Darkness and Daylight   Mildred
Dr. Hathern's Daughters   Mildred's Ambition
Dora Deane   Millbank
Edith Lyle   Mrs. Hallam's Companion
Edna Browning   Paul Ralston
English Orphans, The   Queenie Hetherton
Ethelyn's Mistake   Rena's Experiment
Forrest House   Rosamond
Gretchen   Rose Mather
Homestead on the Hillside Tempest and Sunshine
Hugh Worthington   Tracy Diamonds, The
Jessie Graham   West Lawn

Very Famous Novels at 45c a Copy

Included Are Many Late and Most Popular Titles, All at 45c a Volume—Cloth Bound—Our Restricted Delivery Offer Applies—See Page 4.

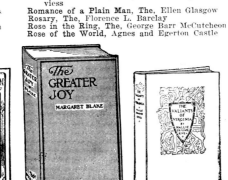

At Good Old Siwash, George Fitch
Anne of Green Gables, L. M. Montgomery
Blue Wall, The, Richard Washburn Child
Bolted Door, The, Geo. Gibbs
Broad Highway, The, Jeffery Farnol
Buck Peters, Ranchman, Clarence E. Mulford
Butterfly Man, The, George Barr McCutcheon
By Right of Purchase, Harold Bindloss
Cab No. 44, R. F. Foster
Calling of Dan Matthews, The, Harold Bell Wright
Call of the Blood, The, Robert Hichens

Call of the Cumberlands, The, Charles Neville Buck
Cape Cod Stories, Joseph C. Lincoln
Cap'n Eri, Joseph C. Lincoln
Cap'n Warren's Wards, Joseph C. Lincoln
Cry in the Wilderness, A, Mary Waller
Destroying Angel, The, Louis Joseph Vance
Gordon Craig, Randall Parrish
Greater Joy, The, Margaret Bland
Greyfriars Bobby, Eleanor Atkinson
Halcyone, Eleanor Glyn
Harvester, The. Gene Stratton-Porter
Havoc, E. Phillips Oppenheim

Heart of Night Wind, The, V. E. Roe
Heather-Moon, The, C. N. & A. M. Williamson
Hollow of Her Hand, The, George Barr McCutcheon
Imposter, The. George Reed Scott
Judgment House, The. Gilbert Parker
Lavender and Old Lace, Myrtle Reed
Lighted Way, The, E. Phillips Oppenheim
Little Knight of the X-Bar B, The, Mary K. Maule
Little Minister, The, James M. Barrie
Little Shepherd of Kingdom Come, The, John Fox, Jr.
Littlest Rebel, The, Edward Peple
Log of a Cowboy, The, Andy Adams
Long Shadow, The, B. M. Bower
Lonesome Trail, The, B. M. Bower
Looking Backward, Edward Bellamy
Lords of High Decision, The, M. Nicholson
Lost Farm Camp, Henry Herbert Knibbs
Marriage, H. G. Wells
Master's Violin, The, Myrtle Reed
Mediator, The, Roy Norton
Melting of Molly, The, Maria Thompson Daviess
Mollie's Prince, Rose Nouchette Carey
Mother Carey's Chickens, Kate Douglas Wiggin
Mountain Girl, The, Payne Erskine

Net, The, Rex Beach
New Chronicles of Rebecca, Kate Douglas Wiggin
Old Rose and Silver, Myrtle Reed
One Wonderful Night, Louis Tracy
Over the Pass, Frederick Palmer
Peg o' My Heart, J. Hartley Manners
Pleasures and Places, Juliet Wilbur Tompkins
Price She Paid, The, David Graham Phillips
Queed, Henry Sydnor Harrison
Rebecca of Sunny Brook Farm, Kate Douglas Wiggin
Redemption of Kenneth Galt, The, Will N. Harben
Red Lane, The, Holman Day
Red Pepper Burns, Grace S. Richmond
Refugees, The, A. Conan Doyle
Rejuvenation of Aunt Mary, The, Anne Warner
Return of Peter Grimm, The, David Belasco
Riders of the Purple Sage, Zane Grey
Rise of Roscoe Paine, The, Joseph C. Lincoln
Road to Providence, The, Maria Thompson Daviess
Romance of a Plain Man, The, Ellen Glasgow
Rosary, The, Florence L. Barclay
Rose in the Ring, The, George Barr McCutcheon
Rose of the World, Agnes and Egerton Castle

Rose of Old Harpeth, The, Maria Thompson Daviess
Round the Corner in Gay Street, Grace S. Richmond
Routledge Rides Alone, Will Levington Comfort
Rue: With a Difference, Rosa N. Carey
Secret Garden, The, Frances Hodgson Burnett
Shepherd of the Hills, The, Harold Bell Wright
Sheriff of Dyke Hole, The, Ridgewell Cullum
Silver Horde, The, Rex Beach
Simon the Jester, William J. Locke
Sins of the Father, The, Thomas Dixon
Stover at Yale, Owen Johnson
Street Called Straight, The, Basil King
Streets of Ascalon, The, Robert W. Chambers
Their Yesterdays, Harold Bell Wright
To Have and to Hold, Mary Johnston
Told by Uncle Remus, J. Chandler Harris
Tono-Bungay, H. G. Wells
Torchy, Sewell Ford
Trail of Ninety-eight, The, Service
Trail of the Lonesome Pine, The, John Fox, Jr.
Traitor, The, Thomas Dixon, Jr.
Trey of Hearts, The, L. J. Vance
True Stories of Crime, Arthur Train
Truxton King, George Barr McCutcheon
Trying Out Torchy, Sewell Ford
Two Little Savages, E. Thompson Seton
Valiants of Virginia, The, Hallie Ermine Rives
Vision of Joy, The, Alexander Corkey
Wall of Men, A, Margaret Hill McCarter
Way of an Eagle, The, E. M. Dell
West Wind, The, Cyrus Townsend Brady
What Happened to Mary, Robt. C. Brown
Wind Before the Dawn, The, Dell H. Munger
Winning of Barbara Worth, The, Harold Bell Wright
Within the Law, Veiller & Dana

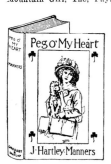

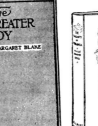

Gimbels Paris, London and American Style Book

The Gimbel Stores Are Musical Centers

Gimbels occupy a unique position among American music lovers. World-famous instruments grace the Gimbel Piano Salons. The best talking machines and records can be had at Gimbels. The Gimbel easy-payment plan, bringing certain of them into the most humble homes, has materially assisted the musical education of America. And what joy a song brings to homes formerly silent because musical advantages seemed denied to the music-hungry through lack of means.

If order is less than $1.00 include 1c. a copy for postage. On orders of a dollar and upwards we deliver free.

POPULAR VOCAL MUSIC—10c. A COPY

Aba Daba Honey-moon.
After the Roses Have Faded Away.
Always Treat Her Like a Baby.
Any Coal?
At That Mississippi Cabaret.
At the Yiddish Wedding Jubilee.

Back to the Carolina You Love.
Back to the Days of Auld Lang Syne.
Ballin' the Jack.
Beautiful Roses.

California and You.
Chinatown, My Chinatown.
Come Back to Me.
Cotton Blossom Time.

Don't Take My Boy Away.

Erin's Isle and You.

Fatima Brown.
Follow the Crowd.
Furnish a Home for Two.

Goodbye, Virginia.
Good Night, Little Girl, Good Night.
Go to Sleep, My Baby.
Gungo Din.

Harmony Bay.
He'd Keep on Saying Good Night.
Here's a Rose for You.
High Cost of Loving.
Honey Rose.

I Can't Get a Girl.
I Can't Stop Loving You.
I Didn't Raise My Boy to be a Soldier.
I'd Like to Be on an Island With You.
If I Could Live to Love You.
If I Could Read Your Heart.
If I Had My Way.
If I Had You.

I Hear You Calling Me, Tennessee.
I'm Glad My Wife's in Europe.
I'm Going to Let the Whole World Know I Love You.
I'm Going to Tell Your Mother.
I'm Not Ashamed of You, Molly.
I'm Waving at You.
Independence Day in Dublintown.
In Spite of All, I Still Love You.
Irish Melodies.
Irish Tango.
Is the Old Love Lamp Still Burning?
It May Be Far to Tipperary, It's a Longer Way to Tennessee.
It's Going to Be a Cold, Cold Winter.
It's Never Too Late to Be Sorry.
It's Too Late Now.
I've Loved You Since You Were a Baby.
I've Only One Idea About the Girls.
I Want to Go Back to Michigan.
I Want to Go to Tokio.
I Want to Linger.
I Want You to Meet My Mother.

Jack o' Lantern Moon.

Land of My Best Girl.
Let Me Guard You While You Slumber.
Let's Fill the Old Oaken Bucket With Love.
Let's Toddle.
Let Them Alone, They're Married.
Light That Lies in a Girlie's Eyes.
Little House on the Hill.
Lucille Love.

My Love Will Live On and On.
My Own Venetian Home.

'Neath the Shadow of the Pyramids.
Nobody Home.
Now She Knows How to Parle-voo.

Old Love Letters.

On the Good Ship "Honey Moon."
On the Road to Loving Town.
On the Shores of Italy.
On the Trail of the Honey Moon.
Over the Alpine Mountains.

Pick of the Family.
Poor Pauline.

Roses Remind Me of Some One.

'S Too High.
She Used to Be the Slowest Girl in Town.
Song of the Ages.
Stay Down Here Where You Belong.
Streets of Old New York.

That Reminds Me.
That's My Idea of Paradise.
There's a Little Spark of Love Still Burning.
Towsee Mongolay.

War in Snider's Grocery Store.
What Did Romeo Say to Juliet?
What'll You Do?
When I Hear a Gun I'm Going to Run.
When It's Moonlight on the Alamo.
When the Angelus Is Ringing.
When the Grown-up Ladies Act Like Babies.
When the Right Girl Comes Along.
When You're a Long, Long Way from Home.
When You Wore a Tulip and I Wore a Big Red Rose.
Winter Nights.

You and I.
You Are My Flower of Love.
You Are the Rose of My Heart.
You Great, Big, Bashful Doll.
You Made My Dreams Come True.
You're Here and I'm Here.
You're Locked in My Heart.

POPULAR INSTRUMENTAL MUSIC—10c. A COPY

After Vespers.
Amapa.
American Patrol.
Army and Navy.
Autumn Leaves.

Ballin' the Jack.
Beautiful Roses.
Beets and Turnips.
Blue Bird.
Boots and Saddles.
Breath of Spring.
Bright Star of Bethlehem.

California Sunshine.
Captain Betty.
Carnation.
Chapel by the Sea.
Chapel Chimes.
Co-ed March.

Country Club.
Cricket.
Cupids and Flowers.

Dance of the Honey Bells.
Dengozo.
Devil.

Egyptian Trop.
Evening Chimes.
Evening Prayer.

Fairy Kisses.
Fascination.
First Love.

Gleaming Star of Heaven.

Hesitation Con Amore.
Humoresque.
Hungarian Rag.

In Love's Garden.

Kissamee.

Laughing Frogs.
Love and Passion.
Love Waltz.

Meadow Brook Fox Trot.
Melody of the Flowers.
Message of Peace.
Moonbeams on the Lake.
Morning Exercise.

National Medley of Patriotic Airs.

Phyllis Tango.
Poem.

Radnor Fox Trot.

Rag-a-Muffin.
Rose That Will Never Die.
Rose Waltz.

Skylark.
Songs of the Nations.
Star of My Dreams.
Student Days.
Sweet Dreams of Heaven.
Sweetie Dear Fox Trot.

Token of Love.
Trip to Niagara.
Twilight Shadow.
Twinkling Stars.

Valse June.

Whispering Roses.
World Peace.

VOCAL AND INSTRUMENTAL MUSIC—30c. A COPY

Good-bye, Girls, I'm Through, from "Chin Chin."

I Hear You Calling Me.
Irish Eyes of Love.

Little Love, a Little Kiss.
Love of the Lorelei, from "The Debutante."
Love's Own Sweet Song, from "Sari."

Macushla.

Oh! Cecilia.
O Promise Me.

Perfect Day.

Rose in the Bud.

Same Sort of Girl, from "Girl from Utah."
Something Seems Tingling, from "High Jinks."
Somewhere a Voice Is Calling.

Song of Songs.
Sympathy, from "The Firefly."

Three for Jack.

When Dreams Come True, from "When Dreams Come True."
When the Moon Slyly Winks, from "Queen of the Movies."
When You're Away, from "The Only Girl."
Who Knows.

New York — Gimbel Brothers — Philadelphia

The Gimbel Music Stores Are Favorites With the Young People

At the Gimbel New York and Gimbel Philadelphia Stores the latest dance music is carried in stock, as well as all the popular and classical music, and a full line of teaching music. The big Gimbel Stores are in close touch with all music publishers in America or abroad and can furnish from stock or procure sheet music, collections and musical scores that are of the rarest, as well as all that is in popular demand. Special music catalogues will be furnished if you state the kind of music you wish, whether elementary or advanced, vocal or instrumental, classical or popular.

Music Rolls and Music Bags, 75c. to $5. Metronomes without bells, $2.25. Metronomes with bells, $3.25.

If order for Sheet Music is less than $1.00 kindly add 1c. a copy for postage. If $1.00 or over, we will send by post at our expense.

Beaux Art Edition of Instrumental Music—5c a Copy

Alpine Hut.
Angel's Dream.

Beautiful Blue Danube Waltzes.
Black Hawk Waltzes.
Bohemian Girl.
Bridal Chorus (Lohengrin).

Cavalleria Rusticana (Intermezzo).
Chapel in the Forest.
Charge of the Uhlans.
Convent Bells.
Corn Flower Waltzes.

Dancing in the Barn.
Danube Waves Waltzes.
Dorothy.
Dying Poet.

Edelweiss.
Evening Star.

Fairy Wedding Waltz.
Far Away.
Farewell to the Piano.
Fifth Nocturne.
Flatterer.
Flower Song.
Funeral March.

Garland of Roses.
General Grant's March.
General Smith's March.
Gertrude's Dreams.
Gypsy Dance.

Heather Bells.
Heather Rose.
Heimweh (Longing for Home).
Home Sweet Home. (Variations.)

Il Trovatore.
Invitation to the Dance.
I Wish I Was in Dixie. (Variations.)

L'Argentine.
La Czarine, Mazurka.
La Fountaine.
La Paloma.
Largo.
Last Hope.
Light Cavalry, Overture.
Little Fairy, March.
Little Fairy, Polka.
Little Fairy, Schottische.
Little Fairy, Waltz.

Loin du Bal (Echoes of the Ball).
Lutspiel, Overture.

Melodies of Scotland.
Melodies of the South.
Melody in F.
Minuet.
My Old Kentucky Home.

Nearer, My God, to Thee.

Old Black Joe.
Old Folks at Home.
Old Oaken Bucket.
On the Meadow.
Orange Blossom Waltzes.
Over the Waves.
Overture of Irish Melodies.

Palms.
Peri Waltzes.
Poet and Peasant, Overture.
Polish Dance.

Qui Vive Galop.

Raymond Overture.
Rustic Dance.

Sack Waltz.
Salut A Pesth March.
Scarf Dance.
Schubert's Serenade.
Second Mazurka.
Serenata.
Sextet from Lucia.
Shepherd Boy.
Spring Song.
Storm.
Sweet Bye and Bye.

Tam O'Shanter.
Tarantelle.
Traumerei.

Under the Double Eagle March.

Valse Bleue.

Waves of the Ocean Galop.
Wedding March.
When You and I Were Young, Maggie.
William Tell, Overture.
Woodland Echoes.

Zampa, Overture.

Beaux Art Edition of Vocal Music—5c a Copy

Anchored.
Anvil Chorus.
Auld Lang Syne.
Ave Maria.

Beauty's Eyes.
Believe Me of All Those Endearing Young Charms.

Calvary.
Carmena.

Celestial Aida.
Come Back to Erin.

Good-Bye.

Home, Sweet Home.

Kathleen Mavourneen.
Killarney.

Last Rose of Summer.
Lead, Kindly Light.
Lost Chord.

Love's Old Sweet Song.

Marseilles Hymn.
Minstrel Boy.

One Sweetly Solemn Thought.
O That We Two Were Maying.

Palms.
Pilgrims' Chorus.

Rocked in the Cradle of the Deep.

Rock of Ages.
Rosary.

Serenade.
Sextet from Lucia.
Spring Song.
Still as the Night.

Then You'll Remember Me.
Toreador Song.

When You and I Were Young, Maggie.

Most Popular Series of Vocal Music—50c a Volume.   Post Paid

Most Popular Army and Navy Songs.
Most Popular College Songs.
Most Popular Home Songs.

Most Popular Hymns.
Most Popular Love Songs.
Most Popular Mother Goose Songs.
Most Popular National Songs.

Most Popular New College Songs.
Most Popular New Songs for Male Quartets.
Most Popular Plantation Songs.

Most Popular Songs for Every Occasion.
Most Popular Songs of the Flag and Nation.

Most Popular Series of Vocal and Instrumental Music—75c a Volume.   Post Paid

Most Popular 'Cello Solos.
Most Popular Children's Piano Duets.
Most Popular Drawing Room and Concert Songs.
Most Popular Flute Solos.
Most Popular Mandolin Dance Folio.

Most Popular Modern Piano Duets.
Most Popular Modern Piano Pieces.
Most Popular New Violin Solos.
Most Popular Piano Folios.
Most Popular Piano Duets.
Most Popular Piano Pieces.

Most Popular Sacred Songs.
Most Popular Selections for the Cornet.
Most Popular Selections for Violin and Piano.
Most Popular Selections from the Most Popular Comic Operas.

Most Popular Selections from the Most Popular Operas.
Most Popular Songs from the Most Popular Comic Operas.
Most Popular Songs from the Most Popular Operas.
Most Popular Violin Dance Pieces.

Vocal and Instrumental Music—10c a Volume

Brilliant Piano Duets.
Castle Society Dance Folios.
Chas. K. Harris's Classical Numbers.
Chas. K. Harris's Dance Albums.
Chas. K. Harris's Vocal Selections.

Crescent Folios of Medium Grade Pieces.

Everybody's Favorite Piano Solos.
Echoes from Danceland.
Eclipse Four Hand Folios.

Motion Picture Music Folios.

Opera Gems. Vols. 1, 2 and 3.
Operatic Dance Folios.

Patriotic Song Folios.

Songs of Ireland.
Standard Duets.

Youth and Beauty Easy Pieces for Beginners.

The Family Music Book—$1.00 a Volume

A collection of five hundred and fifty-two pieces of vocal and piano music of moderate difficulty, selected from the works of classic and modern composers, and including many old favorites universally known.

Gimbels Paris, London and American Style Book

Parasols in the Latest Fashions for Summer 1915

Any Parasol on these pages can be made with collapsible handle to fit into suitcase for 50c. extra.

K—20900. Parasol. Plain silk with Dresden ribbon insertion and border. 16-inch, enamel frame. Pink, light blue, white or green. Natural wood handle. $1.50.

K—20901. Woman's Parasol. Plain colored taffeta. Three rows shirring and shirred border, gilt frame, long carved stick. Rich silk cord and tassel. Green or any color taffeta. $5.00.

K—20902. Parasol.. Plain taffetaline with Dresden ribbon insertion, hemstitch finish. Pink, light blue, white or green. Fancy natural light wood handle with tassel. 14 inches. $1.00.

K—20903. Woman's Parasol. Top Dresden silk with deep messaline shirred border, finished with soutache braid. Colors of borders, green or black. Gilt frame. Long carved handle. $3.00.

K—20904. Woman's Parasol. Plain messaline silk with deep fancy striped moire ribbon insertion. Shirred edge finished with narrow soutache braid. Long carved self-colored handle. 8 ribs. Gilt frame. Green, navy. $3.75.

K—20905. Woman's Parasol. Plain taffeta. "Flopper" style, threefold trimming, stitched with black. Fancy long black stick. 10 ribs. Gilt frame Any color with black edge. Very stylish. Elaborate silk cord and tassel. $5.00.

K—20906. Woman's Parasol. White and black satin striped top with deep plain satin shirred border, finished with narrow soutache braid. Carved stick. Colors of borders, green, black, cerise or purple. 8 ribs. Gilt frame. $3.00.

K—20907. Woman's Parasol. Plain taffeta with deep Dresden ribbon insertion, shirred edge, finished with narrow soutache braid. Any color taffeta. Long carved stylish handle. 8 ribs. Gilt frame. $3.00.

K—20908. Woman's Parasol. Plain taffeta silk top with one-inch white and black satin striped border. Plain black stick, any color taffeta. 8 ribs. $2.00.

K—20909. Child's Parasol. 14 inches, 10 ribs, flowered cotton top with Dresden border. 50c.

K—20910. Woman's Parasol. Mushroom model

—something entirely new. Plain taffeta top with narrow white and black satin striped taffeta border, Long black stick. 16 ribs. Gilt frame, ribs turned under. Fancy silk cord and tassel. Any color taffeta. $5.00.

K—20911. Woman's Parasol. White and black satin stripe taffeta top with deep ribbon insertion and plain messaline border. Shirred edge. Finished with narrow soutache braid. Long carved black handle. $5.00.

K—20912. Woman's Parasol. Plain taffeta silk with deep Dresden ribbon insertion. Bell shape. Long-shaped handle. 22-inch, 8-rib, gilt frame. Any color taffeta. $3.00.

K—20913. Parasol. Silk Dresden taffeta top. Shirred edge, bound with black. 22-inch, 8-rib, gilt frame. Fancy silk cord and tassel. Long black stick, very smart. $3.00.

K—20914. Woman's Parasol. White and black satin striped top and border with deep Dresden ribbon insertion. Shirred edge, finished with narrow soutache braid. Long carved black stick. $3.75.

K—20800 $3.00

K-20801 $3.00

K-20802 $2.50

K-20804 $3.00

K-20805 $1.50

K-20803 $5.50

K-20806 $2.00

K-20807 $1.50

K-20808 85¢

K-20809 $3.75

K—20800. Woman's Parasol. Plain messaline. Bell shape. Gilt ribs. Long carved handle. Green, navy, black or purple. $3.00.

K—20801. Woman's Parasol. White and black Bayadere satin stripe taffeta. Shirred edge. Bound with plain taffeta. Long black stick. $3.00.

K—20802. Woman's Parasol. Taffeta silk with four one-half inch tucks. 8 ribs. Long carved handle. Almost any color taffeta. $2.50.

K—20803. Woman's Parasol. White and black

combination moire ribbon. Shirred edge. Long black stick. $5.50.

K—20804. Woman's Parasol. White linen hand embroidered flower. Scalloped edge. Long carved handle. $3.00.

K—20805. Child's Parasol. 16-inch. Plain silk, shirred edge, 8 ribs. Pink, light blue or white. $1.50.

K—20806. Woman's Parasol. White and black striped messaline, with plain taffeta binding, in any color. Shirred edge. 8 ribs. Also

comes in plain taffeta, shirred edge, any color taffeta, $2.00.

K—20807. Parasol. 18-inch. Plain silk with Dresden border and top. 8 ribs. Enamel frame. White, pink and light blue. $1.50.

K—20808. Parasol. Dresden top with plain border. Any color taffeta. Hemstitched finish. 16 inches. 85c.

K—20809. Woman's Parasol. Black bone tips, white and black satin striped taffeta. Shirred edge. Finished with narrow soutache braid. 8 ribs. Long black carved handle. $3.75.

Parasols in the Latest Fashions for Summer 1915

The Parasol is the completing touch to the smart costume, and it gives distinction to the plain one. It is astonishing what a transformation in one's appearance even an inexpensive, new-style parasol can make.

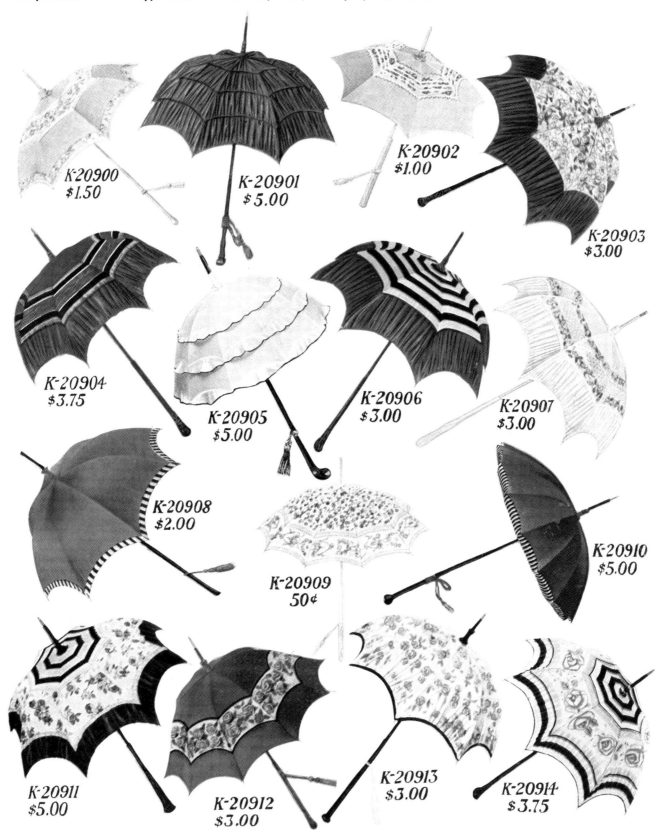

K-20900
$1.50

K-20901
$5.00

K-20902
$1.00

K-20903
$3.00

K-20904
$3.75

K-20905
$5.00

K-20906
$3.00

K-20907
$3.00

K-20908
$2.00

K-20909
50¢

K-20910
$5.00

K-20911
$5.00

K-20912
$3.00

K-20913
$3.00

K-20914
$3.75

For Full Descriptions See Opposite Page

New York — Gimbel Brothers — Philadelphia

[original inside back cover]

Here Is A Fine Showing Of New And Staple Ribbons

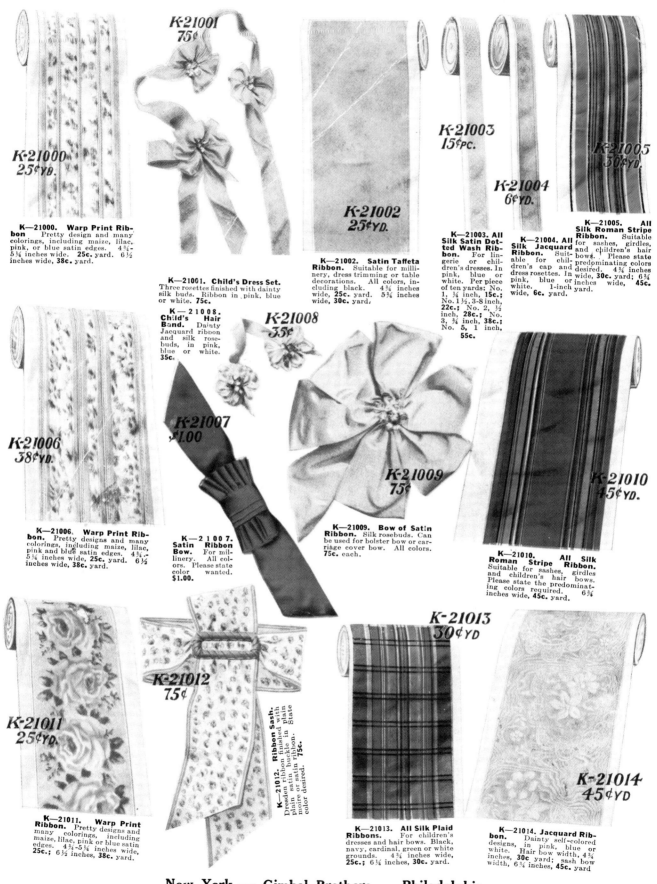

K—21000. *Warp Print Ribbon* Pretty design and many colorings, including maize, lilac, pink, or blue satin edges. 4¾-5¼ inches wide. **25c.** yard. 6½ inches wide, **38c.** yard.

K—21001. *Child's Dress Set.* Three rosettes finished with dainty silk buds. Ribbon in pink, blue or white. **75c.**

K—21008. *Child's Hair Band.* Dainty Jacquard ribbon and silk rosebuds, in pink, blue or white. **35c.**

K—21002. *Satin Taffeta Ribbon.* Suitable for millinery, dress trimming or table decorations. All colors, including black. 4¾ inches wide, **25c.** yard. 5¾ inches wide, **30c.** yard.

K—21003. *All Silk Satin Dotted Wash Ribbon.* For lingerie or children's dresses. In pink, blue or white. Per piece of ten yards: No. 1, ¼ inch, **15c.**; No. 1½, 3-8 inch, **22c.**; No. 2, ½ inch, **28c.**; No. 3, ¾ inch, **38c.**; No. 5, 1 inch, **55c.**

K—21004. *All Silk Jacquard Ribbon.* Suitable for children's cap and dress rosettes. In pink, blue or white. 1-inch wide, **6c.** yard.

K—21005. *All Silk Roman Stripe Ribbon.* Suitable for sashes, girdles, and children's hair bows. Please state predominating colors desired. 4¾ inches wide, **30c.** yard; 6¾ inches wide, **45c.** yard.

K—21006. *Warp Print Ribbon.* Pretty designs and many colorings, including maize, lilac, pink and blue satin edges. 4¾-5¼ inches wide, **25c.** yard. 6½ inches wide, **38c.** yard.

K—21007. *Satin Ribbon Bow.* For millinery. All colors. Please state color wanted. **$1.00.**

K—21009. *Bow of Satin Ribbon.* Silk rosebuds. Can be used for bolster bow or carriage cover bow. All colors. **75c.** each.

K—21010. *All Silk Roman Stripe Ribbon.* Suitable for sashes, girdles and children's hair bows. Please state the predominating colors required. 6¾ inches wide, **45c.** yard.

K—21011. *Warp Print Ribbon.* Pretty designs and many colorings, including maize, lilac, pink or blue satin edges. 4¾-5¼ inches wide, **25c.**; 6½ inches, **38c.** yard.

K—21012. *Ribbon Sash.* Dresden ribbon finished with plain plain satin buckle in plain moire or satin ribbon. State color desired. **75c.**

K—21013. *All Silk Plaid Ribbons.* For children's dresses and hair bows. Black, navy, cardinal, green or white grounds. 4¾ inches wide, **25c.**; 6¼ inches, **30c.** yard.

K—21014. *Jacquard Ribbon.* Dainty self-colored designs, in pink, blue or white. Hair bow width, 4¾ inches, **30c.** yard; sash bow width, 6¾ inches, **45c.** yard

New York — Gimbel Brothers — Philadelphia

[original back cover]